T0271379

The Legal and Economic Analysis of the WTO/FTA System

World Scientific Studies in International Economics
(ISSN: 1793-3641)

The complete list of the published volumes in the series can be found at
http://www.worldscientific.com/series/wssie

50 World Scientific
Studies in
International
Economics

The Legal and Economic Analysis of the WTO/FTA System

Dukgeun Ahn
Seoul National University, Korea

 **World Scientific**

NEW JERSEY · LONDON · SINGAPORE · BEIJING · SHANGHAI · HONG KONG · TAIPEI · CHENNAI · TOKYO

Published by

World Scientific Publishing Co. Pte. Ltd.
5 Toh Tuck Link, Singapore 596224
USA office: 27 Warren Street, Suite 401-402, Hackensack, NJ 07601
UK office: 57 Shelton Street, Covent Garden, London WC2H 9HE

Library of Congress Cataloging-in-Publication Data
Names: An, Tŏk-kŭn, author.
Title: The legal and economic analysis of the WTO/FTA system / Dukgeun Ahn,
    Seoul National University, Korea.
Description: Hackensack, New Jersey : World Scientific, 2015. |
    Series: World Scientific studies in international economics, ISSN 1793-3641 ; 50
Identifiers: LCCN 2015033003| ISBN 9789814704342 | ISBN 9814704342
Subjects: LCSH: World Trade Organization. | Foreign trade regulation. | Free trade. |
    Tariff--Law and legislation.
Classification: LCC K4610 .A955 2015 | DDC 382/.92--dc23
LC record available at http://lccn.loc.gov/2015033003

British Library Cataloguing-in-Publication Data
A catalogue record for this book is available from the British Library.

In-house Editors: Karimah Samsudin/Nisha Rahul

Typeset by Stallion Press
Email: enquiries@stallionpress.com

Printed in Singapore

To my wife, Jiyoung Park, for all those times and supports

Acknowledgments

The works collected in this book have been significantly benefitted by many colleagues, students and professors. Most of all, I cannot thank enough Professor Robert M. Stern for guiding me throughout academic career. His academic leadership has always been the greatest motivation for his students including me. Professor Alan V. Deardorff has been not just academic advisor but also the life time role model for me. I have learned all my academic rigor, devotion and passion from his teaching. Professor John H. Jackson is another beacon of my academic life who opens the whole new world — a legal side of the world trading system. It has always been the most incredible honor and fortune for me to have them together as my teachers and mentors at the University of Michigan. I am also truly indebted to Professor Mitsuo Matsushita for his sincere scholarly guidance since my internship at the WTO Appellate Body. I have always tried to learn his warm heart for students and colleagues as well as persistent commitment to fairness and justice.

For the publication of this book, I express my gratitude to the various publishers for giving copyright permissions to produce the following articles in the book:

Wolters Kluwer Law International: Articles (1) Understanding Non-litigated Disputes in the WTO Dispute settlement System. Journal of World Trade, Vol. 47, No. 5, 2013, co-authored with Jee-Hyeong Park and Jihong Lee, (2) Alternative Approach to Causation Analysis in Trade Remedy Investigations: 'Cost of Production' Test. Journal of World Trade, Vol. 44, No. 5, 2010, co-authored with William J. Moon, (3) Third Country Dumping: Origin, Evolution and

Prospect. Journal of World Trade, Vol. 46, No. 3, 2012, (4) Linkages between International Trade and Financial Institutions: WTO, IMF, and World Bank. Journal of World Trade, Vol. 34, No. 4, 2000, and (5) Analysis of Anti-dumping Use in Free Trade Agreements. Journal of World Trade, Vol. 45, No. 2, 2011, co-authored with Wonkyu Shin.

VoxEU.org: Chapter (1) "Is the Chinese Exchange-rate Regime 'WTO-legal'?" (in *The US-Sino Currency Dispute: New Insights from Politics, Economics and Law*, ed. By Simon Evenett, 2010, Centre for Economic Policy Research, 2010, CEPR, VOX.

Oxford University Press: Articles (1) Korea in the GATT/WTO Dispute Settlement System: Legal Battle for Economic Development. *J Int Economic Law* (2003) 6 (3): 597–633, (2) Foe or Friend of GATT Article XXIV: Diversity in Trade Remedy Rules. *J Int Economic Law* (2008) 11 (1): 107–133 first published online February 1, 2008, and (3) Countervailing Duty against China: Opening a Pandora's Box in the WTO System? *J Int Economic Law* (2011) 14 (2): 329–368 first published online June 24, 2011.

Cameroon May Publishing: Articles (1) Restructuring the WTO Safeguard Mechanism" in *The WTO Trade Remedy System: East Asian Perspectives*, eds. by Mitsuo Matsushita, Dukgeun Ahn & Tain-Jy Chen, Cameron May, 2006, pp. 11–31, and (2) WTO Disciplines under the IMF Program: Congruence or Conflict. in *WTO and East Asia: New Perspectives*, eds. by Mitsuo Matsushita and Dukgeun Ahn, Cameron May, 2004, pp. 25–38.

Cambridge University Press: Article (1) United States — Anti-Dumping Measures on Certain Shrimp and Diamond Sawblades from China: Never Ending Zeroing in the WTO? *World Trade Review*, Vol. 13, No. 2, 2014, co-authored with Patrick Messerlin.

American Society of International Law: Articles (1) International Decision: United States — Definitive Anti-Dumping and Countervailing Duties on Certain Products from China. *American Journal of International Law*, Vol. 105, No. 4, 2011, and (2) Book Review:

International Law in Financial Regulation and Monetary Affairs. *American Journal of International Law*, Vol. 108, No. 1, 2014.

Asian Journal of WTO & International Health Law and Policy: Article (1) Dispute Settlement Systems in Asian FTAs: Issues and Problems. Asian Journal of WTO & International Health Law and Policy, Vol. 8, No. 2, 2013.

Korea Development Institute: Article (1) WTO Legal Issues for North-South Korean Trade. in Multilateral and Regional Frameworks for Globalization: WTO and Free Trade Agreements, eds. by Lim and Torrens, Korea Development Institute, 2005.

I am also very grateful to many excellent students, particularly Wonkyu Shin, Jieun Lee, William J. Moon and Ji Yeong Yoo in preparing this book. I hope this book can be a milestone for my future research.

Dukgeun Ahn

About the Author

 **Dr. Dukgeun Ahn** is Professor of International Trade Law and Policy in Graduate School of International Studies (GSIS), Seoul National University. He also works as Director of Center for International Commerce and Finance in GSIS. Professor Ahn has taught at various other universities including Singapore National University, University of Hong Kong, University of Barcelona in Spain, World Trade Institute in Switzerland and the KDI School of Public Policy and Management in Korea. In addition, he has advised many developing country governments, international organizations as well as various Korean ministries concerning trade law and policy issues such as World Trade Organization (WTO) disputes, trade negotiation and trade policy making. Professor Ahn is currently working as a Commissioner of the Korea Trade Commission and served as a Member of the National Economic Advisory Council, the constitutional body chaired by the President of Korea. He is listed as a panelist candidate for the WTO dispute settlement as well as the Korea-US FTA and the Korea-EU FTA.

His works and contributions have been recognized by many awards, including Award by the Minister of Commerce, Industry and Energy of Republic of Korea, 2004, Award by the Minister of the Interior of Republic of Korea, 2015, Award by the Prime Minister of Republic of Korea, 2005, and Simdang Academic Excellence Award by Korea Association of International Trade Law, 2012. He is an editorial board member for many academic journals, including Journal of International Economic Law (Oxford University Press), Journal of International Area Studies (Seoul National University) and Journal of Korea Trade (Korea Trade Research Association). Professor Ahn holds both Ph.D. in Economics and J.D. (Member of New York Bar) from the University of Michigan, Ann Arbor.

Preface

The establishment of the World Trade Organization (WTO) in 1995 caused the fundamental paradigm shift of methodologies to understand the world trading system. The transformation of a rule-oriented trading system under the General Agreement on Tariffs and Trade (GATT) into a rule-based system by the WTO has significantly enhanced the importance of legal expertise to understand and apply the international trade laws and rules. Nevertheless, the economic nature of international trade relationships still requires economic analyses for many aspects of the WTO system. This reality of the WTO system has increased the importance of interdisciplinary approach to address legal frameworks of economic relationships. This book collects interdisciplinary studies covering a wide range of issues from the WTO dispute settlement system to trade remedy systems and FTA negotiations.

Part One. Dispute Settlement in the WTO System

The dispute settlement system is the core element of the WTO that has significantly fortified the legalistic nature of the world trading system. The impressive development of the "WTO law", since the inception of the WTO, has been continued by growing jurisprudence of panels and the Appellate Body. In fact, WTO rulings have been one of the favorite subjects for legal scholars to analyze and criticize with different legal principles and interpretations.

On the other hand, almost half of the cases brought to the dispute settlement system were not actually litigated to produce the legal rulings. Instead of legal litigations, they were somehow resolved by consultations and implicit or explicit settlements, or often not pursued under the legal proceeding. These non-litigated disputes have not been seriously analyzed since they do not produce any legal ruling. "Understanding Non-litigated Disputes in the WTO Dispute Settlement System" (*Journal of World Trade*, 2013) applies a logistic regression to examine economic determinants of non-litigation in the WTO dispute settlement system on the basis of the bargaining theory. The bargaining theory of asymmetric information suggests that, in the context of WTO disputes, a greater economic size difference reduces the likelihood of voluntary settlement, or conversely increases the likelihood of litigation, if it were to worsen the informational asymmetry. This theoretical prediction is indeed supported by empirical evidence using the WTO dispute data. WTO members also tend to prefer non-litigation when a respondent is smaller than a complainant, has less reputational concern, and faces less retaliatory capacity of the complainant. Our findings suggest a case for reforming the legal rules of the consultation process towards mitigating informational asymmetry or improving communication between disputing parties in the WTO.

"Korea in the GATT/WTO Dispute Settlement System: Legal Battle for Economic Development" (*Journal of International Economic Law*, 2003) reviews the Korean experience of trade disputes that critically contributed to shaping trade policy environments. Although this article focuses on the Korean cases, the manner of handling trade disputes and implementing the GATT/WTO recommendations by the Korean government offer useful implications for other developing country members. For example, GATT Article XVIII:B invoked from the beginning of the accession was dis-invoked only when Korea lost the first GATT dispute in 1988. The fact that the first five WTO disputes were settled by consultation instead of panel proceedings also indicates a typical situation for developing countries with little capacity and experience for substantially legalized dispute settlement procedures in the WTO system. In contrast, the anti-dumping disputes in the GATT and WTO system show how domestic trade policy capacity has been improved by trade dispute settlement experience. The experience of Korea illustrates how legal dispute settlement experiences contributed to enhancing trade policy capacities and infrastructures that are essential to economic development of developing countries.

Part Two. Practices and Theoretical Foundations of the Trade Remedy System

The trade remedy system has been the core element of the world trading system, especially at the inchoate stage of the GATT. However, globalized economy with investment networks and global supply chains has raised fundamental challenges for systemic foundations of trade remedy systems. This part addresses various structural issues concerning trade remedy systems.

"Alternative Approach to Causation Analysis in Trade Remedy Investigations: 'Cost of Production' Test" (*Journal of World Trade*, 2010) seeks to suggest an alternative method for causation analysis of trade remedy investigations. Probably it is the causation analysis that brings the largest gap between legal understanding and economic evaluation in trade remedy investigations. The econometric analysis typically employed for assessing causation by economists is rarely accepted by lawyers who rely on "but for" test to vindicate causation. Considering technical difficulties for trade remedy investigations, we propose a relatively easy and yet more economically sensible method on the basis of production costs.

"Third Country Dumping: Origin, Evolution and Prospect" (*Journal of World Trade*, 2012) revisits the antiquated provision permitting a third country anti-dumping action. Due to the legal requirements to obtain approval by the "Contracting Parties", third country anti-dumping action has become practically useless. Nevertheless, this provision was used especially by Australia and New Zealand whose economies have an exceptionally close relationship. This article analyzes potential importance of this provision in the context of the current world trading system in which proliferating FTAs generate unprecedented economic incentives.

"Restructuring the WTO Safeguard Mechanism" (in *The WTO Trade Remedy System: East Asian Perspectives*, 2006) emphasizes the need to restructure the current WTO safeguard system. The Agreement on Safeguard, established during the Uruguay Round negotiation, played a significant role in rationalizing safeguard measures of the WTO system. However, safeguard measures have been abused by many developing countries that normally do not have much experience in utilizing trade remedy measures. Such problem may be more systemic when the dispute settlement procedures cannot appropriately address safeguard measures of fast track nature. This article explains systemic problems of the Agreement on Safeguard that become more obvious from the experience of application so far.

Proliferating FTAs have recently produced various unprecedented legal developments, notably in terms of trade remedy rules. Although FTAs are exempted from the most-favored-nation obligation with respect to tariff treatment, it is not clear whether discriminatory trade remedy rules can be applied against different FTA partners. "Foe or Friend of GATT Article XXIV: Diversity in Trade Remedy Rules" (*Journal of International Economic Law*, 2008) reviews modified FTA rules and analyzes WTO consistency of diversified trade remedy rules.

"Countervailing Duty against China: Opening a Pandora's Box in the WTO System?" (*Journal of International Economic Law*, 2011) reviews new phenomena in the WTO system that WTO members impose countervailing duties against non-market economies. In particular, the US government traditionally declined to impose countervailing duties against non-market economies such as China, but, after the change of its policies, China has become the most frequent target of the US countervailing actions concurrently applied with antidumping duties. Simultaneous application of countervailing and antidumping duties against imports from China without proper offset procedures caused direct contradiction between the panel and the Appellate Body. This article analyzes whether the legal rulings of the panel and the Appellate Body fit into legal structures and drafting intents of the WTO Agreements. It is argued that despite the desirability of the Appellate Body ruling from the policy perspective, the legal interpretation to prevent concurrent application of countervailing and antidumping duties may raise some issues.

"United States — Anti-Dumping Measures on Certain Shrimp and Diamond Sawblades from China: Never Ending Zeroing in the WTO?" (*World Trade Review*, 2014) explains unique implementation problems of the US government in relation to "zeroing" disputes. This dispute can also be classified as one of those remedial disputes that are required to apply legal rulings to actual antidumping duties. The WTO system recognizes the constitutional differences and peculiarities of the members. But the differences between the United States and the European Union in relation to implementation of "zeroing" rulings raise interesting institutional issues.

"United States — Definitive Anti-Dumping and Countervailing Duties on Certain Products from China" (*American Journal of International Law*, 2011) provides a concise case review that addresses important legal issues for countervailing duties against China, including determination of public body and WTO consistency of double remedy actions.

Part Three. Interrelation between Trade and Finance

International trade and finance are essentially two sides of the same coin. Trade balances affect the international financial situations of trading economies through exchange rate adjustment which in turn influences trade balances. The developments of international trading system and financial system, however, turned out to be very different from each other when the International Monetary Fund (IMF) had to embrace flexible exchange rate systems and the GATT was transformed into the WTO. Most notably, while the international financial system mostly relies on soft law type commitments, the international trading system becomes highly legalistic with the augmented dispute settlement system.

"Linkages between International Trade and Financial Institutions: WTO, IMF, and World Bank" (*Journal of World Trade*, 2000) draws academic attention to linkages between trade and financial institutions. For example, GATT still allows trade restrictions based on balance of payment situations, although it does not establish legal process or authority for evaluating balance of payment status. The legal obligations of the WTO system thus depend on coherent operations with the IMF and the World Bank that hardly work in practice. This article reviews the existing mechanism to link trade and financial institutions, and discusses potential issues for further development.

Other systemic issues between the WTO and IMF include subsidy disciplines for bail out programs employed by countries in financial distress. This potential conflict between international trade rules and international financial policies became a real issue during the Asian financial crisis of 1998–1999. "WTO Disciplines under the IMF Program: Conflict or Congruence: From the Korean Experience" (in *WTO and East Asia: New Perspectives*, 2004) analyzes the Korean case to illustrate the structural problems of WTO subsidy rules in addressing emergency policies undertaken by the IMF conditionality programs. The article's points are still valid for numerous bail-out programs introduced after the global financial crisis of 2008.

The dramatic rise of the Chinese economy in the world trading system during the past couple of decades provoked unprecedented controversies on proper exchange rate policies and the scope of government authorities to deal with them. "Is the Chinese Exchange-rate Regime 'WTO-legal'?" (in *The US-Sino Currency Dispute: New Insights from Politics, Economics and Law*, 2010) examines the potential legal issues to be considered in case the US government takes action through the WTO over China's alleged currency manipulation. This article analyzes three potential legal issues: legality of exchange-rate policy under the GATT rules, legality under the subsidy rules, and the feasibility of non-violation complaints. It concludes that any WTO resolution will be difficult to achieve because the WTO rules are not designed to deal with alleged exchange-rate manipulation.

Peculiar legal situations of the international financial system were extensively analyzed in an effort to draw some implication for future development of international financial law. In September 2010, the *Journal of International Economic Law* published the special issue collecting twenty-two articles that was later published as a book, *International Law in Financial Regulation and Monetary Affairs*. The book review article for "International Law in Financial Regulation and Monetary Affairs" (*American Journal of International Law*, 2014) explains a comprehensive framework to address legal and institutional loopholes. The Bretton Woods system, originally perceived as a trinity of institutions — the IMF, International Bank for Reconstruction and Development, and International Trade Organization (ITO) — could barely survive the demise of the ITO. The post–Bretton Woods system of the twenty-first century may need a more coherent and newly augmented trinity of the WTO, World Bank, and potentially a World Financial Organization that would provide a "rule-oriented" system modeled on the WTO, to supplant the IMF.

Part Four. Legal and Economic Analysis of Free Trade Agreements

International trade law recently experiences notable development by emerging FTA norms. Many interesting, *albeit* not fully consistent, rules have been introduced in FTAs through bilateral or regional compromises. "Dispute Settlement Systems in Asian FTAs: Issues and Problems" (*Asian Journal of WTO & International Health Law and Policy*, 2013) reviews different dispute settlement rules adopted in Asian FTAs. In particular, it is noted that different dispute settlement rules supported — in fact, often insisted in the Doha negotiation — by the United States and the European Union are adopted in the Korea–US FTA and the Korea–EU FTA, respectively. Considering the fact that the United States and the European Union are actively pursuing more FTAs, this kind of rule diversity appears to be inevitable elements for the future world trading system.

The establishment of FTA relationships may generate conflicting economic incentives for trade remedy actions against FTA parties. Whereas the whole purpose of FTA negotiations is to facilitate more trade with FTA partners, increased trade may increase the need and incentives for more trade remedy actions to protect injured domestic industries. Using longitudinal data of major AD user countries from 1995 to 2009, "Analysis of Anti-dumping Use in Free Trade Agreements" (*Journal of World Trade*, 2011) found that there is clearly an inverse relationship between an FTA and AD activities except for Latin American countries. This finding represents the user's tendency to trigger less AD filings against FTA membership, regardless of facing more imports from FTA partners. The estimation results from the dynamic model show that the FTA enactment year clearly has significant effect, suggesting substantial reduction of AD investigations in that year.

"WTO Legal Issues for North-South Korean Trade" (in *Multilateral and Regional Frameworks for Globalization: WTO and Free Trade Agreements*, 2005) explains a peculiar trade relationship between North and South Koreas. One of the major potential problems in the WTO system may be the MFN treatment obligation against other WTO members. This article also explains the difference from the German cases. The only legal solution to resolve this MFN problem of economically very important "internal trade" between North and South Koreas seems to be a free trade agreement, although it may cause another domestic political controversy.

The works collected in this book have been significantly benefitted by many colleagues, students and professors. Most of all, I cannot thank enough Professor Robert M. Stern for guiding me throughout academic career. His academic leadership has always been the greatest motivation for his students including me. Professor Alan V. Deardorff has been not just academic advisor but also the life time role model for me. I have learned all my academic rigor, devotion and passion from his teaching. Professor John H. Jackson is another beacon of my academic life that opens the whole new world — a legal side of the world trading system. It is always the most incredible honor and fortune for me to have them together as my teachers and mentors at the University of Michigan.

I am also very grateful to many excellent students, particularly Wonkyu Shin, Jieun Lee, William J. Moon and Ji Yeong Yoo in preparing this book. I hope this book can be a milestone for my future research.

Table of Contents

Part One

Dispute Settlement in the WTO System

Chapter 1

Understanding Non-litigated Disputes in the WTO Dispute Settlement System

Dukgeun AHN, Jihong LEE &
Jee-Hyeong PARK*

This article focuses on a less scrutinized aspect of the WTO dispute settlement system – non-litigated disputes. Legal rules concerning consultation and settlement during the panel proceedings are analysed with the case laws. We then propose, and empirically analyse, several key economic determinants of non-litigation in the WTO dispute settlement system that are motivated by the theory of bargaining with informational asymmetry. In particular, our logistic regressions show that a greater difference in the size of the pair of disputing countries reduces the likelihood of voluntary settlement or non-litigation. WTO members also tend to prefer non-litigation when the respondent is smaller than the complainant, has less reputational concern, and faces less retaliatory capacity of the complainant. Our findings suggest a case for reforming the legal rules of the consultation process towards mitigating informational asymmetry or improving communication between disputing parties in the WTO.

1 INTRODUCTION

The WTO dispute settlement system has been one of the most actively growing subject areas in international economics as well as in international law. In particular, the whole jurisprudence of international trade law has been developed with numerous rulings by panels and the Appellate Body that constitute important foundation of WTO case law at an unprecedented level of sophistication.[1]

* Dukgeun Ahn, Graduate School of International Studies, Seoul National University. dahn@snu.ac.kr; Jihong Lee, Department of Economics, Seoul National University. jihonglee@snu.ac.kr; Jee-Hyeong Park, Department of Economics, Seoul National University. j-hpark@snu.ac.kr.

We are very grateful to valuable comments by Sungjoon Cho, Chul Chung and Patrick Messerlin. We also thank Minjung Kim, Hyoyoung Lee, Dahee Park, and Jaeyoun Roh for their excellent research assistance. Dukgeun Ahn and Jee-Hyeong Park acknowledge financial support from the National Research Foundation of Korea Grant funded by the Korean government (NRF-2011-330-B00063). Jihong Lee's research was supported by a Korea Research Foundation Grant (KRF-2009-327-B00117). This research was also supported by the Asia Research Foundation Grant funded by the Seoul National University Asia Center (0448A-20130004).

[1] The sheer volumes of WTO rulings are massive. For example, the *World Trade Organization Dispute Settlement Reports* that compile all the formal rulings by panels and the Appellate Body in 2000–2011 contain 69,861 pages. The World Trade Organization Dispute Settlement Reports 2005 alone has 11,752 pages. WTO, *World Trade Organization Dispute Settlement Reports* (Cambridge U. Press various years).

Ahn, Dukgeun; Lee, Jihong & Park, Jee-Hyeong. 'Understanding Non-litigated Disputes In the WTO Dispute Settlement System'. *Journal of World Trade* 47, no. 5 (2013): 985–1012.

In contrast to the vast amount of case law and relevant academic analyses, there are still a significant number of WTO disputes that have drawn less attention from the academia and practitioners. They are WTO disputes that were settled at a consultation stage or during the panel proceeding. Among 419 cases brought to the WTO dispute settlement system until 2010, 230 cases – almost 55% – were not litigated.[2] Since these disputes did not produce any formal rulings by panels or the Appellate Body, they were categorically excluded from the development of the WTO jurisprudence and thereby mostly ignored in serious legal analyses. These non-litigated disputes,[3] however, are not less important with respect to the roles of the WTO dispute settlement system. To the contrary, settling disputes by non-litigation may be a more efficient way to serve the purpose of the WTO dispute settlement system than litigating disputes, especially considering the fact that the WTO litigation has become increasingly more expensive and difficult to ensure prompt compliance.

This article focuses on this less scrutinized aspect of the WTO dispute settlement system – non-litigated disputes. Unlike litigation process of panel proceeding and appellate review, which have been articulated by constant amendments of rules and practices, non-litigation process such as consultation or settlement has not been sufficiently elaborated primarily for the purpose of allowing significant discretion for disputing members. Our objectives are two-fold. First, we present a detailed description of the WTO procedures and rules that govern the disputing parties' decisions on whether or not to litigate the disputes to obtain legal rulings. In particular, we analyse different rule developments for non-litigation or settlement process and explain the structural issues to be addressed by future amendments. Second, we attempt to identify the key economic determinants of the disputing countries' incentives for (non-)litigation from the actual WTO dispute data. Based on the theory of settlement bargaining with asymmetric information, we conjecture how certain economic indicators of the disputing countries affect the likelihood of non-litigation, and conduct an empirical analysis using the WTO dispute data. Our main finding is that the

---

[2] More detailed statistics on the WTO dispute settlement situation are presented in Section 4. In fact, the dispute settlement experience under the GATT system involved a remarkable portion of non-litigated cases. Among 207 cases between 1948 and 1989, 84 cases were settled prior to panel decisions and 27 cases were withdrawn. In other words, almost 54% of the cases were not litigated in the GATT dispute settlement system. Robert Hudec, *Enforcing International Trade Law: The Evolution of the Modern GATT Legal System*, 277–291 (Butterworth Leg. Publishers 1993).

[3] The term 'non-litigated dispute' broadly refers to the disputes that are concluded without formal rulings of panels. More specifically, they include disputes that are settled or left inactive at a consultation stage, withdrawn at a panel proceeding with mutually agreed solution, or terminated due to the lapse of panel establishment authority. Although litigation takes place technically with the beginning of a panel proceeding, we use the term of 'non-litigation' in the sense that a full litigation is not completed.

relative economic sizes of the disputing countries matter in a significant way: a greater disparity between the two countries' Gross Domestic Product (GDP) decreases the likelihood of non-litigation. Furthermore, this effect is stronger when the respondent country has a size advantage over the complainant country. WTO members also tend to prefer non-litigation when the respondent has less reputational concern and faces less retaliatory capacity of the complainant.

The non-litigation aspect of the WTO dispute settlement system has been addressed by only a few economic and legal studies to date.[4] Among these, Guzman and Simmons (2002) also examine the likelihood of non-litigation using the actual WTO dispute data. In contrast to the present article, these authors test the hypothesis that settlement is more likely to occur when a dispute concerns more 'continuous' cases such as tariffs, nonzero quotas and subsidies. Their empirical study is based on a smaller sample of disputes, filed between 1995 and 2000.

The article is organized as follows. Section 2 reviews the legal rules pertinent to non-ligation in the WTO dispute settlement system. Section 3 presents economic rationales for settling the WTO disputes by non-litigation on the basis of bargaining theory and identifies several key determinants of the disputing parties' (non-)litigation incentives. Section 4 presents the results of our logistic regressions on the likelihood of non-litigation using data accumulated under the WTO dispute settlement system during the period of 1995–2010. Section 5 discusses the remaining agenda for future research as well as rule development in the WTO.

2 LEGAL RULES FOR NON-LITIGATION IN THE WTO DISPUTE SETTLEMENT SYSTEM

There are essentially two stages for a WTO dispute to be settled without litigation. First, a request for consultation in the WTO dispute settlement system may

---

[4] The previous research includes, for example, Gary Horlick, *The Consultation Phase of WTO Dispute Resolution: A Private Practitioner's View*, 32 Intl. Law., 685–693 (1998); Marc L. Busch, *Democracy, Consultation, and the Paneling of Disputes under GATT*, 44 J. Conflict Res., 425 (2000); Peiter-Jan Kuijper, *The Pre-litigation Stage in the WTO Dispute Settlement Procedure and in the EC Infringement Procedure*, in *Improving WTO Dispute Settlement Procedures: Issues & Lessons from the Practice of Other International Courts & Tribunals* 67 (Friedl Weiss ed., Cameron 2000); Marc L. Busch & Eric Reinhardt, *Bargaining in the Shadow of the Law: Early Settlement in GATT/WTO Disputes*, 24 Fordham Intl. L. J. 158 (2000); Andrew T. Guzman and Beth A. Simmons, *To Settle or Empanel? An Empirical Analysis of Litigation and Settlement at the WTO*, 31 J. Leg. Stud. S205 (2002); Amelia Porges, *Settling WTO Disputes: What Do Litigation Models Tell Us*, 19 Ohio State J. Dispute Res. 141 (2003); Gabrielle Marceau, *Consultations and the Panel Process in the WTO Dispute Settlement System*, in *Key Issues in WTO Dispute Settlement: The First Ten Years* 29 (Rufus Yerxa & Bruce Wilson eds., Cambridge U. Press 2005).

successfully resolve the dispute. Second, in case they cannot settle a dispute at a consultation stage, disputing parties may resolve a dispute during the panel proceeding and thus prevent the panel from issuing the final legal rulings. In addition, even if disputing parties formally settle a dispute neither in consultation nor during a panel proceeding, a complainant sometimes does not pursue a formal litigation after the consultation request or panel suspension despite the absence of explicit mutual resolution. This inaction on the part of the complainant tacitly implies a settlement between the disputing parties.

The above-mentioned three possible cases of non-litigation are subject to certain procedural rules and disciplines of the WTO. Pursuant to Article 3.5 of the Understanding on Rules and Procedures Governing the Settlement of Disputes (hereinafter 'DSU'), agreed solutions by consultation or settlement shall be consistent with the covered agreements and shall not nullify or impair benefits accruing to any member. However, unlike the Dispute Settlement Body (DSB) recommendations and rulings for which Article 21.5 of the DSU applies to ensure the implementation, there is no procedure to check or monitor whether agreed solutions are properly implemented.

2.1   NON-LITIGATION BY SETTLEMENT IN A CONSULTATION STAGE

2.1[a]   *Rules for Consultation*

When a WTO Member intends to bring a complaint to the dispute settlement system, it must start with consultation except for very special and limited cases such as disputes under the Agreement on Textiles and Clothing (ATC)[5] or complaints under GATT Article XXIII: 1(c).[6] After consultation requests are made by a complainant, a respondent should engage in consultations in good faith. Only in case where the respondent does not respond to the consultation request or the consultation fails to settle the dispute in sixty days,[7] a panel proceeding may begin.

---

[5]   ATC Art. 8.10. If recommendations issued by the Textiles Monitoring Body (TMB) cannot resolve disputes, Members may bring the matter directly to a panel procedure. Since consultation is actually required prior to the TMB recommendation, Members can proceed to a panel procedure without repeating consultation process. The panel in *US – Measure Affecting Imports of Woven Wool Shirts and Blouses from India* (DS33) explained that 'a Member which remains unsatisfied with the TMB recommendations can request the establishment of a panel without having to request consultations under Article 4 of the DSU'. Panel Report, *US – Measure Affecting Imports of Woven Wool Shirts and Blouses from India*, WT/DS33/R, adopted 23 May 1997, para.7.19.

[6]   Consultation is not required because situation complaints under Art. XXIII:1(c) do not necessarily involve a dispute between particular governments. Jeff Waincymer, *WTO Litigation: Procedural Aspects of Formal Dispute Settlement* 214 (Cameron May Publisher 2002).

[7]   In practice, the minimum consultation period takes more than 70 days due to the advance notice requirement for convening the DSB meeting. William Davey, *WTO Dispute Settlement: Segregating*

There were in fact a few cases in which respondents explicitly refused to consult. For example, when Nicaragua brought a complaint against the US trade sanctions or Yugoslavia challenged the EC trade embargo, the respondents refused to consult with complainants.[8] Turkey also did not respond to the consultation requests by India, Hong Kong and Thailand when these countries challenged certain Turkish policies to restrict textile importation as a part of the compliance under the EC–Turkey Customs Union.[9] Respondents may skip or shorten the sixty day consultation period by not responding to consultation requests or agreeing to prompt establishment of a panel. In case of urgency, such as disputes concerning perishable goods, parties should begin consultation within ten days from the consultation request and may move to a panel proceeding after twenty days of consultation.[10]

However, respondents cannot block panel establishment by delaying consultation process, although a complainant may decide not to pursue a panel proceeding. A Member's duty to consult is 'absolute' and is not susceptible to the imposition of any terms and conditions.[11]

A third party that has 'substantial trade interest' may be allowed to participate in the consultation if a respondent agrees. In case third party participation is not permitted, a Member may submit a separate consultation request against the responding party. However, third party participation in consultation is not a prerequisite for third party participation in the subsequent panel proceeding which is based on 'substantial interest' and needs no consent by the responding party.[12]

In fact, consultation is supposed to serve conflicting roles: bilateral settlement oriented process on the one hand and a mandatory pre-litigation procedure on the other hand.[13] For the former purpose, the rules for consultation provides that the contents of consultation be confidential and permits that disputing parties exercise broad discretion regarding the consultation contents and procedures. This is the reason for a panel to reject offers made in the context of consultations as irrelevant evidence for panel proceedings since they are 'of no legal consequence

---

Useful Political Aspects and Avoiding 'Over-Legalisation', in New Directions in International Economic Law: Essays in Honor of John H Jackson 291 (M. Bronkers & R. Quick eds., Kluwer L. Intl. 2000).

[8]   WTO, Analytical Index: Guide to GATT Law and Practice, 672–673 (WTO 1995).

[9]   Panel Report, Turkey – Restrictions on Imports of Textile and Clothing Products, WT/DS34/R, adopted 19 Nov. 1999, paras 9.18–9.24.

[10]   No consultation yet demanded expedited process based on urgency provisions of DSU Arts 4.8 and 4.9. The United States in Canada – Term of Patent Protection (DS170) tried to rely on DSU Art. 4.9 not for consultation but for expedited panel procedure.

[11]   Panel Report, Brazil – Measures Affecting Desiccated Coconut, WT/DS22/R, adopted 20 Mar. 1997, para. 287.

[12]   Third party participation in a panel proceeding is based on rules of DSU Art. 10, rather than the agreement by a responding party.

[13]   Waincymer, supra n. 6, at 222.

to the later stages of dispute settlement'.[14] But the latter purpose demands more articulated rules about the procedural and evidentiary elements of consultation. The Appellate Body in *India – Protection for Pharmaceutical and Agricultural Chemical Products* explained that fact finding is a major function of the consultation process.[15] Thus, the panel in *Mexico – Anti-dumping Investigation of High Fructose Corn Syrup from the United States* held that information obtained in the consultations could be used in subsequent panel proceedings.[16] In *EC – Anti-dumping Duties on Imports of Cotton-Type Bed Linen from India*, the panel accepted even the verbatim report of consultation in the panel proceeding as admissible evidence although it might not be relevant or probative.[17] This seemingly contradictory approach towards information obtained from consultation is in fact the clarification between fact finding and legal deliberation. While panels and the Appellate Body broadly accept more information to assist fact finding for a dispute, they strictly restrict unnecessary legal implications from consultation stages.

Figure 1   Annual Trend of Consultation Requests Leading to Panel Establishment

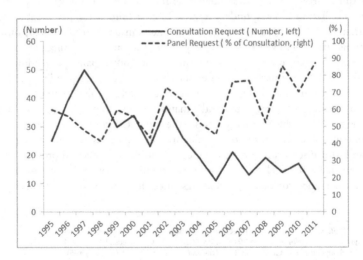

---

14   Panel Report, *United States – Restrictions on Imports of Cotton and Man-Made Fibre Underwear*, WT/DS24/R, adopted 25 Feb. 1997, para. 7.27.
15   Appellate Body Report, *India – Patent Protection for Pharmaceutical and Agricultural Chemical Products*, WT/DS50/AB/R, adopted 2 Sep. 1998, para. 94.
16   Panel Report, *Mexico – Anti-dumping Investigation of High Fructose Corn Syrup from the United States*, WT/DS132/R, adopted 24 Feb. 2000, para. 7.41.
17   Panel Report, *EC – Anti-dumping Duties on Imports of Cotton-Type Bed Linen from India*, WT/DS141/R, adopted 12 Mar. 2001, paras 6.32–6.35.

2.1[b] *Use of Consultation*

Until the end of 2011, almost 42% of the 427 consultation requests were in fact resolved at the consultation stage. Considering ever increasing legal costs for actual WTO litigations and compliance problems, successful resolutions in consultation phases are indeed the very testament of values of the WTO dispute settlement system. It is noted that the ratio of consultation requests reaching to panel establishment has constantly increased as shown in Figure 1. This trend shows that as the WTO dispute settlement system becomes more mature and experienced, WTO members bring less consultation requests but at the same time they are less likely to settle by consultation. For example, in 1998 when 41 consultation requests were brought to the WTO dispute settlement system, only seventeen requests (41% of the total consultation requests) were continued to a panel request. But in 2011 when 8 consultation requests were made, seven requests (87.5%) were led to a panel request.

Therefore, Figure 1 illustrates that the role of consultation in settling the disputes has been significantly weakened in recent years. It also raises an important point for studies regarding consultation. The recent trend by WTO members to settle less during consultation may require revisiting previous studies mostly based on the data until the early 2000s.

2.1[c] *Legal Issues for Consultation*

The role of consultation for dispute settlement was firmly recognized from the very inception of GATT. Article XXII:1 stipulates the duty for a contracting party to 'afford adequate opportunity' for bilateral consultation. In addition, Article XXII:2 that was added by amendment in 1955 allows for multilateral consultation by the CONTACTING PARTIES with any contracting parties.[18] Article XXIII:1 also provides that when a contracting party makes written representations or proposals to other contracting parties, such parties must 'give sympathetic consideration' to representations or proposals. This procedure is considered a prerequisite for formal panel procedures.

The rules for consultation have been gradually articulated. The 'Understanding Regarding Notification, Consultation, Dispute Settlement and Surveillance' adopted on 28 November 1979 clarified the procedural requirement for consultation under Article XXIII:1, which should be tried prior to resorting to

---

[18]   GATT, *Protocol Amending the Preamble and Parts II and III of the GATT, 10 March 1955*, UNTS 278 (1957).

Article XXIII:2.[19] This procedure was further enhanced by the 'Decision of 12 April 1989 on Improvements to the GATT Dispute Settlement Rules and Procedures' that specified time schedules for consultation procedures such as ten days for reply to consultation request, thirty days for entry into consultation, and at least sixty days for consultation periods prior to panel request. Finally, the Uruguay Round negotiation significantly elaborated the provision for consultation in Article 4 of the DSU that practically replaced Article XXII of GATT.[20] In addition, various other covered agreements also stipulated corresponding consultation provisions that are explicitly enunciated in Footnote 4 of the DSU. The panel in *Turkey – Restrictions on Imports of Textiles and Clothing Products* noted that consultations are a crucial and integral part of the DSU and are intended to facilitate a mutually satisfactory settlement of the dispute.[21]

As regards to the application of Article 4 of the DSU, one of the fundamental issues relates to the adequacy of consultations. In fact, what substantive requirements are in terms of consultation is not clear. For example, Article 4.2 provides that a WTO member should 'afford adequate opportunity for consultation'. The panel in *Korea – Taxes on Alcoholic Beverages* explained that the only requirement for consultation under the DSU is not to inquire as to what actually occurred during the consultations but to check whether consultations were in fact held.[22] The Appellate Body noted in *US – Subsidies on Upland Cotton* that examining what took place in the consultations would seem contrary to Article 4.6 of the DSU, which provides that '[c]onsultations shall be confidential, and without prejudice to the rights of any Member in any further proceedings'.[23]

One anomaly for the consultation rules is the lack of formal withdrawal procedure. Unlike the panel procedure which is to be lapsed after a specified period of suspension, consultation requests, if it is not pursued by complainants, continues to be technically open instead of being lapsed.[24]

Another legal problem for settlement through consultation is the lack of enforcement mechanism. While the recommendations by panels and the Appellate Body are enforced ultimately by retaliation authority, settlement arrangements by

[19] GATT, *Understanding regarding notification consultation, dispute settlement and surveillance*, L/4907 adopted on 28 Nov. 1979.
[20] Legally speaking, Art. XXII of GATT can work as a special consultation clause for disputes arising from GATT, while Art. 4 of DSU applies for consultation under the general WTO dispute settlement.
[21] Panel Report, *Turkey – Restrictions on Imports of Textile and Clothing Products*, WT/DS34/R, adopted 19 Nov. 1999, para. 9.24.
[22] Panel Report, *Korea – Taxes on Alcoholic Beverages*, WT/DS75,84/R, adopted 17 Feb. 1999, para. 10.19.
[23] Appellate Body Report, *United States- Subsidies on Upland Cotton, Recourse by Brazil to Article 21.5*, WT/DS267/AB/R, adopted 21 Mar. 2005, para. 287.
[24] Rüdiger Wolfrum et al., *WTO- Institutions and Dispute Settlement 326* (Martinus Nijhoff Publishers 2006).

consultation have no means to be rigorously enforced. That partly explains why consultations are often not formally withdrawn. Consultation requests not withdrawn may signal the complainant's intent to re-initiate dispute settlement procedures when agreed solutions are not properly undertaken.

2.2 Non-litigation by settlement in a panel process

When parties cannot resolve the disputes in a consultation phase, they begin the panel proceeding with a request for panel establishment. But the parties in the panel proceeding are allowed at any stage to suspend the formal procedure and, instead, resort to consultation in order to settle the dispute. Article 12.12 of the DSU provides that a panel may suspend the panel procedure for a period not exceeding twelve months. If the panel procedure is suspended for more than twelve months, the authority for panel establishment shall lapse.

About 24% (56 out of 230 cases) of the non-litigated WTO disputes until 2010 could still be settled after consultation failed.[25] Among fifty-six cases, thirty-five cases were settled after panel requests were submitted and twenty-one cases were settled even after panels were actually established. It is noted that about 15% of the non-litigated disputes were settled after the panel requests were submitted but still before the panels were established. In other words, a panel request itself seems to work as an additional incentive for a respondent to settle the dispute because the panel request indicates the serious commitments by the respondent to pursue litigation procedures.

The first panel proceeding suspended in the middle of litigation was *EC – Trade Description of Scallops* brought by Canada (DS7), Peru (DS12) and Chile (DS14).[26] After the panel issued the interim report on 14 March 1996, the parties notified the DSB of a mutually agreed solution on 5 July 1996. Settlement during the panel proceeding took places in divergent stages. For example, in *EC – Measures Affecting Butter Products*, the panel issued its final report to the parties on 23 December 1998 but could not circulate it to all the members due to the settlement by parties on 11 November 1999.[27] In *Korea – Measures Affecting the Importation of Bovine Meat and Meat Products from Canada*, the parties notified a mutually agreed solution on 19 June 2012 after the panel issued the descriptive

---

[25] More detailed statistics are provided in Section 4.

[26] Panel Report, *EC – Trade Description of Scallops*, WT/DS7,12,14/R, mutually agreed solution, circulated 5 Aug. 1996.

[27] Panel Report, *EC – Measures Affecting Butter Products*, WT/DS72/R, mutually agreed solution, circulated 24 Nov. 1999.

part of the draft interim report on 10 December 2010.[28] In *Japan – Import Quotas on Dried Laver and Seasoned Laver*, the parties settled the dispute on 23 January 2006 when the panel scheduled to issue the interim report on 27 January 2006.[29] In *US – Anti-dumping Duty on Dynamic Random Access Memory Semiconductors of One Megabit or above from Korea*, parties reached a mutually agreed solution after the Article 21.5 panel was constituted.[30] Until the end of 2010, twenty-one panel proceedings had been suspended or settled before the panel reports were formally issued.

Although the DSU does not provide similar provisions for suspending the appellate review, Rule 30.1 of the 'Working Procedures for Appellate Review' also permits appellants to withdraw at any time during the appeal. However, no appellate review has ever been suspended as of March 2013.

3   ECONOMIC PRINCIPLES FOR NON-LITIGATION IN THE WTO DISPUTE SETTLEMENT SYSTEM: SETTLEMENT BARGAINING

Following the discussion of the procedures and rules that govern the disputing countries' (non-)litigation incentives under the WTO dispute settlement system, we now turn to another set of determinants of these incentives: economic variables. In this section, we first present a brief overview of economic theories of non-litigation based on the settlement bargaining literature and then motivate several factors of non-litigation that will be used in our empirical study below. While the WTO dispute settlement system lacks the full enforcement power of domestic courts, it is fair to say that its decisions impose non-negligible consequences on the litigating countries.[31] Therefore, a worthwhile comparison can be drawn from the settlement bargaining literature, and this will identify

---

[28]   Panel Report, *Korea – Measures Affecting the Importation of Bovine Meat and Meat Products from Canada*, WT/DS391/R, mutually agreed solution, circulated 19 Jun. 2012, paras 13–24.

[29]   Panel Report, *Japan – Import Quotas on Dried Laver and Seasoned Lave*, WT/DS323/R, mutually agreed solution, circulated 23 Jan. 2006, paras 10–14.

[30]   Panel Report, *US – Anti-dumping Duty on Dynamic Random Access Memory Semiconductors of One Megabit or above from Korea, Recourse to Article 21.5 of the DSU by Korea*, WT/DS99/RW, mutually agreed solution, circulated 07 Nov. 2000.

[31]   The WTO authorizes the use of retaliation by a complainant against a respondent not complying with the rulings of the WTO. Using a repeated game framework, many studies explore the enforcement issues associated with international trade agreements since the pioneering work by Dixit (1987). Avinash Dixit, *Strategic Aspects of Trade Policy*, in *Advances in Economic Theory: Fifth World Congress* (Truman F. Bewley, ed., Cambridge U. Press 1987). In relation to the role of the WTO, Maggi (1999) emphasizes the importance of multilateral retaliation, and more recently Park (2011) analyzes the WTO's role by relaxing the incentive constraint associated with utilizing retaliation in the presence of imperfect private monitoring of the WTO rule violation. Giovanni Maggi, *The Role of Multilateral Institutions in International Trade Cooperation*, 89 American Econ. Rev., 190–214 (1999); Jee-Hyeong Park, *Enforcing International Trade Agreements with Imperfect Private Monitoring*, 78 Rev. Econ. Stud., 1102–1134 (2011).

several key determinants of the bargaining outcome between trading countries in the WTO system. There are indeed a number of excellent surveys on litigation and bargaining that offer more extensive coverage of the relevant topics; see, for example, Spier (2007).[32]

3.1 BASIC THEORETICAL FRAMEWORK FOR SETTLEMENT BARGAINING

The basic economic model of settlement bargaining has the following ingredients. There are two players in dispute over some issue. Two trading countries, exporter and importer, have conflicting interests regarding the tariff levied by the importing country on the exporting country's product. The two players negotiate over a settlement, e.g., renewed tariff level, in the shadow of a third party: breakdown of the negotiation by either player leads to a decision by an independent judicial procedure such as the WTO dispute settlement system. Voluntary settlement may arise but the details of bargaining behaviour and outcome are affected substantially by the possibility of the independent judicial procedure.[33]

An exporting country's decision to initiate a WTO dispute settlement procedure against its importing counterpart depends on the benefits from pursuing the case as well as its costs. The complainant's benefits come from the expected reduction in the level of tariff recommended by the DSB. The costs of litigation can arise from multiple sources, ranging from preparation of legal documents and other required materials to hiring legal advisors. These costs may also reflect the sheer time that it takes the WTO to reach its verdict, as well as various political costs that arise domestically for the government to obtain public approval towards such a diplomatic conflict.[34]

Before bringing the case formally to the WTO, the countries negotiate over a voluntary settlement. These negotiations may be costly themselves but, if successful, would save significant costs that will follow a breakdown. Indeed, in absence of any transaction costs, economic theory based on rational decision

---

[32] Kathryn E. Spier, *Litigation* in *The Handbook of Law and Economics* (A. Mitchell Polinsky & Steven Shavell, eds., North Holland 2007).

[33] Beshkar and Park (2012) analyse the pre-trial settlement bargaining in the WTO dispute settlement procedure as a signalling game with non-transferable utility in which the defending country knows the likelihood of winning in the court and the complaining country receives only an imperfect signal about the likelihood of the court outcome. They show that the bargaining outcome is affected both by the accuracy of the WTO ruling and by the accuracy of the complaining country's private signal. In contrast to their analysis in which risk-aversion drives countries to settle in the absence of any other cost associated with litigation, the theoretical framework in our discussion can be more general in the sense that it can include various types of costs associated with litigation. Mostafa Beshkar & Jee-Hyeong Park, *Pre-trial Settlement with Imperfect Private Monitoring*, mimeo (2012).

[34] A negative litigation outcome can be politically burdensome. A settlement between governments is often less transparent to the public and hence reduces political risk.

makers predicts that all the gains from trade will be exploited leaving no deadweight loss and hence the WTO litigation will never be invoked – this is the essence of the 'Coase theorem.' Therefore, in order to understand the determinants of the countries' incentives to proceed with a formal litigation process rather than reaching a voluntary agreement themselves, one needs to delve into identifying the sources of transaction costs.

In reality, a considerable proportion of legal disputes end up in court litigations; likewise, many trade conflicts are resolved via the WTO litigations. An important explanation for breakdown of settlement negotiations and bargaining inefficiency is informational asymmetry: the full extents of the bargaining parties' costs and benefits from a WTO verdict on a renewed tariff level are privately known. The exporting country, for example, may have first-hand knowledge of the extent of welfare loss that it has suffered as a result of the high tariff imposed by the importing country, which may similarly possess private knowledge about the full consequences of tariff reduction on its own domestic constituents. Typically, the governments in these cross-border disputes represent complex, and often opaque, chains of political interests domestically in addition to more transparent economic gains and losses.

In the presence of asymmetric information, the countries cannot fine-tune their demands to internalize the inefficient costs associated with resorting to the WTO litigation and, as a consequence, incompatible bargaining postures arise. To make the discourse concrete, suppose that the importer expects the WTO panel to order a tariff reduction that will lead to a welfare loss of X, while the cost of litigation is C. If the complainant knew these costs and benefits, she could demand a new tariff level that corresponds to the amount X+C, leaving the respondent indifferent between voluntary agreement and expected WTO verdict. However, such an offer cannot be engineered if the complainant faces uncertainty over X or C, or indeed both. Rejection of settlement, and hence, formal litigation would follow if the complainant were to ask too much from the respondent, relative to what the respondent privately expects herself from the WTO litigation.

It should be noted that the sample of cases that do end up going to the WTO litigation under asymmetric information is not a random sample – a country that is more confident about winning possibility at the WTO litigations is more likely to reject the settlement offer and take up the third party verdict. The issue is more subtle, however, because in reality one should accept that the informational asymmetry applies both ways. What drives the incompatibility of bargaining postures in bargaining theory with asymmetric information is not each party's own estimation of her net benefit from the WTO litigation per se but the disparity between the parties' perception of each other's legal strength. The larger is this disparity the more likely is the dispute to end up being litigated via the WTO dispute settlement system.

The thrust of our paper is to scrutinize the determinants of non-litigation from the actual dispute data collected from the WTO. While the bargaining theory proposes a critical role of asymmetric information, an empirical test of its predictions runs into a major challenge in measuring the degree of asymmetric information over each pair of disputing countries' costs and benefits from the WTO litigation; they are, by definition, private information. Nonetheless, the bargaining theory of informational asymmetry enables us to motivate several potentially important determinants of non-litigation in the WTO context that can be addressed in the data. We turn to this issue next.

3.2   POSSIBLE FACTORS OF SETTLEMENT BARGAINING

3.2[a]   *Disparity in Economic Size*

A key question in the analysis of bargaining seeks to identify the source of relative bargaining power between the negotiating parties. In the context of WTO disputes, a natural link can be drawn between a country's bargaining power and its economic size. However, it is a priori unclear how the difference in the size of the pair of disputing countries influences the outcome of settlement bargaining: Would a dispute between a large country and a small country more or less likely end up being litigated than one between countries with more balanced sizes?

The bargaining theory of asymmetric information suggests the following possible mechanism: a greater size difference reduces the likelihood of voluntary settlement, or conversely increases the likelihood of litigation, if it were to worsen the informational asymmetry. Two assumptions can motivate how the difference in the economic size of the pair of disputing countries is positively related to the disparity between the parties' private perception of each other's strength in the WTO panel proceeding. First, the complexity of domestic politics that eventually matters for calculating the costs and benefits associated with the panel decision is likely to be correlated with the size of a country. Given this assumption, an increase in the size of a country will make her opponent's estimation of her litigation stake harder, raising the possibility of perception disparity due to imprecise estimates. Second, the economic size of a country determines the set of tools and resources at her disposal in dealing with a dispute, from gathering information and legally preparing the litigations to politically influencing the panel. With more tools and resources, an increase in the size of a country enables her to derive a more accurate estimate of her opponent's stake in the litigation. Thus, this second assumption can induce the degree of asymmetric information over each pair of disputing countries to remain constant as both countries get larger, whereas the informational asymmetry increases with a rise in the size difference of the disputing pair.

The following simple thought experiment demonstrates how the above two assumptions may lead to a positive relationship between the difference in the size of disputing countries and the likelihood of litigation caused by bargaining failure. Denote the economic sizes of country A and country B by S_A and S_B, respectively. The two assumptions imply that the likelihood of bargaining failure caused by country A's inaccurate estimation of country B's litigation strength is positively related with S_B/S_A: recall that the disparity between the disputing parties' perception of each other's litigation strength gives a rise to the possibility of litigation. Because the failure of bargaining may also occur due to country B's imprecise estimation, the likelihood of WTO litigation will be positively related with $S_B/S_A + S_A/S_B$, which in turn equals to $[(S_B)^2 + (S_A)^2]/(S_A \times S_B)$. By defining $r_B \equiv S_B/S_A$, the relative size of country B, we can easily show that $[(S_B)^2 + (S_A)^2]/(S_A \times S_B) = r_B + 1/r_B$. The value of $r_B + 1/r_B$ reaches its minimum when $r_B = 1$ and its value rises either when r_B increases above 1 or when r_B decreases below 1. According to this simple thought experiment, thus, the likelihood of litigation increases with an increase in the size difference between disputing countries, and this likelihood is minimized for an equal-sized disputing pair.

3.2[b]   *Asymmetry in Panel Decision and Implementation*

In most of WTO disputes, the complainant is an exporter, seeking reduction or elimination of some protective measures raised by the respondent, such as anti-dumping duties, subsidies or countervailing duties, escape-clause protection, import prohibition based on environment, public health or technical regulations, and so forth. The panel deliberation mostly focuses on legitimacy of such protective measures, which often depends on various economic and regulatory aspects of the respondent. In estimating the outcome of the panel decision which is a crucial part in evaluating the litigation strength of disputing parties, thus, the information about the respondent is more important than that about the complainant. This implies that the inaccuracy of information about the respondent can play a more important role in causing the disparity between the parties' perception of each other's litigation strength than the one about the complainant in WTO disputes.

Also note that the WTO panel verdict has to be implemented by the respondent, if the ruling is adopted by the DSB. This creates a potentially important asymmetry in bargaining posture and outcome across the two parties because, unlike domestic courts, a WTO verdict is not fully binding. It is the respondent who eventually decides upon whether to implement a WTO verdict or not, which in turn largely depends on various economic and political conditions of the respondent. This uncertainty about implementation would magnify the inaccuracy of parties' perception of each other's litigation strength, once again having the inaccuracy of information about the respondent play a more important role in causing bargaining failure than the one about the complainant.

The above discussion of asymmetry in panel decision and implementation implies that the same imperfectness of information is more likely to cause bargaining failure when it concerns the respondent rather than the complainant. This leads us to test the following hypothesis: A greater difference in the size of the pair of disputing countries reduces the likelihood of voluntary settlement even more when the difference is caused by the respondent being larger than the complainant.

3.2[c]   *Retaliatory Power*

In relation to the previous concern, the power to retaliate against a disobeying respondent may vary across countries, and this may also significantly affect the bargaining outcome. It is not clear, however, whether a stronger retaliatory power of a complainant would lead to a higher or lower likelihood of voluntary settlement. On the one hand, a stronger retaliatory power will reduce the possibility of non-implementation of the panel verdict, which in turn reduces uncertainty and associated imperfectness of information about the respondent. On the other hand, a stronger retaliatory power may increase uncertainty about a complainant because whether to retaliate or not is a private choice that the complainant makes.

3.2[d]   *Reputation Concerns*

A large country that imports (or exports) many products from (or to) many countries has to be concerned with how the outcome of the current dispute may affect potential future disputes. In order to discourage future complainants, it may then be in her interests to promote a reputation for being a tough bargainer by litigating a case that she otherwise would not. Lee and Liu (2013) provide a recent theoretical study of the role of such bargaining externalities.

3.2[e]   *Other Sources of Asymmetric Information*

Asymmetric information between two countries may arise from multiple sources. For example, two countries that share the same language may have greater information about each other. We include a common language dummy in the following empirical analysis of factors that determines the likelihood of litigation in WTO disputes.

4   REALITIES AND PECULIARITIES OF NON-LITIGATION IN THE WTO DISPUTE SETTLEMENT SYSTEM

4.1   DESCRIPTIVE CHARACTERISTICS OF NON-LITIGATED CASES IN THE WTO

Prior to conducting an empirical analysis of the possible determinants of non-litigation suggested by our theoretical discussion in the preceding section, we provide descriptive statistics on non-litigated WTO disputes filed from 1995 to 2010.[35] Out of 419 disputes filed during this period, 230 cases (54.9%) were not actually litigated, demonstrating the relevance of non-litigation in the WTO dispute settlement system. We categorize non-litigated cases according to the stage of settlement in their dispute settlement proceeding: (1) during consultation; (2) after panel request; (3) after panel establishment. We also classify non-litigated cases according to the degree of explicitness of settlement: (i) no formal notification of settlement/termination/withdrawal; (ii) formal notification of settlement/termination/withdrawal without publicizing terms of settlement; (iii) formal notification of mutually agreed settlement, publicizing terms of settlement. Table 1 shows how 230 non-litigated cases are classified into these categories:

---

[35]   Since it typically takes more than a year to complete a panel proceeding, we limit our empirical analysis to the WTO disputes filed from the year of WTO establishment in 1995 to the end of 2010, of which we know for sure whether a filed case has been withdrawn or not.

Table 1   Classification of Non-Litigated WTO Disputes: 1995–2010

		Stage of Settlement			
		During Consultation	After Panel Request	After Panel Establishment	Total
Degree of Explicitness of Settlement	No Formal Notification	129	16	14	159 (69%)
	Formal Notification without Publicizing Terms of Settlement	7	10	1	18 (8%)
	Formal Notification with Publicized Terms of Settlement	38	9	6	53 (23%)
	Total	**174 (76%)**	**35(15%)**	**21(9%)**	**230**

As shown in Table 1, 76% of non-litigated cases were settled during consultation. In other words, a vast majority of non-litigated cases did not even proceed to requesting a panel establishment. This indicates that most of non-litigated cases led to some sort of settlement at a very early stage of their dispute settlement proceeding, even though 129 among such 174 non-litigated cases generated no formal notification of settlement.[36] Only about 9% of non-litigated cases have reached the stage of establishment of a panel that ended without generating any ruling. While a sizable number of non-litigated cases, 53 (23%) out of 230, have notified the terms of their settlement to the DSB that publicized them, we do not know the terms of settlement for the rest of non-litigated cases.

Another way to characterize the WTO disputes is to classify them based on economic characteristics of complainant and respondent countries. We classify countries into G2 (US and EU), IND (Industrial), LDC (Least Developed), and DEV (Developing) countries, where IND, LDC, and DEV follow the classification of Horn and Mavroidis (2008), as shown by Table A1 in Appendix. Using this characterization, Table 2 shows the number of the WTO disputes according to their country types.

---

[36] Non-litigated cases are not necessarily 'resolved' by a mutually agreed resolution: it may be that the case gets withdrawn or stalls without further progress for a variety of reasons Nonetheless, we can still treat such cases as non-litigated in the sense that at least one party has 'voluntarily' given up her option to proceed to obtain the panel decision.

Table 2   Country-Type Based Classification of WTO Disputes: 1995–2010

Number of All Disputed Cases		Respondent Country Classification				
		G2	IND	LDC	DEV	Total
Complainant	G2	63	52	0	63	**178**
Country	IND	59	24	0	24	**107**
Classification	LDC	0	0	0	1	**1**
	DEV	68	16	0	49	**133**
	Total	**190**	**92**	**0**	**137**	**419**

Note: Appendix Table A1 lists all the countries in each category.

The number of WTO disputes involving G2 countries as a respondent is 190 out of 419 cases, and 178 cases had one of G2 countries as a complainant. While these numbers account for a disproportionately large share of G2 countries in the WTO disputes, it is not that surprising given the fact that G2's share in the world economy is about one half of it during the period of 1995–2010. Another notable situation is that there is almost no involvement of LDC countries in the WTO dispute settlement system, except only one case in which a LDC filed a case against a DEV country.[37] Even though LDC's share in the world economy is very small, almost no utilization of the WTO dispute settlement system by and against LDC countries is still a notable fact, which deserves more attention so as to enhance the legitimacy of the WTO.[38] To the contrary, both IND and DEV countries have been active participants of the WTO dispute settlement system, particularly considering their levels of trade.

Table 3 presents the number of non-litigated disputes according to disputing country types, showing the percentage of non-litigation based on the total disputes for each combination of complainant and respondent country types in parenthesis. For example, there are thirty-seven non-litigated cases among sixty-three disputes between G2 country as a complainant and G2 country as a respondent. So, 58.7% of G2-G2 disputes were not litigated. Likewise, when G2 brought a dispute against industrial countries (IND), 51.9% (27 out of the total 52) of the disputes were not litigated. The percentage of non-litigation for G2 complaining disputes reaches 61.9% when G2 complained against developing countries (DEV).

---

[37]   This unique case is *India – Anti-dumping Measure on Batteries from Bangladesh* (DS306).
[38]   One potential explanation is the existence of a significant fixed cost associated with filing a WTO dispute case. In the presence of such a cost, filing a dispute to the WTO requires the amount of potential damage caused by a violation of the WTO rule to exceed a certain level. The amount of imports and exports of LDC may not be large enough to have the potential damage exceed such a critical level. Further investigation into this phenomenon, however, is beyond the scope of this paper.

Table 3   Country-Type Based Classification of Non-Litigated WTO Cases: 1995–2010

Number (%) of Non-litigated Cases		Respondent Country Classification				
		G2	IND	LDC	DEV	Total
Complainant Country Classification	G2	37 (58.7%)	27 (51.9%)	0 (N/A)	39 (61.9%)	**103 (57.9%)**
	IND	19 (32.2%)	14 (58.3%)	0 (N/A)	14 (58.3%)	**47 (43.9%)**
	LDC	0 (N/A)	0 (N/A)	0 (N/A)	1 (100%)	**1 (100%)**
	DEV	30 (44.1%)	11 (68.6%)	0 (N/A)	38 (77.6%)	**79 (59.4%)**
	Total	**86 (45.3%)**	**52 (56.5%)**	**0 (N/A)**	**92 (67.1%)**	**230 (54.9%)**

Recall that the likelihood of non-litigation is higher between countries with similar economic sizes according to the theoretical predictions in section 3. Assuming that countries have similar economic sizes when they belong to the same group of countries, Table 3 offers a glimpse of how the size disparity affects the likelihood of litigation. Note that the percentage of non-litigation between countries of the same group is higher than the average non-litigation percentage either as a complainant or as a respondent: for example, the non-litigation percentage between G2, 58.7%, is higher than the average non-litigation percentage, 57.9%, as a complainant, and 45.3%, as a respondent. The same tendencies can be observed for IND-IND and DEV-DEV pairs. The exception occurs for LDC countries, which has only one dispute case that is not litigated.

In section 3.2 above, we discussed a possible channel, based on the theory of asymmetric information, via which the likelihood of non-litigation decreases as the difference in the economic sizes of countries in dispute increases. Assuming that GDPs of countries belonging to IND are larger than those of countries belonging to DEV, the non-litigation percentage for DEV complaining disputes decreases from 77.6% to 68.6%, then to 44.1%, when the respondent countries change from DEV to IND, then to G2. We fail to have such a monotone change for the cases in which G2 countries are complainants. However, some countries in the DEV group are actually larger than some IND countries, and there are other factors that would also influence the likelihood of non-litigation, as discussed in section 3.2. In order to rigorously delineate the determinants of non-litigation, we carry out a regression analysis.

4.2   AN ECONOMETRIC ANALYSIS: LOGISTIC REGRESSION

The main focus of our empirical analysis is to scrutinize the following relationship: a greater difference in the economic size of the pair of disputing countries reduces

JOURNAL OF WORLD TRADE

the likelihood of non-litigation. To measure the economic size of a country, we use real GDP as reported by the World Bank.[39] Because the dependent variable is the non-litigation dummy, which takes 1 if non-litigation occurs and 0 otherwise, we use the logistic regression for our econometric analysis. Table 4 summarizes the regression results.

Table 4   Logistic Regression Results

Explanatory Variables	Variations for Testing Non-litigation Decisions			
	(1)	(2)	(3)	(4)
GDP-Diff	-8.01e-14 (2.17e-14)★★★	-7.61e-14 (2.20e-14)★★★	-7.31e-14 (2.28e-14)★★★	-6.57e-14 (2.30e-14)★★★
D-Dummy		-.6539801 (.2025215)★★★	-.573636 (.2093156)★★★	-.885459 (.224587)★★★
D-Import			-3.07e-09 (1.28e-09)★★	
Export-Share				-1.783413 (.7955965)★★
Observations	419	419	403[40]	411[41]
R-Squared	0.0244	0.0427	0.0525	0.0537

Note: Standard deviation is inside parenthesis; ★ represents significance at 10% level, ★★ represents significance at 5% level, and ★★★ represents significance at 1% level.

The first explanatory variable is the absolute value of the difference in the size of real GDP (GDP-Diff) of the pair of disputing countries. The coefficient on GDP-Diff in the first column of Table 4 is negative and statistically significant at 1% level, indeed supporting the claim that an increase in their size difference raises the possibility of settlement bargaining to fail.

There are other factors that may affect the likelihood of non-litigation, as discussed in section 3.2. Due to asymmetry in panel decision and implementation, a greater difference in the size of the pair of disputing countries decreases the likelihood of non-litigation even more when the difference is caused by the respondent being larger than the complainant. To capture this possibility, we add a dummy variable, which takes 1 if the respondent's size is larger than the

---

[39]   We have used the real GDP of the disputing countries for the year before the actual filing year. We note that the real GDP is mostly stable over a year period.
[40]   The reduction in the number of observations is due to the lack of import data of some countries.
[41]   The reduction in the number of observations is due to the lack of export data of some countries.

complainant's, and 0 otherwise, denoting it by D-Dummy. As shown in the second column of Table 4, the coefficient on D-Dummy is negative and statistically significant, with the coefficient on GDP-Diff continuing to be negative and statistically significant at 1% level, thus supporting our prediction.

To measure the degree of reputational concerns of a respondent, we use the amount of total imports of the respondent from the complainant, denoting it by D-Import.[42] The respondent that imports many products from the complainant is likely to have a greater concern about how the outcome of the current dispute may affect potential future disputes with the same complainant. In order to discourage future complaints by the complainant, it may then be in her interests to promote a reputation for being a tough bargainer by litigating a case that she otherwise would not. Thus, we expect a negative coefficient on D-Import, and indeed the regression result on the third column supports such a prediction, with statistical significance at 5% level.

As a measure of retaliatory power of a complainant against potential non-compliance of a respondent, we use the ratio of the respondent's export to the complainant over the respondent's total export, representing the complainant's importance as the respondent's export destination, denoting it by Export-Share.[43] The sign on Export-Share can either be positive or negative, depending on whether a stronger retaliatory power of the complainant mitigates or magnifies the effect of informational asymmetry across countries in dispute. The regression result in the fourth column includes Export-Share as an explanatory variable in addition to GDP-Diff and D-Dummy.[44] The coefficient on Export-Share is negative and statistically significant at 5% level, indicating that the stronger retaliatory power may magnify the effect of informational asymmetry, raising the possibility of bargaining failure.[45]

---

[42] D-import data come from the trade data of UN Comtrade for the year that precedes the filing year of a dispute under consideration. While we could have used D-import data for the filing year instead of the one for the preceding year, it is unlikely to affect the outcome of our analysis as D-import data are mostly stable over a year period.

[43] The export share data comes from the trade data of UN Comtrade, for the year in which the last action took place in the WTO dispute settlement process in the case of non-litigation, and for the year of panel ruling in the case of litigation.

[44] We also run the regression with all four variables of GDP-Diff, D-Dummy, D-Import, and Export-Share, having the same signs on the coefficients. But the signs on D-Import and Export-Share were no longer statistically significant.

[45] We also ran a regression including a language dummy, which takes one if countries in dispute use a common language or zero otherwise. While the sign of the coefficient on the language dummy was positive as expected, it was not statistically significant and hence omitted from Table 4.

4.3 Implication and Limitation of the Econometric Analysis

According to economic theory, settlement bargaining may fail and thus litigation may occur due to informational asymmetry that generates a disparity between the disputing parties' perception of each other's legal strength. By linking such informational asymmetry with the difference in the size of countries in dispute, the theory then suggests a channel via which the likelihood of non-litigation decreases with an increase in the size difference. We find an empirical evidence for this prediction using the WTO dispute data. Other variables that can also be motivated by the theory of asymmetric information turn out to have significant effects in the expected directions.

Figure 1 in Introduction illustrates that both the number of dispute cases filed and the percentage of non-litigated cases have actually been decreasing over time in the WTO dispute settlement system. There has been a clear trend that WTO members are more determined to litigate a dispute once the dispute formally reaches the WTO dispute settlement system. How can we interpret these phenomena based on our findings? Does the reduction in the percentage of non-litigated disputes imply an increase in the informational asymmetry across countries over time? It should be noted here that the decline in the number of disputes filed to the WTO may imply not only a possible reduction in non-compliance of the WTO rules, but also a possible increase in dispute resolution among members prior to formal dispute filing to the WTO. If the latter is the primary cause for the phenomena in Figure 1, then the upward trend in the frequency of litigation does not necessarily imply an increase in the cross-country informational asymmetry about the legal strength of their disputed cases.

5 WAYS FORWARD TO MAKE MORE SENSE OF NON-LITIGATION

Our legal and economic analysis of non-litigated disputes in the WTO system opens up a number of avenues for further research. For example, as explained in section 2, non-litigated disputes can be divided into two groups: cases settled during the consultation stage and cases settled during the panel process. Economic incentives may differ depending on when settlement takes place. A more sophisticated bargaining model may explain the forces that determine the disputing countries' incentives on when to drop litigation. Moreover, a future research may explain when a member decides to bring a case to the WTO dispute settlement system and when it tries to resolve a dispute even without resorting to the WTO altogether. Lessons from theoretical development in bargaining analysis would play an important role in elucidating legal decisions of WTO members with respect to settlement versus litigation.

The discussion of Figure 1 in section 2.1 also emphasizes a point that our analysis has not fully explored: what is the role of the consultation stage in the WTO dispute settlement system if countries can settle prior to bringing their disputes to the WTO? The stated goal of having the consultation stage is to promote settlement among countries, thus to avoid costly litigation and potential conflicts between members. But, if countries can settle a dispute even prior to bringing it to the WTO, the utilization of the consultation stage as an opportunity to settle would have been clearly declining. Our economic analysis of non-litigation should be expanded and complemented by more articulated models to provide a better understanding for the role of the consultation stage in the WTO disputes.

Another aspect of consultation to examine is the role for disseminating information about potentially disputable issues to other members. Consultation requests by complainants can actually draw other members' attention to the disputed issues. Such requests will provide other members with an opportunity to decide whether they would also initiate separate challenges or join merely as third parties. A bargaining model to explain sequential decision making for litigation may also shed light on the reasons why multiple members try to bring complaints on essentially the same matters undertaken by a respondent. Future research in this regard may help understand the strategic incentives to separately join in the WTO litigation despite the possibility of free riding on the other complainants' litigations.

The finding in this paper, as discussed in section 4, can also raise an important practical implication for future directions of the WTO dispute settlement system. If the informational asymmetry problem can be reduced, disputing members will be able to avoid litigation more easily since both parties understand each other's situation better. In this regard, the role of consultation should be appreciated more seriously since its primary function is to facilitate communication between disputing parties. Furthermore, refining the consultation process, in order to mitigate informational asymmetry or improve better communication between disputing parties, would be able to substantially contribute to nurturing settlement instead of costly litigation in the WTO. There are previous studies that suggest more transparency – or less privacy – during consultation would actually discourage settlement because disputing parties would then have less latitude to strike a deal.[46] Our results do not necessarily contradict this view: it is the

---

[46]   See, e.g., M. Busch and E. Reinhardt, *Bargaining in the Shadow of the Law: Early Settlement in GATT/WTO Disputes*, 24 Fordham Intl. L. J. 158, 170–172 (2000).

facilitation of information sharing not with non-disputing WTO members or general public but *between disputing parties* that reduces informational asymmetry problem.

Unfortunately, although there were a few proposals to amend and upgrade the consultation process in the Doha rules negotiation, no proposal was made to improve communication or fact finding functions among disputing parties. For example, there was an amending proposal that a member requesting consultation 'shall notify to the DSB as to the status of the consultations'.[47] This will clearly enhance information sharing among WTO members on the disputing situations, but not necessarily between disputing parties. Current DSU negotiations need to pay more attention to the non-litigated aspects of the WTO dispute settlement system so that it can contribute to the legitimacy and stability of the WTO system.

REFERENCES

Beshkar, M. & J-H. Park. *Pre-trial Settlement with Imperfect Private Monitoring.* Mimeo, 2012.

Bown, Chad P. 'Participation in WTO Dispute Settlement: Complainants, Interested Parties, and Free Riders'. *World Bank Economic Review* 19 (2005): 287.

Busch, Marc L. 'Democracy, Consultation, and the Paneling of Disputes under GATT'. *Journal of Conflict Resolution* 44 (2000): 425.

Busch, Marc L. & Eric Reinhardt. 'Bargaining in the Shadow of the Law: Early Settlement in GATT/WTO Disputes'. *Fordham International Law Journal* 24 (2000): 158.

Davey, William J. 'Proposals for Improving the Working Procedures of WTO Dispute Settlement Panels'. In *The WTO Dispute Settlement System 1995-2003*, edited by Federico Ortino & Ernst-Ulrich Petersmann. Kluwer Law International, 2004.

Dixit, A. 1987, 'Strategic Aspects of Trade Policy'. In *Advances in Economic Theory: Fifth World Congress*, Cambridge University Press.

Guzman, Andrew T. & Beth A. Simmons. 'To Settle or Empanel? An Empirical Analysis of Litigation and Settlement at the WTO'. *Journal of Legal Studies* 31 (2002): S205.

Horlick, Gary N. 'The Consultation Phase of WTO Dispute Resolution: A Private Practitioner's View'. *International Law* 32 (1998): 685.

Horn, H. & Mavroidis. *The WTO Dispute Settlement System 1995–2006: Some Descriptive Statistics.* Mimeo, 2008.

---

[47]   WTO, TN/DS/25, para. 6a.

Jansen, Bernard. 'Scope of Jurisdiction in GATT/WTO Dispute Settlement: Consultations and Panel Requests'. In *Improving WTO Dispute Settlement Procedures: Issues & Lessons from the Practice of Other International Courts & Tribunals*, edited by Friedl Weiss. Cameron May, 2000.

Kuijper, Peiter-Jan. 'The Pre-litigation Stage in the WTO Dispute Settlement Procedure and in the EC Infringement Procedure'. In *Improving WTO Dispute Settlement Procedures: Issues & Lessons from the Practice of Other International Courts & Tribunals*, edited by Friedl Weiss. Cameron May, 2000.

Lee, J. & Q. Liu. 'Gambling Reputation: Repeated Bargaining with Outside Options'. *Econometrica* 81 (2013): 1601.

Maggi, G. 'The Role of Multilateral Institutions in International Trade Cooperation'. *American Economic Review* 89 (1999): 190.

Marceau, Gabrielle. 'Consultations and the Panel Process in the WTO Dispute Settlement System'. In *Key Issues in WTO Dispute Settlement: The First Ten Years*, edited by Rufus Yerxa & Bruce Wilson. Cambridge University Press, 2005.

Olin, Wethington L. 'Commentary on the Consultation Mechanism under the WTO Dispute Settlement Understanding during the First Five Years'. *Law and Policy International Business* 31 (1999): 583.

Palmeter, David & Petros C. Mavroidis. *Dispute Settlement in the World Trade Organization: Practice and Procedure*, Cambridge University Press, 2004.

Park, J-H. 'Enforcing International Trade Agreements with Imperfect Private Monitoring'. *Review of Economic Studies* 78 (2011): 1102.

Parlin, Christopher. 'Operation of Consultations, Deterrence, and Mediation'. *Law and Policy International Business* 31 (1999): 565.

Porges, Amelia. 'Settling WTO Disputes: What Do Litigation Models Tell Us'. *Ohio State Journal on Dispute Resolution* 19 (2003): 141.

Spier, K.E. 'Litigation'. In *The Handbook of Law and Economics*, edited by A. Mitchell Polinsky & Steven Shavell. North Holland, 2007.

Yerxa, Rufus & Bruce Wilson. *Key Issues in WTO Dispute Settlement: The First Ten Years*. Cambridge University Press, 2005.

WTO. *A Handbook on the WTO Dispute Settlement System*. Cambridge University Press, 2004.

APPENDIX

Table A1   *Country Classification*

G2	LDC	DEV		
EC	Angola	Albania	India	Tanzania
US	Bangladesh	Antigua and	Indonesia	Thailand
		Barbuda		
	Benin Burkina	Argentina	Jamaica	Trinidad and
	Faso Burundi	Armenia	Jordan	Tobago
IND	Cambodia	Bahrain	Kenya Kuwait	Tunisia
	Central Afr.	Barbados	Kyrgyz Republic	Unit. Arab
Australia	Rep	Belize	Macao – China	Emirates
Bulgaria	Chad	Bolivia	Malaysia	Uruguay
Canada	Dem. Rep.	Botswana	Mauritius	Venezuela
Croatia	Congo	Brazil	Moldova	Zimbabwe
Cyprus	Djibouti	Brunei	Mongolia	
Czech Republic	Gambia	Darussalam	Morocco	
Estonia	Guinea	Cameroon	Namibia	
Hong Kong –	Guinea-Bissau	Chile	Nicaragua	
Ch. Hungary	Haiti Lesotho	China	Nigeria	
Iceland	Madagascar	Colombia	Oman	
Israel	Malawi	Congo	Pakistan	
Japan	Maldives	Costa Rica	Panama	
Korea	Mali	Côte d'Ivoire	Papua New	
Latvia	Mauritania	Cuba Dominica	Guinea	
Liechtenstein	Mozambique	Dominican	Paraguay	
Lithuania	Myanmar	Republic	Peru	
Malta	Nepal	Ecuador	Philippines	
Mexico	Niger	Egypt	Qatar	
New Zealand	Rwanda	El Salvador	St Kitts and Nevis	
Norway	Senegal	Fiji	St Lucia	
Poland	Sierra Leone	F.Yug. Rep	St Vincent & the	
Romania	Solomon	Maced.	Gr.	
Singapore	Islands	Gabon	Saudi Arabia	
Slovak Republic	Togo	Georgia	South Africa	
	Uganda	Ghana	Sri Lanka	
		Grenada		

G2	LDC	DEV		
Slovenia	Zambia	Guatemala	Suriname	
Switzerland		Guyana	Swaziland	
Turkey		Honduras	Chinese Taipei	

Source: Horn and Mavroidis (2008): 'The WTO Dispute Settlement System 1995–2006: Some Descriptive Statistics'

Note: The group G2 needs no further explanation, except that they counted EC-15 as one of its two constituent members. The LDC group corresponds largely to the list of LDCs according to the United Nations. A more discretionary line is drawn between IND and DEV. Horn and Mavroidis (2008) have here classified OECD Member under IND; they have also classified under IND, non-OECD Members which have become members of the EC, or are at an advanced stage of their accession negotiations. Finally, under IND they have also classified countries which are not OECD Members but have a very high per capita income, countries such as Singapore. The DEV group consists of all countries which do not fit into either of the above-mentioned categories.

Table A2   Logistic Regression Variables and Data

	Description	Data Sources	Prediction
Dependent Variable			
Non-litigation	1 if non-litigation occurs; 0 otherwise (i.e. if the final panel reports have been circulated).	The chronological list of disputes cases on WTO website.	
Explanatory Variables			
GDP-Diff	The absolute value of the difference in real GDP of disputing country pairs for the year before the actual filing year.	World Bank	Higher GDP-Diff reduces the likelihood of non-litigation.
D-dummy	1 if the respondent's size is larger than the complainant's; 0 otherwise.	World Bank	D-dummy=1 reduces the likelihood of non-litigation.
D-Import	The amount of total import of the respondent from the complainant for the year before the actual filing year.	UN Comtrade	Higher D-Import reduces the likelihood of non-litigation.

	Description	*Data Sources*	*Prediction*
Export-Share	The ratio of the respondent's export to the complainant over the respondent's total export for the year when the last action took place in the WTO dispute settlement process.	UN Comtrade	Higher Export-Share reduces the likelihood of non-litigation.
L-Dummy	1 if the disputing countries share a common language; 0 otherwise.	World Atlas	Common language increases the likelihood of non-litigation.

Journal of International Economic Law 6(3), 597–633 © Oxford University Press 2003; all rights reserved

Chapter 2

KOREA IN THE GATT/WTO DISPUTE SETTLEMENT SYSTEM: LEGAL BATTLE FOR ECONOMIC DEVELOPMENT

*Dukgeun Ahn**

ABSTRACT

Korea's economic development saga, which amazed economists and policy-makers, has been filled with numerous trade disputes with its major trading partners. Despite the prevalence of such bilateral trade disputes, Korea had shown unequivocal resistance to resorting to the multilateral dispute settlement forum under the GATT system. Since the inception of the WTO, however, Korea has dramatically changed its attitude toward trade dispute settlement. The Korean experience of trade dispute settlement, therefore, seems a salient example of how the newly augmented system under the WTO is perceived and how it has been effectively utilized by average WTO Member countries in order to address international trade problems.

INTRODUCTION

International trade is an indispensable element for explaining Korea's economic development during the past three decades,[1] marking a remarkable accomplishment that has amazed many economists[2] and policymakers.[3] From a legal perspective, however, Korea's economic development saga has been filled with numerous trade disputes with its major trading partners. When

---

* Assistant Professor of trade law and policy, KDI School of Public Policy and Management, Korea. I am grateful to participants at the international symposium on 'WTO and East Asia', especially John H. Jackson, Misuo Matsushita, Ho-Young Ahn and Doo-Sik Kim, for useful comments on the earlier drafts.

[1] See generally Il Sakong, *Korea in the World Economy* (Washington, DC: Institute for International Economics, 1993).

[2] Professor Robert Lucas, 1995 Nobel laureate in economics, wrote that 'simply advising a society to "follow the Korean model" is a little like advising an aspiring basketball player to "follow the Michael Jordan model"'. Robert E. Lucas, Jr, 'Making a Miracle', 61 Econometrica 251 (1993), at 252.

[3] For example, a report by the Korea International Trade Association (KITA) estimates that the contribution of merchandise export to total economic growth in 2001 amounted to 53.6%. However, this significant ratio was partly due to the substantial reduction of the total growth rate, that is estimated to have been 2.8% in 2001 while it was 8.8% in 2000. The economic growth attributed to the merchandise export is estimated to be 3.5% in 2000 and 1.5% in 2001. Korea International Trade Association, 'Effect of Exports on the National Economy in 2001' (Feb. 2002, in Korean).

31

export volumes and the diversity of products from Korea have grown, its primary exporting items have been routinely targeted by various trade remedy actions such as anti-dumping, countervailing, and safeguard measures in the major markets, especially since the 1980s.[4]

Despite the prevalence of such bilateral trade disputes, however, Korea had not been eager to utilize the multilateral dispute settlement system established under the GATT. This general tendency of the Korean government to avoid legal confrontation in the multilateral forum and instead to resort to bilateral diplomatic settlements has dramatically changed with the development of the WTO dispute settlement system. Thus, the Korean experience of trade dispute settlement seems a salient example of how the newly augmented system under the WTO has been perceived and effectively utilized by many less visible WTO Member countries in order to address international trade problems.

This article briefly reviews the Korean experience of dispute settlements in the GATT/WTO system and also discusses non-legal implication of legal adjudication. But, rather than delving into the legal issues disputed in individual cases that are too diverse to be scrutinized in one paper, this article focuses on the overall progress of trade dispute resolution and implementation thereof. Sections I and II analyze the trade dispute settlement involving Korea under the GATT and WTO systems, respectively. Systemic issues regarding the current WTO dispute settlement system drawn from the Korean experience for the Doha Round negotiations are discussed in Section III. Finally, the last section concludes with some observations.

I. DISPUTE SETTLEMENT DURING THE GATT PERIOD (1967–1994)

A. Korea's accession to the GATT

The Korean government first sought to join the GATT in 1950, when it eagerly tried to be recognized as an independent state in the international community after liberation from Japan. At that time, the Korean government delegation sent to Torquay, England, finished the GATT accession negotiation and signed the relevant documents.[5] This first attempt, however, failed when the Korean government could not complete the requisite domestic ratification procedures due to the Korean War during 1950–1953.[6]

---

[4] During the 1980s, at least 171 trade remedy measures against Korean exports were reported. See below Figure 2 in Section I.C. See generally N. Han *et al.*, *Cases of Trade Disputes of the Korean Industries* (Seoul: POSRI, 1999, in Korean) 37.

[5] GATT, *Basic Instruments and Selected Documents* (hereinafter '*BISD*'), Vol. II (1952) 33–34. At that meeting, Austria, Peru, Philippines, and Turkey also finished the accession negotiation. While Austria, Peru, and Turkey formally became contracting parties in 1951, the Philippines formally joined the GATT on 27 December 1979.

[6] Tae-Hyuk Hahm, 'Reflections on the GATT Accession Negotiations', *Diplomatic Negotiation Case* 94-1 (1994, in Korean), at 5.

The GATT regime underwent substantial changes to embrace development issues more explicitly during the late 1960s. The efforts to demonstrate a more forceful commitment to the interests of developing countries within the GATT system led to the adoption of the new provisions, Articles XXXVI–XXXVIII, as Part IV of the GATT.[7] In addition, the GATT as a whole tried to be perceived as a more favorable forum for developing countries. For example, the 1964 GATT publication entitled 'The Role of GATT in Relation to Trade and Development' emphasized considerable legal freedom for developing countries, such as non-reciprocity, infant industry protection for industrial development, and balance-of-payment protection measures.[8] These factors clearly demonstrated a strong GATT policy to expand its membership with developing countries. Moreover, in terms of the legal disciplines of the GATT, the late 1960s was probably the lowest point in the GATT's history.[9] During the period of 1959–1970, the GATT dispute settlement activities had dramatically declined, becoming virtually dormant in the late 1960s.[10] Such developments created undoubtedly a more favorable environment for developing countries to consider joining the GATT. In fact, the GATT membership increased most during the 1960s, in which 39 countries acceded (see Table 1).[11]

With such a favorable backdrop to developing countries within the GATT, the Korean government resumed its effort to accede to the GATT in 1965 when it vigorously pursued export promotion as the primary element of economic development policies. The revision of the GATT to include Part IV to deal with development issues also played an important role in inducing Korea to reconsider the GATT accession at that time. After extensive internal discussion on potential economic benefits and costs, the Korean government finally submitted its accession application to the GATT Secretariat on 20 May 1966, and conducted the tariff negotiations with 12 contracting parties from September to 2 December 1966.[12]

Korea officially acceded to the GATT in 1967, in accordance with Article XXXIII of the GATT.[13] More specifically, on 16 December 1966, the Council of Representatives adopted the 'Report of the Working Party' for

---

[7] The Protocol Amending the General Agreement on Tariffs and Trade to Introduce a Part IV on Trade and Development, which was adopted on 8 February 1965, entered into force on 27 June 1966. WTO, *Analytical Index: Guide to GATT Law and Practice* (Geneva, 1995) 1040.

[8] Robert E. Hudec, *Developing Countries in the GATT Legal System* (Trade Policy Research Center, 1987) 59–60.

[9] Ibid, at 65.

[10] Robert E. Hudec, *The GATT Legal System and World Trade Diplomacy* (2nd edn, Butterworth Legal Publishers, 1990) 235–50.

[11] The accession to the GATT was also substantially increased in the early 1990s during which the Uruguay Round negotiation had been conducted. See generally WTO, n 7, at 1136.

[12] The Working Party for Korea's accession included 14 contracting parties. Hahm, above n 6, 23.

[13] GATT, 'Korea – Accession under Article XXXIII: Decision of 2 March 1967', BISD, No 15 (1968) 60.

Table 1. The Statistics for Accession to the GATT.

Years	1948–1949	1950s	1960s	1970s	1980s	1990–1994	Total
Number of acceding countries	19	17	39	9	11	33	128

Table 2. GATT Disputes Involving Korea

Case name	Complainants	Panel decision	Notes
As respondent			
Korea – Restrictions on Imports of Beef	Australia, New Zealand, US	BISD 36S/202, 36S/234, 36S/268 (adopted on 7 Nov. 1989)	Cases under Article XXIII
Korea – Anti-Dumping Duties on Imports of Polyacetal Resins from the United States	US	BISD 40S/205 (adopted on 27 April 1993)	Case under the Tokyo Round Anti-dumping Code
As complainant			
EC – Article XIX Action on Imports into the UK of Television Sets from Korea	Korea	None (Settled)	Cases under Article XXIII

the GATT accession.[14] After the Korean government completed the domestic ratification procedure, the 'Protocol for the Accession of Korea' to the GATT entered into force on 14 April 1967.[15] On the other hand, Korea invoked Article XXXV for non-application of GATT with respect to Cuba,[16] Czechoslovakia,[17] Poland,[18] and Yugoslavia.[19] These Article XXXV invocations were all simultaneously withdrawn in September 1971.[20]

Korea began its formal participation as a contracting party at the Tokyo Round of the multilateral trade negotiation, although it was merely as a minor player.[21] Subsequently, Korea joined the four so-called 'Side Codes': Subsidies Code,[22] Standards Code,[23] Customs Valuation Code,[24] and Anti-Dumping Code.[25]

Korea had never joined the sectoral agreements on bovine meat, dairy products, and civil aircraft, nor the Agreement on Import Licensing Procedures as a plurilateral agreement. Korea joined the Agreement on Government Procurement during the Uruguay Round and implemented it only from 1 January 1997, while all other signatories except for Hong Kong applied it from 1 January 1996.[26]

B. GATT disputes concerning Korea

The Korean government's experience of dispute settlement under the GATT system is fairly limited (see Table 2).[27] Korea was challenged only

---

[14] GATT, above n 13, at 106.

[15] GATT, above n 13, at 44.

[16] GATT, L/2783 (1967).

[17] GATT, L/2783 (1967).

[18] GATT, L/2874 (1967)

[19] GATT, L/2783 (1967).

[20] GATT, L/3580 (1971). See also WTO, above n 7, at 1034–1036. On the other hand, it is noted that 50 contracting parties invoked Article XXXV in respect of Japan at its accession in 1955. Ibid.

[21] Chulsu Kim, 'Korea in the Multilateral Trading System: From Obscurity to Prominence', in *The Kluwer Companion to the WTO Agreement* (The Hague: Kluwer Law International, forthcoming).

[22] The Agreement on Interpretation and Application of Articles VI, XVI, and XXIII. In Korea, it was signed on 10 June 1980 and entered into force on 10 July 1980 as Treaty No 709. See Ministry of Foreign Affairs, *Compilation of Multilateral Treaties*, Vol 5 (in Korean).

[23] The Agreement on Technical Barriers to Trade. In Korea, it was signed on 3 September 1980 and entered into force on 2 October 1980 as Treaty No 715. Ibid.

[24] The Agreement on Implementation of Article VII. The Customs Valuation Code entered into force on 1 January 1981 while the other three Codes entered into force on 1 January 1980. GATT, BISD, No 28 (1982) 40. In Korea, it was entered into force on 6 January 1981 as Treaty No 729. Ministry of Foreign Affairs, above n 22.

[25] The Agreement on Implementation of Article VI. Korea accepted the Anti-Dumping Code on 24 February 1986 and the Code entered into force for Korea on 26 March 1986 as Treaty No 877. GATT, BISD, No 33 (1987) 207. See also Ministry of Foreign Affairs, *Compilation of Multilateral Treaties*, Vol 8 (in Korean).

[26] WTO, Agreement on Government Procurement, Article XXIV:3. Hong Kong also had one more year for implementation to apply from 1 January 1997.

[27] For the GATT panel reports, see generally Pierre Pescatore *et al.*, *Handbook of WTO/GATT Dispute*

once under Article XXIII of the GATT in 1988 and later one more time under the Tokyo Round Anti-Dumping Code in 1992. The former case, *Korea – Restrictions on Imports of Beef* ('*Korea – Beef I*'),[28] however, had an enormous impact on the subsequent Korean trading system by dismantling Article XVIII:B cover for import restriction. The latter case, *Korea – Anti-Dumping Duties on Imports of Polyacetal Resins from the United States* ('*Korea – Polyacetal Resins*'), also set an important precedent for the inchoate Korean trade remedy system.[29]

In 1978, Korea brought the first case as a complainant under Article XXIII against the European Communities regarding a safeguard action. This case, *EC – Article XIX Action on Imports into the U.K. of Television Sets from Korea*,[30] did not, however, produce an actual ruling since Korea agreed with the European Communities on a voluntary export restraint arrangement and withdrew its complaint in 1979.[31]

Since the late 1980s, Korea began to participate in the GATT dispute settlement procedures as a third party. The first case as a third party was *US – Section 337 of the Tariff Act of 1930*,[32] in which the European Communities brought a case against the United States concerning a discriminatory patent protection mechanism. In that case, Canada, Japan, and Switzerland also joined as third parties. When the US intellectual property system was challenged in the GATT dispute settlement system, the Korean government determined to exercise its third-party right because it was immediately after Korea had been targeted by Section 301 for the lack of effective protection of US intellectual property rights.[33] The second case was *EEC – Regulation on Imports of Parts and Components*,[34] in which Japan challenged the European Communities' anti-circumvention duties on certain manufactured products. In this case, Korea was a third party along with Australia, Canada, Hong Kong, Singapore, and the United States.

Furthermore, Korean government officials also occasionally contributed to panel works for GATT dispute settlements. In 1973, Eun Tak Lee was elected as one of the four panelists in the *UK – Import Restrictions on Cotton*

Settlement (looseleaf). On-line access to the GATT panel reports is available at <http://www.world-tradelaw.net/reports/gattpanels> (visited 25 March 2003) and <http://www.wto.org/english/tratop_e/dispu_e/gt47ds_e.htm> (visited 25 March 2003).

[28] GATT, BISD, No 36 (1990) 202, 234, 268, adopted 7 November 1989.

[29] GATT, BISD, No 40 (1995) 205, adopted 27 April 1993.

[30] GATT, C/M/124 (1978).

[31] GATT, C/M/134 (1979). See also Robert E. Hudec, *Enforcing International Trade Law: The Evolution of the Modern GATT Legal System* (Butterworth Legal Publishers, 1993) 283, 471.

[32] GATT, BISD, No 36 (1990) 345, adopted 7 November 1989.

[33] The section 301 investigation was terminated on 14 August 1986 when the US government concluded an agreement with Korea that would dramatically improve protection of intellectual property rights. US Fed. Reg. 29445, 14 August 1986.

[34] GATT, BISD, No 37 (1991) 132, adopted 16 May 1990.

Textiles case.[35] Ki-Choo Lee later worked as a panelist for *EC – Refunds on Exports of Sugar*[36] and *EEC – UK Application of EEC Directives to Imports of Poultry from the US.*[37]

1. Korea – Beef I case: opening the real GATT period

Since its accession to the GATT in 1967, Korea had imposed various import restrictive measures on the basis of the balance-of-payment (hereinafter 'BOP') exception under Article XVIII:B. In fact, it was the BOP exception that crucially motivated the Korean government to apply for the GATT accession despite serious concerns regarding consequential import liberalization.[38] As of 1988, the Korean government still maintained such measures on 358 items, including beef.

Korea began the importation of beef in 1976 and made a GATT concession for a 20% bound tariff in 1979. In October 1984 when the price of domestic cows plummeted,[39] the Korean government limited commercial imports of beef to the general market in order to protect domestic beef farmers, and from May 1985, even high-quality beef for the hotel market. Between May 1985 and August 1988, virtually no commercial imports of beef took place. Incidentally, from 1986 Korea had accumulated, for the first time in its history, a trade surplus, until it was later reversed in 1990.

On 16 February 1988, the American Meat Institute filed a Section 301 petition and the USTR initiated a Section 301 investigation on 18 March 1988.[40] Australia, New Zealand, and the United States also brought complaints against Korea to the GATT dispute settlement system and thereby three panels were separately established, although the memberships of the panels were identical.[41] The Korean government decided to address the three panels separately because it thought it would be more advantageous to deal with complainants one-by-one, rather than confront the three counterparts simultaneously.[42] Interestingly, the Korean government was permitted to

---

[35] GATT, BISD, No 20 (1974) 237, adopted 5 February 1973.

[36] GATT, BISD, No 27 (1981) 69, adopted 10 November 1980.

[37] GATT, BISD, No 28 (1982) 90, adopted 11 June 1981.

[38] The Korean government consulted with the GATT Secretariat prior to the accession application and was assured that, under Article XVIII:B, it might maintain the existing import restraints for even more than a decade. Hahm, above n 6, 10.

[39] The fluctuation in cow prices was indeed enormous during the early 1980s in Korea. The price for a cow was about $900 in 1981, $1,600 in 1983 and $1,000 in 1985. The price for a calf fluctuated even more substantially: about $180 in 1981, $900 in 1983 and $380 in 1985. Nevertheless, the domestic beef price remained relatively stable, showing about 15% change during 1981-1985. Hu and Lee, 'Economic Assessment of Beef Industry and Policy Development', 8 Rural Economy 9 (1985, in Korean), at 10.

[40] USTR, *Section 301 Table of Cases*, Beef (301_65) <http://www.ustr.gov/html/act301.htm>.

[41] GATT, above n 28.

[42] Interview with Young-Rae Lee, President of Korea 4-H (then Director General of Ministry of Agriculture, Forest and Fishery) (13 Aug. 2002). This strategy turned out to be burdensome in its

38

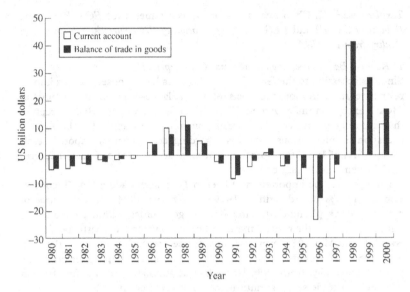

Figure 1. Trend of Balance of Payments in Korea

Bank of Korea, Statistics Database <http://www.bok.or.kr> (visited on 2 April 2003).

bring a foreign private counsel to assist its oral hearings during the panel proceedings.[43]

On the basis of the BOP Committee consultation and the IMF opinion provided thereto, the panel held that the import restriction by Korea was not consistent with the GATT and could not be justified under the BOP exception of Article XVIII:B. The panel rejected the Korean government's argument that this issue should be confined to the determination not by the dispute settlement panel but by the BOP Committee.[44]

---

procedural aspect, by requiring the duplicative oral hearings with three parties. The only other GATT cases in which separate panels were established basically on the same matter for different complainants are the cases concerning 'Income Tax Practices' maintained by France, Belgium, and the Netherlands. GATT, BISD, No 23 (1977) 114, 127, 137.

[43] A European lawyer was allowed to attend a sitting of an oral hearing without a right to make a statement. The Korean government requested that a meeting be suspended whenever it needed to consult with the foreign legal counsel. Interview with Young-Rae Lee, President of Korea 4-H (then Director-General of Ministry of Agriculture, Forest and Fishery) (13 Aug. 2002). Under the WTO system, the participation of a private counsel became a well-established matter of law. See generally M. Bronckers and John Jackson, 'Editorial Comment: Outside Counsel in WTO Dispute Processes', 2 JIEL 155 (1999).

[44] The case raised an important issue of a proper jurisdictional dichotomy between panel and committees. For more detailed discussion on the institutional balance, see Frieder Roessler, 'The Institutional Balance between the Judicial and the Political Organs of the WTO', in Marco Bronckers

Accordingly, the panel recommended that Korea eliminate the import measures on beef and hold consultations with Australia, New Zealand, and the United States to work out a timetable for the removal of import restrictions on beef that had been imposed on the basis of BOP reasons. This panel report was circulated to the GATT Contracting Parties on 24 May 1989. Korea repeatedly objected to adopting the panel reports in the subsequent Council meetings held on 22–23 June, 19 July and 11 October 1989, raising serious reservations about some of the panels' findings and conclusions. In particular, Korea argued that the panels had prejudged the result of the BOP Committee's work by making a ruling on the compatibility of BOP restrictions before the BOP Committee could have reached a conclusion.

On the other hand, in September 1989, the USTR made a positive determination[45] on the Section 301 investigation regarding Korea's beef import sanction and subsequently announced that if there were no substantial movement toward a resolution by mid-November, a proposed retaliation list would be published. In response to this threat of Section 301 retaliation, Korea finally agreed to the adoption of the panel reports at the Council meeting on 7 November 1989,[46] when the BOP consultation was indeed concluded. As a consequence, Korea agreed to disinvoke Article XVIII:B by 1 January 1990.[47] On 21 March 1990, Korea signed a memorandum of understanding with the United States on beef imports and formally exchanged the letter on 26 April 1990, which terminated the Section 301 investigation.[48] Noting that the remaining restrictions were largely concentrated in the agricultural sector, Korea was permitted by the BOP Committee to phase out the remaining restrictions or otherwise bring them into conformity with GATT provisions by 1 July 1997. However, the BOP Committee's decision on the transition period was later superseded by the Agreement on Agriculture in the Uruguay Round.[49]

---

and Reinhard Quick: *New Directions in International Economic Law – Essays in Honour of John H. Jackson* (The Hague: Kluwer Law International, 2000) 325. See also Dukgeun Ahn, 'Linkages between International Financial and Trade Institutions – IMF, World Bank and WTO', 34(4) Journal of World Trade 1 (2000), at 16–23.

[45] US Fed. Reg. 40769, 28 September 1989.

[46] GATT, C/M/237, dated 28 November 1989, at 19.

[47] GATT, BOP/R/183/Add.1, dated 27 October 1989, at 2. Since then, Korea has been perceived as having 'graduated' from Article XVIII:B. Despite the persistent trade deficit during the most of 1990s, Korea never reinvoked Article XVIII:B.

In fact, Korea was the first developing country to dismantle the BOP exception cover in the GATT. Subsequently, there have been many gradual termination of the BOP exceptions in GATT/WTO history. For example, 11 GATT contracting parties disinvoked the BOP exceptions under Articles XII or XVIII:B since 1979. See WTO, above n 7, 395. After the WTO was established, 11 WTO Members disinvoked the BOP exceptions. Only a handful of WTO Members, such as Bangladesh and Pakistan, are still invoking such exceptions. See generally WTO, WT/BOP/R/19, 37, 44, 47, 55.

[48] US Fed. Reg. 20376, 26 April 1990.

[49] Kim, above n 21, 8.

40

Journal of International Economic Law (JIEL) 6(3)

The consequence of *Korea – Beef I* case was a legal completion of import liberalization in Korea. Although some import-restrictive measures, notably the 'Import Diversification Program' to limit importation from Japan, remained in practice, a legal justification for overall import constraints was no longer available. Subsequently, by abrogating the Import Diversification Program on 30 June 1999, the Korean government abolished all the legal and practical grounds to constrain importation.

2. Korea – Polyacetal Resins: shaping the trade remedy system

The *Korea – Polyacetal Resins* case is interesting because the underlying anti-dumping action was the very first formal decision taken by the main trade remedy authority, the Korean Trade Commission ('KTC').[50] Following the Korean companies' petition on 8 May 1990, the KTC formally initiated an anti-dumping investigation involving two US and one Japanese polyacetal resins producers on 25 August 1990.[51] On 20 February 1991, the Office of Customs Administration found dumping margins ranging from 20.6 to 107.6% for the three respondents.[52] On 24 April 1991, the KTC made a positive determination on material injury to the domestic industry. Subsequently, on 30 September 1991, the Ministry of Finance imposed anti-dumping duties that were due to expire on 3 October 1993.

On 21 June 1991, before the actual anti-dumping measure was imposed, the United States requested consultations regarding the anti-dumping decision under the Tokyo Round Anti-dumping Code. When the two consultation meetings on 24 July and 30 September 1991 failed, the Committee on Anti-Dumping Practices agreed to establish a panel on 17 February 1992. Canada, the European Communities, and Japan joined the dispute as third parties. In this case, the panel ruled that various aspects of the KTC's determination on present material injury, a threat thereof and material retardation were inconsistent with disciplines and obligations under the Anti-dumping Code. The panel report was issued to the parties to the disputes on 10 March 1993 and circulated to the Committee on 2 April 1993.[53] This ruling was adopted by the Committee on 29 April 1993.[54]

---

[50] The KTC was established pursuant to Article 37 of the Foreign Trade Act in 1987. The KTC was originally composed of one chairman (part-time member) and four Commissioners (only one full-time member). Currently, the KTC has one chairman and seven Commissioners with one full-time member.

[51] This case was the fourth anti-dumping case for the KTC. But, it was in this case that the KTC began a formal investigation based on the pertinent regulations and made a positive determination to impose anti-dumping duties. See generally Korea Trade Commission, *A History of 10 Years for the KTC* (1997, in Korean) 280.

[52] The authority to make a dumping margin determination was transferred to the KTC in 1996 by the revision of the 'Regulations for Implementation of the Customs Duties Act'. See President Order No 14871 (dated 30 December 1995). Since then, the KTC has maintained the authority to make determinations on both dumping margin and injury.

[53] GATT, ADP/M/40, para 181.

[54] GATT, BISD, No 40 (1995) 198.

Korea strongly disagreed with the panel's decision, particularly regarding the denial of evidentiary value of the transcript of the KTC's voting session on 24 April 1991 for the simple reason that it was not notified publicly. However, Korea did not object to the adoption of the panel report, saying it was refraining 'because it believed that the multilateral dispute settlement system provided the best way to solve trade issues, and because it had in the past strongly supported the strengthening of the multilateral dispute settlement system'.[55] In any case, the original due date of the pertinent anti-dumping duties remained only a little more than 5 months.

The dispute settlement experience from this case made an important contribution to refine the KTC in particular and the Korean trade remedy system in general, especially at the infant stage. The panel's ruling of violation mostly concerned itself with deficiency of proper analysis or sufficient explanation for injury determination. It was, therefore, basically perceived as a recommendation to augment and discipline transparency aspects of incipient trade remedy procedures.[56] Accordingly, the KTC tried to accommodate the multilateral obligations in all aspects of trade remedy actions including safeguard as well as anti-dumping measures and enhance functional expertise in a substantive set of practices. This case, however, did not result in any substantial regulatory modification regarding anti-dumping actions.

C. Assessment

Under the GATT system, Japan has been perceived as 'one of those countries that leaned toward pragmatism as opposed to other countries, notably the United States, that favoured legalism'.[57] Obviously, Korea was even more pragmatic.[58] It tried to avoid formal dispute settlement or litigation as much as it could.

The fact that Korea rarely utilized the GATT dispute settlement system, however, should not be misunderstood to imply that Korea had hardly experienced much trouble with foreign trade barriers under the GATT system. As illustrated in Figure 2, exports from Korea during the GATT era routinely faced various trade restrictive measures by other GATT contracting parties, particularly the United States, the European Communities, Canada, and Australia. From 1960 to 1994, at least 291 foreign trade remedy measures against Korean exports were reported,[59] about 94% of them imposed by the

---

[55] GATT, ADP/M/40, para 185.

[56] Interview with Wan-soon Kim, Investment Ombudsman, Korea Trade-Investment Promotion Agency (then Chairman of the KTC) (14 Aug. 2002).

[57] Yuji Iwasawa, 'WTO Dispute Settlement and Japan', in Bronckers and Quick, above n 44, at 474.

[58] For the Japanese experience of the GATT dispute settlement, see generally Saadia M. Pekkanen, 'Aggressive Legalism: The Rules of the WTO and Japan's Emerging Trade Strategy', 24 World Economy 707 (2001).

[59] Han *et al.*, above n 4, 37.

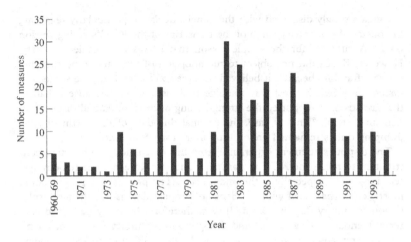

Figure 2. Trade Remedy Measures against Korean Exports (1960–1994)
Statistics drawn from Han *et al.*, above n 4, 37.

aforementioned countries. Furthermore, among 98 Section 301 cases initiated from 1975 until the end of 1994, Korea had been targeted 10 times.[60]

Considering such turbulent experiences and history, the Korean government was astonishingly hesitant to utilize the GATT dispute settlement system to cope with chronic foreign trade barriers. This may be explained partly by the fact that the Korean government lacked sufficiently competent officials to deal with the legal technicality of the GATT dispute settlement system. The different legal culture that used to consider legal confrontation as the demise of diplomatic or normal relations may also have some validity in explaining significant dispute aversion of Korea during the GATT period. But, it seems more importantly linked to the fact that Korea typically scored vast trade surpluses, at least in terms of trade in goods, with those major countries that had routinely imposed trade remedy measures. The substantial trade surpluses in major foreign markets generally undermined the political positions of the Korean government in asserting its legal rights under the GATT and led to a high propensity to avoid any legal confrontation. In other words, the persistent trade imbalance seemed to play a key role in

---

[60] These cases include: Thrown Silk Agreement with Japan (301_12), Insurance (301_20), Non-Rubber Footwear Import Restrictions (301_37), Steel Wire Rope Subsidies and Trademark Infringement (301_39), Insurance (301_51), Intellectual Property Rights (301_52), Cigarettes (301_64), Beef (301_65), Wine (301_67), Agricultural Market Access Restrictions (301_95). After the WTO was established in 1995, one more Section 301 case was initiated against Korea regarding Barriers to Auto Imports (301_115) in October 1997. See USTR, *Section 301 Table of Cases: Initiated Cases* <http://www.ustr.gov/html/act301.htm> (visited 9 April 2003).

Table 3. Trade Remedy Measures against Korean Exports by Countries[1]

	1960s	1970–74	1975–79	1980–84	1985–89	1990–94	Total
US	1	2	8	29	39	17	96
Canada	1	2	4	12	11	3	33
EC	2	10	22	7	19	12	72
Australia	0	0	3	36	14	19	72
Japan	1	4	4	2	2	0	13
Others	0	0	0	0	0	5	5
Total	5	18	41	86	85	56	291

[1] Han *et al.*, above n 4, 39.

setting the overall attitude towards the legal settlement of disputes under the multilateral trading system. It also explains why Japan, the trading partner that has constantly recorded huge trade surpluses against Korea, hardly ever raised trade remedy measures against Korean exports, especially since the 1980s (see Table 3).[61]

II. DISPUTE SETTLEMENT DURING THE WTO PERIOD

The Uruguay Round negotiation crucially augmented the GATT dispute settlement system, rectifying several systemic problems by instituting, *inter alia*, a quasi-automatic adoption mechanism, an appellate procedure, and a single unified system.[62] Generally speaking, the new WTO dispute settlement system has so far turned out to be a very effective and reliable instrument in resolving trade disputes for the Member countries. As of 31 March 2003, 286 cases have been brought to the WTO dispute settlement body. Among them, 69 panel and Appellate Body reports were adopted, while 40 cases were resolved with mutually agreed solutions and 24 cases were settled or inactive.[63]

Under the WTO system, the Korean government changed from a dispute aversion attitude and has become considerably more active in asserting its rights through the dispute settlement mechanism. Incidentally, since the

[61] Japan's less aggressive attitude toward formal trade dispute settlement is also explained by permanent trade surplus. See Hiroko Yamane, 'The WTO Dispute Settlement Mechanism and Japanese Traders', 1 JIEL 683 (1998), at 689.

[62] For detailed discussion on the WTO dispute settlement system, see generally John H. Jackson, *The World Trade Organization: Constitution and Jurisprudence* (London: Royal Institute of International Affairs, 1998); David Palmeter and Petros C. Mavroidis, *Dispute Settlement in the World Trade Organization: Practice and Procedure* (The Hague: Kluwer Law International, 1999); E.-U. Petersmann, *The GATT/WTO Dispute Settlement System: International Law, International Organizations and Dispute Settlement* (The Hague: Kluwer Law International, 1997); 'Special Issue: WTO Dispute Settlement System', 1(2) JIEL (1998); Jeff Waincymer, *WTO Litigation: Procedural Aspects of Formal Dispute Settlement* (London: Cameron May, 2002).

[63] WTO, WT/DS/OV/12, dated 7 April 2003, ii. See also Kara Leitner and Simon Lester, 'WTO Dispute Settlement 1995–2002: A Statistical Analysis', 6 JIEL 251 (2003).

mid-1990s, the trade balances with those major trading partners have been reversed and showed substantial deficits. For example, the trade deficit of Korea with respect to the United States began to occur from 1994 and remained throughout 1997, reaching $8.5 billion in 1997. This trend was again reversed in 1998, primarily due to the financial crisis which caused imports to plummet. Although there were some differences in the magnitude of the trade imbalances, the overall trends of trade balance were very much the same with respect to other major trading partners. As of March 2003, Korea has brought complaints to the WTO dispute settlement system in seven cases while being challenged by 12 complaints. The details of the relevant cases are discussed below.

A. Korea as respondent

As of March 2003, Korea was challenged by 12 complaints on nine distinct matters, as summarized in Table 4. It is noted that complaints against Korea have so far been raised mostly by the United States and the European Communities. The only two other complaints were filed by Australia and Canada. Since the Korean government commenced the litigation of WTO cases in *Korea – Taxes on Alcoholic Beverages*, it seems predetermined to exhaust the full procedure of the dispute settlement system, at least if contested by other Members.

1. Settlement by consultation: not yet ready to litigate

Korea was a respondent in some of the very early cases in the WTO dispute settlement, which concerned somewhat unfamiliar obligations under the SPS and TBT Agreements. The United States made a consultation request against Korea on 6 April 1995 (DS3) and basically on the same matter again on 24 May 1996 (DS41).[64] Both cases were suspended because the United States did not take additional steps.

On 5 May 1995, the United States made a consultation request regarding the regulation on the shelf-life of products (DS5). This case was settled with a mutually acceptable solution.[65] The Canadian request for consultation regarding the Korean regulation on the shelf-life and disinfection treatment of bottled water was also settled with a mutually satisfactory solution (DS20).[66] These four complaints were based on the SPS and TBT Agreements in addition to the GATT and could be settled promptly.

On 9 May 1996, the European Communities made a request for con-

---

[64] The second consultation request by the United States encompassed all amendments, revisions, and new measures adopted by the Korean government after the first consultation request. WTO, WT/DS41/1, dated 31 May 1996.

[65] WTO, WT/DS5/5, dated 31 July 1995.

[66] WTO, WT/DS20/6, dated 6 May 1996.

Table 4. WTO Cases Involving Korea as Respondent

Case name	Complainant	Dispute number
Korea – Measures Concerning the Testing and Inspection of Agricultural Products	US	DS3 & DS41
Korea – Measures Concerning the Shelf-Life of Products	US	DS5
Korea – Measures Concerning Bottled Water	Canada	DS20
Korea – Laws, Regulations and Practices in the Telecommunications Procurement Sector	EC	DS40
*Korea – Taxes on Alcoholic Beverages (Korea – Soju)	EC, US	DS75 & DS84
*Korea – Definitive Safeguard Measure on Imports of Certain Dairy Products (Korea – Dairy Product)	EC	DS98
*Korea – Measures Affecting Imports of Fresh, Chilled and Frozen Beef (Korea – Beef II)	US, Australia	DS161 & DS169
*Korea – Measures Affecting Government Procurement	US	DS163
Korea – Measures Affecting Trade in Commercial Vessels	EC	DS273

* Cases for which panel reports were issued.

sultations, alleging that the procurement practices for the Korean tele-communications sector were discriminatory against foreign suppliers, and that the bilateral agreement with the United States was preferential (DS40). The parties also agreed on a mutually satisfactory solution during the consultation.[67]

The Korean government basically tried to settle the first five complaints, rather than actually litigate the cases. This is partly because the merits of the cases were relatively clear and partly because the economic stakes at issue were not substantial. In addition, the Korean government was not sufficiently prepared to handle the newly instituted WTO dispute settlement system in the procedural aspect and unfamiliar legal issues concerning the SPS and TBT Agreements in the substantive aspect.

2. Full litigation: fight to the end

The very first case in which Korea experienced the whole WTO dispute settlement procedure was the *Korea – Taxes on Alcoholic Beverages* ('*Korea – Soju*') case (DS75 and DS84). The European Communities and the United States contended that the Korean liquor taxes of 100% on whisky and 35% on diluted *soju* were not consistent with the national treatment obligation

---

[67] WTO, WT/DS40/2, dated 29 October 1997. Korea and the European Communities signed the 'Agreement on Telecommunications Procurement between the Republic of Korea and the European Community' on 29 October 1997 and the Agreement entered into force on 1 November 1997. Subsequently, Korea entered into a similar bilateral agreement for telecommunications equipment procurement with Canada. See also Han-young Lie and Dukgeun Ahn, 'Legal Issues of Privatization in Government Procurement Agreements: Experience of Korea from Bilateral and WTO Agreements', 9(2) *International Trade Law & Regulation* 54 (2003).

46

under Article III of the GATT. Basically, this case was considered as a 'revisited' *Japan – Taxes on Alcoholic Beverages* (*'Japan – Shochu'*) case (DS8, DS10, and DS11), in which the Japanese tax system of discriminating against imported alcoholic beverages over *shochu* was found to be in violation of Article III of the GATT. As a legal strategy to distinguish this case from the *Japan – Shochu* case, the Korean government tried to inject more antitrust law principles and experts in the panel proceeding because a large price gap between *soju* and whisky might be deemed to represent a non-competitive relationship of pertinent products in the antitrust law context.[68]

The panel and the Appellate Body held that the Korean taxes on *soju* and whisky were discriminatory and the Dispute Settlement Body (hereinafter 'DSB') adopted this ruling on 17 February 1999. The reasonable period for implementation was determined to be 11 months and two weeks, that is, from 17 February 1999 to 31 January 2000.[69] Subsequently, Korea amended the Liquor Tax Law and the Education Tax Law to impose flat rates of 72% in liquor tax and 30% in education tax, that entered into force on 1 January 2000.[70] The DSB recommendation was successfully implemented a month earlier than the due date.

This case awakened the Korean public to the role and influence of the WTO dispute settlement system. The media and newspapers closely covered every step pertaining to this case, from the consultation request to the panel proceeding and the Appellate Body ruling. It was not just because this case was the first WTO dispute settlement proceeding for Korea, but also because the popularity of the product concerned, *soju*, was probably incomparable to any other product in Korea. Despite objections by the general public as well as by *soju* manufacturers, the Korean government amended the tax laws to substantially increase liquor taxes on *soju*, instead of reducing the liquor tax on whisky to the original level on *soju*, in order to eliminate the WTO-illegal tax gap while minimizing the potential adverse impact on public health and consequent social costs.[71] In 2000, the tax revenue from the liquor tax, $1.72 billion, accounted for 2.4% of the total tax revenue.[72] The share of the tax revenue from *soju* increased from 17.3% in 1999 to 23.2%, whereas that from whisky was reduced from 10.8% to 8.3%.[73] By

---

[68] For example, the Korean government tried to include antitrust law experts regardless of their nationality as panelists, but failed due to the objection by the complainants. Hyun Chong Kim, 'The WTO Dispute Settlement Process: A Primer', 2 JIEL 457 (1999), at 465–66. Except for this case, the Korean government as a respondent did not resort to the Director-General for the panel selection.

[69] WTO, WT/DS75/16, WT/DS84/14, dated 4 June 1999.

[70] WTO, WT/DS75/18, WT/DS84/16, dated 17 January 2000.

[71] See generally Korea Institute of Public Finance, *Monthly Public Finance Forum* (September 1999, in Korean) 82–102.

[72] National Tax Service, *Statistical Yearbook of National Tax 2001* (2001). The dollar amount was calculated based on $1 = W1,300.

[73] Korea Institute of Public Finance, *Monthly Public Finance Forum* (September 2001, in Korean) 114.

experiencing the impact of the WTO dispute settlement decision probably at the deepest and widest level of daily life, this case played a crucial role in enhancing awareness of the WTO in Korea.

This case also contributed to setting the procedural practice of permitting private counsel in a dispute settlement proceeding, particularly a panel proceeding. The Korean government was not yet capable of dealing with complicated WTO litigation and thereby was very eager to rely on assistance by foreign private counsel.[74] Since the Appellate Body already ruled in favor of permission of private counsel for an appellate proceeding[75] and the panel in the *Indonesia – Auto* case allowed private counsel in a preliminary ruling on 3 December 1997,[76] the panel composed on 5 December 1997 in *Korea – Soju* did not oppose the request by the Korean government.[77] After the confirmation of the panel as regards the permissibility of private counsel in the *Korea – Soju* case, it has become a part of well-established dispute settlement practices under the WTO system.

The first dispute settlement case under the Agreement on Safeguards also involved the Korean safeguard measure concerning dairy products (DS98).[78] On 12 August 1997, the European Communities requested consultations with Korea regarding the safeguard quotas that went into effect on 7 March 1997 and were to remain in force until 28 February 2001.[79] The panel and the Appellate Body held that the Korean safeguard measures were inconsistent with the obligations under the Agreement on Safeguards. The DSB adopted those rulings on 12 January 2000 and it was agreed that the reasonable implementation period would expire on 20 May 2000. Korea, through its administrative procedures, effectively lifted the safeguard measure on imports of the dairy products as of 20 May 2000.

Since its inception in 1987, through to 1994, the KTC had relied more on safeguard measures than on anti-dumping measures to address injury to domestic industries incurred by importation.[80] During 1987–1994, the KTC engaged in 25 safeguard and 12 anti-dumping investigations that resulted in 16 safe-

---

[74] See also above, n 43, and the accompanying text.

[75] WTO Appellate Body Report, *European Communities – Regimes for the Importation, Sale and Distribution of Bananas*, WT/DS27/AB/R, adopted 25 September 1997, paras 10–12.

[76] WTO Panel Report, *Indonesia – Certain Measures Affecting the Automobile Industry*, WT/DS54, DS55, DS59, DS64/R, adopted 23 July 1998, para 14.1.

[77] Panel Report, *Korea – Soju*, WT/DS75, DS84/R, adopted 17 February 1999, para 10.31.

[78] The first complaint brought under the Agreement on Safeguards was *US – Safeguard Measure against Imports of Corn Brooms*. WTO, WT/DS78/1, dated 1 May 1997. This case was resolved without litigation although it remained technically pending. The actual panel decision concerning safeguard measures was issued for the first time in *Korea – Dairy Safeguards*. WTO, WT/DS98/R, adopted 12 January 2000.

[79] WTO, G/SG/N/10/KOR/1, dated 27 January 1997 and G/SG/N/10/KOR/1/Supp 1, dated 1 April 1997.

[80] On the other hand, the KTC has never even initiated a countervailing investigation to date. See Korea Trade Commission, above n 51, 280–99.

[81] Ibid.

614 *Journal of International Economic Law (JIEL) 6(3)*

guard and 8 anti-dumping measures.[81] After this case, however, the KTC markedly abstained from using a safeguard measure whereas it substantially increased anti-dumping actions. For example, from 1997 to 2002, there were only four safeguard investigations but 46 anti-dumping cases.[82] Accordingly, subsequent safeguard actions by the KTC appeared seriously disciplined by the WTO dispute settlement system. The safeguard mechanism in Korea was further elaborated with new laws and regulations on trade remedy actions.[83]

On the other hand, it was reported that the importation of dairy products at issue was reduced by about $70 million during the period in which the safeguard measure remained in force. This result, along with the outcome from the *Argentina – Safeguard Measures on Imports of Footwear* ('*Argentina – Footwear*')[84] case whose proceedings were conducted almost concomitantly, raised an important systemic issue for the WTO safeguard system. In the *Korea – Definitive Safeguard Measure on Imports of Certain Dairy Products* case, the termination of illegal safeguard measures pursuant to the DSB recommendation was undertaken only 9 months prior to the original due date of the measures. In the *Argentina – Footwear* case, the implementation of the DSB recommendation by repealing the safeguard measure coincided with the original due date of the measure. Thus, the experience from these early safeguard cases raised imminent need for considering expeditious or accelerated dispute settlement procedures.[85]

On 1 February 1999, the United States requested consultations with Korea in respect of a dual retail system for beef ('*Korea – Beef II*'; DS161). On 13 April 1999, Australia also requested consultations on the same basis (DS169). On 10 January 2001, the DSB adopted the panel and the Appellate Body reports that held the Korean measures to be inconsistent with the WTO obligation. The parties to the dispute agreed that a reasonable implementation period would be 8 months and thus expire on 10 September 2001.[86] The Korean government subsequently revised the 'Management Guideline for Imported Beef' to abolish the beef import system operated by the Livestock Products Marketing Organization.[87] In addition, on 10 September 2001, the Korean government eliminated the dual retail system for beef by entirely abolishing the 'Management Guideline for Imported Beef'.[88] Thus,

---

[82] Korea Trade Commission, *Summary Report of Trade Remedy Action* (February 2003, in Korean) 1.

[83] Act on Investigation of Unfair Trade Practice and Trade Remedy Measures, Law 6417; Implementing Regulation, Presidential Order No 17222.

[84] WTO, WT/DS121/AB/R, adopted 12 January 2000. See also WTO, WT/DSB/M/75, dated 7 March 2000, at 2.

[85] See below n 147 and the accompanying text.

[86] WTO, WT/DS161, DS169/12, dated 24 April 2001.

[87] Ministry of Agriculture Notification 2000-82.

[88] Ministry of Agriculture Notification 2001-54.

[89] WTO, WT/DSB/M/110, dated 22 October 2001.

Korea considered that it had fully implemented the DSB's recommendation in this case.[89]

In terms of policy implementation, the *Korea – Beef II* case made an important contribution towards underlining the national treatment obligation for domestic regulations and their *de facto* application. Unlike the *Korea – Soju* case that addressed relatively clear discriminative treatment by vastly different tax rates, this case set an important precedent for a much broader scope of the national treatment principle, especially dealing with a retail distribution system often convoluted by ingenious regulations.

The only dispute settlement case concerning the Agreement on Government Procurement ('GPA') to date is *Korea – Measures Affecting Government Procurement* (DS163).[90] On 16 February 1999, the United States requested consultations regarding certain procurement practices of the Korean Airport Construction Authority ('KOACA'). The panel ultimately ruled that the KOACA was not a covered entity under Korea's Appendix I of the GPA, even if the panel noted that the conduct of the Korean government with respect to the US inquiries in the course of pertinent negotiation '[could], at best, be described as inadequate'.[91] The United States did not make an appeal and the panel report was adopted on 19 June 2000.[92] One of the important lessons from this case for the Korean government was about the discrepancy between its organizational mechanism for governmental offices that is based on decision-making structures and the WTO concession practice that is based on the institutional 'entities' in the context of the GPA. The Government Organization Act of the Republic of Korea prescribes various government entities that actually constitute mere positions of certain level. Moreover, the Korean government has often established a special 'task force', 'group', or 'committee' with specific mandates, whose legal foundations are obscure.[93] This issue of how to determine the scope of covered entities in relation to a newly established governmental organ may require a more elaborate approach in the context of the GPA.

On 24 October 2000, the Committee of European Union Shipbuilders Associations filed a complaint under the trade barriers regulation ('TBR') procedure concerning divergent financial arrangements for Korean shipbuilding industries. Although the Commission was mindful of

---

[90] This case is the fourth complaint concerning government procurement. The first complaint, *Japan – Procurement of a Navigation Satellite* (DS73), was settled with a mutually satisfactory solution. The second and third complaints, *US – Measure Affecting Government Procurement* (DS88, DS95), were in respect of the same issue. The panel's authority lapsed as of 11 February 2000, when it was not requested to resume the proceeding after suspension of the works. WTO, WT/DS88, DS95/6 (dated 14 Feb. 2000).

[91] WTO, WT/DS163/R (adopted on 19 June 2000), para 7.80.

[92] WTO, WT/DS163/7 (dated 6 Nov. 2000).

[93] Young-Joon Cho, 'Review of the Panel Report for 'Korea – Measures Affecting Government Procurement', 33 International Trade Law 127 (2000, in Korean), at 152.

the extraordinary situation in Korea that was caused by the financial crisis in 1997, it found that parts of corporate restructuring programs and assistance through taxation for shipbuilding companies constituted prohibited subsidies within the meaning of the WTO Agreement on Subsidies and Countervailing Measures ('SCM Agreement').[94] Subsequent to the affirmative determination of the TBR procedure, the two parties had two rounds of bilateral negotiations in August and September 2002. On 21 October 2002, the European Communities made a formal request for a consultation with Korea under the WTO dispute settlement system on various corporate restructuring measures for the shipbuilding industry, alleging that they constituted prohibited subsidies under the SCM Agreement.[95]

This case was merely the beginning of much more controversial trade conflicts as regards corporate restructuring programs undertaken by the Korean government as parts of the IMF program to overcome the financial crisis. On 25 July 2002, the European Commission initiated a countervailing investigation on the Korean semiconductor producers, alleging that the governmental intervention in terms of debt-for-equity swaps and debt forgiveness for pertinent companies established illegal subsidies.[96] Apart from the EC's action against the Korean government, the United States had also closely monitored the Korean government's roles in financial and corporate restructuring programs.[97] Concerning various aspects of corporate restructuring programs for Korean semiconductor manufacturers, the US authorities initiated a countervailing investigation in November 2002 that ended up with a preliminary determination for countervailing duties up to 57.73%.[98] As of 21 March 2003, it was reported that the European Commission would also make a preliminary countervailing determination of 30–35% on basically the identical matter.[99] These concomitant actions in the two major markets, if sustained in the final determinations, would risk the whole fate of the third largest semiconductor producer in the world. Furthermore, the legal validity of those actions would have significant implications for many other Korean industries that experienced similar restructuring programs in the course of the IMF program during the past few years. The Korean government seems to have no other choice than resorting to the WTO dispute settlement process to vindicate the legitimacy of its systemic and structural measures adopted during the IMF program. The outcome of the WTO dispute settlement

---

[94] Commission Decision 2002/818/EC, OJ 2002 L 281/15.

[95] WTO, WT/DS273/1, dated 24 October 2002.

[96] WTO, G/SCM/N/93/EEC, dated 12 March 2003.

[97] See, for example, USTR, *Subsidies Enforcement Annual Report to the Congress* (February 1999), 7–8.

[98] US Department of Commerce, *Preliminary Affirmative Countervailing Duty Determination: Dynamic Random Access Memory Semiconductors from the Republic of Korea*, <http://ia.ita.doc.gov/download/drams-korea-draft-prelim-fr-notice.pdf> (visited on 12 April 2003).

[99] 'Hynix faces 30–35% EU import duties', *Financial Times* (21 March 2003), 17.

related to this dispute would certainly be an interesting and important addition to the WTO jurisprudence.

3. Overall comments

Considering the experience so far as a respondent in the WTO dispute settlement, the reaction by the Korean government appears to show a typical pattern as an average WTO Member. For half of the complaints, Korea tried to settle the trade disputes without resorting to legal procedures. But, as it obtained more experience and the WTO jurisprudence became more sophisticated, Korea has become determined to take a more legalistic approach in dealing with complaints by other Members.

When engaged in a WTO legal proceeding, Korea has been in full compliance with DSB recommendations. For all three cases in which Korea was found to be inconsistent with the WTO Agreements, Korea fully implemented the DSB recommendations within the determined or agreed reasonable periods of time, even in politically loaded areas such as taxes and agriculture. It is also noted that Korea made appeals for all three cases in which the panels found some violations for its own measures. Lastly, it should also be noted that the areas challenged by other Member countries are fairly diverse, ranging from SPS and TBT measures to government procurement, safeguard, domestic taxes, and retailing distribution systems. This is starkly contrasted with the cases in which Korea brought complaints, which concentrated mainly on anti-dumping measures. Overall, the dispute settlement experience of Korea as a respondent in such divergent areas under the auspice of the WTO has played a significant role in enhancing public recognition of the importance of the multilateral trade norms in all aspects of economic activities and policy-making.

B. Korea as complainant

So far, the Korean complaints in the WTO dispute settlement system have focused primarily on the US anti-dumping measures (see Table 5). Five out of the total seven complaints were concerned with anti-dumping matters and six complaints were against the United States. Only one case was against the Philippines and two cases were concerning safeguard measures. In other words, the Korean complaints to the WTO dispute settlement system to date can be simply summarized as exclusive concentration on trade remedy issues, predominantly caused by US anti-dumping measures.

While Korea had been challenged in the WTO dispute settlement system from a very early period,[100] Korea appeared quite hesitant in bringing complaints against other WTO Member countries. It was only in July

---

[100] In 1995, three consultation requests were brought against Korea. The first two requests for *Korea – Measures Concerning the Testing and Inspection of Agricultural Products* (DS3) and *Korea – Measures Concerning the Shelf-Life of Products* (DS5) were made on 6 April and 5 May 1995.

Table 5. WTO Cases Involving Korea as Complainant

Case name	Complainant	Dispute number
US – *Imposition of Anti-Dumping Duties on Imports of Color Television Receivers from Korea*	US	DS89
US – Anti-Dumping Duty on Dynamic Random Access Memory Semiconductors (DRAMS) of One Megabit or Above from Korea (US – DRAMS)	US	DS99
US – Anti-Dumping Measures on Stainless Steel Plate in Coils and Stainless Steel Sheet and Strip from Korea	US	DS179
US – Definitive Safeguard Measures on Imports of Circular Welded Carbon Quality Line Pipe from Korea (US – Line Pipe)	US	DS202
Philippines – Anti-Dumping Measures regarding Polypropylene Resins from Korea	Philippines	DS215
US – Continued Dumping and Subsidy Offset Ac of 2000	US	DS217
US – *Definitive Safeguard Measures on Imports of Certain Steel Products*	US	DS251

* Cases for which panel reports were issued.

1997 that Korea began to use the WTO dispute settlement system as a complainant. The first WTO case Korea brought to the DSB was in respect of the US anti-dumping duties on Samsung color television receivers. On 10 July 1997, Korea requested a consultation, alleging that the United States had maintained an anti-dumping duty order for the past 12 years despite the cessation of exports as well as the absence of dumping. Subsequently, in response to the US preliminary determination of 19 December 1997 to revoke the anti-dumping duty order, Korea withdrew its request for a panel. On 27 August 1998, the United States made a final determination to revoke the anti-dumping duty order which had been imposed on Samsung color television receivers since 1984. At the DSB meeting on 22 September 1998, Korea announced that it definitively withdrew the request for a panel because the imposition of anti-dumping duties had been revoked.[101]

For a similar case regarding anti-dumping duty orders on DRAMS, however, the United States did not readily revoke the orders and, on 6 November 1997, Korea requested the establishment of a panel. The DSB established a panel at its meeting on 16 January 1998. On 19 March 1998, the Director-General completed the panel composition and thereby Korea began its first panel proceeding as a complainant. The Panel found the measures at issue

---

[101] WTO, WT/DS89/9, dated 18 September 1998.

to be in violation of Article 11.2 of the WTO Anti-Dumping Agreement.[102] The United States did not make an appeal and the DSB adopted the panel report on 19 March 1999.

Incidentally, this first 'win' as a complainant in *US – DRAMS* came just 11 days after Korea lost its first WTO litigation as a respondent in *Korea – Soju*.[103] This somewhat fortunate timing of winning a WTO case contributed to alleviating the general concern and resistance of the Korean public about the fairness and objectivity of the WTO dispute settlement system.

The two parties agreed on an implementation period of 8 months, expiring on 19 November 1999. At the DSB meeting on 27 January 2000, the United States stated that it had implemented the DSB recommendations by amending the pertinent Department of Commerce ('DOC') regulation, more specifically, by deleting the 'not likely' standard and incorporating the 'necessary' standard of the WTO Antidumping Agreement. The DOC, however, issued a revised 'Final Results of Re-determination' in the third administrative review on 4 November 1999, concluding that, because a resumption of dumping was likely, it was necessary to leave the anti-dumping order in place. On 6 April 2000, Korea requested the referral of this matter to the original panel pursuant to Article 21.5 of the DSU and the European Communities reserved its third-party right. On 19 September 2000, Korea requested that the panel suspend its work and, on 20 October 2000, the parties notified the DSB of a mutually satisfactory solution to the matter, involving the revocation of the anti-dumping order at issue as the result of a five-year 'sunset' review by the DOC.[104]

This case was the first case ever in which Korea won a favorable panel decision throughout the GATT/WTO system. Although it took one and half more years for the United States to satisfactorily comply with the DSB recommendation after the adoption of the panel report, the sheer fact of winning a WTO dispute concerning chronic trade barriers of the major trading partners furnished the Korean government with confidence in the new WTO dispute settlement system. Unfortunately, however, the dismal implementation by the United States after the panel proceeding compromised the confidence of a relatively new user concerning the effectiveness and fairness of the WTO dispute settlement system.[105] In any case,

---

[102] WTO Panel Report, *United States – Anti-Dumping Duty on Dynamic Random Access Memory Semiconductors (DRAMS) of One Megabit or Above from Korea* ('*US – DRAMS*'), WT/DS99/R, adopted 19 March 1999.

[103] The Appellate Body Report for *Korea – Soju* case was circulated on 18 January 1999, while the panel report for *US – DRAMS* case was circulated on 29 January 1999. See WTO, *Korea – Soju*, WT/DS75, DS84/AB/R, adopted 17 February 1999 and above n 98.

[104] WTO, WT/DS99/12, dated 25 October 2000.

[105] For more positive assessment for Article 21.5 proceedings, see generally Jason Kearns and Steve Charnovitz, 'Adjudicating Compliance in the WTO: A Review of DSU Article 21.5', 5 JIEL 331 (2002).

US – DRAMS clearly led the Korean government to adopt a more legal approach by utilizing the WTO dispute settlement system to address foreign trade barriers in subsequent cases. In other words, the experience and confidence gained from this case clearly led the Korean government to move to the direction of 'aggressive legalism' in handling subsequent trade disputes.[106]

The *US – Anti-Dumping Measures on Stainless Steel Plate in Coils and Stainless Steel Sheet and Strip from Korea* ('*Korea – Stainless Steel*') case dealt with two separate anti-dumping actions by the US authorities concerning stainless steel plate in coils ('plate') and stainless steel sheet and strip in coils ('sheet'). For the anti-dumping case on plate, the DOC selected 1 January to 31 December 1997 as the period of investigation. The DOC issued the preliminary dumping margin of 2.77% for Korean exporters including Pohang Iron and Steel Company ('POSCO'). But, the DOC later issued the final dumping margin of 16.26%. The anti-dumping case for sheet covered 1 April 1997 through 31 March 1998 as the period of investigation. The DOC issued the preliminary dumping margin of 58.79% for Taihan steel company and 12.35% for other Korean exporters including POSCO. Upon the allegation of miscalculation, the dumping margin for POSCO was revised to 3.92%. But, the DOC issued the final dumping margin of 58.79% for Taihan and 12.12% for other Korean exporters including POSCO. Regarding these anti-dumping measures, the Korean government requested consultations with the United States on 30 July 1999 and the panel establishment on 14 October 1999. The European Communities and Japan joined the panel proceeding as third parties. In this case, the panel was established on 19 November 1999 but actually composed on 24 March 2000.[107]

The underlying economic situation for this case is remarkably aberrational.[108] The pertinent investigation periods included unprecedented fluctuation of exchange rates caused by the financial crisis. As illustrated in Figure 3, the value of the Korean currency, Won, precipitated to a half in a time span of just three months. The WTO panel found that the methodology adopted by the DOC to deal with such abnormity, including double currency conversion and the use of multiple averaging periods, was not consistent with the WTO obligations. Without the US' appeal, the DSB adopted the panel report on 1 February 2001. They had agreed on the reasonable period of 7 months, to expire on 1 September 2001. On 28 August 2001, the International Trade Administration of the DOC issued the 'Notice of

---

[106] For the discussion of 'aggressive legalism' by the Japanese government to deal with trade disputes, see Pekkanen, above n 58, at 707–37.

[107] It took 126 days to compose the panel, which is so far the longest period of time required for the panel appointment in cases involving Korea.

[108] Timothy Lane *et al.*, 'IMF-Supported Programs in Indonesia, Korea and Thailand: A Preliminary Assessment', *Occasional Paper 178* (Washington DC: International Monetary Fund, 1999).

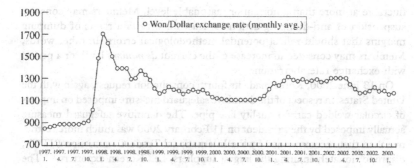

Figure 3. Won/Dollar Exchange Rate Trends

Bank of Korea, *Principal Economic Indicators* (March 2003).
See also <http://www.bok.or.kr> (visited 25 March 2003).

Table 6. The Changes of Dumping Margins

Exporter/Manufacturer	Original Dumping Margin (%)		Recalculated Dumping Margin (%)	
	SSPC	SSSS	SSPC	SSSS
Pohang Iron & Steel Co. Ltd	16.26	12.12	6.08	2.49
Inchon Iron & Steel Co. Ltd	16.26	0.00	6.08	0.00
Taihan Electric Wire Co. Ltd	16.26	58.79	6.08	58.79
All others	16.26	12.12	6.08	2.49

Amendment of Final Determinations' on the relevant anti-dumping duty order, in which the recalculation of dumping margins substantially reduced anti-dumping duties (see Table 6).[109] At the DSB's meeting of 10 September 2001, the United States announced that it had implemented the DSB's recommendation and Korea acknowledged the satisfactory implementation.[110]

This case showed how vulnerable exporters might be in terms of anti-dumping actions as the exchange rates became abnormally fluctuating. Since dumping margin calculation permits various price adjustment to find 'ex-factory' prices but no modification for volatile exchange rates except for averaging, unstable exchange rates can cause serious distortion in calculating dumping margins. This systemic problem may expose more exporters in developing countries that suffer from vacillating exchange rates to additional risks of being targeted by anti-dumping actions. Based on the Korean experience during the financial crisis, in which foreign exchange rates

[109] US Fed. Reg. 45279, 28 August 2001. For the original dumping margin determination, see US Fed. Reg. 15443, 31 March 1999 for SSPC and US Fed. Reg. 30664, 8 June 1999 for SSSS.

[110] WTO, WT/DSB/26, dated 12 October 2001, 18.

fluctuate at more than a normal or reasonable level, Members may consider suspension of anti-dumping actions at least for a certain range of dumping margins that should reflect potential methodological errors. In other words, Members may consider an increase of the current *de minimis* level for a period with exchange rate aberration.

On 13 June 2000, Korea made its fourth consultation request, again with the United States, in respect of the definitive safeguard measure imposed on imports of circular welded carbon quality line pipe. The definitive safeguard measure actually imposed by the President on 11 February 2000 was much more restrictive than that recommended by the International Trade Commission ('ITC'), disproportionately injuring the largest suppliers, i.e., Korean exporters.[111] The exemption of Mexican and Canadian suppliers from the safeguard measure led them to become the largest and third-largest suppliers.

Korea considered that the US procedures and determinations that led to the imposition of the safeguard measure, as well as the measure itself, contravened various obligations under the Agreement on Safeguards and the GATT 1994. The panel was established on 23 October 2000 and composed by the Director-General on 22 January 2001. Australia, Canada, European Communities, Japan, and Mexico reserved their third-party rights. In the panel report circulated on 29 October 2001, the panel concluded that the US measure was imposed in a manner inconsistent with the WTO obligations. In the Appellate Body proceeding,[112] Korea's argument on the permissible extent of a safeguard measure was accepted, which seems to be one of the key findings for WTO jurisprudence on safeguard.[113]

It is also noted that this appellate proceeding was the first WTO dispute settlement litigation handled entirely by Korean government officials. It was a substantial development for Korea in terms of capacity building for WTO dispute settlement, particularly considering the previous cases in which foreign legal counsels played primary roles in WTO litigations. Moreover, when considering the fact that Korea is one of the WTO Members that did contribute to set the procedural practices to permit private counsel in a dispute settlement proceeding, the outcome of the *US – Line Pipe* appellate proceeding substantially enhanced self-confidence and capacity in terms of much-needed legal expertise.

When both parties agreed on the reasonable period of time for imple-

---

[111] The imports above the first 9,000 short tons from each country would be subject to a 19%, 15% and 11% duty for the first, second, and third year. See WTO Panel Report, *United States – Definitive Safeguard Measures on Imports of Circular Welded Carbon Quality Line Pipe from Korea* ('*US – Line Pipe*'), WT/DS202/R, adopted 8 March 2002, para 2.5.

[112] WTO Appellate Body Report, *US – Line Pipe*, WT/DS202/AB/R, adopted 8 March 2002. The United States initially filed an appeal on 6 November 2001 (WT/DS202/7), but withdrew it for scheduling reasons on 13 November (WT/DS202/8). The appeal was re-filed on 19 November 2001 (WT/DS202/9).

[113] See generally Dukgeun Ahn, 'Critical Review of the WTO Jurisprudence on Safeguard' (mimeo).

mentation with expiration on 1 September 2002, the arbitration under DSU Article 21.3 was suspended.[114] The US government agreed to increase the in-quota volume of imports to 17,500 tons and lower the safeguard tariff to 11%, with the termination due of 1 March 2003.[115] But, considering the original due date of the safeguard measure that was set at 24 February 2003, the practical impact of the WTO dispute settlement system was to increase the in-quota volume from 9,000 to 17,500 tons only for the period of 1 September 2002 to 24 February 2003, while the latter measure remained until the end of February 2003. Thus, this case again illustrated the systemic problem for implementation in a safeguard dispute.

On 15 December 2000, Korea requested consultations with the Philippines concerning the dumping decision of the Tariff Commission of the Philippines on polypropylene resins. This anti-dumping order was actually the first anti-dumping measure by the Philippines against Korean exporters, since the first anti-dumping investigation against Korean electrolytic tinplates was dismissed for lack of merit.[116] The Tariff Commission of the Philippines imposed the provisional anti-dumping duties on polypropylene resins ranging from 4.20% to 40.53% and subsequently the final duties at slightly lowered levels.[117] Following the consultation on 19 January 2001 under the purview of the WTO dispute settlement system, the Philippines withdrew the anti-dumping order on 8 November 2001 and Korea did not pursue further action in the DSB.[118] This case is so far the only trade dispute for Korea elevated to the formal dispute settlement procedure as opposed to a developing country.

The fifth WTO complaint by Korea against the United States was also related to anti-dumping matters. On 21 December 2000, Korea, along with Australia, Brazil, Chile, European Communities, India, Indonesia, Japan, and Thailand, requested consultations with the United States concerning the amendment to the Tariff Act of 1930, entitled 'Continued Dumping and Subsidy Offset Act of 2000', which is usually referred to as the 'Byrd Amendment'. By distributing the anti-dumping and countervailing duties to domestic petitioners, the Byrd Amendment aimed to create more incentives to bring trade remedy actions. As the third frequent target for anti-dumping and countervailing measures in the US market, Korean exporters were very keen on the outcome of this case.[119]

---

[114] WTO, WT/DS202/17, dated 26 July 2002.

[115] WTO, WT/DS202/18, dated 31 July 2002.

[116] WTO, G/ADP/N/65/PHL, dated 21 September 2000.

[117] WTO, G/ADP/N/72/PHL, dated 6 March 2001.

[118] WTO, G/ADP/N/85/PHL, dated 22 February 2002.

[119] For anti-dumping measures, exporters from China and Japan are more frequent targets than those from Korea in the US market. US countervailing measures have targeted Italy, India, Korea, and France. WTO, 'Statistics on Anti-dumping', <http://www.wto.org/english/tratop_e/adp_e/adp_e.htm> and 'Statistics on Subsidies and Countervailing Measures', <http://www.wto.org/english/tratop_e/scm_e/scm_stattab8_e.htm> (visited 9 April 2003).

The panel established by the requests from 9 Members was later merged with the panel requested by Canada and Mexico. The panel and the Appellate Body found that the Byrd Amendment is inconsistent with the Anti-dumping and SCM Agreement. Furthermore, the panel suggested that the United States bring the Byrd Amendment into conformity by repealing it. On 2 April 2003, the arbitrator was appointed to determine a reasonable period of implementation under DSU Article 21.3.

Ironically, a subsidiary company of a Korean manufacturer received a substantial 'offset' disbursement under the Byrd Amendment. Zenith Electronics owned by LG Electronics received the disbursement of $24.3 million in 2001 and $9 million in 2002 from anti-dumping duties collected on Japanese television imports. The offset payment for Zenith Electronics in 2001 was indeed more than 10% of the total disbursement of $231.2 million in 2001.[120] In 2002, the total disbursement under the Byrd Amendment was increased to $329.8 million.[121]

On 20 March 2002, Korea requested consultation with the United States regarding the definitive safeguard measures on the imports of certain steel products and the related laws including Section 201 of the Trade Act of 1974 and Section 311 of the NAFTA Implementation Act. The DSB established a single panel to include complaints by other Members such as the European Communities, Japan, China, Switzerland, Norway, New Zealand, and Brazil.[122] In addition to most complainants that reserved third-party rights, Chinese Taipei, Cuba, Malaysia, Mexico, Thailand, Turkey, and Venezuela also participated as third parties in the proceeding. On 25 July 2002, the Director-General composed the panel. Chinese Taipei later determined to become a more active participant and made an independent consultation request with the United States on 1 November 2002.[123]

Concerning this US Section 201 action, the Korean government made the first trade compensation request pursuant to Article 8 of the Agreement on Safeguards.[124] When the US government did not agree on satisfactory com-

---

[120] US Customs and Border Protection, 'CDSOA FY2001 Disbursements Final', <http://www.customs.ustreas.gov/xp/cgov/import/add_cvd/> (visited 10 April 2003). On the other hand, it is noted that only two ball bearing companies, Torrington and MPB (The Timken Company), received more offset payments in gross than Zenith Electronics in 2001. Their total disbursements amount to $62.8 million and $25 million, respectively. But, the disbursement for Zenith Electronics is the second largest one in terms of individual claims, following $34.7 million offset payment for Torrington in relation to ball bearings dumping from Japan.

[121] US Customs and Border Protection, 'CDSOA FY2002 Disbursements Final', <http://www.customs.ustreas.gov/xp/cgov/import/add_cvd/> (visited 10 April 2003).

[122] WTO, WT/DS251/10, dated 12 August 2002.

[123] WTO, WT/DS274/1, dated 11 November 2002.

[124] About 12% of trade remedy measures against Korean exports are safeguard actions. For example, as of 31 December 2002, Korean exporters are subject to 10 safeguard measures and 5 investigations in India, United States, Venezuela, China, Argentina, Canada, and European Communities. Korea Trade Investment Promotion Agency (KOTRA), 'Summary of Import Restrictions against Korean Exports 2002' (December, 2002, in Korean).

pensatory arrangements, several WTO Members, such as the European Communities,[125] Japan,[126] Norway,[127] China,[128] and Switzerland,[129] notified the Council for Trade in Goods of proposed suspension of concessions. Instead of proposing suspension of concessions, the Korean government notified the Council for Trade in Goods of the agreement that the 90-day period set forth in Article 8.2 of the Agreement on Safeguards and Article XIX:3(a) of the GATT shall be considered to expire on 19 March 2005.[130] This agreement to postpone potential retaliation for about three years, however, practically eradicates all real impact on balancing trade interests, since the original safeguard measure is supposed to end on 20 March 2005.[131] In other words, the Korean government tried to avoid the possibility of actually exercising the suspension of concessions against one of its major trading partners without the DSB authorization, while it still maintained a political gesture that it exercised a legal authority specifically enunciated under the Agreement on Safeguards.

As described above, Korea has had major problems regarding the US anti-dumping practices. In some sense, its experience as a complainant in the WTO dispute settlement system almost exclusively against US anti-dumping practices is puzzling because, during the period of 1 January 1995 to 20 June 2002, it was the European Communities that initiated the most anti-dumping investigations against exported products from Korea, and it was South Africa and India that actually imposed the most anti-dumping measures (See Table 7).[132] This fact seems to imply that the US market still occupies an unbalanced economic importance for Korea.[133] Currently, Korea is actively engaged in pushing the agenda to revise the Anti-dumping Agreement in the Doha Development Agenda.[134]

For three cases in which the entire dispute settlement procedure including implementation ended, the major problem Korea faced was the failure

---

[125] WTO, G/C/10, dated 15 May 2002.

[126] WTO, G/C/15, dated 21 May 2002.

[127] WTO, G/C/16, dated 21 May 2002.

[128] WTO, G/C/17, dated 21 May 2002.

[129] WTO, G/C/18, dated 22 May 2002.

[130] WTO, G/C/12, dated 16 May 2002. On the other hand, Australia, Brazil, and New Zealand extended the deadline for retaliation to 20 March 2005. See WTO, G/C/11, dated 16 May 2002 and G/C/13, 14, dated 17 May 2002.

[131] WTO, G/SG/N/10/USA/6, dated 14 March 2002.

[132] WTO, 'Statistics on Anti-dumping', <http://www.wto.org/english/tratop_e/adp_e/adp_e.htm> (visited 9 April 2003).

[133] On the other hand, Japan, a country with similar trade structure and attitude toward trade dispute settlement, has shown much diverse interest as a complainant concerning its target markets. See generally Iwasawa, above n 57, 473.

[134] For the Korean proposal regarding anti-dumping issues, see, for example, WTO, WT/GC/W/235/Rev.1, dated 12 July 1999; TN/RL/W/6, dated 26 April 2002; TN/RL/W/10, dated 28 June 2002.

Table 7. AD Actions against Korea (From 01/01/95 to 31/12/02)

	Argentina	Australia	EC	India	South Africa	US	Others	Total
AD initiation	9	14	21	21	13	20	62	160
AD measures	7	5	10	16	14	11	20	83

to ensure prompt and effective implementation by a respondent. The implementation for the *US – DRAMS* and *US – Line Pipe* cases was in fact not much more than the mere expiration of the original trade remedy measures. This result raises concern for effectiveness and fairness of the WTO dispute settlement system, especially when dealing with the WTO litigation demands sizeable financial and human resources. In particular, the lack of legal systems to represent private parties' interest in line with Section 301 and TBR procedures would inevitably result in a less enthusiastic approach for resorting to legal activism for many WTO Members including Korea, because government officials in charge of WTO disputes may not have an incentive to initiate all those costly procedures merely for 'winning on paper'.

C. Korea as a third party

The DSU allows a third-party Member with substantial trade interests to join consultations[135] as well as the panel[136] and Appellate Body proceedings[137] between disputing parties. To date, Korea has joined, as a third party, 7 consultations and 13 panel proceedings (see Table 8). For three cases, *Indonesia – Automobiles* (DS54, DS55, DS59), *EC – LAN* (DS62, DS67) and *US – Steel Safeguard* (DS248, DS249, DS252, DS253, DS254, DS258, DS259) cases, Korea joined both consultations and panel proceedings.

As a third party, the Korean government demonstrated primary interests in disputes related to the major industrial sectors such as automobile, steel, and computers (see Table 9). Korea has not yet participated as a third party in disputes regarding, *inter alia*, GATT, agricultural products, SPS measures, TBT measures, services, or TRIPS. Although the recent practices of the WTO panels in attaching most of the party submissions as well as relevant documents for the proceeding to panel reports dwindle the exclusive benefit of a third-party participation to secure an access to those documents, a more timely and direct participation to present its views and economic interests may still be very beneficial for Korea in building the WTO jurisprudence.

---

[135] DSU, Art. 4.11.

[136] DSU, Art. 10.2.

[137] DSU, Art. 17.4. Articles 10.2 and 17.4 only mention 'substantial interest', but the difference from 'substantial trade interest' under Article 4.11 has not drawn much attention.

Table 8. Korea as Third Party in a Panel Proceeding

Case Name	Complainant	Dispute number
*Indonesia – Certain Measures Affecting the Automobile Industry	EC	DS54
	Japan	DS55
	US	DS59
*EC – Customs Classification of Some Computer Equipment	US	DS62
	US	DS67
Canada – Certain Automotive Industry Measures	Japan	DS139
	EC	DS142
US – Sections 301–310 of the Trade Act of 1974	EC	DS152
India – Measures Relating to Trade and Investment in the Motor Vehicle Sector	US	DS175
US – Anti-Dumping Measures on Certain Hot-Rolled Steel Products from Japan	Japan	DS184
US – Definitive Safeguard Measures on Imports of and Circular Welded Carbon Quality Line Pipe	EC	DS214
US – Continued Dumping and Subsidy Offset Act of 2000	Canada	Mexico
US – Sunset Review of Anti-Dumping Duties on Corrosion-Resistant Carbon Steel Flat Products from Japan	Japan	DS244
*US – Definitive Safeguard Measures on Imports of Steel Wire Rod and Circular Welded Carbon Quality Line Pipe	EC	DS248
	Japan	DS249
	China	DS252
	Switzerland	DS253
	Norway	DS254
	New Zealand	DS258
	Brazil	DS259
EC – Provisional Safeguard Measures on Imports of Certain Steel Products	US	DS260
**Brazil – Export Financing Programme for Aircraft	Canada	DS46/RW/2
**EC – Anti-Dumping Duties on Imports of Cotton-Type Bed Linen from India	India	DS141/RW

* Cases for which Korea also joined consultations.
** Compliance Panel

III. SYSTEMIC CONCERN FOR THE WTO DISPUTE SETTLEMENT SYSTEM

Despite the overall consensus of satisfactory operation of the WTO dispute settlement system, the WTO Member countries are currently engaged in active discussion and negotiation to improve the rules and procedures concerning the dispute settlement process. In fact, a ministerial decision adopted on 15 December 1993 'invited the Ministerial Conference to complete a full review of dispute settlement rules and procedures under the World Trade

Table 9. Korea in Joint Consultation

Case Name	Complainant	Dispute number
Brazil – Certain Automotive Investment Measures	Japan	DS51
Brazil – Certain Measures Affecting Trade and Investment in the Automotive Sector	US	DS52
*Indonesia – Certain Measures Affecting the Automobile Industry	EC	DS54
	Japan	DS55
	US	DS59
*EC – Customs Classification of Some Computer Equipment	US	DS62
	US	DS67
Brazil – Measures Affecting Payment Terms for Imports	EC	DS116
US – Continued Dumping and Subsidy Offset Act of 2000	Canada & Mexico	DS234
*US – Definitive Safeguard Measures on Imports of Steel Wire Rod and Circular Welded Carbon Quality Line Pipe	EC	DS248
	New Zealand	DS258
	Brazil	DS259

* Cases for which Korea also joined the panel proceedings.

Organization within four years after the entry into force of the Agreement Establishing the World Trade Organization, and to take a decision on the occasion of its first meeting after the completion of the review, whether to continue, modify, or terminate such dispute settlement rules and procedures'.[138] After the failure in the Seattle Ministerial Conference to complete the DSU revision, the WTO Members agreed to finish the negotiation for the DSU improvements and clarifications not later than May 2003 as a part of the Doha Round negotiation.[139] As of April 2003, many WTO Members including Korea, individually or jointly, have submitted their proposals on the DSU improvement.

The formal proposal submitted by Korea primarily concerned prompt compliance with recommendations or rulings of the DSB.[140] While Korea agrees on the basic principle that a multilateral determination on the WTO-consistency of an implementation measure should precede a request for retaliation,[141] it suggested expediting other parts of the implementation stage, especially considering the possibility of additional delay caused by appellate review procedure for compliance panel rulings.[142] More specifically, Korea

---

[138] Decision on the Application and Review of the Understanding on Rules and Procedures Governing the Settlement of Disputes. WTO, *The Results of the Uruguay Round of Multilateral Trade Negotiations: Legal Text* (Geneva, 1994) 465.

[139] Ministerial Declaration. WTO, WT/MIN(01)/DEC/1, dated 20 November 2001, para 30.

[140] WTO, TN/DS/W/11, dated 11 July 2002.

[141] In this regard, Korea co-sponsored a concept paper on the sequencing issue. WTO, JOB(02)/45, dated 31 May 2002.

[142] As of April 2003, eight Article 21.5 panel rulings were appealed and the Appellate Body issued rulings on those cases.

proposed the deletion of the 30-day requirement for notification of the intention to implement after the DSB adoption, and also suggested concomitant determination of the level of nullification or impairment by a compliance panel.[143]

Based on the practical experience of Korea, another obstacle for the prompt resolution of WTO disputes has been caused by a panel selection process that demands an increasingly longer period of time. In particular, it took much more time to select panelists when Korea engaged in WTO disputes as a complainant than as a respondent, ranging from 62 to 126 days.[144] This problem may be mitigated by the appointment of permanent panelists, for example, as proposed by the European Communities,[145] or by mandating specific due dates for panel selection such as 'within 30 days after the panel establishment'.

Another systemic issue concerning the current dispute settlement procedure drawn from the Korean experience is the need to adopt an accelerated procedure for safeguard measures.[146] In the *Korea – Dairy Products* case, the safeguard measure in the form of quotas went into effect from 7 March 1997, with a duration of four years. On the other hand, the panel requested by the European Communities was established on 22 July 1998 and the subsequent panel and the Appellate Body proceeding ended on 14 December 1999. After the adoption of those reports by the DSB on 12 January 2000, the reasonable period of time for implementation was agreed to end on 20 May 2000. Hence, even with successful implementation of the DSB recommendation by repealing it, the 'illegal' safeguard measure had been in force for more than three years. As explained above, this problem is not unique to Korean safeguard measures, nor the consequence of lack of implementation intent by Korea. In fact, the implementation period agreed in the *Korea – Dairy Product* case is the shortest one so far for WTO safeguard disputes.[147] In the *US – Line Pipe* case in which Korea was a complainant, the United States imposed the safeguard duty on 1 March 2000 with a duration of three years and one day.[148] After the DSB adopted the panel and Appellate Body reports, both parties agreed on the reasonable period of implementation that was to expire on 1 September 2002, merely six months earlier than the original due date of the safeguard measure. But, practically, the US measure was maintained until the end of February 2003, surpassing the original due date of

---

[143] WTO, TN/DS/W/35, dated 22 January 2003.

[144] WTO, TN/DS/W/7, 11–13 (dated 30 May 2002).

[145] WTO, TN/DS/W/1 (dated 13 March 2002).

[146] In fact, Australia made the proposal regarding this issue. WTO, TN/DS/W/8 (dated 8 July 2002).

[147] In *Argentina – Footwear* case, Argentina revoked the WTO-inconsistent safeguard measure on 25 February 2000, after the DSB adoption of the panel and Appellate Body reports on 12 January 2000. The safeguard measure was, however, due to expire on 25 February 2000 and thus Argentina did not even engage in negotiation or arbitration to determine the implementation period.

[148] WTO, G/SG/N/10/USA/5/Rev.1, dated 28 March 2000.

the safeguard measure set on 24 February 2003. In the *US – Definitive Safeguard Measures on Imports of Wheat Gluten from the European Communities* case, the actual due dates of the original safeguard measures coincided with the expiry of the reasonable period of implementation.[149] Therefore, the effectiveness of the current WTO dispute settlement system seems seriously undermined particularly in the context of 'temporary' safeguard actions. An accelerated dispute settlement procedure, in line with those currently available for prohibited or actionable subsidy, would be able to discipline prevalent abuse of safeguard measures under the WTO system.[150]

CONCLUDING COMMENTS

During the past half century, Korea achieved a remarkable economic development and became one of the major trading countries in the world. For example, in 2001, Korea was ranked as the eighth exporter and importer in the world according to the statistics on merchandise trade that exclude intra-EU trade.[151] Accordingly, Korea made the thirteenth largest contribution to the budget of the WTO by providing 2.381% of the budget in 2002.[152] Considering such a position in the world trading system, it is not surprising that Korea has become more active in asserting its rights under the WTO Agreements, although it initially showed a strong tendency to avoid legal confrontation with its major trading partners. In that regard, the Korean government became recently keener to monitor the foreign trade barriers and environment.[153]

From the practical aspect of dispute settlement, the Korean government has relied heavily on foreign private counsels to deal with the GATT/WTO disputes, particularly when the cases have been actually litigated at a panel or the Appellate Body level.[154] This situation, therefore, raised serious concern about building 'in-house' expertise to deal with WTO litigation. Indeed, when the Ministry of Foreign Affairs was expanded to become the Ministry of Foreign Affairs and Trade by establishing the Office of Trade

---

[149] WTO, WT/DS166/12, dated 12 April 2001.

[150] Active utilization of safeguard measures by developing countries, notably India, Chile, and Czech Republic, is one of the salient features of the WTO system, in contrast with the GATT system. See Dukgeun Ahn, 'WTO Safeguard System: Present and Perspective', in *Korea–China Joint Workshop Proceeding for Trade Remedy Institutions* 3 (2002, in Korean).

[151] WTO, *International Trade Statistics 2002* (Geneva, 2002) 26.

[152] WTO, *Annual Report 2002* (Geneva, 2002) 165–67. The United States made the largest contribution by providing 15.723% of the budget. China's contribution accounted for 2.973% in the 2002 WTO budget. Ibid.

[153] The Korean Ministry of Foreign Affairs and Trade began to publish 'A Comprehensive Survey of the Trade Environment' since 1998. This can be viewed as a Korean version of 'National Trade Estimate Report' by the USTR, but without Section 301 linkage.

[154] In fact, this situation is not peculiar to Korea. The legal technicality and formality of WTO dispute settlement proceedings has become increasingly complicated. Many developing countries find themselves without the proper capacity to deal with trade disputes under the WTO system. In this

Negotiation in 1998,[155] a special body entitled the 'International Trade Law Team' was created with the mandate to provide legal support regarding the WTO Agreements and, more broadly, legal matters on international economic relations. The role of this special team in relation to handling WTO dispute settlement cases, however, has not been very visible except for the very recent cases. On the other hand, Korean experts began to contribute to WTO panel works more actively in recent years.[156]

Assessing the experience to date, Korea appears to have been in quite a defensive position in dispute settlements. According to the statistics until the end of 2002, no other WTO Member country, except for Argentina, has been so disproportionately challenged by the dispute settlement system.[157] And yet, Korea has been fully cooperative in implementing the DSB recommendations. The overall Korean practice in terms of the WTO dispute settlement would be viewed as exemplary in its contribution to enhancing the international economic order.[158] Conversely, the role of the WTO dispute settlement system for future economic development for Korea would remain vital.

---

regard, 32 countries agreed to establish the 'Advisory Centre on WTO Law', an independent body to assist its signatories on WTO dispute settlement. Korea is not yet a signatory to this Centre. See <http://www.acwl.ch> (visited 25 March 2003).

[155] The Presidential Order, No 15710 (28 February 1998).

[156] As of April 2003, Korean experts worked as a panelist in three cases. Korean legal experts also contributed to the works of the WTO Secretariat in relation to trade disputes. No Appellate Body Member has been elected from Korea.

[157] Until the end of 2002, Argentina was challenged in 15 cases whereas it brought only 8 cases.

[158] Professor Jackson raised this question to assess how the Japanese international law practice was related to the maintenance of international economic order. John H. Jackson, 'Western View of Japanese International Law Practice for the Maintenance of the International Economic Order', in Nisuke Ando: *Japan and International Law: Past, Present and Future* (The Hague: Kluwer Law International, 1999) 208.

APPENDICES. PROFILES OF THE WTO CASES INVOLVING KOREA

Appendix 1. WTO Cases Involving Korea as Respondent

Cases name	Complainant	Dispute number	Panelists	Appellate Body Division	Adoption date
Korea – Measures Concerning the Testing and Inspection of Agricultural Products	US	DS3 & DS41	Pending consultation		
Korea – Measures Concerning the Shelf-Life of Products	US	DS5	Settled		
Korea – Measures Concerning Bottled Water	Canada	DS20	Settled		
Korea – Laws, Regulations and Practices in the Telecommunications Procurement Sector	EC	DS40	Settled		
*Korea – Taxes on Alcoholic Beverages	EC, US	DS75 & DS84	Mr Åke Lindén (Chairperson), Professor Frédéric Jenny, Mr Carlos da Rocha Parahnos	Matsushita (Presiding Member), Ehlermann, Feliciano	17 February 1999
*Korea – Definitive Safeguard Measure on Imports of Certain Dairy Products	EC	DS98	Mr Ole Lundby (Chairperson), Ms Leora Blumberg, Ms Luz Elena Reyes	El-Naggar (Presiding Member), Ehlermann, Feliciano	12 January 2000
*Korea – Measures Affecting Imports of Fresh, Chilled and Frozen Beef	US, Australia	DS161 & DS169	Lars Anell (Chairperson), Paul Demaret, Alan Matthews	Ehlermann (Presiding Member), Abi-Saab, Feliciano	10 January 2001
*Korea – Measures Affecting Government Procurement	US	DS163	Mr Michael D. Cartland Ms Marie-Gabrielle Ineichen-Fleisch (Chairperson) Mr Peter-Armin Trepte	Not Appealed	19 June 2000

* Cases for which panel reports were issued.

Appendix.2. WTO Cases Involving Korea as Complainant

Cases name	Respondent	Dispute number	Panelists	Appellate Body Division	Adoption date
United States – Imposition of Anti-Dumping Duties on Imports of Color Television Receivers from Korea	US	DS89	Withdrawal		
United States – Anti-Dumping Duty on Dynamic Random Access Memory Semiconductors (DRAMS) of One Megabit or Above from Korea	US	DS99	Mr Crawford Falconer (Chairperson), Mr Meinhard Hilf, Ms Marta Lemme	Not Appealed	19 March 1999
United States – Anti-Dumping Measures on Stainless Steel Plate in Coils and Stainless Steel Sheet and Strip from Korea	US	DS179	Mr José Antonio S. Buencamino (Chairperson), Mr G. Bruce Cullen, Ms Enie Neri de Ross	Not Appealed	1 February 2001
United States – Definitive Safeguard Measures on Imports of Circular Welded Carbon Quality Line Pipe from Korea	US	DS202	Mr Dariusz Rosati (Chairperson), Mr Roberto Azevedo, Mr Eduardo Bianchi	Lacarte-Muro, Bacchus, (Presiding Member,) Abi-Saab	8 March 2002
Philippines – Anti-Dumping Measures regarding Polypropylene Resins from Korea	Philippines	DS215	Pending Consultation		
United States – Continued Dumping and Subsidy Offset Act of 2000	US	DS217	Mr Luzius Wasescha, Mr Maamoun Abdel-Fattah, Mr William Falconer	Sacerdoti (Presiding Member), Baptista, Lockhart	27 January 2003
United States – Definitive Safeguard Measures on Imports of Certain Steel Products	US	DS251	Mr Stefan Johannesson, Mr Mohan Kumar, Ms Margaret Liang		Ongoing

* Cases for which panel reports were issued.

Part Two

Practices and Theoretical Foundations of the Trade Remedy System

Chapter 3

Alternative Approach to Causation Analysis in Trade Remedy Investigations: 'Cost of Production' Test

Dukgeun AHN[*] and William J. MOON[**]

Causation requirement in trade remedy investigations has produced significant controversy in terms of legal interpretation and economic analysis. Deficient treaty texts and confusing legal ruling have exacerbated practical difficulty for investigating authorities to ensure World Trade Organization (WTO) consistency. Various analytical models that were proposed on the basis of more articulated economics often turn out to be too complicated to apply in broader cases or critically contingent on data availability. We suggest an alternative approach that utilizes firm production costs to complement the previous models.

1. INTRODUCTION

The multilateral trade agreements such as General Agreement on Tariffs and Trade (GATT) and World Trade Organization (WTO) Agreements as well as national regulations dealing with trade remedy systems stipulate a 'causation' requirement as one of the essential elements for utilizing trade remedy measures. Imports, whether dumped, subsidized, or increased due to market liberalization, must be shown to have 'caused' injury to domestic industries producing like or directly competitive products. This seemingly simple task has been the focal point for long controversy among economists and lawyers because there is no explicit guidance as to how causation requirements should be applied in trade remedy investigations.[1] The lack of more articulated criteria is indeed puzzling, given that other legal elements involving dumping and subsidy margin calculation or injury determination are substantially articulated and causation is an essential requirement as important as those elements.[2]

The key question still to be resolved is how to determine whether the increase in imports is the true cause of injury to the domestic industry and not a consequence of that

---

[*] Associate Professor of International Trade Law and Policy, Graduate School of International Studies, Seoul National University. E-mail: dahn@snu.ac.kr.
[**] Research Associate, Centre for International Commerce and Finance, Seoul National University & J.D. Candidate, Yale Law School. E-mail: william.moon@yale.edu.
[1] An excellent summary and explanation on this issue are provided in Alan O. Sykes, *The WTO Agreement on Safeguards: A Commentary* (Oxford: Oxford University Press, 2006), 156–210. The logic for a safeguard measure can be mostly extended to anti-dumping and countervailing cases.
[2] See, e.g., J. Czako et al., *A Handbook on Anti-dumping Investigations* (Cambridge: Cambridge University Press, 2003).

Ahn, Dukgeun & William J. Moon. 'Alternative Approach to Causation Analysis in Trade Remedy Investigations: 'Cost of Production' Test'. *Journal of World Trade* 44, no. 5 (2010): 1023–1052.
© 2010 Kluwer Law International BV, The Netherlands

JOURNAL OF WORLD TRADE

injury. The economic analysis on the causal relationship between imports and the pertinent domestic industry does not seem to conform to the legal interpretation of causation requirements, or vice versa. For example, the panel's ruling in *Argentina – Footwear* illustrates that coincidence between an upward trend in imports and downward trends in the injury factors is important evidence for causation determination.[3] Such a finding of coincidence, however, does contradict the most elementary economic lesson for causation analysis. The panel in *US – Steel Safeguard*, for example, emphasized the need for a more articulated econometric analysis in relation to causation determination.[4]

Truth be told, correlation and causation have been a philosophical conundrum for centuries and a central question that remains to be debated in many academic disciplines. In this article, we propose an additional tool that can be used to refine causation analysis for trade remedy systems. First, building on Kelly's model, we introduce the 'Cost of Production Test' that addresses the problems stemming from one of the false assumptions adopted in the original model. Our new approach, as it turns out, also helps meet the non-attribution requirement. Second, we suggest applying the 'Insufficient and Non-redundant Parts of Unnecessary but Sufficient Cause (INUS)' condition to ascertain the philosophical definition of 'genuine and substantial relationship of cause and effect' that is required for safeguard actions, presenting a viable alternative to prior – and often criticized – standards for safeguard action.

2.   Rules in WTO, United States and EU

2.1.   Anti-dumping regulation

The WTO Anti-dumping (AD) Agreement requires the 'demonstration of a causal relationship between the dumped imports and the injury to the domestic industry' and the non-attribution analysis for other known factors injuring the domestic industry. The AD Agreement agreed at the Kennedy Round negotiation, which did not enter into force due to the opposition by the US Congress, showed an important difference in terms of causation requirements for anti-dumping actions. The relevant articles are given as follows:[5]

Article 3. Determination of Injury

(a) A determination of injury shall be made only when the authorities concerned are satisfied that the dumped imports are *demonstrably the principal cause* of material injury or of threat of material injury to a domestic industry or *the principal cause* of material retardation of the establishment of such an industry. In reaching their decision the authorities shall weigh, on one hand, the effect of the dumping and, on the other hand, all other factors taken together which may be adversely affecting the industry. The determination shall in all cases be based on positive findings and not on mere allegations or hypothetical possibilities. [. . .]

---

[3] Panel Report, *Argentina – Safeguard Measures on Imports of Footwear* (*Argentina – Footwear*), WT/DS121/R, para. 8.229.
[4] Panel Report, *Definitive Safeguard Measures on Imports of Certain Steel Products* (*US – Steel Safeguards*), WT/DS248,249,251,252,253,254,258,259/R, para. 10.342. See *infra* s. 3.3.
[5] GATT, Basic Instruments and Selected Documents, 15S/24 (1968).

(b) In order to establish whether dumped imports have caused injury, all other factors which, individually or in combination, may be adversely affecting the industry shall be examined, for example: the volume and prices of undumped imports of the product in question, competition between the domestic producers themselves, contraction in demand due to substitution of other products or to changes in consumer tastes.

In the original wording, causal relationship between dumped imports and industry injury is stipulated as 'demonstrably the principal cause'. Moreover, it demands weighing the effects of the dumping versus 'all other factors taken together which may be adversely affecting the industry', although the provision does not elaborate on how to conduct a comparison between dumping and all other factors. 'All other factors' include 'the volume and prices of undumped imports of the product in question, competition between the domestic producers themselves, contraction in demand due to substitution of other products or to changes in consumer tastes' that are indeed typical elements to aggravate or create domestic industry injury.

However, this principal causality test contradicted the existing US anti-dumping regulations, which specifically required 'a causal link but...not...that dumped imports must be a principal cause, or a major cause, or a substantial cause of injury caused by all factors contributing to overall injury to an industry'.[6] That was in fact the main reason for the US Congress to veto the first AD Agreement concluded under the auspice of the GATT. Another problem of the above provision is that it was susceptible to different interpretations, creating ambiguity to the critical element of an anti-dumping system. For example, it was not clear whether dumped imports must be themselves the cause of material injury or the principal causal factor for material injury resulted by all injurious factors.[7]

The Tokyo Round negotiation modified several parts of the original AD Agreement so that it could be accepted by major GATT contracting parties including the United States. One of the critical changes was the causation requirement, which was finalized as below:[8]

Article 3. Determination of Injury

(c) It must be demonstrated that the dumped imports are, through the effects of dumping, causing injury within the meaning of this Code. There may be other factors which at the same time are injuring the industry, and the injuries caused by other factors must not be attributed to the dumped imports.

(d) The effect of the dumped imports shall be assessed in relation to the domestic production of the like product when available data permit the separate identification of production in terms of such criteria as: the production process, the producers' realizations, profits. When the domestic production of the like product has no separate identity in these terms the effects of the dumped imports shall be

---

[6] S. Rep. No. 1298, 93rd Cong., 2nd Sess. 180 (1974). See also M. Trebilcock & R. Howse, *The Regulation of International Trade*, 3rd edn New York: Routledge, (2005), 233–234.
[7] R. Bierwagen, *GATT Article VI and the Protectionist Bias in Anti-dumping Laws* (1990), 87–89.
[8] GATT, Basic Instruments and Selected Documents, 26 S/171 (1980). See also <www.worldtradelaw.net/tokyoround/antidumpingcode.pdf>, (visited on 3 Mar. 2010).

assessed by the examination of the production of the narrowest group or range of products, which includes the like product, for which the necessary information can be provided.

The principal causation requirement was eliminated and instead replaced with the demonstration of mere 'causation'. Moreover, the requirement to 'weigh' the effect of the dumping and all other factors was discarded and replaced with mere non-attribution analysis. This provision was further elaborated during the Uruguay Round negotiation to require the demonstration of a causal relationship between the dumped imports and the injury 'based on an examination of all relevant evidence before the authorities'. The investigating authorities must examine 'any known factors other than the dumped imports which at the same time are injuring the domestic industry', which include 'the volume and prices of imports not sold at dumping prices, contraction in demand or changes in the patterns of consumption, trade restrictive practices of and competition between the foreign and domestic producers, developments in technology and the export performance and productivity of the domestic industry'.

The European Community (EC) adopted essentially the same provision as the WTO AD Agreement with respect to causation requirement.[9] In contrast, section 1673 of the US Trade Act stipulates that injury must occur 'by reason of' dumped merchandise. Although the legal discrepancy between 'cause' and 'by reason of' tests is not obvious, it is generally understood that the US anti-dumping act stipulates the same standard as the WTO AD Agreement. In other words, there is no need for dumping to be the sole or principal cause of injury and to be weighed against other factors.[10] In fact, the legislative guidelines such as the Statements of Administrative Action or the Senate Report for the Trade Agreements Act of 1979 emphasized that the 'by reason of' standard did not require dumped imports to be the 'principal', 'major', 'substantial', or a 'significant' cause.[11] In addition, the US Court of International Trade repeatedly confirmed that the International Trade Commission (ITC) was precluded from weighing causes of injury[12] and that the existence of other contributing causes of injury was irrelevant if there was substantial evidence that a causal nexus existed between imports and injury.[13]

2.2. COUNTERVAILING REGULATION

The provisions for countervailing regulations are almost identical to anti-dumping rules, particularly with respect to causation element. For example, Article 15.5 of the Subsidies

---

[9] Council Regulation (EC) No. 384/96 of 22 Dec. 1995 on protection against dumped imports from countries not members of the European Community (hereinafter 'EC AD Regulation').

[10] Raj Bhala & Kevin Kennedy, *World Trade Law* (1998), 882–885; Joseph E. Pattison, *Anti-dumping and Countervailing Laws* (1995), ss 4.03–4.05; Gary N. Horlick, 'The United States Anti-dumping System', in *Anti-dumping Law and Practice*, ed. John H. Jackson & Edwin A. Vermulst (1989), 160.

[11] Statements of Administrative Action, H.R. Doc. No. 153, Part II, 434 and Senate Report, No. 249, 96th Cong., 1st Sess. 75. See also William D. DeGrandis, 'Proving Causation in Anti-dumping Cases', *The International Lawyer* 20, no. 2 (1986): 563, 568–569.

[12] See, e.g., *British Steel Corp. v. US*, 593 F. Supp. 405, 413 (1984).

[13] See, e.g., *Atlantic Sugar, Ltd v. US*, 519 F. Supp. 916, 922 (1981).

Table 1. Causation Requirements in Anti-dumping Regulations

WTO	**Article 3: Determination of Injury**

3.5. It must be demonstrated that the dumped imports are, through the effects of dumping, as set forth in paragraphs 2 and 4, causing injury within the meaning of this Agreement. The demonstration of a causal relationship between the dumped imports and the injury to the domestic industry shall be based on an examination of all relevant evidence before the authorities. The authorities shall also examine any known factors other than the dumped imports which at the same time are injuring the domestic industry, and the injuries caused by these other factors must not be attributed to the dumped imports. Factors which may be relevant in this respect include, *inter alia*, the volume and prices of imports not sold at dumping prices, contraction in demand or changes in the patterns of consumption, trade restrictive practices of and competition between the foreign and domestic producers, developments in technology and the export performance and productivity of the domestic industry.

United States[14] — If —

(2) the Commission determines that —

  (A) an industry in the US —

    (i) is materially injured, or

    (ii) is threatened with material injury, or

  (B) the establishment of an industry in the US is materially retarded, by reason of imports of that merchandise or by reason of sales (or the likelihood of sales) of that merchandise for importation, then there shall be imposed upon such merchandise an anti-dumping duty, in addition to any other duty imposed, in an amount equal to the amount by which the normal value exceeds the export price (or the constructed export price) for the merchandise. For purposes of this section and section 1673d (b)(1) of this title, a reference to the sale of foreign merchandise includes the entering into of any leasing arrangement regarding the merchandise that is equivalent to the sale of the merchandise.

EU[15] — **Article 3 – Determination of Injury**

6. It must be demonstrated, from all the relevant evidence presented in relation to paragraph 2, that the dumped imports are causing injury within the meaning of this Regulation. Specifically, this shall entail a demonstration that the volume and/or price levels identified pursuant to paragraph 3 are responsible for an impact on the Community industry as provided for in paragraph 5, and that this impact exists to a degree which enables it to be classified as material.

7. Known factors other than the dumped imports which at the same time are injuring the Community industry shall also be examined to ensure that injury caused by these other factors is not attributed to the dumped imports under paragraph 6. Factors which may be considered in this respect include the volume and prices of imports not sold at dumping prices, contraction in demand or changes in the patterns of consumption, restrictive trade practices of, and competition between, third country and Community producers, developments in technology and the export performance and productivity of the Community industry.

---

[14] USC, s. 1673.
[15] EC AD Regulation.

and Countervailing Measures (SCM) Agreement is parallel to Article 3.5 of the AD Agreement. Causation-related provisions in US laws[16] and EC Regulations[17] also stipulate the same legal requirement. Therefore, there is no difference from the above discussion for anti-dumping regulation in terms of interpretation and application of causation requirement.

Unlike AD Agreement, the SCM Agreement was first concluded only in the Tokyo Round negotiation. So, the causation requirement that was controversial in the Kennedy Round AD Code was already modified in accordance with the Tokyo Round AD Code.

2.3.   SAFEGUARD REGULATION

The legal text of the Safeguard Agreement concerning causation requirement does not differ from those of the AD Agreement or the SCM Agreement. The treaty text requires the increased imports to 'cause' or 'threaten to cause' serious injury to a domestic industry. The interpretation of this causation requirement, however, perhaps raised the most controversial issue about the WTO safeguard system.[18] The main reason for this controversy is that safeguard action does not require any unfair trade practices. So the argument that the causation requirement in the context of safeguard actions should be stricter than that for anti-dumping or countervailing actions appears to be very compelling. Moreover, Article 4 of the Safeguard Agreement stipulates non-attribution requirement, which is basically identical to those of anti-dumping and countervailing actions.

On the other hand, it is noteworthy that the causation requirements of the US and Canadian safeguard regulations are different from the WTO Safeguard Agreement. As quoted in Table 2, the US trade laws stipulate that imports must be 'substantial cause' of serious injury. This substantial cause requirement is interpreted as 'a cause which is important and not less than any other cause'. The same legal requirement for causation – 'an important cause that is no less important than any other cause of the serious injury or threat' – appears in the Canadian regulation,[19] although a different term of 'principal cause' is used.[20]

3.   LEGAL PRACTICES AND INTERPRETATION

The legal application of causation requirement for trade remedy actions is divided into two elements: (i) causal relationship between imports – dumped, subsidized, or merely increased imports – and injury to a domestic industry, and (ii) non-attribution of injury caused by

---

[16] USC, s. 1671.
[17] Council Regulation (EC) No. 2026/97 of 6 Oct. 1997 on protection against subsidized imports from countries not members of the European Community.
[18] See, for example, Sykes, *supra* n. 1, at 156–210 or Dukgeun Ahn, 'Restructuring the WTO Safeguard System', in *The WTO Trade Remedy System: East Asian Perspective*, ed. M. Matsushita, D. Ahn & T. Chen (2006), at 17–19.
[19] Article 27, Canadian International Trade Tribunal Act.
[20] Ahn, *supra* n. 18, at 18.

Table 2. Causation Requirements in Safeguard Regulations

WTO	**Article 4: Determination of Serious Injury or Threat Thereof**

2. (a) In the investigation to determine whether increased imports have caused or are threatening to cause serious injury to a domestic industry under the terms of this Agreement, the competent authorities shall evaluate all relevant factors of an objective and quantifiable nature having a bearing on the situation of that industry, in particular, the rate and amount of the increase in imports of the product concerned in absolute and relative terms, the share of the domestic market taken by increased imports, changes in the level of sales, production, productivity, capacity utilization, profits and losses, and employment.

(b) The determination referred to in subparagraph (a) shall not be made unless this investigation demonstrates, on the basis of objective evidence, the existence of the causal link between increased imports of the product concerned and serious injury or threat thereof. When factors other than increased imports are causing injury to the domestic industry at the same time, such injury shall not be attributed to increased imports.

Unite States[21]

Section 2251. Action to facilitate positive adjustment to import competition

(a) Presidential action

If the United States International Trade Commission (hereinafter referred to in this part as the 'Commission') determines under section 2252(b) of this title that an article is being imported into the US in such increased quantities as to be a substantial cause of serious injury, or the threat thereof, to the domestic industry producing an article like or directly competitive with the imported article, the President, in accordance with this part, shall take all appropriate and feasible action within his power which the President determines will facilitate efforts by the domestic industry to make a positive adjustment to import competition and provide greater economic and social benefits than costs.

Section 2252. Investigations, determinations, and recommendations by Commission

(b) Investigations and determinations by Commission

(1) (B) For purposes of this section, the term 'substantial cause' means a cause which is important and not less than any other cause.

(c) Factors applied in making determinations

(1) In making determinations under subsection (b) of this section, the Commission shall take into account all economic factors which it considers relevant, including (but not limited to)

(C) with respect to substantial cause, an increase in imports (either actual or relative to domestic production) and a decline in the proportion of the domestic market supplied by domestic producers.

EU[22]

Article 5

2. Using as a basis the factors described in Article 10, the investigation shall seek to determine whether imports of the product in question are causing or threatening to cause serious injury to the Community producers concerned.

Continued on next page

[21] USC, ss 2251 and 2252.
[22] EU AD Regulation.

Table 2. Continued

Article 10

Examination of the trend of imports, of the conditions in which they take place and of serious injury or threat of serious injury to Community producers resulting from such imports shall cover in particular the following factors:

  a. the volume of imports, in particular where there has been a significant increase, either in absolute terms or relative to production or consumption in the Community;

  b. the price of imports, in particular where there has been a significant price undercutting as compared with the price of a like product in the Community;

  c. the consequent impact on Community producers as indicated by trends in certain economic factors such as:
    –production;
    –capacity utilization;
    –stocks;
    –sales;
    –market share;
    –prices (i.e. depression of prices or prevention of price increases which would normally have occurred);
    –profits;
    –return on capital employed;
    –cash flow;
    –employment.

  d. factors other than trends in imports which are causing or may have caused injury to the Community producers concerned.

---

factors other than imports. These legal elements bring about much controversy over, for example, how to prove causal relationship, and what is to be shown for finding factors other than imports that cause injury to meet the non-attribution requirement.

The main principles for legal application drawn from WTO jurisprudence are as follows: first, apply non-attribution principle and, second, establish causal relationship between imports and domestic injury. The crucial rulings by the WTO panels and Appellate Body related to these issues are summarized and analysed below.

3.1. AD AGREEMENT

3.1.1. *Non-attribution*

In *US – Hot-Rolled Steel*,[23] the panel opined that non-attribution does not require investigating authority to identify the extent of injury caused by other factors in order to isolate

---

[23] Panel Report, *US – Anti-dumping Measures on Certain Hot-Rolled Steel Products from Japan* (*US – Hot-rolled Steel*), WT/DS184/R, adopted 23 Aug. 2001 modified by Appellate Body Report WT/DS184/AB/R, DSR 2001:X, 4769.

the injury caused by them from the injury caused by dumped imports.[24] Instead, the panel ruled that the investigating authority was required to conduct an examination sufficient to ensure that material injury was not caused by factors other than these imports.[25] This rather loose interpretation by a GATT panel was reversed by the Appellate Body.

The Appellate Body in *US – Hot-rolled Steel* ruled that non-attribution analysis 'must involve separating and distinguishing the injurious effects of the other factors from the injurious effects of the dumped imports',[26] while the particular methods and approaches to carry out the process of separating and distinguishing the injurious effects of dumped imports from the injurious effects of other known causal factors are not prescribed by the *AD Agreement*.[27] The Appellate Body further explained that it requires 'a satisfactory explanation of the nature and extent of the injurious effects of the other factors, as distinguished from the injurious effects of the dumped imports',[28] no matter how difficult it may be as a practical matter.

The implication of this ruling is profound. It appears that quantitative methodology such as econometric analysis is now indispensable to provide 'a satisfactory explanation of both the nature and extent of the injurious effects' of other factors as well as dumped imports. Only rigorous quantifiable analysis would be able to satisfy such detailed prescription for non-attribution requirements.

Moreover, this decision naturally raises a relevant question of whether the non-attribution analysis requires the comparison of injurious effects of other factors as opposed to dumped imports, probably as the next step of separation and distinction of injurious effects. In this regard, *EC – Tube or Pipe Fitting* raised the issue of whether the non-attribution provision requires an investigating authority to examine the effects of the other causal factors *collectively* after having examined them *individually*.[29]

In fact, the EC identified other factors such as imports from third countries not subject to investigation, decline in consumption, and substitution.[30] With respect to each of the factors, the EC concluded that the extent of the contribution to injury was not significant and thereby not such as to have broken the causal link between dumped imports and material injury. Brazil claimed that this 'significant contribution test' as applied to individual factor was inconsistent with Article 3.5 because the collective effect of insignificant factors might collectively constitute a significant cause of injury. In other words, the EC and Brazil contested how to weigh or compare the extent of injurious effects between dumped imports and other factors.

---

[24] This is actually drawn from the decision in *US – Imposition of Anti-dumping Duties on Imports of Fresh and Chilled Atlantic Salmon for Norway*, ADP/87 (27 Apr. 1994), at 555.
[25] Panel Report, *US – Hot-rolled Steel*, para. 7.254.
[26] Appellate Body Report, *US – Hot-rolled Steel*, WT/DS184/AB/R, para. 223.
[27] *Ibid.*, para 224.
[28] *Ibid.*, para. 226.
[29] Appellate Body Report, *European Communities – Anti-dumping Duties on Malleable Cast Iron Tube or Pipe Fittings from Brazil (EC – Tube or Pipe Fittings)*, WT/DS219/AB/R, adopted 18 Aug. 2003, DSR 2003:VI, 2613, para. 187.
[30] Panel Report, *EC – Tube or Pipe Fittings*, para. 7.367.

The Appellate Body, however, ruled that 'Article 3.5 does not compel, *in every case*, an assessment of the *collective* effects of other causal factors, because such an assessment is not always necessary to conclude that injuries ascribed to dumped imports are actually caused by those imports'.[31] Thus, the Appellate Body clarified that the crucial element of the non-attribution analysis is to separate and distinguish injurious effects of other factors from that of dumped import; not to make a quantitative comparison among them. This ruling may be understood as an attempt to qualify potentially too difficult of a requirement implied by the decision in *US – Hot-rolled Steel.*

In all, the Appellate Body decisions concerning the non-attribution requirement have made the relevant analysis unnecessarily or disproportionately complicated considering its purpose or utility. Even after scrutinizing the nature and extent of injurious effects of individual factors, the separation of their effects is the ultimate goal. As long as dumped imports can be shown to have a causal relationship with injury after such non-attribution, the anti-dumping duty is typically determined by the whole dumping margin – or injury margin in countries that adopt the lesser duty rule – regardless of the extent of injurious effect of dumped imports.[32] The lack of the linkage between causation and anti-dumping measures is contrasted to the case of safeguard actions.

3.1.2.   *Causal Relationship*

The AD Agreement does not specify what should be shown to vindicate the causal relationship between dumped imports and domestic injury. In addition, the AD Agreement does not require the investigating authority to determine that dumped imports are the sole cause of injury. The panel in *US – Hot-Rolled Steel* ruled that there is no obligation in Article 3.5 of the AD Agreement that an investigating authority 'demonstrate that dumped imports alone have caused material injury by deducting the injury caused by other factors from the overall injury found to exist, in order to determine whether the remaining injury rises to the level of material injury'.[33]

Despite substantial elaboration of the AD Agreement through rulings for the WTO disputes, no case has directly addressed the issue of what must be shown for causal relationship under Article 3.5. In fact, the WTO disputes raising causation issues normally focused on non-attribution analysis or other known factors instead of causal relationship per se.[34] For example, in *US – Softwood Lumber VI*,[35] the panel ruled that the causal analysis was inconsistent with the AD Agreement because the determination of substantially

---

[31] Appellate Body Report, *EC – Tube or Pipe Fittings*, para. 191.
[32] Some commentators wrote that 'causal requirement has been read in a proceduralist manner'. P. Mavroidis et al., *The Law and Economics of Contingent Protection in the WTO* (2008), 123.
[33] Panel Report, *US – Hot-rolled Steel*, at para. 7.260.
[34] In this respect, the GATT cases are not exceptional. Ten GATT rulings concerning anti-dumping disputes included no part concerning causal relationship issues. For GATT AD cases, see <www.worldtradelaw.net/dsc/database/ad.asp>.
[35] Panel Report, *US – Investigation of the International Trade Commission in Softwood Lumber from Canada (US – Softwood Lumber VI)*, WT/DS277/R, adopted 26 Apr. 2004, DSR 2004:VI, 2485.

increased imports was already in violation. Likewise, in *Thailand – H-Beams*,[36] the panel found Thailand's determination of a causal relationship to be in error under Articles 3.5 in light of the earlier finding that price effects was inconsistent. In *EC – Bed Linen (Article 21.5-India)*,[37] the panel rejected India's claim on EC's causation analysis because the market share figures referred to by India were not those on which the EC decision was based. In other words, the panel concluded that India failed to demonstrate the prima facie case that an unbiased and objective investigating authority could have reached the EC causation determination.

3.2. SCM AGREEMENT

3.2.1. *Causal Relationship*

The WTO jurisprudence has not yet clarified what kind or extent of causal link must be shown to satisfy causation requirement. However, the panel in *US – Lumber VI* explained that the causation determination must be based at least on correct factual proof.[38] Given that ITC's determination of substantially increased imports was found to be in violation of the SCM Agreement, the panel concluded that the causal analysis cannot be consistent with the SCM Agreement because a fundamental element of causal analysis is flawed.

3.2.2. *Non-attribution*

The panel in *US – Lumber VI* explained that 'although it has not been specifically considered in a countervailing duty case, given that the relevant provisions in the two Agreements are identical, and in light of the Declaration of Ministers relating to Dispute Settlement under the AD and SCM Agreements, it is clear to us that the requirement is the same in the context of both anti-dumping and countervailing duty investigations'.[39] Therefore, rulings concerning the non-attribution element in the AD cases are to be applied for SCM disputes. In addition to the AD jurisprudence, the cases relating to the SCM Agreement contain a few more elaboration.

First, the panel in *EC – Countervailing Measures on DRAM Chips*[40] emphasized the need for a quantitative analysis to embrace the Appellate Body ruling that the

---

[36] Panel Report, *Thailand – Anti-dumping Duties on Angles, Shapes and Sections of Iron or Non-alloy Steel and H-Beams from Poland (Thailand – H-Beams)*, WT/DS122/R, adopted 5 Apr. 2001, as modified by Appellate Body Report WT/DS122/AB/R, DSR 2001:VII, 2741.

[37] Panel Report, *European Communities – Anti-dumping Duties on Imports of Cotton-Type Bed Linen from India – Recourse to Article 21.5 of the DSU by India*, WT/DS141/RW, adopted 24 Apr. 2003, as modified by Appellate Body Report WT/DS141/AB/RW, DSR 2003:IV, 1269.

[38] Panel Report, *US – Softwood Lumber VI*, para. 7.122.

[39] *Ibid.*, para. 7.129.

[40] Panel Report, *European Communities – Countervailing Measures on Dynamic Random Access Memory Chips from Korea (EC – Countervailing Measures on DRAM Chips)*, WT/DS299/R, adopted 3 Aug. 2005, DSR 2005:XVIII, 8671.

non-attribution requirement mandates the finding of the extent as well as the nature of the injurious effects of the other factors. The panel ruled that:

> it does not suffice for an investigating authority merely to 'check the box'. An investigating authority must do more than simply list other known factors, and then dismiss their role with bare qualitative assertions, such as 'the factor did not contribute in any significant way to the injury', or 'the factor did not break the causal link between subsidized imports and material injury.' In our view, an investigating authority must make a better effort to quantify the impact of other known factors, relative to subsidized imports, preferably using elementary economic constructs or models. At the very least, the non-attribution language of Article 15.5 requires from an investigating authority a satisfactory explanation of the nature *and extent* of the injurious effects of the other factors, as distinguished from the injurious effects of the subsidized imports.[41] (Italic in the original report)

Based on the above explanation, the panel noted that the EC failed to examine the extent of the negative effects of economic downturn in the market, overcapacity, and other non-subsidized import, although those factors are acknowledged as relevant factors to cause injury. Such decision may be one of the most economics-oriented approaches that embrace a quantitative analysis as an essential element for non-attribution requirements.

Second, the failure of an investigating authority to evaluate factors whose relevance is explicitly acknowledged constitutes a breach of the non-attribution obligation. For example, in the *US – Lumber VI* case, the panel ruled that the failure of the United States International Trade Commission (USITC) to discuss the likely future effects of domestic supplies of lumber was a 'glaring omission' and thereby violation of Article 15.5 of the SCM Agreement.[42] This ruling does not specifically address how much 'relevant' other factors should be taken into account for non-attribution analysis. However, insofar as the relevance of a factor is acknowledged by an investigating authority, the effect of that factor must be examined and explained with adequate reasoning.

3.2.3. *Causation Issues for Serious Prejudice*

Although it is not prescribed as expressly as in a countervailing investigation case, actionable subsidy may be challenged if serious prejudice to another WTO member's interest is shown to be caused by a subsidy. Article 6.3 of the SCM Agreement implies the causation requirement for serious prejudice determination by providing that 'the effect of the subsidy' is to displace or impede trade, price undercutting or depression, or increase of market share.

In fact, the panel in *Korea – Commercial Vessels* noted that there must be a causal relationship between the subsidy and the effects described in Article 6.3 of SCM Agreement.[43] The same panel explained that the text of Article 6.3 implies a 'but for' approach to causation and requires a counterfactual examination, that is, determining what trade or

---

[41] Panel Report, *EC – Countervailing Measures on DRAM Chips*, para. 7.405.
[42] Panel Report, *US – Lumber VI*, paras 7.135–7.137.
[43] Panel Report, *Korea – Measures Affecting Trade in Commercial Vessels (Korea – Commercial Vessels)*, WT/DS273/R, adopted 11 Apr. 2005, DSR 2005:VII, 2749, para. 7.604.

prices would have been in the absence of the subsidy.[44] The actual application of this 'but for' test is more clearly shown in *US – Upland Cotton*.[45] The panel concluded that four main factors – (i) substantial proportionate influence of the United States in the world upland cotton market; (ii) US subsidy programmes directly linked to world prices for upland cotton; (iii) discernable temporal coincidence of suppressed world market prices and the price-contingent US subsidies; and (iv) credible evidence concerning the divergence between US upland cotton producers' total production costs and sales revenue since 1997 – supported 'the proposition that US upland cotton producers would not have been economically capable of remaining in the production of upland cotton had it not been for the US subsidies at issue and that the effect of the subsidies was to allow US producers to sell upland cotton at a price lower than would otherwise have been necessary to cover their total costs'.[46]

Notwithstanding any textual basis in the SCM Agreement, the panel in *US – Upland Cotton* applied the non-attribution analysis to serious prejudice determination.[47] The panel in *Korea – Commercial Vessels* also considered that a non-attribution analysis in the context of serious prejudice determination is 'logical and appropriate'.[48] In other words, the panel is required to analyse the effects of identified factors other than the subsidies with a view to determining whether such factors would attenuate any affirmative causal link or render insignificant the effects of the subsidy. These positions were approved by the Appellate Body in *US – Upland Cotton* as follows:

> [] we agree with the Panel that it is necessary to ensure that the effects of other factors on prices are not improperly attributed to the challenged subsidies. Pursuant to Article 6.3(c) of the *SCM Agreement*, '[s]erious prejudice in the sense of paragraph (c) of Article 5 may arise' when 'the effect of *the subsidy* is. . .significant price suppression'. (Emphasis added.) If the significant price suppression found in the world market for upland cotton were caused by factors other than the challenged subsidies, then that price suppression would not be 'the effect of' the challenged subsidies in the sense of Article 6.3(c). Therefore, we do not find fault with the Panel's approach of 'examin[ing] whether or not "the effect of the subsidy" is the significant price suppression which [it had] found to exist in the same world market' and separately 'consider[ing] the role of other alleged causal factors in the record before [it] which may affect [the] analysis of the causal link between the United States subsidies and the significant price suppression'.[49]

Based on the above reasoning, the Appellate Body in *US – Upland Cotton* found no legal error in the panel's non-attribution analysis to address 'other causal factors' such as planting decisions, increased textile imports, weakness in world demand for upland cotton, the strong US dollar, and the release of government upland cotton stocks between 1999 and 2001 in China. However, it is noted that the Appellate Body was not fully satisfied with the

[44] Panel Report, *Korea – Commercial Vessels*, para. 7.612.
[45] Panel Report, *US – Subsidies on Upland Cotton (US – Upland Cotton)*, WT/DS267/R, Corr.1, and Add.1 to Add.3, adopted 21 Mar. 2005, as modified by Appellate Body Report WT/DS267/AB/R, DSR 2005:II, 299, paras 7.1347–7.1356.
[46] Panel Report, *US – Upland Cotton*, paras 7.1348–7.1353.
[47] *Ibid.*, para. 7.1344.
[48] Panel Report, *Korea – Commercial Vessels*, para. 7.618.
[49] Appellate Body Report, *US – Upland Cotton*, para. 437.

panel's reasoning. The Appellate Body explained that the panel 'could have provided a more detailed explanation of its analysis of the complex facts and economic arguments' arising in the dispute in order to 'demonstrate precisely how it evaluated the different factors bearing on the relationship between the price-contingent subsidies and significant price suppression'.[50]

3.3. SAFEGUARD AGREEMENT

The causation requirement for a safeguard measure is particularly important because increased import itself without any wrongful activities from exporting countries becomes the basis of safeguard application:

> Applying our standard of review, we will consider whether Argentina's causation analysis meets these requirements on the basis of (i) whether an upward trend in imports coincides with downward trends in the injury factors, and if not, whether a reasoned explanation is provided as to why nevertheless the data show causation; (ii) whether the conditions of competition in the Argentine footwear market between imported and domestic footwear as analysed demonstrate, on the basis of objective evidence, a causal link of the imports to any injury; and (iii) whether other relevant factors have been analysed and whether it is established that injury caused by factors other than imports has not been attributed to imports.

3.3.1. Non-attribution

The Appellate Body explained that the interpretation for non-attribution requirements in the AD Agreement and the Safeguard Agreement provides guidance for each other.[51] Therefore, investigating authorities are required to 'identify the nature and extent of the injurious effects of the known factors other than increased imports, as well as explain satisfactorily the nature and extent of the injurious effects of those other factors as distinguished from the injurious effects of the increased imports'.[52] The Appellate Body also clarified that the non-attribution analysis must be undertaken before the final determination about the existence of the causal link between increased imports and serious injury.[53]

It is noteworthy that the panel in *US – Steel Safeguards* emphasized the importance of quantitative analysis for non-attribution analysis. The panel ruled that 'a competent authority may find itself in situations where quantification and some form of economic analysis are necessary to rebut allegedly plausible alternative explanations that have been put

---

[50] *Ibid.*, para. 458.
[51] Appellate Body Report, *US – Definitive Safeguard Measures on Imports of Circular Welded Carbon Quality Line Pipe from Korea (US – Line Pipe)*, WT/DS202/AB/R, adopted 8 Mar. 2002, DSR 2002:IV, 1403, para. 214.
[52] Appellate Body Report, *US – Line Pipe*, para. 215.
[53] Appellate Body Report, *US – Safeguard Measures on Imports of Fresh, Chilled or Frozen Lamb Meat from New Zealand and Australia (US – Lamb)*, WT/DS177/AB/R, WT/DS178/AB/R, adopted 16 May 2001, DSR 2001:IX, 4051, para. 180.

forward',[54] although 'the results of such quantification may not necessarily be determinative'.[55] Regarding the criteria for quantitative analysis, the panel provides that[56]:

> Regarding argumentation by the parties as to the form which quantification should take, the Panel considers that this will depend again upon the complexity of the situation under consideration. The approach adopted should enable a competent authority to apportion, even roughly, the injury attributable to factors other than increased imports that may come into play in the context of a particular industry. The more complex the situation, the more necessary a sophisticated analysis becomes. Whatever approach or model is adopted, it should be applied in good faith and with due diligence. It seems to us that this is demanded by the good faith interpretation and application of Articles 2.1, 4.2(b) and 3.1 of the Agreement on Safeguards.

The above explanation implies the need to adopt econometric methods for non-attribution analysis. This ruling demanding more rigorous scrutiny can be understood in relation to the decision concerning the permitted level of safeguard measures. Contrary to the cases for anti-dumping and countervailing duties, the Appellate Body concluded that a safeguard measure should be applied so as to address only the consequences of imports, not the entirety of the serious injury.[57] Since the level of a safeguard measure is now contingent on the effects of imports to serious injury, the quantitative evaluation of effects of all contributing factors becomes critical in implementing safeguard measures. The application of non-attribution approach to the imposition of a safeguard measure cannot be taken in the imposition of anti-dumping or countervailing duty that is based on dumping or subsidy margin instead of injury margin, unless an investigating authority voluntarily employs a lesser duty rule.[58]

3.3.2.   Causal Relationship

The panel in *US – Wheat Gluten* ruled that, following the non-attribution analysis, the effects caused by other factors must be excluded totally from the determination of serious injury so as to ensure that these effects are not 'attributed' to the increased imports and the effects caused by increased imports alone must be capable of causing serious injury.[59] In other words, the panel explained that the increased imports must be sufficient, in and of themselves, to cause serious injury. Rejecting this interpretation, the Appellate Body ruled that the investigating authority must show 'the causal link' between increased imports and serious injury, which means 'a genuine and substantial relationship of cause and effect' between these two elements.[60] How to establish a genuine and substantial relationship of

---

[54] Panel Reports, *US – Definitive Safeguard Measures on Imports of Certain Steel Products (US – Steel Safeguards)*, WT/DS248/R, WT/DS249/R, WT/DS251/R, WT/DS252/R, WT/DS253/R, WT/DS254/R, WT/DS258/R, WT/DS259/R, and Corr.1, adopted 10 Dec. 2003, as modified by Appellate Body Report WT/DS248/AB/R, WT/DS249/AB/R, WT/DS251/AB/R, WT/DS252/AB/R, WT/DS253/AB/R, WT/DS254/AB/R, WT/DS258/AB/R, WT/DS259/AB/R, DSR 2003:VIII, 3273, para. 10.340.

[55] Panel Report, *US – Steel Safeguards*, para. 10.341.

[56] *Ibid.*, para. 10.342.

[57] Appellate Body Report, *US – Line Pipe*, paras 252 and 258.

[58] P. Mavroidis et al., *The Law and Economics of Contingent Protection in the WTO* (2008), 559–560.

[59] Appellate Body Report, *US – Definitive Safeguard Measures on Imports of Wheat Gluten from the European Communities (US – Wheat Gluten)*, WT/DS166/AB/R, adopted 19 Jan. 2001, DSR 2001:II, 717, para. 66. See also Panel Report, *US – Wheat Gluten*, para. 8.138.

[60] Appellate Body Report, *US – Wheat Gluten*, para. 69.

cause and effect between increased imports and serious injury remains to be elaborated in future cases.

4. ECONOMIC ANALYSIS FOR CAUSATION ANALYSIS

4.1. ECONOMETRIC MODEL

One of the most frequently adopted economic models to analyse causation issue is the econometric analysis that is supposed to show the degree of causal relationship between pre-chosen factors and a dependent variable.

Grossman developed an estimated equation that can be used for counterfactual analysis, which can determine the sensitivity of domestic production to the relative price of imports, the relative price of inputs, and overall demand.[61] Based on the empirical relationship between employment figures and its determinants,[62] he used the model to test the steel industry as an example. In his conclusion, he argues that the USITC claims of Bethlehem Steel Corporation and the United Steel Workers of America were unwarranted, since his counterfactual test found secular factors (e.g., faster than average growth of employment and productivity in the high-technology and service sectors) to be a more important factor than imports in causing employment loss. Rotemberg and Pindyck, using the copper industry as an example, also developed a similar framework using Granger causality regressions to ascertain the amount of injury caused by imports.[63]

The econometric approach offers a detailed quantitative approach to causation analysis and offers answers to attribution. Yet, it also suffers from many limitations. As Sykes points out, there is the practical difficulty of gathering all the necessary data to perform accurate calculations.[64] This is especially true for smaller or under-scrutinized industries, where very limited information is available. As Irwin points out, there is also no clear-cut way of determining which factors are appropriate for the empirical model.[65] Such limitations have contributed to the relatively infrequent application of econometric tools in trade remedy decisions.

4.2. ELASTICITY/PARTIAL EQUILIBRIUM MODEL

Another model frequently used for causation analysis is a partial equilibrium model that is based on supply and demand conditions of the market. This method often requires estimation of elasticity to ascertain market supply and demand.

---

[61] Gene M. Grossman, 'Imports as a Cause of Injury: The Case of the US Steel Industry', *Journal of International Economics* 20 (1986): 201.

[62] For the purposes of his study, Grossman only focuses on employment loss as representing domestic industry harm.

[63] Julio J. Rotemberg & Robert Pindyck, 'Are Imports to Blame?: Attribution of Injury under the 1974 Trade Act', *Journal of Law and Economics* 30 (1987): 101.

[64] Sykes, *supra* n. 1, at 199.

[65] Douglas A. Irwin, 'Causing Problems? The WTO Review of Causation and Injury Attribution in US Section 201 Cases', *World Trade Review* 2 (2003): 297, at 316.

In a seminal work using this method, Kelly advocated a model that attributes change in domestic production into three factors – shift in import supply, shift in domestic demand, and shift in domestic supply.[66] With informed guesses about relevant elasticity, Kelly estimated the effects of import supply curve relative to other factors. Irwin expanded upon Kelly's 1988 study to articulate a more refined causation standard. For example, Irwin observed that in the *Lamb* case, 'domestic price rose (and import prices rose substantially) and consumption fell while domestic production declined and imports increased'.[67] According to Irwin, such result is more consistent with domestic supply curve inward shift rather than import increase being an independent causal factor.

This approach has the advantages that it does not require econometric estimations and that it is applicable to three divergent market settings – a competitive market where imports and domestic goods are perfect substitutes, a competitive market in which imports and domestic goods are imperfect substitutes, and a market where the domestic firm has market power.[68] Another advantage of this model is the practicality stemming from simplicity of its data requirement: it only requires market data – consumption level, domestic production level, imports, unit value – and the elasticity value for domestic demand curve, domestic supply curve, and import supply curve. The major shortcomings of this model are twofold: first, it still necessitates the use of subjective judgments in remedy investigations; second, it assumes that correlation is a necessary condition for causation, which depicts false reality, as discussed in section 5.

5. ALTERNATIVE APPROACH FOR CAUSATION ANALYSIS

5.1. FALSE ASSUMPTIONS IN THE EXTANT WTO CASE LAW

Article 2 of the SG Agreement allows for safeguards when 'a product is being imported in such increased quantities, absolute, or relative to domestic production, and under such conditions as to cause or threaten serious injury'. Generally speaking, the causation test used to determine the legality of safeguard measures in WTO case law has centred upon analysing the overall coincidence between import surge and domestic industry harm. In *Argentina-Footwear*, for example, the Appellate Body affirmed that in an analysis of causation, 'It is the relationship between the movements in imports and the movements in injury factors that must be central to a causation analysis and determination.'[69] Irwin observed that in the current state of affairs, 'both the ITC and WTO panels seem to agree that the coincidence of a higher level of import and a lower level of domestic activity usually constitutes sufficient evidence that imports have caused injury'.[70] In other words, causation analysis often means no more than the finding of mere correlation.

---

[66] Kenneth Kelly, 'The Analysis of Causality in Escape Clause Cases', *Journal of Industrial Economics* 37 (1988): 187.
[67] Irwin, *supra* n. 65, at 312.
[68] Sykes, *supra* n. 1, at 200.
[69] Appellate Body Report, *Argentina – Safeguard Measures on Imports of Footwear* (*Argentina – Footwear*), WT/DS121/AB/R, adopted 12 Jan. 2000, DSR 2000:I, 515, para. 144.
[70] Irwin, *supra* n. 65, at 301.

This approach is systematically flawed for the purpose of causation analysis in trade remedy investigations. Specifically, equating correlation to causation would eliminate from consideration two distinct – yet important – cases where clear injury could occur as a result of imports, yet no correlation can be established.

First is the case where firms that did well *despite injury* would not seek remedy because they cannot establish correlation (and investigating agencies such as the USITC would not bring it up because they categorically exclude these firms as having been injured). For example, an industry might have grown by 300% had there been no import harm, but because of dumping or illegal subsidies by another nation, it may have just grown by 50%. In this case, there was import increase and unfair trade practices, but no industry *decline*. This illustrates a false assumption in the extant causation analysis model that industries must be at low state of profitability or at a stage of decline to qualify for protection under the trade remedy system. That seems far from reality. It is certainly possible that firms that have high profit margins or even an industry that is rapidly growing (e.g., infant-stage industries) could be suffering from dumping or subsidization from other countries.

For the purpose of safeguard, this is not an important consideration. After all, the very purpose of safeguard actions is to permit temporary protection for declining or seriously injured domestic industries. However, the purpose of anti-dumping and countervailing duties is to punish cheaters – not to have temporary 'reorganizing time' for declining industries. Indeed, the language of the agreements support this view: anti-dumping and countervailing policies only require 'material injury', while safeguard requires 'serious injury'.

Second is the case where correlation cannot be established because of the very nature of profit driven firms. The often-used index that measures harm in domestic industries is the level of production and industry employment data.[71] Microeconomic theory of production tells us that these figures may not reflect upon actual industry harm, at least in the short run. According to the theory, any profit-maximizing firm, in the short run,[72] will produce up to the point where marginal cost equals that of marginal revenue (e.g., market-clearing price of the good), since fixed costs cannot be altered in the short run.[73] That is, rational firms will produce even if they will be making negative profits because of sunk cost. In the long run, however, firms need to consider fixed cost and will only produce up to the point where marginal revenue equals the average cost of production.

This tells us that correlation between increased imports and decreased production in a strict temporal sense will only appear when the marginal revenue of domestic firms drops so

---

[71] *Ibid.*; Grossman, *supra* n. 61.

[72] Short run is a time frame where at least one factor of production is fixed, whereas long run is the time where all production formula can be altered. See N. Gregory Mankiw, *Principles of Economics*, 4th edn (Madison, OH: Thomson, 2007), at 280.

[73] Fixed costs include costs like labour and overhead costs, which are often unalterable in the short run by employment contracts and the nature of sunk costs.

significantly so that it will be below those firms' average costs, or if the firms are in a particular industry where all production formula can be altered rapidly. By the same token, this means that firms whose long run constitutes several years and firms that happen to have large fixed costs will have difficulty showing the evidence of declining production even though they are in fact suffering from dumping or subsidization. In other words, those firms may be categorically denied of trade remedy protection due to the nature of production and cost structures of rational firms.[74]

The fact that production decisions of firms may critically depend on time horizon suggests more rigorous consideration of short run versus long run. Otherwise, firms may not show symptoms of decline during the time period of import increase, thus potentially denying declining industry with legally deserving trade remedy measures.

5.2.   ALTERNATIVE APPROACH TO SOLVE THE CAUSATION CONUNDRUM: 'COST OF PRODUCTION TEST'

As many philosophers have come to terms with, there is simply no way to prove or directly observe causation; only correlation can be observed. Therefore, correlation is an exceedingly valuable figure that can be complemented by relevant facts to infer causality. In that sense, Irwin and Kelly's causation model that uses correlation as one of the underlying framework for causation analysis can be a good starting point in causation analysis.

We propose an alternative approach that modifies and builds on the model used by Irwin and Kelly to address the concerns raised in section 5.1. A critical assumption made in Irwin and Kelly's model is that the causal link 'requires objective evidence that harm to an industry coincides with a period of increased imports or import penetration'.[75] In logical terms, this is stating that correlation is necessary – but not sufficient in itself – to prove causation. We reject this assumption. We argue that correlation, in a strict temporal sense, is neither a sufficient nor a necessary condition to prove causation. That is, because of the two rationales stated above, correlation will not be observed in many instances, even when there is genuine harm caused by increase in imports.[76] Correlation, for example, will not be observed when rational firms show symptoms of decline five years after the increase in imports, because they take into account the ubiquity of sunk cost. Correlation may also simply be a temporal coincidence to industry decline, rather than a cause. To ameliorate

---

[74] In *US – Steel Safeguards*, the dispute panel even acknowledged that temporal lag may exist between import increase and injury 'in certain cases'.

[75] Irwin, *supra* n. 65, at 301.

[76] Since causation may be proved without proving strict temporal correlation, correlation is not a necessary condition to prove causation.

this problem, we propose an additional tool that can be used as complement to Elasticity/ Partial Equilibrium Model. We propose the following hypotheses:

HYPOTHESIS 1 (H1)

If the price of imports is less than the domestic marginal cost of production, we should see an immediate decline in production that is attributable to import surge.

HYPOTHESIS 2 (H2)

If the price of imports is greater than the domestic marginal cost of production but lower than the domestic average cost of production, we should not observe immediate decline in production that is attributable to import surge; instead, we should expect decline sometime in the future.

HYPOTHESIS 3 (H3)

If the import price is greater than the domestic average cost of production, we should not see an immediate nor future decline that is attributable to import increase.

Figure 1. Cost of Production Test for Causation Analysis

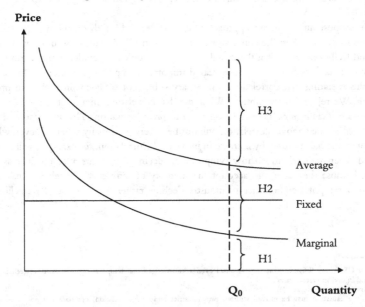

Figure 1 shows how a firm's cost structure can be utilized in relation to causation analysis. At any given level of production, Q_0, an import price lower than the marginal cost of production would cause immediate production decline and thereby become the primary causal factor for industry injury. To the contrary, an import price higher than the average cost of production would not generally be considered as the main causal factor for industry injury.

This model is widely applicable,[77] including competitive markets and markets where domestic firms have market power, since output decisions based on production costs are the same regardless of the market power possessed by firms.[78] Below, we present five cases that illustrate the usefullness of our model.

The first is a safeguard case from 2003, *Certain Circular Welded Carbon Quality Line Pipe*. Table 3 summarizes the data provided by the USITC investigation.

This case fits the criteria for Hypothesis 1, where the unit price of imports is lower than the domestic marginal cost of production. As the hypothesis predicted, US firms experienced immediate decline every year from 2000 to 2002, which should at least partially be attributed to import increase. In fact, both capacity utilization and total sales fell drastically during this time, despite the fact that the US consumption quantity stayed levelled. In the corresponding WTO dispute case, *US-Line Pipe*, the grounds for Korea's challenge of US safeguard measures rested on the interpretation of the phrase 'serious injury or the threat of serious injury', and not on the causation issues.

Table 3. Price and Costs for Certain Circular Welded Carbon Quality Line Pipe Case[79]

	2000	2001	2002
Domestic industry sales (short tons)	566,868	458,288	390,758
US production (short tons)	592,856	476,240	409,292
Total imports (short tons)	154,188	140,005	200,151
Per unit sales price	USD 495.04	USD 478.65	USD 473.22
Marginal cost of production per short ton	USD 455.68	USD 448.99	USD 461.32
Average cost of production per short ton[80]	USD 478.01	USD 471.94	USD 485.64
Price of imports	USD 417.67	USD 432.92	USD 378.62

---

[77] This model, for example, can be introduced for the purpose of meeting the 'threat of serious injury' requirement of Safeguard agreement, which is defined as 'serious injury that is clearly imminent'. Art. 4: Safeguard agreements 1 (b). Specifically, according to Hypothesis 2, if the price of imports is greater than the marginal cost of production but lower than the average cost of production, we would not see an immediate industry decline but an inevitable decline sometime in the future since firms cannot sustain economic losses for an infinite amount of time. This meets the 'clearly imminent' part of the requirement. Depending on how serious that injury is going to be, firms may be able to seek remedy under the Safeguard agreement.

[78] In both cases, firms will produce up to the point where the marginal cost of production equals marginal revenue.

[79] 'Certain Circular Welded Carbon Quality Line Pipe: Evaluation of the Effectiveness of Import Relief', <www.usitc.gov/trade_remedy/731_ad_701_cvd/investigations/2003/204_line_pipe/PDF/PUB3628.pdf>, 19 Jun. 2009. This figure does not include numbers for Japan and Germany, which were not provided by the USITC.

[80] Average cost of production was calculated by adding per unit Selling, General, and Administrative (SG&A) expenses to the marginal cost of production figure.

Table 4. Price and Costs for Certain Steel Wire Rod Case

	2000	2001	2002
Domestic industry sales (short tons)	2,178,717	1,843,418	1,952,168
US total production (short tons)	2,271,816	1,779,465	2,016,845
Total imports (short tons)	2,561,949	2,719,785	3,368,159
Per unit sales price	USD 330.62	USD 336.51	USD 363.14
Marginal cost of production	USD 317	USD 331	USD 336
Average cost of production	USD 330	USD 348	USD 354
Price of imports	USD 294.06	USD 274.37	USD 289.11

Table 4 shows data for the case of *Certain Steel Wire Rod*, which again fits under the definition of Hypothesis 1.[81]

This example is interesting because despite the fact that the price of imports was below the marginal cost of production (meaning that imports did indeed cause industry injury), the price increase and US total consumption increase between 2001 and 2002 suggests that the demand curve shifted to the right. So while we can blame import surge for some of the domestic industry harm, import increase cannot be the sole blame for domestic industry decline between 2001 and 2002.[82]

Next is the *Carbon and Alloy Long Steel (Hot Bar)* case, illustrated in Table 5.[83] In this case, the price of imports was higher than the average cost of production, fitting the rubric of Hypothesis 3. According to Hypothesis 3, we should not see domestic industry decline attributed to imports, since firms will continue to produce as long as their economic profit is greater than 0. In this case, domestic consumption stayed level or increased, and more importantly, import price was higher than the average cost of production. It is very difficult to argue in these cases that imports were causing domestic industry harm.

In the case of *Welded Pipe*,[84] the situation is more complicated but still well explained by our framework. In the years of 2001, 2002, and 2004, this case falls under the criteria for Hypothesis 2, while 2003 falls under the criteria for Hypothesis 1.

Such discrepancy provides a good case study for analysing causal relationship between import surge and domestic industry harm. Imports, in absolute terms, actually declined between 2001 and 2003, both in absolute and relative terms. Even if imports increased, there are multiple reasons to believe that imports did not cause domestic industry harm. In particular, according to Hypothesis 2, the domestic production decline (in short tons) observed between 2001 and 2002 should not have been observed if it was due to imports, since firms would not have significantly alter their production decisions in the short run, as long as price of imports are above their marginal costs. It seems more likely that increase

---

[81] 'Certain Steel Wire Rod: Evaluation of the Effectiveness of Import Relief', <www.usitc.gov/trade_remedy/731_ad_701_cvd/investigations/2003/204_wire_rod/PDF/PUB3629.pdf>, 19 Jun. 2009.
[82] While there is no absolute decline for domestic industry between 2001 and 2002, the size of the market grew significantly more, making the domestic industry's share of the market decline.
[83] 'Steel: Evaluation of the Effectiveness of Import Relief', <www.usitc.gov/trade_remedy/731_ad_701_cvd/investigations/2005/204_steel/PDF/Pub3797.pdf>, 19 Jun. 2009.
[84] *Ibid.*

Table 5. *Price and Costs for Carbon and Alloy Long Steel (Hot Bar) Case*

	2001	2002	2003	2004
Domestic industry sales (short tons)	7,788,822	7,966,707	7,445,886	8,095,888
US total production (short tons)	8,821,048	9,110,314	8,880,720	10,304,626
Total imports (short tons)	1,950,917	2,019,577	1,996,476	2,250,220
Per unit sales price	USD 383.00	USD 377.00	USD 404.00	USD 578.00
Marginal cost of production	USD 359	USD 350	USD 370	USD 496
Average cost of production	USD 381	USD 372	USD 392	USD 519
Price of imports	USD 434.00	USD 432.00	USD 453.00	USD 577.00

Table 6. *Price and Costs for Welded Pipe Case*

	2001	2002	2003	2004
Domestic industry sales (short tons)	4,644,252	4,261,552	4,259,372	4,389,279
US total production (short tons)	4,579,045	4,380,184	4,185,801	4,475,508
Total imports (short tons)	2,829,403	2,525,295	2,127,143	2,604,972
Per unit sales price	USD 570.00	USD 605.00	USD 604.00	USD 887.00
Marginal cost of production	USD 495.00	USD 518.00	USD 551.00	USD 718.00
Average cost of production	USD 538.00	USD 564.00	USD 589.00	USD 766.00
Price of imports	USD 502.00	USD 539.00	USD 542.00	USD 738.00
Ratio of imports/domestic consumption	0.37858357	0.37208662	0.33306788	0.37244474

in cost of raw material – as stated by the USITC – played a larger role in loss of output.[85] The output loss in 2003 seems more attributable to imports, since costs of imports were now lower than domestic marginal cost of production. In fact, capital expenditure for domestic firms declined significantly, from USD 103,662,000 in 2002 to USD 67,801,000 in 2003. This stays consistent with Hypothesis 1, in which firms alter their long-term production capacity if prices fall below their marginal cost.

The *Fittings*[86] case provides an excellent application of Hypothesis 3, where the price of imports is higher than the domestic average cost of production. This is the case in both 2002 and 2004. In 2001 and 2003, import price is higher than marginal cost but lower than average cost, which calls for application of Hypothesis 2. We see a total sales decline, in terms of dollars, from 2001 to 2003. Even assuming that significant import increase took place,[87] the domestic industry harm, it seems, cannot be attributed to imports. As Hypothesis 3 calls for, there should not be an immediate – nor long-term – decline in production attributed to

---

[85] *Ibid.*
[86] *Ibid.*
[87] In absolute terms, imports actually declined in the periods of 2001–2003.

JOURNAL OF WORLD TRADE

Table 7. Price and Costs for Fittings Case

	2001	2002	2003	2004
Domestic industry sales (short tons)	77,196	77,705	73,239	79,529
US total production (short tons)	91,795	93,608	87,830	110,807
Total imports (short tons)	169,605	143,051	127,459	151,769
Per unit sales price	USD 2,214.00	USD 2,160.00	USD 2,175.00	USD 2,534.00
Marginal cost of production	USD 1,804.00	USD 1,775.00	USD 1,814.00	USD 1,937.00
Average cost of production	USD 2,147.00	USD 2,096.00	USD 2,170.00	USD 2,295.00
Price of imports	USD 2,042.00	USD 2,170.00	USD 1,990.00	USD 2,313.00

imports for 2002. In addition, since decline in production should not have taken place immediately in 2003, it seems unlikely that imports were responsible for causing domestic industry decline from 2001 to 2003.

As illustrated by the case examples, the 'Cost of Production Test' is useful because it, by design, helps address the burden of non-attribution, which is important for all cases where the price of imports are lower than the average cost of production for domestic firms. For example, if the price of import is greater than the domestic marginal cost of production but lower than the average cost of production, we can objectively attribute immediate industry decline to a factor other than import increase, since firms will not alter their production in the short run and, therefore, *not* show symptoms of decline attributable to import surge. If the price of import is lower than the marginal cost of production, we would see an immediate industry decline that should at least partially be attributed to import increase. This approach is also practically feasible. Cost of production figures are publicly available data published in financial statements in all publicly traded companies and in many privately owned companies. Unlike figures like the elasticity of goods that are almost always going to be subject to debate, cost of production figures cannot be easily manipulated for the purpose of seeking trade remedy, offering a degree of objectivity.

We acknowledge the following limits to our model. First, we assume that firms act rationality – which is often not the case. Yet, at the aggregate level, assuming firm rationality often best depicts the real world.[88] Second, although we improve upon Irwin and Kelly's model, there are still limitations associated with the original Elasticity Model: namely, subjective judgment goes into determining causality. Third, different industries have different long terms and short terms, which may hinder using a 'one-size-fits-all' test when using the 'Cost of Production Test'. For example, some industries may experience relatively quicker decline if the import price is higher than marginal cost and lower than

---

[88] Christine Jolls, Cass R. Sunstein & Richard H. Thaler, 'A Behavioral Approach to Law and Economics', in *Behavioral Law and Economics*, ed. Cass R. Sunstein (Cambridge: Cambridge University Press: 2000), at 19.

average cost than other industries whose fixed costs are not alterable in a short span of time. Even given all of that, our model improves upon Kelly and Irwin's original model in terms of practicality and objectivity.

Observing the production costs also help reinforce the importance of examining cost of production that are central to anti-dumping and countervailing measures. Specifically, both investigative agencies and dispute panels should reject the assumption that only declining industries are entitled to anti-dumping and countervailing protection. The text of agreements for anti-dumping and countervailing requires, respectively, that 'significant increase in dumped imports, either in absolute or relative terms' and 'a significant increase in subsidized imports'.[89] Nowhere in the text requires actual industry decline. While the Safeguard Agreements clearly define 'serious injury' as 'a significant overall impairment in the position of a domestic industry',[90] AD Agreement and SCM Agreement allow for a broad interpretation of harm: 'The examination of the impact. . .on the domestic industry shall include an evaluation of all relevant economic factors and indices having a bearing on the state of the industry.'[91] That should include harms that occur to highly profitable industries as well as industries that are showing growth.

That being said, we are not advocating that national governments levy countervailing duties and anti-dumping duties whenever it is legally sanctioned. Many economists view subsidized imports and dumped imports as economically advantageous for importing nations and believe that only economic efficiency should guide international trade.[92] In fact, it may seem counter-intuitive that dumping – which is a form of subsidization for consumers – is penalized under international trade law, since firms often price discriminate for different markets. Yet, national governments need to weigh more than economic efficiency in rendering policy decisions. The trade remedy system is founded on this very premise. Insofar as a country maintains and utilizes a trade remedy system pursuant to the WTO Agreements, our framework gives each country a better criteria to address causation analysis that is the critical element and yet terribly confusing. The Cost of Production Test provides WTO Members with an additional tool to meet legally deserving trade remedies, which can be exercised after weighing social, economic, and political costs into consideration.

5.3. Solving the causation conundrum: The INUS test

As reviewed in section 5.1, another problem raised by equating correlation and causation is when serious harm is done to growing or economically viable industries. This calls for

---

[89] AD Agreement 3.5; Art. 15: Determination of Injury 15.2 SCM Agreement.
[90] Article 4: Safeguard agreements 1 (a).
[91] AD Agreement 3.5; Art. 15: Determination of Injury 15.2 SCM Agreement.
[92] Adam Smith, in *The Wealth of Nations*, famously articulated that 'if a foreign country can supply us with a commodity cheaper than we ourselves can make it, better buy it of them with some part of the produce of our own industry employed in a way in which we have some advantage'. Adam Smith, *An Inquiry into the Nature and Causes of the Wealth of Nations* (Edinburgh: Adam and Charles Black, 1863), at 200; see also Michael P. Gallaway, Bruce A. Blonigen & Joseph E. Flynn, 'Welfare Costs of the US Anti-dumping and Countervailing Duty Laws', *Journal of International Economics* 49 (1999): 211.

examining the divergent purpose of different trade remedy measures. Specifically, we argue that the AD Agreement and SCM Agreement are in place for a very different reason than Safeguard Agreement. Anti-dumping and countervailing duties are in place to punish cheaters of the system if it causes or threatens to cause material injury to the importing nation.[93] Safeguard measures, on the other hand, is a measure that can be used even when everyone has acted appropriately under trade agreements.[94] Although there are many rationales for its existence, the strongest rationale presented seems to be that it offers a temporary shield to declining domestic industries, which 'reduce the risk of trade concessions under conditions of political uncertainty, and thereby facilitate more of them'.[95]

That point is so important because it implies that we should set different causal proof burden for the two different scenarios. For anti-dumping and countervailing duties, *smaller* amount of harm – compared to safeguard cases –may be punished. In these cases, it matters less that domestic industries were seriously harmed or on the verge on collapse; it matters more that a party cheated, even in cases where correlation would not show because the harm is done to a prospering industry. For safeguard, the burden of proof for link between increased imports and serious injury is greater. The wording in Article 4.2(b) requires that imports establish a 'genuine and substantial relationship of cause and effect', while the US statutory burden is to prove 'substantial causation'. According to the USITC, substantial causation means greater than any other causes, which is defined by the Trade Act of 1974. This is rather arbitrary. Of course, the definition is inclusive to the scenario where imports could account for 51% of the cause. If, however, there were 100 causes of domestic industry collapse, ninety-nine of which accounting for 0.99% each but import surge accounting for 1.99%, the current system would still view imports as the culprit. Irwin assesses that such system is non-explicit and loosely reasoned, producing some decisions that seem 'arbitrary and simply based on assertions'.[96]

Indeed, this standard has caused problems at a number of trade disputes, which points out a need for a more fine-tuned definition of 'genuine and substantial relationship of cause and effect'. One of the approaches suggested is mandating that increased imports itself is necessary and sufficient cause of serious injury, as ruled by the panel in *US – Wheat Gluten Safeguard*. This standard was reversed by the Appellate Body, and for good reason: while it is possible that the import be *sufficient* for serious harm, it is, in our minds, impossible that imports increase alone may be *necessary* for serious injury. Necessary condition means that no other factor – such as overall economic downturn, consumer taste shift, or natural disasters – could possibly be responsible for serious injury. Logically speaking, this is impossible, even if the standard allows that imports need not, by themselves, cause a threat of serious injury.

---

[93] Peter Van den Bossche, *The Law and Policy of the World Trade Organization* (Cambridge: Cambridge University Press: 2005), at 42.

[94] Safeguard provisions were adopted largely at the request of the United States, during the Uruguay Round negotiations. Many scholars view safeguard provisions as an insurance for trading nations that encourage more liberal trade policies.

[95] Sykes, *supra* n. 1, at xxx.

[96] Irwin, *supra* n. 65, at 303.

Another suggestion is a standard proposed by the Appellate Body that reversed the panel decision in *US – Lamb Meat*, which upheld their own decision in *US – Wheat Gluten*. In the decision, the Appellate Body stated that the *Agreement on Safeguards* did not require that increased imports be neither 'sufficient' nor 'alone' to cause or threaten to cause serious injury. This ruling seems equally mysterious to the standard proposed by the original ruling in *Wheat Gluten*. As Sykes points out intuitively, there is no point of non-attribution requirement if increased imports need not be sufficient to cause serious injury.[97]

We articulate a logically consistent yet practically feasible standard for causation by applying and modifying the INUS model. The INUS test, introduced by philosopher John Mackie in 1965, attempts to explicate causality in terms of necessary and sufficient conditions.[98] According to this test, C is a cause of E if and only if:

(1)   C and E are both actual.
(2)   C occurs before E.
(3)   C is an INUS condition of E.

Here, the notion of an INUS condition is spelled out as follows:

C is an INUS condition of E if and only if C is an **I**nsufficient but **N**on-redundant part of a Condition, which is itself **U**nnecessary but exclusively **S**ufficient for E in the circumstances.

For the purposes of trade causation analysis, 'insufficient' implies that the import could not have caused harm alone – such as settlement of labour unions that allowed the goods to be produced in the first place. It is non-redundant; if absent this factor, the effect could not have possibly occurred within that cluster. It is unnecessary, because surely other factors can be combined as a cluster to cause the harm (say, for example, an economic downturn that eliminate demand for certain industries). The following provides an illustration:

    (A&B&C or D&E or G&H) ↔ Z
    A = Import surge of TV
    B = Production of the imported TV abroad
    C = Low fuel cost that allowed the production parts of TV to be acquired sufficiently cheap
    D = The Federal Reserve Bank's decision to increase interest rates by 0.5%
    E = Investors' preference to save money instead of buying TV due to the interest rate change
    G = Wal-Mart's decision not to sell domestic TV
    H = Other retail stores' decision not to increase their stock of domestic TV
    Z = Domestic TV Industry decline.

In this case, absent B or C, import surge would not have occurred. At the same time, B and C are not sufficient by themselves to cause Z. Yet, import surge is not a necessary condition to cause Z, since other factors, like combination of D&E or G&H could also cause Z. In that sense, if it can sufficiently cause harm, then we can view import increase as a

---

[97] Sykes, *supra* n. 1, at 179.
[98] John Mackie, 'Causes and Conditions', *American Philosophical Quarterly* 2, no. 4 (1965): 245, at 245–255; Leon Horsten & Erik Weber, 'INUS Conditions', in *Encyclopedia of Statistics in Behavioural Science*, ed. Brian S. Everitt & David C. Howell, Chichester: Wiley, (2005) at 955.

'substantial cause' of domestic industry decline. This burden of proof suits the safeguard agreement in accordance to the purpose of the agreements. In pure logical terms, this would eliminate cases where domestic industries merely took a role in causing industry decline – even if they are greater cause than any other cause – but not a cause that would be sufficient in itself to cause the industry decline. Instead, being sufficient but not necessary to cause harm requires that the disputing party show that import surge was the dispositive factor in causing industry harm.

Take the *Wheat Gluten* case, for example. In a written submission to the WTO panel, the USITC argued that imports were a substantial causation of harm by establishing temporal correlation: 'Correlating with this decline in industry performance, the USITC report found that imports of wheat gluten increased dramatically from their steady 1993–1995 level of 128 million pounds to 156 million pounds in 1996, and still further to 177 million pounds in 1997.'[99] Then, the USITC qualitatively compared import surge with alternative causes, including increase in raw material costs, competition among domestic producers, and changes in co-products. They concluded that import surge was a greater cause than each one of these causes. That seems rather strange, because in the same report, the USITC admitted that, 'raw material costs did increase during the Period of Investigation (POI), particularly in 1996 and 1997'.[100] If the premise of the import surge was mere temporal correlation, what precludes the correlation between raw material price increase and domestic industry harm from also being the culprit?[101] Aside from that logical inconsistency, USITC's test also failed the INUS condition, since they compared imports to each of the alternative causes, neglecting to consider the harm done by aggregates of other causes. Reference the following illustration:

$(A\&B \text{ or } C\&D\&E\&F\&G^{102}) \leftrightarrow Z$

A = import surge of wheat gluten
B = the homogeneity of wheat gluten that allows imports to be perfect substitutes of domestic products
C = changes in co-product markets
D = domestic producers' importation of wheat gluten
E = competition among domestic producers
F = increased capacity
G = rising raw materials costs (wheat gluten and wheat flour)
Z = domestic wheat gluten industry decline.

In this case, by comparing A to C, D, E, F, and G independently, the USITC committed a serious error in neglecting to consider the combined effect of C, D, E, F, and G, which may have been sufficient *as a cluster* to cause the industry harm observed. Granted, the INUS condition allows for cases where multiple clusters may be responsible for an observed

---

[99] Panel Report, *US – Wheat Gluten*, at 233.
[100] *Ibid.*, at 236.
[101] Although the USITC brushes off such striking correlation by arguing that firms should have been able to pass the rising cost of goods to the consumer absent import surge, there is less credibility to this argument since wheat gluten is a homogeneous good competing in a perfectly competitive market.
[102] Causes C, D, E, F, and G are the actual alternate causes proposed by the USITC.

outcome.[103] However, unless the USITC can supply more information than mere temporal correlation, it is hard to view imports as a sufficient cause of the import harm. In fact, as reasoned by the panel, 'injury factors were declining prior to the surge in imports found by the USITC in 1996–1997',[104] giving more reason to believe that the alternate causes had more to do with the industry decline than the import surge.

Granted, the INUS condition is a practically difficult standard to apply. For example, how do we define sufficiency? Should imports account for specific numerical percentage point of harm to be deemed the culprit? Assigning a specific number is always going to be controversial and likely lead to cherry-picking of data by disputed parties to conjure numbers that fit their argument. At the end of the day, scholars and practitioners alike should accept that some level of subjective judgments is unavoidable. Rather, they should pay attention to factual circumstances in each case and treat prior rulings as persuasive precedents to guide their judgment. While we think that the subjectivity of the INUS condition is its weakness, we also note its superiority to the standards presented in the panel ruling of *US – Wheat Gluten* (which is logically impossible) and the Appellate Body decision in *US – Lamb* (which undermines the very purpose of non-attribution requirement).

6. CONCLUSION

David Hume, in *An Enquiry Concerning Human Understanding*, famously argued that causation itself is a meaningless phenomenon – a series of conjoined events that we presume to be causally related, but one that may equally be presumed not causally related.[105] For example, even given the empirically strong preceding of a rooster's crow to sunrise, a reasonable person would not believe that a rooster's crow caused the sun to rise. To put it bluntly, causation is a phenomenon that cannot be proven; only correlation can be observed, which, coupled with strong reasoning and evidence, can be deduced to be causally related.

In the field of international trade law, causation is a central element in many trade remedy measures. Although sophisticated tools – from the Elasticity Model to the Partial Equilibrium Model – have been developed to address the need to assess causal relationships, the assumption that correlation equals causation has been widespread in previous WTO case law and extant literature in the field. In this article, we elucidate problems that stem from that assumption. First is the case where temporal correlation between dumping/illegal subsidizing and industry decline would not show even when there is genuine harm, simply because the industry is growing or is a lucrative industry. Second is the case where due to

---

[103] For example, if Adam and Sarah shot a deer at the same time, and each of the bullets were sufficient to kill the deer, gunshots of both Adam and Sarah were independently sufficient to cause the death of the deer. This is the difference between the INUS condition and the condition articulated in the panel ruling in *US – Wheat Gluten*, the latter standard that argues that import surge must be both sufficient and necessary condition of the industry decline.

[104] Panel Report, *US – Wheat Gluten*, para. 8.100.

[105] David Hume, *An Enquiry Concerning Human Understanding* (Filiquarian, 2007).

the ubiquity of sunk costs, temporal correlation would not be shown due to lag in the decision-making processes of rational firms.

   This piece attempts to tackle such problem by improving upon Kelly's elasticity model. We first introduce the 'Cost of Production Test', which predicts the following: if the import price is below marginal cost, we should observe immediate decline attributed at least partially to imports; if the import price is between marginal cost and average cost, we should see some time lag in the harm done by imports; if the import price is higher than the average cost, industry decline cannot be attributed to import surge. Second, we suggest importing the INUS condition to define the 'genuine and substantial relationship of cause and effect' requirement mandated by the safeguard agreement. This condition, although subjective in its own right, is a significant improvement from the previous definitions that were either logically infeasible or pointless in terms of meeting the non-attribution requirement.

Chapter 4

Third Country Dumping: Origin, Evolution and Prospect

Dukgeun Ahn[*]

Third country anti-dumping actions were envisioned at the very inception of the General Agreement on Tariffs and Trade (GATT) and yet almost completely neglected by most governments throughout the GATT/World Trade Organization (WTO) history. The requirement for prior approval by multilateral trade institutions became a formidable procedural obstacle for any country seeking third country anti-dumping duty (AD) actions. Despite such difficulties, there were only few attempts to effectively employ such actions and several legal arrangements to refine the rules for third country AD actions. This article investigates the origin and historical development concerning third country AD actions and examines their implications for the current WTO system that is congested with numerous Free Trade Agreements (FTAs).

1 INTRODUCTION

When GATT contracting parties agreed to condemn dumping practices and permit AD actions for importing countries to protect their domestic industries, they also allowed AD actions to importing countries on behalf of a third country's domestic industries.[1] The rationale seems to be that if dumping is to be condemned because of its injurious effects on a certain industry, injuries incurred to other exporting countries, rather than importing countries, should also be accounted for under the anti-dumping system. Nevertheless, the fact that the importing country has to limit importation on behalf of a third country's industry raises unique and fundamental questions on how and when AD actions should be allowed. This explains why Article VI:6 allows 'AD actions on behalf of a third country (hereinafter third country AD actions)', but only under unusual conditions. For example, GATT Article VI:6(b) provides that 'the Contracting Parties' need to waive otherwise pertinent normal legal elements for invoking AD actions, implying that third country AD actions are in fact multilateral

---

[*] Associate Professor of International Trade Law and Policy, Graduate School of International Studies/Law School, Seoul National University; Visiting Scholar, Institute of International Economic Law, Georgetown Law Center. E-mail: dahn@snu.ac.kr. I am very grateful to Sahar Hosni, Sungjoon Cho and John H. Jackson for valuable comments and supports. I also appreciate research assistance by Hyoyoung Lee, Nathan Pak, Pia Kim, and SSK research grant.
[1] See, e.g., Art. 34.6 of the Havana Charter and Art. VI:5 of GATT.

Ahn Dukgeun. 'Third Country Dumping: Origin, Evolution and Prospect'. *Journal of World Trade* 46, no. 3 (2012): 635–656.
© 2012 Kluwer Law International BV, The Netherlands

actions rather than bilateral actions. This multilateral aspect of third country AD actions has revealed itself as one of the major hurdles for GATT contracting parties in employing such actions against other contracting parties.[2]

The rarity of third country AD actions due to their legal burden in the GATT system and the lack of commercial incentives from the standpoint of importing countries have made GATT Article VI:6 and pertinent provisions in the AD Agreement practically void.[3] Third country AD actions, however, have not been completely forgotten or unnoticed in the GATT/WTO system. There have been several attempts by GATT/WTO Members to use third country AD actions and even proposals addressing such actions during the current Doha negotiations. Moreover, private sectors are also mindful of this provision. For example, in October 2007, the National Council of Textile Organizations (NCTO) in the United States proposed the expansion of third country dumping provisions for the NAFTA region.[4]

This study reviews the historical development of domestic and international rules concerning third country AD actions. Actual third country AD cases are examined and explained to draw some implications regarding the practicality of current rules. After analysing the rationale and theoretical foundations for these rules, proposals in the Doha negotiations are examined.

In fact, GATT Article VI:6 stipulates not only AD but also countervailing duty (CVD) actions on behalf of a third country. Third country CVD actions appear particularly controversial due to the political implications of such actions and thereby would be even rarer – indeed, no case has ever been reported in GATT/WTO history. To legally challenge a trading partner's subsidy policies to protect the industries of another exporting countries would hardly seem possible unless there were some exceptionally close economic and political links between the importing country and the beneficiary of third country CVD actions. It may explain why the Agreement on Interpretation and Application of Articles VI, XVI and XXIII of the General Agreement on Tariffs and Trade (Subsidies Code) and the Agreement on Subsidies and Countervailing Measures (SCM Agreement) do not include parallel elaboration of third country CVD actions. In fact, although elaboration of Article VI:6 in terms of CVD actions was proposed during the Uruguay Round negotiations, no serious discussion or follow-ups ensued.[5] Accordingly, this study focuses on third country AD actions.

---

[2] Edwin Vermulst & F. Graafsma, *Customs and Trade Laws as Tools of Protection: Selected Essays*, 429-445(Cameron May 2002).

[3] For example, see GATT, C/W/420 (June 27, 1983).

[4] *Witness Statement for NCTO in US International Trade Commission* (Oct. 30, 2007), http://www.ncto.org/Newsroom/itc.pdf (accessed Jan. 20, 2011).

[5] For example, Australia proposed that "The Subsidies Group should also review the operation of Article VI:6 of the GATT with a view to introducing more effective provisions enabling contracting

2 HISTORICAL DEVELOPMENT OF RULES

2.1 GATT/WTO

2.1.[a]   *Evolution of GATT Article VI:5*

Although rarely practiced, the third country dumping issue was addressed from the very beginning of world trade rules. Article 34.6 of the Havana Charter stipulated that '[t]he Organization may waive the requirements of this paragraph so as to permit a Member to levy an anti-dumping or countervailing duty on the importation of any product for the purpose of offsetting dumping or subsidization which causes or threatens material injury to an industry in another Member country exporting the product concerned to the importing Member country.'[6] In fact, this provision was drawn from the original GATT text.

It is noteworthy, however, that early negotiation drafts of the GATT did not include this provision.[7] Even the New York Draft of the GATT, which broadly formulated the legal framework of world trade, made no mention or provision for third country dumping.[8] In May 1947, somewhat surprisingly, Syria and Lebanon submitted the proposal to add the following new paragraph to the article on anti-dumping:

> 'If a Member exporting the like product considers that its interests are adversely affected by the dumping practised by another Member, it may bring the matter before the Organization. The latter shall proceed to an investigation and make appropriate recommendations to the Member concerned. If the Organization finds that the Member is not carrying out its recommendations, it shall recognise the right of the complaining Member to refuse the tariff concessions agreed on in respect of the trade of the defaulting Member.'[9]

Presumably pursuant to the above suggestion, the 'Report of the Tariff Negotiations Working Party' in July 1947 included the third country dumping provision in the draft text for the very first time.[10] Subsequently, the draft charter issued in August 1947 included the third country dumping provision that was adopted in the Havana Charter almost in verbatim.[11] This provision was reflected

---

parties to take countervailing action on behalf of third countries." GATT, MTN.GNG/NG10/W/15 (Nov. 30, 1987).

[6] UN, E/Conf.2/78 (Apr. 1948).

[7] See for example, GATT, E/PC/T/C.6/85/Rev.1 (Feb. 20, 1947).

[8] UN, E/PC/T/34 (Mar. 5, 1947).

[9] UN, E/PC/T/W/66 (May 14, 1947).

[10] UN, E/PC/T/135 (July 24, 1947).

[11] UN, E/PC/T/142 (Aug. 1, 1947). The AD provision was one of the few commercial policy articles drawn from the Geneva ITO draft yet with substantial changes. John H. Jackson, *World Trade and the Law of GATT* 405 (The Michie Company 1969).

in the Geneva Draft for GATT[12] and several other drafts issued in September 1947.[13] This provision was adopted virtually intact in the final GATT text as Article VI:5, which provided:

> The CONTRACTING PARTIES may waive the requirements of this paragraph so as to permit a contracting party to levy an anti-dumping or countervailing duty on the importation of any product for the purpose of offsetting dumping or subsidization which causes or threatens material injury to an industry in the territory of another contracting party exporting the product concerned to the territory of the importing contracting party.[14]

It is noteworthy that, unlike a normal anti-dumping duty, which is bilateral in nature, a third country anti-dumping duty necessitates permission or approval by the Contracting Parties, which indicates the multilateral nature of this action. In addition, an injury requirement was imposed on the industry of an exporting country instead of an importing country.

The amendment of GATT in 1955 revised the third country dumping provision in Article VI:5.[15] The first addition was to Ad Article VI, para.6(b), which clarifies that waivers are granted only on application by the contracting party proposing to levy an anti-dumping or countervailing duty. A notable addition was made in Article VI:6(b), imposing a mandatory waiver for injury requirement in cases 'in which [the CONTRACTING PARTIES] find that a subsidy is causing or threatening material injury to an industry in the territory of another contracting party exporting the product concerned to the territory of the importing contracting party'. This amendment, however, did not lead to further development in the SCM Agreement.

Although Australia and New Zealand proposed at that time to remove the requirement of prior approval by the Contracting Parties, which was, from a practical standpoint, the most onerous procedural burden for third country AD actions, this suggestion was not widely supported by other GATT contracting parties.[16] The amended procedure was equally unattractive. For example, Ad Article VI, para.6(b) required an importing country to initiate the approval procedure by the Contracting Parties while the main beneficiary of third country AD actions would be an exporting country competing with a third country. Consequently, the amendment of 1955 could not help the GATT contracting

---

[12] UN, E/PC/T/189 (Aug. 30, 1947).
[13] See UN, E/PC/T/186 (Sept. 10, 1947), E/PC/T/196 (Sept. 13, 1947), and E/PC/T/212 (Sept. 22, 1947). The expression of 'organization' was replaced with 'Contracting Parties.'
[14] UN, E/PC/T/214/Add.1/Rev.1.
[15] Protocol Amending the Preamble and Parts II and III of General Agreements (Agreement No. 33 in App.C, Mar. 10, 1955). See also John Jackson, *supra* n. 11, at 406.
[16] GATT, L/334 (Mar. 1, 1955).

parties take the third country AD actions more seriously into account in relation to their trade policies.

2.1[b]   *Elaboration in the Anti-dumping Agreements*

In January 1960, the Group of Experts on Anti-dumping and Countervailing Duties issued a second report that addressed many legal agendas concerning the procedural and substantive aspects of AD and CVD.[17] The report mentioned, in relation to third country dumping, the following:

> 23. In order to avoid any misunderstanding, the Group wished to stress that a third country, in order to justify a request to an importing country to impose measures against another country, should produce evidence that the dumping engaged in by the other country was causing material injury to its domestic industry and not only to the exports of the industry of that third country. However, in cases where the importing country granted a request from a third country, anti-dumping measures should not be imposed until and unless the CONTRACTING PARTIES had approved the proposed measure (Article VI, paragraph 6).

> 24. The Group, while noting that such cases might be infrequent, called the attention of the CONTRACTING PARTIES to the possibility that this procedure might be too slow for the approved measures to be fully effective. The Group felt that it should be left to the CONTRACTING PARTIES to determine whether it would be desirable to propose methods to expedite any decision which might have to be taken, for instance, by instituting a panel which could meet at short notice whenever necessary.

> 25. In any case, there was no doubt that the initiation of the procedures of resorting to the CONTRACTING PARTIES laid down in Article VI, paragraph 6, should be left to the discretion of the importing country. Consequently, the Group was of the opinion that where the importing country found it impossible or undesirable to grant the request from a third country which claimed injury, the third country had no right to retaliatory measures but could have resort to Articles XXII and XXIII of the General Agreement.[18]

Based on the above proposal, Article VI:6 of GATT was substantially elaborated when the Kennedy Round negotiators drafted the very first international treaty dealing specifically with anti-dumping matters – 'Agreement on Implementation of Article VI of the General Agreement on Tariffs and Trade (hereinafter Kennedy Round AD code)'. In fact, when the United Kingdom

---

[17]   The Group consisted of twenty-six peoples from fourteen countries. GATT, L/1141, Annex (Jan. 29, 1960). The first report also addressed key concepts such as export prices, normal values, like products, material injury, and provisional measures. GATT, L/978 (Apr. 24, 1959).

[18]   *Id.*

prepared the first draft text for the 'International Code on Anti-Dumping Procedures and Practice',[19] the above report provided the essential basis for the text of Provisions 22–24 that addressed AD action on behalf of third countries.[20] The proposed articles for third country AD actions were by no means a major issue and thus received only minor attention from contracting parties. For example, Canada opined that the third country dumping provisions should be retained in a 'permissive' form.[21] Finland argued that the decision whether or not to proceed with a third country dumping case must rest with an importing country.[22] Some countries addressed more specific issues. For example, Japan stated that the causal relationship between dumped imports and the material injury of a third country must be clearly established and based on the same strict criteria as a normal dumping case.[23] Sweden opined that the injury should be determined in relation to the total amount of sales of a third country industry.[24] Interestingly, taking a contrary position to other countries, Australia proposed that third countries should be free to request third country AD actions in their interests.[25] Whereas, the United States did not make any comments on third country dumping in its comprehensive anti-dumping checklist that raised many legal issues on the proposed text.[26] Neither did the European Economic Community make any comments on third country dumping.[27]

In August 1966, when the GATT Secretariat summarized 'Possible Elements to be Considered for Inclusion in an Anti-dumping Code', the provision on third country AD actions had already been drawn up without much controversy.[28] That provision was finally confirmed as Article 12 in Part E of the Kennedy Round AD Code.'[29]

Although the Kennedy Round AD Code was not successfully implemented,[30] Article 12 in Part E 'Anti-dumping action on behalf of a third

---

[19]   GATT, Spec(65)86.
[20]   GATT, TN.64/NTB/W/2 (Nov. 23, 1965), para.19.
[21]   GATT, TN.64/NTB/W/12/Add.3 (June 29, 1966), para.X.
[22]   GATT, TN.64/NTB/W/12/Add.4 (June 30, 1966), para.X.
[23]   GATT, TN.64/NTB/W/12/Add.6 (July 1, 1966), para.X.
[24]   GATT, TN.64/NTB/W/12/Add.8 (July 7, 1966), para.X.
[25]   GATT, TN.64/NTB/W/12/Add.9 (July 8, 1966), Item X. Australia turned out to be the major country to use third country AD actions. See *infra* Section III.
[26]   GATT, TN.64/NTB/W/12/Add.5 (June 30, 1966).
[27]   GATT, TN.64/NTB/W/12/Add.2 (June 24, 1966).
[28]   GATT, TN.64/NTB/W/13 (Aug. 23, 1966), 11-12.
[29]   GATT, L/2812 (July 12, 1967), 13.
[30]   The Kennedy Round AD Code entered into force on July 1, 1968, with sixteen parties including the United States. GATT, L/3036 (July 4, 1968). But, when the US Tariff Commission failed to implement the Code – particularly the provision for material injury – due to the legislation by the US Congress, the Code was practically abandoned. See John Jackson, *The World Trading System* 256 (2d ed., MIT Press 1997); see also Thomas Curtis & John Vastine, Jr., *The Kennedy Round and the Future of American Trade*, 213-214 (Praeger Publishers 1971).

country' became, in verbatim, the basis for Article 12 of the Tokyo Round AD Code and finally Article 14 of the WTO AD Agreement, which provides as follows:

Article 14: Anti-Dumping Action on Behalf of a Third Country

14.1 An application for anti-dumping action on behalf of a third country shall be made by the authorities of the third country requesting action.

14.2 Such an application shall be supported by price information to show that the imports are being dumped and by detailed information to show that the alleged dumping is causing injury to the domestic industry concerned in the third country. The government of the third country shall afford all assistance to the authorities of the importing country to obtain any further information which the latter may require.

14.3 In considering such an application, the authorities of the importing country shall consider the effects of the alleged dumping on the industry concerned as a whole in the third country; that is to say, the injury shall not be assessed in relation only to the effect of the alleged dumping on the industry's exports to the importing country or even on the industry's total exports.

14.4 The decision whether or not to proceed with a case shall rest with the importing country. If the importing country decides that it is prepared to take action, the initiation of the approach to the Council for Trade in Goods seeking its approval for such action shall rest with the importing country.

While the Uruguay Round negotiations substantially amended the Tokyo Round AD Code, Article 14 was virtually set aside from the whole negotiation process.[31]

As enunciated in Article 14 of the WTO AD Agreement, actions against a third country dumping must be initiated through an application by the exporting country's authorities. In other words, this provides a key difference with regular AD actions, which are initiated by the application of injured domestic companies. Also, Article 14.3 clarifies that the investigation should consider the effects of alleged dumping on the industry concerned as a whole, not merely on the exports of the industry. This injury requirement is equivalent to that of regular AD actions, in that the overall industry situation should be considered. But, apparently, 'threat of an injury' cannot provide a basis for AD actions under Article 14. In addition, injury 'being caused' by alleged dumping under Article 14 does not include material retardation of the establishment of a domestic industry, since otherwise the material retardation part would have appeared in the text, as

---

[31] For example, the Chairman's report issued in July 1990 did not mention any discussion or proposal concerning anti-dumping action on behalf of a third country. See MTN.GNG/NG8/W/83/Add.5 (July 23, 1990). See also generally Terence Stewart, *The GATT/Uruguay Round: A Negotiating history (1986-1992), Vol. II: Commentary*, 1389-1710 (Kluwer Law & Taxation Publishers 1993).

in Article VI:6(a) of the WTO AD Agreement. Article 14.4 stipulates that whereas an importing country has complete discretion over whether or not to take actions against third country dumping, that country must have the prior approval of the Council for Trade in Goods. This legal element is the most serious procedural burden, because consensus-based decision-making in the Council for Trade in Goods makes approval almost impossible when a third country AD action is proposed against any member of the Council. Conversely, the approval of third country AD actions by the Council for Trade in Goods may be possible against non-WTO members that do not have opportunities to block consensus decision-making. This possibility, however, is becoming slimmer as membership to the WTO continues to grow.

In contrast to Article 14 of the Agreement on Implementation of Article VI of the General Agreement on Tariffs and Trade (AD Agreement), the SCM Agreement and previously the Tokyo Round Subsidies Code, do not include any specific provision for CVD actions dealing with third country subsidization. The lack of such rules appears to be mainly because the subsidy disciplines articulate the rules for directly challenging export subsidization under the GATT/WTO dispute settlement system. For example, Article 9 of the Tokyo Round Subsidies Code prohibited export subsidies on products other than primary products. Likewise, Part II of the SCM Agreement permits direct challenge under the WTO dispute settlement system even without showing domestic injury if a WTO member uses subsidies contingent upon export performance. Moreover, Article 6.3(b) of the SCM Agreement specifically indicates that serious prejudice for the interests of a Member may arise when a subsidy displaces or impedes the exports of a like product of that Member from a third country market. If so, subsidies may be challenged under actionable subsidy rules in Part III of the SCM Agreement. Therefore, CVD actions on behalf of a third country seem practically abandoned, particularly considering the onerous legal requirement of prior approval by the Council for Trade in Goods.

2.2 NATIONAL LAWS

Despite the codification of the GATT/WTO rules, many WTO Members, including *inter alia* the European Union, Canada, China, Japan, Korea, and Mexico, do not include third country dumping provisions in their domestic AD regulations. In principle, these countries all embrace third country dumping provisions, since the WTO Agreement must be incorporated into their domestic laws and regulations. However, their domestic regulations which are actually applicable to AD actions often dismiss third country dumping actions primarily due to the low probability for actual utilization.

But, some WTO Members do have third country dumping rules. For example, the United States incorporated the third country dumping rule in Section 1318 of the Omnibus Trade and Competitiveness Act of 1988, or Section 1677k of the US Code.[32] Under this Section, a domestic industry may submit a petition to the United States Trade Representative (USTR) to request GATT contracting parties to take action on behalf of the domestic industry. If the USTR, on the basis of the information contained in a petition, determines that there is a reasonable basis for the allegations in the petition, it shall process an application pursuant to Article 12 of the AD Agreement. The Department of Commerce (DOC) and the US International Trade Commission (ITC) are supposed to assist the USTR in preparing the application. It should be noted that while the authorities for domestic AD actions are the DOC and the ITC, third country AD action is officially supposed to be handled by the USTR.

In case the importing country refuses to undertake anti-dumping measures, the USTR 'shall promptly consult with the domestic industry on whether action under any other law of the United States is appropriate'.[33] This last provision implying potential retaliation, for example, under Section 301, raised concerns among GATT contracting parties. In fact, Hong Kong inquired specifically on whether the refusal to take third country anti-dumping actions could be construed as a violation under Section 301.[34] Singapore also raised the question in the Committee on Anti-dumping Practices, on exactly what kind of actions the US government was considering.[35] The US government replied by stating simply that no policies were developed with respect to the implementation of this provision since no requests for actions were made.[36]

Section 1677k of the US Code is solely concerned with procedures for US firms to initiate third country AD actions in other countries, not the facilitation of such actions in the United States.[37] Therefore, when the Uruguay Round negotiations were finished, the Tariff Act of 1930 was amended by Section 783 to deal with third country AD petitions.[38] This provision allows WTO Members to file a petition with the USTR for a third country dumping problem. Prior to initiation of third country AD actions, the USTR must consult with the DOC and the ITC, solicit public comments and obtain approval of the WTO Council

---

[32] P.L.100–418.
[33] US Code, S. 1677k(e).
[34] GATT, ADP/W/244 (Oct. 19, 1989).
[35] GATT, ADP/W/251 (Nov. 20, 1989).
[36] GATT, ADP/W/272 (May 25, 1990) and ADP/W/273 (June 8, 1990).
[37] Martin Richadson, *Third Party Anti-dumping: A Tentative Rationale*, 22 European J. Political Economy 759, 761 (2006).
[38] Pub. L. No. 103–465, 108 Stat. 4897.

for Trade in Goods. The USTR is required to articulate procedural and substantive rules pursuant to the following detailed guideline:

'The Administration intends that the Trade Representative will develop consistent, transparent standards of general applicability that provide meaningful guidance to the agencies, while according them the necessary flexibility to develop appropriate procedures. With respect to procedural issues, the Trade Representative will indicate the deadlines (if any) applicable to such investigations, the persons who may participate as parties in such investigations, and the applicability of requirements such as hearings and exchanges of information pursuant to administrative protective order. The Trade Representative will articulate the extent to which substantive rules (particularly with respect to Commission injury investigations) applicable to anti-dumping investigations filed on behalf of U.S. industries – such as like product, related parties, and cumulation – are also applicable in third country investigations. The Administration intends that these standards should, to a considerable extent, permit the Commission to incorporate by analogy the standards it uses concerning injury to U.S. industries. Nevertheless, certain concepts, such as regional industries, may have little applicability in third country investigations. In such circumstances, the Commission should have the flexibility in third country investigations to deviate from the standards used in anti-dumping investigations of U.S. industries.'[39]

Despite such a clear mandate, the USTR has not yet completed its task.

Australia and New Zealand, the only two countries with actual experience in attempting third country AD actions, have domestic regulations which are relatively more articulated. In particular, Australia has the most detailed rules concerning third country countervailing as well as anti-dumping duties. Section 269TH of the Customs Act of 1901 dealing with third country AD actions stipulates the precise definition of third country dumping, notice procedures, and calculation methods. Whereas, third country dumping duties are not applied to the goods that are produced or manufactured in New Zealand.[40] Australia also has third country countervailing duty rules that are very similar in many aspects to third country anti-dumping duty rules.[41]

In Article 18 of the Dumping and Countervailing Duties Amendment Act 1994, New Zealand stipulates rules concerning third country dumping and subsidization. The interesting element in the New Zealand AD laws is that they allow material retardation of domestic industry as the injury requirement for third country AD and CVD actions.

---

[39]   Uruguay Round Trade Agreements, Texts of Agreements, Implementing Bill, Statement of Administrative Action, and Required Supporting Statements, House Document 103-316, Vol. 1, 846 (1994).
[40]   S. 9 of the Customs Tariff (Anti-dumping) Act of 1975. WTO, G/ADP/N/1/AUS/1 (Apr. 6, 1995).
[41]   S. 11 of the Customs Tariff (Anti-dumping) Act of 1975 and S. 269TK of the Customs Act of 1901.

2.3   FREE TRADE AGREEMENTS

Parties in free trade agreements (FTA) tend to care more about collective or combined markets established by the FTAs. Therefore, these countries are more likely to consider third country AD provisions in an effort to protect bilateral market access. In fact, some FTAs explicitly stipulated provisions for third country AD actions.

The first FTA to specifically address the third country dumping issue was the Australia-New Zealand Closer Economic Relations Trade Agreement (ANZCERTA). Article 15.8 of ANZCERTA provides that if 'a Member State is of the opinion that goods imported into the territory of the other Member State from outside the Area are being dumped and that this dumping is causing material injury or threatening to cause material injury to an industry located in the first Member State, the other Member State shall, at the written request of the first Member State, examine the possibility of taking action, consistent with its international obligations, to prevent material injury.'[42] While this provision highlighted third country AD actions for the benefits of an FTA party, the substantive rules for such action were subject to international obligations, i.e., GATT Article VI:6 and Article 12 of the Tokyo Round AD Code. In other words, this provision was technically a repetition of the GATT rules. And yet, Australia and New Zealand indeed encouraged each other to utilize third country AD actions through the provisions of an FTA. Pursuant to this provision, these two countries actually attempted to use third country AD actions later.

In addition, Article 14 of ANZCERTA further stipulates third country AD actions to address intermediate goods problems. When 'the policies of either Member State or the application by one or both Member States of assistance or other measures' enable the Member State's own producers to obtain intermediate goods at lower costs such that 'it gives rise to a trend in trade which frustrates or threatens to frustrate the achievement of equal opportunities for producers or manufacturers in both Member States', third country AD or CVD actions are allowed, 'in so far as this action would be consistent with other international obligations of the other Member State and in so far as the first Member State had taken such action itself or would have taken such action had the goods from the third countries been imported in similar circumstances into its territory.' This provision, however, requires 'the policies of either Member State or the application by one or both Member States of assistance or other measures' as a condition to initiate third country AD or CVD actions.

---

[42]   WT/REG111 (entered into force on Jan. 1, 1983).

The Andean Community also has an anti-dumping regulation that permits third country AD actions. Article 2 of 'Decision 283: Rules for preventing or correcting distortions in competition caused by dumping or subsidy practices' provide that 'Member Countries or firms with a legitimate interest may ask the Board for authorization or a mandate to take measures to prevent or correct distortions in competition in the Sub-regional market caused by dumping . . . [w]hen practices originating in a country outside the Sub-region threaten to cause or do cause material injury to national production intended for export to another Member Country.'[43] It is noted that rules under the Andean Community do not mandate GATT/WTO approval for third country AD actions.

Another FTA to explicitly mention third country anti-dumping actions is the North America Free Trade Agreement (NAFTA). Article 317 of NAFTA, titled 'Third Country Dumping', affirms 'the importance of cooperation with respect to actions under Article 12 of the Agreement on Implementation of Article VI of the General Agreement on Tariffs and Trade'. Moreover, if a party presents an application to another party requesting anti-dumping action on its behalf, those parties 'shall consult within 30 days respecting the factual basis of the request, and the requested [p]arty shall give full consideration to the request.' This provision sets forth the requirement of consultation within thirty days of third country anti-dumping application, which is an additional element to the GATT rules. But again, all substantive GATT rules on third country AD actions are still binding upon the NAFTA parties.

The opposite approach is to prohibit third country AD actions in FTAs despite the WTO AD Agreement. For example, Article 2.8.1(d) of the Jordan-Singapore FTA stipulates that 'Article 14 of the WTO Anti-Dumping Agreement on third country dumping shall not be applied by the Parties.'

3 APPLICATIONS AND DISPUTES

3.1 THIRD COUNTRY AD ACTIONS

Known cases of third country AD actions are very rare because the procedural difficulties prevented the imposition of actual measures. However, de facto third country AD actions occurred even before anti-dumping rules were elaborated by the separate Anti-dumping Code. There is at least one case in which a third country AD measure was imposed in the early 1960s. It is reported that the United Kingdom maintained anti-dumping duties against imports of butter from

---

[43] http://www.sice.oas.org/trade/JUNAC/decisiones/dec283e.asp (accessed Jan. 20, 2011).

the Irish Republic following a request from New Zealand, albeit the details of this case were not readily available.[44]

More recent cases are summarized in Table 1. The very first, and probably the only, actual third country AD measure after the GATT Article VI was elaborated into the Anti-dumping Code was imposed by Venezuela against France on the request of Ecuador, another Andean Community member.[45] Venezuela later suspended this AD duty when it joined the GATT. In August 2002, the Andean Community decided to re-initiate AD investigations on sorbitol from France. The European Commission (EC) raised 'serious doubts about the legality of this proceeding' due to, among other reasons, failure of proper notification about the constitution of the Andean Community and relevant rules, including AD regulations as well as lack of common external tariffs.[46] With no formal WTO authorization granted, this case appeared to be resolved.[47]

New Zealand initiated four third country anti-dumping investigations, all of which were applied by Australia. None of the four New Zealand cases led to the imposition of AD duties, since such actions were required to comply with the GATT/WTO obligations of prior approval by the GATT contracting parties or WTO Council for Trade in Goods. It is, however, noteworthy that the dumping investigation initiated by Australia in 1992 resulted in price undertaking. Whereas, in 1993 and 1994, the New Zealand government referred the third country AD applications by Alcan New Zealand Limited to the Australian authority but later withdrew them even before initiating the investigations.[48] It is somewhat puzzling that New Zealand did not seriously pursue third country AD actions to Australia, particularly considering the reciprocal nature of bilateral trade structures between Australia and New Zealand.

In 1996, Canada also brought the third country AD action to the United States against Japan.[49] This case was suspended when the US government and the Japanese exporters reached a suspension agreement.[50]

---

[44] John Singleton & Paul Robertson, 'Britain, Butter and European Integration', 50 The Economic History Review, 327-347, 343 (1997). See also Gerarad Curzon, Multilateral Commercial Diplomacy 198 (Praeger Publishers 1965). It is not known whether and how the UK's third country AD measure was approved by the GATT.

[45] Gary Horlick & Bart Szewczyk, Article 14, in Rudiger Wolfrum, Peter-Tobias Stoll, and Michael Koebele, WTO Trade Remedies, 185-186 (Martinus Nijhoff Publishers 2009).

[46] Customs duties applied are 15% in Ecuador and Colombia, 10% in Venezuela and Bolivia and 4% in Peru. European Commission, Report for the 133 Committee (Ref. 199/03, Apr. 9, 2003), at 32.

[47] Horlick and Szewczyk, supra n. 45, at 186.

[48] See Grant W. David, 'Dumping on Your Mates: A Trans-Tasman Experience', Australian J. Intl. L. 134, 150 (1998).

[49] 61 Fed. Reg. 33148 (June 26, 1996).

[50] 62 Fed. Reg. 973 (Jan. 7, 1997). See also Canadian Department of Foreign Affairs and International Trade, US Trade Remedy Law: The Canadian Experience 28 (2d ed., 1985-2000, 2002).

Table 1   Third Country Anti-dumping Actions[51]

Investigating Country/Case	Year	Complainant	Action
Venezuela*/Andean Community	1990/2002	Ecuador	AD Measures
New Zealand/Plaster of Paris bandages from Germany	1992	Australia	Threat of injury/ Price undertaking
US/Sodium Azide from Japan	1996	Canada	Suspension Agreement
New Zealand/Clear Float Glass from China, Indonesia and Thailand	1997	Australia	No consensus/No action
New Zealand/ACE Inhibitors from Germany and Switzerland	1999	Australia	Withdrawal
*New Zealand/Primary Carpet Backing Fabric from Saudi Arabia**	2000	Australia	No material injury/ Termination

* indicates that the country was then not a WTO Member.

As shown in Table 1, all third country AD actions so far have been initiated by the requests of particularly interdependent economic neighbours, especially FTA partners that are also geographically proximate. In fact, the Andean Community, ANZCERTA, as well as the NAFTA represent some of the strongest cooperative arrangements amongst numerous FTAs, incorporating special economic and political unity amongst signatories.

3.2   MONITORING THIRD COUNTRY DUMPING: EXPORT PRICE COLLUSION

Third country AD actions are designed to protect innocuous exporters from third countries' dumping by permitting importing countries to undertake AD actions. The alternate way of handling third country dumping problems is to directly address the third country that is engaged in dumping exportation. In this regard, a direct monitoring system adopted by the United States is noteworthy, since it is still the only measure actually implemented to address a dumping third country.

---

http://www.international.gc.ca/trade-agreements-accords-commerciaux/assets/pdfs/USlaw-e.pdf (accessed Feb. 12, 2011).

[51] This table includes only the cases for which the formal AD investigations were conducted. But, as shown in the New Zealand examples, there are the cases in which third country AD application was made but did not result in formal investigation.

In September 1986, the United States and Japan concluded the 'Arrangement between the Government of Japan and the Government of the United States of America Concerning Trade in Semiconductor Products' (US-Japan Semiconductor Agreement) to resolve aggravating trade conflicts between the two major producing countries.[52] As part of the arrangement to prevent the problem of dumping, the United States and Japan both agreed to monitor third country markets. Article II:3 of the US-Japan Semiconductor Agreement stated that '[b]oth governments recognize the need to prevent dumping in accordance with relevant provisions of the GATT and encourage respective industries to conform with the above principles.' It also added that '[i]n order to prevent dumping, the Government of Japan will monitor, as appropriate, cost and export prices on the products exported by Japanese semi-conductor firms from Japan.'[53]

Pursuant to this commitment, Japan, as an administrative matter, monitored semiconductor exports to most significant markets accounting for 97% of Japanese exports.[54] Japanese manufacturers and exporters were required to report data on export prices, and periodically report on costs to the Ministry of International Trade and Industry (MITI). When MITI found cases in which export prices were 'extremely below costs', it would inform the relevant companies of the facts and of MITI's 'concern'. Although MITI never set minimum export prices and the communications by MITI to the companies were not legally binding, companies were 'expected to understand that it was in their own self-interest to prevent dumping, and to take action accordingly'.[55] In March 1987, the US President announced trade sanctions of 100% tariffs on major Japanese products on the basis of non-compliance with third country dumping provisions.[56] In response, Japan took the case to the GATT dispute settlement system.[57] But, when the Japanese semiconductor manufacturers later

---

[52] The rapidly increasing market shares of Japanese producers provoked serious legal and political challenges by US producers using the procedures under Section 301 and anti-dumping laws. See for example Douglas Irwin, 'The US-Japan Semiconductor Trade Conflict', in The Political Economy of Trade Protection, 5-13 (Anne O. Krueger ed., U. Chicago Press 1996); Douglas Irwin, 'The Semiconductor Industry', Brookings Trade Forum 173-200 (1998); Richard E. Baldwin, 'The impact of the 1986 US—Japan semiconductor agreement', 6 Japan & the World Economy 129 (1994).

[53] GATT, L/6076, 7 (Nov. 6, 1986).

[54] These markets included Brazil, Canada, China, France, Germany F.R., Hong Kong, Ireland, Italy, Korea, Malaysia, Mexico, the Philippines, Singapore, Sweden, Taiwan and the United Kingdom. GATT, L/6309, footnote 2 (adopted May 4, 1988).

[55] Id., at para.23.

[56] See Michael P. Ryan, Playing by the Rules: American Trade Power and Diplomacy in the Pacific 97-110 (Georgetown U. Press 1995).

[57] GATT, United States – Unilateral Measures on Imports of Certain Japanese Products, L/6159 (Apr. 21, 1987). See also WTO, Analytical Index: Guide to GATT Law and Practices, vol. 2, 781 (1995).

increased the prices, the US government terminated its trade sanctions.[58] Japan thereby dropped the GATT dispute case.

Whereas, the European Economic Community (EEC) challenged this monitoring measure for third country markets through the GATT dispute settlement system, claiming that it contravened Articles VI and XI.[59] The EEC's main concern was that this arrangement increased the price of 'indispensable and irreplaceable' inputs to its own downstream industries. The panel found that the third country monitoring system was indeed inconsistent with Article XI, due essentially to the nature of export control and restriction.[60] Regarding Article VI, however, the panel found that this provision was silent on actions by exporting countries. Accordingly, the panel ruled that Article VI did not provide a justification for measures restricting exportation inconsistently with Article XI:1, nor did it provide the legal basis for exporting countries to make arrangements to control exportation.[61]

This ruling raised an important point regarding third country AD actions in the GATT/WTO system. The third country monitoring system is, in fact, a supply-side version of third country AD actions for which an importing country is supposed to have the full authority to exercise. Exporting countries are monitoring and sharing price information so that potentially differential prices would be eliminated. However, the legal implications for this arrangement are critically different from third country AD actions. The third country monitoring system virtually constitutes a government-sanctioned international cartel by price-fixing. This mechanism of fixing prices for particular semiconductors in specific markets might be used to suppress comparative advantage for finished products incorporating those semi-conductors in other markets and to distort international trade to favour products of related or vertically integrated producers.[62] In 1991, the US government deleted the third country monitoring provision when interest groups for downstream industries – especially computer producers – lobbied against semiconductor producers.[63]

4 RATIONALE AND PROBLEMS

Granting an exporting country the right to apply AD investigations in an importing country against other exporting countries introduces peculiar problems to the AD system. In principle, if dumping is to be condemned due to

---

[58]   52 Fed. Reg. 22,693 (June 15, 1987) and 52 Fed. Reg. 43,146 (Nov. 9, 1987).
[59]   GATT, *Japan – Trade in Semi-Conductors*, L/6309 (adopted May 4, 1988).
[60]   *Id.* at paras 117–118.
[61]   *Id.* at para.120.
[62]   The Australian government also raised this point in the third party submission. *Id.* at para. 85.
[63]   Douglas Irwin, *supra* n. 52, at 5.

the material injury it causes to domestic industries, third country dumping causing injuries to other exporting countries might be equally condemnable. However, third country AD actions would cause an increase in import prices that tends to harm the social welfare of importing countries. In fact, working as a mechanism to indirectly induce price collusion among exporters, third country AD actions benefit an exporting country at the expense of the importing country.[64] Nevertheless, are there any economic reasons for an importing country to voluntarily agree on welfare-reducing AD actions seemingly to benefit other exporting countries, let alone bother trying to secure consensual support for its own actions from the WTO?

There are at least three reasons or scenarios that may justify third country AD actions. First, an injured exporter in Country A may not be 'foreign' to the importing Country B. In other words, exporters in Country A may be subsidiary companies of firms in Country B that are intended to bring manufactured products back to their home country. In such a case, industry injuries to Country A due to third country dumping may be perceived as industry injuries to Country B. One important point in this situation is that the Country A government, as a petitioner, should be able to show material injury for its own whole industry, not just the injury to that particular subsidiary company. Thus, although the home company in Country B wants Country A to initiate a third country AD action, it may not be easy for the home company to persuade Country A's government.

Second, Country A and Country B may want to protect from a third country their integrated markets, a result occurring from historical colonial occupation until the Second World War, which is nowadays also typical under FTA arrangements.[65] Suppose that the MFN tariff for Country B is 10%. After the establishment of an FTA between Countries A and B, Country C exporters would not be able to compete in Country B's market unless they reduce their export prices to the level that the FTA arrangement would benefit Country A exporters. So, artificially created price advantages by free trade under an FTA would induce non-FTA parties to engage in more aggressive pricing – often, dumping practices. Therefore, FTA parties may share mutual incentives to protect their markets by third country AD actions from non-party exportation. More generally speaking, an FTA member may want to take third country AD actions

---

[64] Petros Mavroidis, Patrick Messerlin & Jasper Wauters, *The Law and Economics of Contingent Protection in the WTO*, 24–25 (Edward Elgar 2008).

[65] Horlick and Szewczyk also pointed out that third country AD actions are likely to remain negligible and concentrated in regions that are becoming increasingly integrated economically and that develop regional political institutions to authorize such measures. Horlick & Szewczyk, *supra* n. 45, at 187.

to encourage rationalization and specialization among producers within a free trade area which will induce the efficiency and benefits of such an agreement.[66]

Third, when the industries of two countries are closely intertwined and use intermediate goods from each other for further processing, an importing country may have an incentive to protect the importation of those intermediate goods from third country dumping. Actually, Article 14 of ANZCERTA envisioned this very situation and stipulated that if the Member States do not reach a mutually acceptable solution involving the alteration of assistance or other measures giving rise to a prejudicial intermediate goods situation,[67] 'initiation by the other Member State of anti-dumping or countervailing action in respect of goods imported from third countries in so far as this action would be consistent with other international obligations of the other Member State and in so far as the first Member State had taken such action itself or would have taken such action had the goods from the third countries been imported in similar circumstances into its territory'.

5   PROGRESS IN THE DOHA DEVELOPMENT AGENDA

The rules negotiation in the Doha Development Agenda (DDA) have sought to refine and elaborate various procedural as well as substantive issues for trade remedy rules which have 'caused controversy and confusion under the WTO system. Despite numerous proposals on almost every aspect of anti-dumping rules and practices, WTO Members had not seriously discussed third country dumping until the mid-2000s. In September 1999, New Zealand suggested that, in preparation for the Seattle Ministerial Conference, any review of the AD Agreement should examine Article 14 to consider the continued desirability and feasibility of this provision.[68] But, when the chairman of the Negotiating Group on Rules issued a very comprehensive document compiling all the issues and

---

[66]   See also Grant W. David, '*Dumping on Your Mates: A Trans-Tasman Experience*', Australian J. Intl. L. 134, 149 (1998).

[67]   Art. 14.1 of ANZCERTA defines a "prejudicial intermediate goods situation" as the situation when:
  '(a) the policies of either Member State or the application by one or both Member States of assistance or other measures enables producers or manufacturers of goods in the territory of one Member State to obtain intermediate goods at lower prices or on other more favourable terms and conditions than are available to the producers or manufacturers of like goods in the territory of the other Member State; and
  (b) the extent of advantage referred to in sub-paragraph (a) of this paragraph in relation to the total cost for the production or manufacture and the sale of the relevant final goods is such that it gives rise to a trend in trade which frustrates or threatens to frustrate the achievement of equal opportunities for producers or manufacturers in both Member States.'

[68]   WTO, WT/GC/W/338 (Sep. 23, 1999).

proposals identified by WTO members in 2003, the third country dumping provision was not even mentioned.[69]

In 2006, Mexico made a specific proposal to delete the approval requirement by the Council for Trade in Goods in Article 14.4 in order to afford Members a real opportunity to carry out procedures whereby anti-dumping action on behalf of a third country could actually be effected.[70] The draft-consolidated chair text of November 2007 included the following proposal:[71]

> 14.4 Notwithstanding the provisions of Article VI:6(b) of GATT 1994, the decision whether or not to proceed with a case shall rest solely with the importing country; provided, that the importing country shall notify the Council for Trade in Goods of its decision to initiate such an investigation.

The views of WTO Members on the above proposal were widely varied; ranging from those seeking to make the provision effectively operational to those questioning the very desirability of this provision. One delegation noted that since more transnational corporations had tended to supply their home market exclusively from offshore production bases in recent years, the use of such a provision might be more likely.[72] The working document of the chairman in May 2008 deleted Article 14.4 altogether and added '[[The decision whether or not to proceed with a case shall rest with the importing country.]]' to the last part of Article 14.3.[73] Without any progress on this issue, the 'New Draft Consolidated Chair Text' issued in December 2008 erased all amendment proposals and simply added the following comments to Article 14:[74]

> [THIRD COUNTRY DUMPING: Some delegations support new rules on third country dumping, as in their view the current rules are unworkable, although it was emphasized that many other issues would have to be addressed if this provision were to be operationalised. Other delegations question whether it is desirable to operationalise this provision at all, with one delegation preferring that the provision be deleted entirely.]

Considering the lack of enthusiasm to amend this provision, and the huge political controversy that would inevitably follow any attempt to modify the AD Agreement, Article 14 appears very likely to remain in its current form. As of February 2011, there was still no consensus among the WTO Members about how to amend Article 14.

---

[69] WTO, TN/RL/W/143 (Aug. 22, 2003).
[70] WTO, TN/RL/GEN/116 (Apr. 21, 2006).
[71] WTO, TN/RL/W/213 (Nov. 30, 2007).
[72] WTO, TN/RL/W/232, A-141 (May 28, 2008).
[73] Id.
[74] WTO, TN/RL/W/236 (Dec. 19, 2008).

6   CONCLUDING REMARKS

In some sense, it is a mystery why the third country AD action provision in GATT VI:6 remained neglected for so long, having been neither refined nor deleted after several rules and negotiations. When countries are competing economically in the best interests of their unequivocal territorial boundaries, third country AD actions do not make much sense, since importing countries imposing AD actions are likely to harm their own domestic economies. However, as global investment dramatically increases and thereby supply chains get more closely intertwined, using AD actions on behalf of strategic partners may come to deserve more careful attention. The implication of third country AD actions becomes particularly important when proliferating FTAs create more tightly integrated markets between or among strategically chosen FTA parties. In other words, the unprecedented phenomena of the world trading system caused by FTAs may revive the potential meaning of the long-forgotten provision on third country AD actions.

This paper does not argue that the WTO rules concerning third country AD actions should be amended so as to be effective in the WTO system. Instead, this paper explains how the third country AD rules originated and remained unexploited due to structural drawbacks. Although it is the WTO Members' decision whether to amend the third country AD provision or not, I hope the analysis of this paper provides an opportunity to cautiously reconsider the utility of resuscitating it.

BIBLIOGRAPHY

Richard E. Baldwin, *The impact of the 1986 US—Japan semiconductor agreement*, 6 Japan & World Econ. 129–152 (1994).

Raj Bhala, *Modern GATT Law: A Treatise on the General Agreement on Tariffs and Trade* (Sweet & Maxwell 2005).

Marco Bronckers, & Gary Horlick, *WTO Jurisprudence and Policy: Practitioners' Perspective* (Cameron May 2005).

Dan Ciuriak, *Anti-dumping at 100 Years and Counting: A Canadian Perspective*, 28 The World Econ. 641–649 (2005).

Thomas Curtis, & John Vastine, Jr., *The Kennedy Round and the Future of American Trade* (Praeger Publishers 1971).

Gerard Curzon, *Multilateral Commercial Diplomacy* (Praeger Publishers 1966).

Grant W. David, '*Dumping on Your Mates: A Trans-Tasman Experience*', Australian Journal of International Law 134–154 (1998).

Michael Finger, *Antidumping: How It Works and Who Gets Hurt* (U Mich. Press 1993).

Gary Horlick, *WTO and NAFTA Rules and Dispute Resolution* (Cameron May 2003).

Gary Horlick, & Bart Szewczyk, *Article 14*, in *WTO Trade Remedies*, Rudiger Wolfrum, Peter–Tobias Stoll &Michael Koebele eds. (Martinus Nijhoff Publishers 2009).

Douglas Irwin, *The Rise of US Anti-dumping Activity in Historical Perspective*, 28 World Econ. 651-668 (2005).

Douglas Irwin, *The US-Japan Semiconductor Trade Conflict*, in *Political Economy of Trade Protection* (Anne Krueger ed., U. Chicago Press 1996).

Douglas Irwin, *The Semiconductor Industry*, Brookings Trade Forum 173-200 (1998).

John Jackson, *World Trade and the Law of GATT* (The Michie Company 1969).

John Jackson, & Edwin Vermulst, *Anti-dumping Law Practice* (U. Mich. Press 1990).

John Jackson, *The World Trading System: Law and Policy of International Economic Relations* (MIT Press 1997).

Petros Mavroidis, Patrick Messerlin & Jasper Wauters, *The Law and Economics of Contingent Protection in the WTO* (Edward Elgar 2008).

Martin Richadson, '*Third Party Anti-dumping: A Tentative Rationale*', 22 European J. Political Econ. 759-770 (2006).

Michael P. Ryan, *Playing by the Rules: American Trade Power and Diplomacy in the Pacific* (Georgetown U. Press 1995).

John Singleton & Paul Robertson, *Britain, Butter and European Integration*, 50 Econ. History Rev. 327-347 (1997).

Terence Stewart, *The GATT/Uruguay Round: A Negotiating history (1986-1992), Vol. II: Commentary* (Kluwer Law & Taxation Publishers 1993).

Edwin Vermulst, *Anti-dumping Law and Practice in the United States and the European Communities* (Elsevier Science 1987).

Edwin Vermulst, & F. Graafsma, *Customs and Trade Laws as Tools of Protection: Selected Essays* (Cameron May 2002).

Edwin Vermulst, Edwin, *Customs and Trade Laws as Tools of Protectionism: Selected Essays* (Cameron May 2005).

Edwin Vermulst, *The WTO Anti-dumping Agreement: A Commentary* (Oxford U. Press 2005).

Jacob Viner, *Dumping: A Problem in International Trade* (U. of Chicago Press 1923).

Chapter 5

RESTRUCTURING THE WTO SAFEGUARD SYSTEM

Dukgeun Ahn[*]

I.   Introduction

A safeguard mechanism for an international trade agreement is the core element to secure market access commitments in trade negotiations and effectively sustain trade liberalization despite domestic resistance from comparatively disadvantaged economic sectors.[1] A safeguard system is not only essential to provide safety nets for overly excessive importation within such a short period of time, but also critical to facilitate structural adjustment induced by import competition.

A formal safeguard provision for an international trade agreement was first introduced in the US-Mexico Trade Agreement in 1942.[2] Pursuant to the Executive Order by President Truman that mandated safeguard systems for international trade agreements,[3] a similar safeguard provision was later adopted in the GATT as Article XIX.

The first attempt by the GATT contracting parties to establish a separate agreement on safeguard along with the Anti-dumping Code and the Subsidy Code failed during the Tokyo Round negotiation. The WTO Agreement on Safeguard (hereinafter "Safeguard Agreement") was later concluded during the Uruguay Round negotiation and entered into force in 1995 with the inception of the WTO. In 2004, 133 out of 148 WTO Members notified their safeguard laws and regulations.[4]

Although there were only two dispute settlement cases relating to Article XIX of the GATT during the GATT system,[5] as of July 2005, 33 complaints

---

[*] Professor of International Trade Law and Policy, Graduate School of International Studies, Seoul National University, Korea. dahn@snu.ac.kr. I would like to thank participants at "2005 International Conference on Trade Remedy System: East Asian Perspectives", especially Professors Catherine Li, Marco Bronckers, Mitsuo Matsushita and William Davey for useful comments.
[1] For general discussion on the rationales of a safeguard system, see John H. Jackson, *World Trade and the Law of GATT*, 553-573 (1969); Jackson et al, *Legal Problems of International Economic Relations: Cases, Materials and Text*, 604-675 (4th ed, 2002); Dukgeun Ahn, *Treatise on the WTO Safeguard System* (2005, in Korean); Bhala and Kennedy, *World Trade Law* (1998).
[2] John H. Jackson, *World Trade and the Law of GATT*, 554 (1969).
[3] See Executive Order No 9832 of February 25, 1947, 3 CFR 624 (1947).
[4] In 1995, only 52 Members made such notification on safeguard related laws and regulations.
[5] They are *United States – Withdrawal of a tariff concession under Art. XIX* (adopted on October 22, 1951; CP/106) and *Norway – Restrictions on imports of certain textile products* (adopted on June 18, 1980; BISD 27S/119).

11

124

concerning safeguard measures were brought to the WTO dispute settlement procedure. Among them, 16 cases ended up with 8 panel and 7 Appellate Body reports that contributed substantially to building WTO jurisprudence for implementation of the safeguard mechanism.[6] In particular, the Appellate Body rulings on various legal elements of the Safeguard Agreement elucidated important criteria for interpreting and applying the newly established WTO disciplines.

Unfortunately, however, the current structure of the WTO safeguard system has not been sufficiently articulated to prevent abusive safeguard protection by many Members.[7] Moreover, the WTO jurisprudence concerning the Safeguard Agreement has raised several controversial issues that have not been welcomed by WTO constituents, neither as complainants nor as defendants. When 7 out of 8 panel reports were reviewed by the Appellate Body, some of the legal rulings and interpretations by the Appellate Body drew much attention and indeed criticism.[8] Some of the more fundament issues, procedural and substantive, will be discussed below to shed some light on the establishment of a better safeguard mechanism in the future.

II.   Problems in the Structure of the WTO Safeguard System

A.   Structural Deficiency in Resorting to the WTO Dispute Settlement System: Lack of Fast-track Procedures

The structural problem of the WTO safeguard system manifested by the experience up to date is the ineffectiveness of a normal WTO dispute settlement procedure to address unjustifiable safeguard measures. While a safeguard measure is by nature an emergency action with temporary duration, the current WTO Dispute Settlement Understanding (hereinafter "DSU") does not provide adequate procedures to address such an "emergency" character of measures at issue. It is contrasted to the Agreement on Subsidies and Countervailing Measures (hereinafter "SCM Agreement") for which the current DSU stipulates fast-track procedures regarding prohibited and actionable subsidies.[9] The

---

[6] *United States– Definitive Safeguard Measures on Imports of Certain Steel Products* case combined the following eight complaints: DS248, 249, 251, 252, 253, 254, 258, 259.

[7] See, for example, Henrik Horn and Petros C. Mavroidis, "United States – Safeguard Measures on Imports of Fresh, Chilled o Frozen Lamb Meat from New Zealand and Australia: what should be required of a safeguard investigation?", 2 *World Trade Review* 395 (2003).

[8] See, for example, Alan O. Sykes, "The Safeguards Mess: A Critique of WTO Jurisprudence", 2 *World Trade Review* 261-295 (2003); and Dukgeun Ahn, *Treatise on the WTO Safeguard System*, Part. IV.3 (2006, forthcoming, in Korean).

[9] Understanding on Rules and Procedures Governing the Settlement of Disputes (DSU), Appendix 2. For example, the DSU stipulates that time- periods applicable for prohibited subsidy cases shall be, roughly speaking, half the time prescribed for normal cases.

structural problem of failure to ensure procedural expediency for safeguard cases is illustrated in Table 1 that shows the duration of safeguard measures and the timing of the WTO dispute settlement.

As shown in Table 1, the ineffectiveness of the current WTO dispute settlement system is apparently serious. All of the listed WTO cases in Table 1 found the safeguard measures at issue to be inconsistent with the WTO obligation. Yet, in many cases, unjustifiable safeguard measures were maintained for a substantial period of time, which renders the resolution through the WTO dispute settlement system practically meaningless.[10] For example, in two cases – *Argentina – Footwear* case and *US – Wheat Gluten* case, the expiration dates for the original safeguard measures coincided with the due dates for the implementation periods determined by the WTO dispute settlement procedure. In the *Argentina – Peach* case, the implementation due date determined by the WTO dispute settlement procedure lapsed merely about two weeks before the original due date of the safeguard measure at issue. In the *Korea – Dairy Product* case, the WTO inconsistent safeguard measure could be maintained for more than three years despite the WTO dispute settlement resolution. In that regard, the repeal of the safeguard measures within less than two years in the *US – Steel* case was actually a rare exception.

Table 1: Timing for Safeguard Measures and Relevant WTO Dispute Settlement

	Length of Safeguard Measure	Period for Dispute Settlement[1]	The End of Implementation Period
Argentina – Footwear	3 years (97.2.25 – 00.2.25)	98.6.10 – 00.1.12	00.2.25
Argentina – Peach	3 years (01.1.19 – 04.1.18)	01.12.06 – 03.4.15	03.12.31
Chile – Price Band	1 year + 1 year extension (99.11.26 – 01.11.26)	01.1.19 – 02.10.23	03.12.23
Korea – Dairy Product	4 years (97.3.1 – 01.2.28)	98.6.10 – 00.1.12	00.5.20
US – Lamb Meat	3 years (99.7.22 – 02.7.22)	99.10.14 – 01.5.16	01.11.15
US – Line Pipe	3 years (00.2.23 – 03.2.24)	00.9.14 – 02.3.8	02.7.24 (Mutual Agreement)
US – Wheat Gluten	3 years (98.6.1 – 01.6.1)	99.6.3 – 01.1.19	01.6.2
US – Steel	4 years (02.3.20 – 06.3.20)	02.5.7 – 03.12.10	Withdrawal on 03.12.4

1) The "period for dispute settlement" in the above table is the period from the panel request to the adoption of panel/Appellate Body reports.

---

[10] Of course, the WTO dispute settlement resolution can prevent unnecessary and unjustifiable extension of a safeguard measure. But, the current WTO dispute settlement resolution whose procedures have been routinely delayed has not properly addressed "temporary" safeguard actions.

The WTO Trade Remedy System: East Asian Perspectives

Unfortunately, this problem of ineffective dispute resolution is systemic. Based on statistics of the WTO dispute settlement proceedings up to June 2005, it takes, on average, about 545 days to complete a dispute settlement proceeding from panel establishment to the adoption of the Appellate Body reports.[11] If a consultation period of the minimum 60 days and an implementation period – maximum 15 months – are added to a normal dispute settlement proceeding, it can easily be extended to two and a half years or more.[12] It implies that unjustifiable safeguard actions with a duration of two or even three years may not be properly disciplined by the current WTO dispute settlement procedure.

Figure 1: Safeguard Actions notified to the WTO as of July 2005

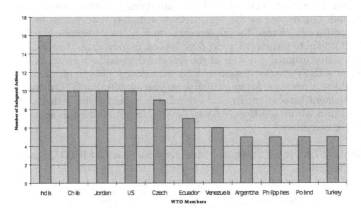

This systemic problem may partly explain why, in the WTO system, safeguard actions have been primarily abused by developing Members that have little experience in implementing safeguard systems. It is starkly contrasted to the GATT situation. During 1950 to 1995, 150 safeguard measures in total were notified to GATT. Those measures were adopted mostly by EC (43), Australia (38), US (27), Canada (23), accounting for about 87 per cent of all measures.[13] However, about 85 per cent of all safeguard actions notified to the WTO were imposed by developing country members.

As of July 2005, the major safeguard users included India (16), Chile (10), Jordan (10), Czech Republic (9), Ecuador (7) and Venezuela (6), in

---

[11] http://www.worldtradelaw.net/dsc/stats.htm (visited on June 26, 2005).

[12] In fact, the average implementation periods are about 12 months for arbitration cases under DSU Article 21.3(c) and nine months for settlement cases under DSU Article 21.3(b). http://www.worldtradelaw.net/dsc/database/implementaverage.asp (visited on June 26, 2005).

[13] WTO, Analytical Index: Guide to GATT Law, Vol I, (1996).

addition to the US (10). Other traditional main users – EC (4), Australia (1) and Canada (2) – have been relatively reluctant to use safeguard measures in the WTO system. Whereas many developing countries do not hesitate to employ questionable safeguard actions, most of those actions were simply disregarded or not bothered by other Members partly because the current WTO dispute settlement system would not effectively discipline them.

Therefore, this systemic problem should be addressed by establishing a more expeditious dispute settlement procedure, preferably in line with those already enunciated for subsidy disputes.

B.   Lack of a Legal Standing for Safeguard Investigation

Unlike the WTO Anti-dumping Agreement and SCM Agreement that provide specific legal standing requirements, the Safeguard Agreement remains silent concerning this issue.[14] Considering the fact that safeguard actions are to be based on serious injury that is a higher level of injury than material injury demanded for anti-dumping and countervailing actions, the standing requirement to ensure legitimate representativeness for a relevant domestic industry should also be mandated for a safeguard investigation at a higher level than anti-dumping and countervailing investigation.

A proper level of a standing requirement does not seem to be a matter of analytical calculation rather than political negotiation. In that regard, it is noteworthy that a draft text of Free Trade Area of the Americas (FTAA) contains "50per cent of the total production of the like or directly competitive good" as a standing requirement for the FTAA safeguard system.[15]

---

[14] Article 5.4 of Anti-dumping Agreement and Article 11.4 of SCM Agreement provide that:

> An investigation shall not be initiated pursuant to paragraph 1 unless the authorities have determined, on the basis of an examination of the degree of support for, or opposition to, the application expressed by domestic producers of the like product, that the application has been made by or on behalf of the domestic industry. The application shall be considered to have been made "by or on behalf of the domestic industry" if it is supported by those domestic producers whose collective output constitutes more than 50 per cent of the total production of the like product produced by that portion of the domestic industry expressing either support for or opposition to the application. However, no investigation shall be initiated when domestic producers expressly supporting the application account for less than 25 per cent of total production of the like product produced by the domestic industry.

[15] Article 6.4 of Chapter XIV, FTAA.TNC/W/133/Rev.3 (dated November 21, 2003).

III. Problems in Implementing the WTO Safeguard Agreement

A. Applying "Unforeseen Development" Requirement

Article XIX:1(a) of the GATT stipulates "unforeseen development" as a precondition for invoking emergency action against imports by providing that: "[i]f, as a result of unforeseen developments and of the effect of the obligations incurred by a contracting party under this Agreement, including tariff concessions, any product is being imported into the territory of that contracting party in such increased quantities and under such conditions as to cause or threaten serious injury to domestic producers in that territory of like or directly competitive products, the contracting party shall be free, in respect of such product, and to the extent and for such time as may be necessary to prevent or remedy such injury, to suspend the obligation in whole or in part or to withdraw or modify the concession."[16] After the GATT Contracting Parties in *Hatter's Fur* ruled very broadly to embrace virtually almost every circumstance for the legal requirement of unforeseen development,[17] this legal element was considered to have no practical legal meaning.[18] It was also dropped out of the textual languages of the WTO Safeguard Agreement during the Uruguay Round negotiation.

It explains primarily why even conventionally active user countries such as the United States, the European Community, Canada and Australia, do not include the "unforeseen development" provision in their most recently amended safeguard laws and regulations.[19] Therefore, many WTO Members still use *ad hoc* procedures or simply rely on practical guidelines to accommodate this element in their investigations. For example, as shown in *US – Steel*, the USTR had to request additional findings on "unforeseen development" to the USITC after the USITC issued its original final report without examining that element.[20]

---

[16] For the discussion on the conflict between economic rationale and legal principles concerning the application of "unforeseen development", see Henrik Horn and Petros C. Mavroidis, "United States – Safeguard Measures on Imports of Fresh, Chilled or Frozen Lamb Meat from New Zealand and Australia: what should be required of a safeguard investigation?", 2 *World Trade Review* 395, 406-408 (2003).

[17] *United States – Withdrawal of a tariff concession under Art. XIX* (adopted on October 22, 1951; CP/106).

[18] John H. Jackson, *World Trade and the Law of GATT* (1969), 553-574.

[19] These laws typically mandate the finding of serious injury and threat thereof, but do not mention "unforeseen development".

[20] Panel Report on *United States – Definitive Safeguard Measures on Imports of Certain Steel Products* (WT/DS248, 249, 251, 252, 253, 254, 258, 259/R; adopted on December 10, 2003), paras 1.222-1.26. The panel found no violation for the timing of the USITC's "subsequent" finding of unforeseen development since it was made before the safeguard measure was applied. But, substantively, the USITC finding of unforeseen development was found to be inconsistent with the WTO obligation.

On the other hand, the Appellate Body substantially elaborated – or complicated – the rules for applying "unforeseen development" provisions in *US – Steel*. It ruled that, in addition to confirming standard of review that requires a reasoned and adequate explanation, unforeseen development resulting in increased imports must be demonstrated for each safeguard measure at issue, rather than for overall economic circumstances. Although this interpretation may fortify the rigor of legal jurisprudence, the vast discrepancy between practices of administering authorities and unbearable legal requirements of the WTO disciplines would strengthen the need for clarifying and augmenting the current system.

B. Causality Requirement

For invoking a safeguard measure, it should be proven that "any product is being imported into the territory of that Member in such increased quantities and under such conditions as to cause or threaten serious injury to domestic producers in that territory of like or directly competitive products". In other words, there must be a causality relationship between increased imports and domestic injury. The analysis of a causality relationship, however, illuminates a vast and fundamental difference between an economic theory and a legal application. While the economic theory requires increased imports to be not merely a proximate but an ultimate cause of injury as a reasonable basis for invoking safeguard actions, the legal interpretation of causality does not fully reflect such an economic distinction.[21]

Although Article XIX of the GATT and the Safeguard Agreement do not specifically provide what kind of causality relationship should be construed, the panel in *US – Wheat Gluten* ruled that the increased imports, under the conditions extant in the market place, *in and of themselves*, caused *serious* injury.[22] Likewise, the panel in *US – Lamb Meat* determined that "increased imports must not only be *necessary*, but also *sufficient* to cause or threaten a degree of injury that is '*serious*' enough to constitute a significant overall impairment in the situation of the domestic industry".[23] In other words, the panels' views are basically primary causality between increased imports and serious injury in that import alone should be able to cause serious injury.

---

[21] See generally Douglas A. Irwin, "Causing problems? The WO Review of Causation and Injury Attribution in US Section 201 cases", 2 *World Trade Review* 297 (2003); and Henrik Horn and Petros C. Mavroidis, "United States – Safeguard Measures on Imports of Fresh, Chilled or Frozen Lamb Meat from New Zealand and Australia: what should be required of a safeguard investigation?", 2 *World Trade Review* 395 (2003).
[22] Panel Report on *United States – Definitive Safeguard Measures on Imports of Wheat Gluten from the European Communities* (adopted on January 19, 2001; WT/DS166/R), para 8.139.
[23] Panel Report on *United States – Safeguard Measures on Imports of Fresh, Chilled or Frozen Lamb Meat from New Zealand and Australia* (adopted on May 16, 2001; WT/DS177, 178/R), para 7.238.

These interpretations and rulings were reversed by the Appellate Body. The Appellate Body ruled that "the competent authorities determine [...] whether 'the causal link' exists between increased imports and serious injury, and whether this causal link involves a *genuine and substantial relationship* of cause and effect between these two elements".[24] This ruling seems to overturn completely the economic justification of safeguard measures. It has been the conventional understanding that a safeguard measure may be invoked as a safety net when import surges induced by trade liberalization cause serious domestic injury. Indeed, for example, Section 202 of the Trade Act of 1974 in the United States enunciates "substantial cause of serious injury" where substantial cause means "a cause which is important and not less than any other cause".[25] In Canada, the causality relationship between increased imports and serious injury is given as "principal cause" that is defined to be "an important cause that is no less important than any other cause of the serious injury or threat".[26] It is also noted that many recent FTAs adopt explicit provisions requiring "substantial cause" for bilateral safeguard mechanisms.

But, according to the rulings by the Appellate Body, serious injury to a domestic industry, however it happened, may be safeguarded as opposed to imports insofar as increased import has "genuine and substantial relationship" with serious domestic injury. For a rough numerical example, suppose that import accounts merely for 5 per cent of injury and that over-investment and earthquakes cause 40 per cent of injury, respectively. Pursuant to the Appellate Body interpretation, it would still be possible to invoke safeguard action if the nature of the causal relationship is genuine and substantial, whereas a safeguard action is not permitted under a panel interpretation or under the US law. If the numbers in the above example are changed to 40 per cent for import, 5 per cent for over-investment and 40 per cent for earthquake, the United States and Canada would allow a safeguard action, whereas panels in *US – Wheat* or *US – Lamb Meat* would not. A very strict standard presented by panels in *US – Wheat* or *US – Lamb Meat* would be satisfied only if import can account at least for 50 per cent or more of injury. The economic justification to permit safeguard measures for limiting importation becomes weaker in a reverse order at the above example.

---

[24] Appellate Body Report on *United States - Definitive Safeguard Measures on Imports of Wheat Gluten from the European Communities* (adopted on January 19, 2001; WT/DS166/AB /R), para. 69.
[25] US Government Printing Office, Overview and Compilation of US Trade Statutes: 2001 edition (June 2001), 664.
[26] Article 27, Canadian International Trade Tribunal Act. See WTO, G/SG/N/1/CAN/3 (dated August 10, 2004).

This unreasonable outcome is generated by the confusion of "nature" of causality and "degree" of causality. In terms of nature of causality, a genuine and substantial relationship between cause and effect seems to make a good legal sense. It is also true that, in that regard, causation and correlation share many common economic phenomena and normally go hand in hand. But, how much causal effects should be required is a question to be clarified by policy consideration for safeguard mechanisms since the textual languages do not provide any clear guidance. Unless judicial activism exercised by the Appellate Body clarifies this problem, the practical difficulty to adopt econometric analyses in legal deliberation and rulings for determining causality relationship would typically lead the Appellate Body to set forth a legal conclusion on causality that is fatally confused with "correlation".[27]

On the other hand, the Appellate Body tried to link causality requirements to a degree of safeguard measures. In *US – Line Pipe* case, the Appellate Body concluded that it would be illogical to require authorities to ensure that the "causal link" not be based on the share of injury attributed to factors other than increased imports, while at the same time permitting a Member to apply a safeguard measure addressing injury caused by all factors.[28] Therefore, the Appellate Body concluded that safeguard measures might be applied only to the extent that they address serious injury "attributed to increased imports".[29]

Even if this ruling seems very plausible in a legal sense, the application of this legal interpretation with respect to safeguard measures appears patently difficult to render it almost useless. Suppose that increased imports cause 10 per cent of serious injury for the domestic industry. The Appellate Body ruling suggests that safeguard measures in this case can only be applied to that 10 per cent injury. Contrary to its seemingly simple and clear criteria, it is not obvious how only 10 per cent of injury should be safeguarded. For example, it is not clear at all whether this 10 per cent injury justifies a safeguard action on the entire imports, or the entire increased volumes of import, or simply 10 per cent of increased volumes of imports. Let alone tremendous difficulty to quantify injury and thereby determine a proper level of a safeguard action, the conceptual ambiguity of safeguarding "injury attributed to increase imports" must be promptly resolved to prevent practical demise of legitimate safeguard measures.

[27] See also Alan O. Sykes, "The 'Safeguards Mess' Revisited – A Reply to Professor Jones", 3 *World Trade Review* 93 (2004), 96.

[28] Appellate Body Report on *United States - Definitive Safeguard Measures on Imports of Circular Welded Carbon Quality Line Pipe from Korea* (adopted on March 8, 2002; WT/DS202/AB/R), paras. 250-252.

[29] Appellate Body Report on *United States - Definitive Safeguard Measures on Imports of Circular Welded Carbon Quality Line Pipe from Korea* (adopted on March 8, 2002; WT/DS202/AB/R), paras. 260.

C.   Parallelism Doctrine

Following the NAFTA model[30], more and more FTAs including Canada-Chile FTA[31] and US-Singapore FTA[32] adopt provisions to exempt FTA parties from WTO safeguard measures. In fact, the exemption of FTA parties from the WTO safeguard actions has been persistent issues for WTO dispute settlement cases.[33]

The selective application of a safeguard measure was indeed one of the most controversial issues during the Uruguay Round negotiation.[34] But, there was no specific agreement or decision on whether Article XXIV of the GATT permits exempting FTA partners from the scope of the MFN application of safeguard measures. To address this issue, the WTO dispute settlement body has relied on invented concept of "parallelism" that requires the imports included in the injury determination to correspond to those covered by the safeguard measure. The parallelism doctrine has worked as one of the most stringent disciplines by striking down all measures reviewed so far.[35]

This parallelism doctrine, however, may create a serious loophole for the MFN application of a safeguard measure. Suppose that the country A is importing from five other countries whose exportation has individually genuine and substantial relationship with serious injury of the country A. Then, pursuant to the parallelism doctrine, the country A can exempt any – or any group – of the five trading partners from its safeguard action by matching products under the investigation and under safeguard measures. In practice, panels and the Appellate Body have adopted the most serious strict scrutiny with regard to parallelism doctrine to prevent abusive selective safeguard actions. But, meticulous preparation of Members' authorities will soon overcome the legal hurdle of parallelism doctrine.

---

[30] Article 802:1 of the NAFTA provides, in a relevant part, that:
    Any Party taking an emergency action under Article XIX or any such agreement shall exclude imports of a good from each other Party from the action unless:
    (a) imports from a Party, considered individually, account for a substantial share of total imports; and
    (b) imports from a Party, considered individually, or in exceptional circumstances imports from Parties considered collectively, contribute importantly to the serious injury, or threat thereof, caused by imports.

[31] Article F-02.

[32] Article 7.5.

[33] Four panel/Appellate Body reports, one regarding Argentine safeguard action and three US safeguard actions, addressed the "parallelism" issue.

[34] Terence P. Stewart, The GATT Uruguay Round: A Negotiating History (1986-1992), vol. II, 1711 – 1800 (1993).

[35] For example, in *US –Steel* safeguard case, the panel and the Appellate Body found the violation of parallelism doctrine for all ten safeguard measures.

The Appellate Body in *US – Line Pipe* case opined that:

> The question of whether Article XXIV of the GATT 1994
> serves as an exception to Article 2.2 of the *Agreement on
> Safeguards* becomes relevant in only two possible
> circumstances. One is when, in the investigation by the
> competent authorities of a WTO Member, the imports that
> are exempted from the safeguard measure *are not
> considered* in the determination of serious injury. The other
> is when, in such an investigation, the imports that are
> exempted from the safeguard measure *are considered* in
> the determination of serious injury, *and* the competent
> authorities have *also* established explicitly, through a
> reasoned and adequate explanation, that imports from
> sources outside the free-trade area, alone, satisfied the
> conditions for the application of a safeguard measure, as
> set out in Article 2.1 and elaborated in Article 4.2.[36]

Considering the Uruguay Round negotiating history, it is not clear whether the Appellate Body is a proper forum to decide the above question. Before the proliferating FTAs cause serious discriminatory safeguard problems, this fundamental issue must be addressed somehow in the WTO.

D.   Legal Requirement of Structural Adjustment

The crucial element of a safeguard system that has been neglected collectively by all the WTO Members is the legal requirement for implementing structural adjustment measures.   The Safeguard Agreement clarifies that any safeguard action shall be applied to the extent necessary to facilitate adjustment, not merely to remedy serious injury. Article 5 of the Safeguard Agreement provides that "[a] Member shall apply safeguard measures only to the extent necessary to prevent or remedy serious injury *and to facilitate adjustment.*" This principle is reiterated in Article 7 as follows: "A Member shall apply safeguard measures only for such period of time as may be necessary to prevent or remedy serious injury *and to facilitate adjustment.*" Moreover, an extension of a safeguard measure must be based on the evidence that the industry is actually adjusting. In other words, the legal element of facilitation of structural adjustment is one of the core parts of the WTO safeguard system.

---

[36] Appellate Body Report on *United States - Definitive Safeguard Measures on Imports of Circular Welded Carbon Quality Line Pipe from Korea* (adopted on March 8, 2002; WT/DS202/AB/R), para. 198.

Despite such a clear textual requirement, that part of legal requirement has not been seriously addressed by most of WTO Members. Administering authorities of WTO Members have rarely paid their attention to whether and how safeguard measures do facilitate structural adjustment of pertinent domestic industries.[37] In fact, this legal element – along with obvious wrongful practices of WTO Members – has never been formally raised at the WTO dispute settlement system and thereby not been elaborated by subsequent jurisprudence. Therefore, this clear legal element still remains practically dead languages. It is particularly unusual when we consider a highly strict literal approach by the Appellate Body that resuscitated even the "unforeseen development" provision.

This legal requirement indeed raises a fundamental issue regarding the safeguard system. The intrinsic character of a safeguard measure is to secure certain period of time in which temporarily protected industries can expedite structural adjustment to trade liberalization. Therefore, a more effective enforcement of the legal requirement concerning facilitation of structural adjustment would substantially contribute to refinement of the WTO safeguard system.

IV. China Specific Safeguard Action: Transitional Product-Specific Safeguard Mechanism

The accession by China to the WTO added a peculiar element to the safeguard system: Transitional Product-Specific Safeguard Mechanism (hereinafter "TPSSM"). Whereas TPSSM shares some commonality with a safeguard system, it differs fundamentally from normal safeguard mechanisms in several important aspects.

Firstly, TPSSM is invoked exclusively against China. In other words, the MFN application of safeguard measures are not required when a WTO Member invokes TPSSM against China.[38] Under the current WTO

---

[37] In most WTO Members, final rulings or recommendations by administering authorities do not even mention this legal requirement. Currently, the United States seems the only country that at least tries to enforce this legal element. For example, the USITC addressed the issue whether pertinent firms undertook structural adjustment measures in the extension case regarding wheat gluten. Although the USITC mentioned several economic facts, even the mere promises or vague future plans were accepted as sufficient evidence to demonstrate sufficiency of implementing adjustment measures. USITC, Wheat Gluten: Extension of Action (Investigation No. TA-204-4), Publication No. 3407 (April 2001).

[38] In fact, a country specific safeguard system is not unprecedented in the GATT/WO system. Similar provisions were adopted when Eastern European countries such as Hungary, Poland, and Romania joined the GATT in the 1960s and 1970s. GATT, Basic Instruments and Selected Documents, 15th Supplement (1968), 46-52; 18th Supplement (1972), 3-10; 20th Supplement (1974), 3-8. See also Fabio Spadi, "Discriminatory Safeguards in the Light of the Admission of the People's Republic of China to the world Trade Organization", 5 *Journal of International Economic Law* 421 (2002), 426-428.

system, it is the only formal mechanism to permit discriminatory safeguard actions.

Secondly, instead of "serious injury" requirement, TPSSM is invoked on the basis of "market disruption or threat thereof". Market disruption deems to exist "whenever imports of an article, like or directly competitive with an article produced by the domestic industry, are increasing rapidly, either absolutely or relatively, so as to be *a significant cause of material injury, or threat of material injury* to the domestic industry". Compared to other trade remedy cases, the threshold of "significant cause of material injury" for invoking import restriction is very lenient, particularly for safeguard actions.

Thirdly, TPSSM permits even more lenient safeguard actions to third countries for preventing "significant diversions of trade" into their markets. Unlike a direct safeguard measure by an importing country to remedy market disruption that still mandates injury determination – albeit at a much lower level, an indirect safeguard measure to remedy trade diversion by third countries does not require any injury determination. Accordingly, this aspect of TPSSM may raise much more serious chain reaction in terms of trade restriction against products from China.

Lastly, unlike normal safeguard measures, TPSSM does not have a specific time limit for measures. So, practically, it seems possible to maintain, extend or re-invoke anytime TPSSM until 2013 when this special arrangement will terminate.

This special arrangement to discriminate China in the WTO system was rapidly incorporated into many WTO Members' trade remedy systems, although there is considerable variance in technical aspects of implementing TPSSM.[39] Considering its porous structure potentially vulnerable to abusive utilization, the record up to date demonstrates remarkably prudent use – or no use – by WTO Members. In the United States, the USITC conducted four investigations, issuing three affirmative determinations[40] and one negative determination[41]. But, in all three affirmative cases, the US President declined to take actual safeguard measures since he considered that the overall social cost of imposing

---

[39] For the excellent comparison between the US and EC systems, see Marco Bronckers, "The Special Safeguards Clause in WTO Trade Relations with China: (How) Will It Work?", in WTO and East Asia: New Perspectives (eds. Mitsuo Matsushita and Dukgeun Ahn, 2004) 39-50.

[40] Pedestal Actuators from China (Investigations No. TA-421-1); Certain Steel Wire Garment Hangers from China (Investigations No. TA-421-2.1); and Certain Ductile Iron Waterworks Fittings from China (Investigations No. TA-421-4).

[41] Certain Brake Drums and Rotors from China (Investigations No. TA-421-3).

trade restrictive measures for the products at issues would prevail the benefits accruing to the protected sectors. These results are noteworthy because public interest consideration has not been such a decisive factor in the US trade remedy regimes. In July 2003, the European Commission undertook one TPSSM investigation under Regulation 427/2003, interestingly along with two parallel investigations under the normal safeguard procedure (Regulation 3285/94) and the safeguard procedure for non-market economies (Regulation 519/94).[42] Later, the European Commission withdrew the TPSSM investigation when it found that the normal safeguard procedure was sufficient to address the domestic industry injury.[43]

Despite the remarkable track record for TPSSM so far, the recent economic situation including the termination of the textile quota regime as of the end of 2004 and a growing concern on the allegedly undue exchange rate management of China appears to intensify more political pressure from domestic industries of the WTO Members to actually utilize a special protective and yet WTO consistent devise. Moreover, the bilateral pressure by China to dismantle the non-market economy provision in its WTO Accession Protocol make other Members dependent more upon TPSSM as the last resort to address imports from China. Since one Member country's invocation of a TPSSM can provoke numerous other Members' chain reaction, the concerted efforts in the multilateral context are necessary for prudent utilization.

V.   Conclusion

Despite various problems manifested in the course of implementing the current WTO safeguard mechanism, the rectification of the problems is not likely to come in the foreseeable future. Unlike other trade remedy issues, safeguard matters are not squarely addressed in the Doha Development Agenda.[44] It leaves a much more difficult task to WTO Members than amending the current text of the Safeguard Agreement. In order to sustain the whole WTO trading system with structurally deficient safeguard system, the WTO Members should exert more

[42] Marco Bronckers, "The Special Safeguards Clause in WTO Trade Relations with China: How) Will It Work?", in *WTO and East Asia: New Perspectives* (eds. Mitsuo Matsushita and Dukgeun Ahn, published by Cameron May Ltd in 2004) 39, 48.

[43] Commission Decision of 9 December 2003 terminating the transitional product-specific Safeguard proceeding concerning imports of certain prepared or preserved citrus fruits namely mandarins, etc.) originating in the People's Republic of China (2003/855/EC), OJ L323/11 (Dec. 10, 2003).

[44] The only issue raised so far in the Doha Development Agenda is about *de minimis* standard for developing countries. Venezuela proposed the modification of Article 9.1 of the current safeguard Agreement by increasing the thresholds to 7% and 15% from 3% and 9%, respectively. This proposal, however, did not obtain consensus support from Members and thereby was not accepted. WTO, G/SG/59 (dated Jan. 17, 2003).

sensible efforts to confine abusive attempts and develop reasonable standards for adequate implementation. After all, solutions for these problems are at the hands of the WTO Members.

Appendix 1. WTO Disputes Relating to the Safeguard Agreement

Name of Dispute	Complainant
1997	
1. United States - Safeguard Measure Against Imports of Broom Corn Brooms	Colombia DS78
2. Korea - Definitive Safeguard Measure on Imports of Certain Dairy Products	EC DS/98
1998	
3. Argentina - Safeguard Measures on Imports of Footwear	EC DS121
4. Argentina - Safeguard Measures on Imports of Footwear	Indonesia DS123
1999	
5. Hungary - Safeguard Measure on Imports of Steel Products from the Czech Republic	Czech Republic DS159
6. Argentina - Measures Affecting Imports of Footwear	US DS164
7. United States - Definitive Safeguard Measures on Imports of Wheat Gluten from the European Communities	EC DS166
8. United States - Safeguard Measure on Imports of Fresh, Chilled or Frozen Lamb from New Zealand	New Zealand DS177
9. United States - Safeguard Measure on Imports of Lamb Meat from Australia	Australia DS178
2000	
10. United States - Definitive Safeguard Measures on Imports of Circular Welded Carbon Quality Line Pipe from Korea	Korea DS202
11. Chile - Price Band System and Safeguard Measures Relating to Certain Agricultural Products	Argentina DS207
12. United States- Definitive Safeguard Measures on Imports of Steel Wire Rod and Circular Welded Quality Line Pipe	EC DS214
2001	
13. Chile - Price Band System and Safeguard Measures Relating to Certain Agricultural Products	Guatemala DS220
14. European Communities- Tariff-Rate Quota on Corn Gluten Feed from the United States	United States DS223
15. Chile – Provisional Safeguard Measure on Mixtures of Edible Oils	Argentina DS226
16. Chile- Safeguards on Sugar	Colombia DS228
17. Chile - Safeguard Measures and Modification of Schedules Regarding Sugar	Colombia DS230
18. Slovakia - Safeguard Measure on Imports of Sugar	Poland DS235
19. Argentina – Definitive Safeguard Measure on Imports of Preserved Peaches	Chile DS238
2002	
20. United States – Definitive Safeguard Measures on Imports of Certain Steel Products	EC DS248
21. United States – Definitive Safeguard Measures on Imports of Certain Steel Products	Japan DS249
22. United States – Definitive Safeguard Measures on Imports of Certain Steel Products	Korea DS251
23. United States – Definitive Safeguard Measures on Imports of Certain Steel Products	China DS252
24. United States – Definitive Safeguard Measures on Imports of Certain Steel Products	Switzerland DS253
25. United States – Definitive Safeguard Measures on Imports of Certain Steel Products	Norway DS254

26. United States – Definitive Safeguard Measures on Imports of Certain Steel Products	New Zealand **DS258**
27. United States – Definitive Safeguard Measures on Imports of Certain Steel Products	Brazil **DS259**
28. European Communities – Provisional Safeguard Measures on Imports of Certain Steel Products	US **DS260**
29. United States – Definitive Safeguard Measures on Imports of Certain Steel Products	Chinese Taipei **DS274**
30. Chile –Definitive Safeguard Measure on Imports of Fructose	Argentina **DS278**
2003	
31. Ecuador - Definitive Safeguard Measure on Imports of Medium Density Fibreboard	Chile **DS303**
2005	
32. European Communities - Definitive Safeguard Measure on Salmon	Chile **DS326**
33. European Communities - Definitive Safeguard Measure on Salmon	Norway **DS328**

Appendix 2. WTO Panel/Appellate Body Reports Relating to the Safeguard Agreement (1 January 1995 – 20 June 2005)

Dispute	Panel Established	Panel Report Circulated	Notice of Appeal	Panel Report Adopted	Appellate Body Report Circulated	Appellate Body Report Adopted
1. Korea - Definitive Safeguard Measure on Imports of Certain Dairy Products	22.07.98 EC WT/DS98	21.06.99 WT/DS98/R	15.09.99 WT/DS98/7	12.01.00 WT/DS98/10	14.12.99 WT/DS98/AB/R	12.01.00 WT/DS98/10
2. Argentina - Safeguard Measures on Imports of Footwear	23.07.98 EC WT/DS121	25.06.99 WT/DS121/R	15.09.99 WT/DS121/6 and Corr.1	12.01.00 WT/DS121/9	14.12.99 WT/DS121/AB/R	12.01.00 WT/DS121/9
3. United States - Definitive Safeguard Measures on Imports of Wheat Gluten from the European Communities	26.07.99 EC WT/DS166	31.07.00 WT/DS166/R	26.09.00 WT/DS166/7	19.01.01 WT/DS166/10	22.12.00 WT/DS166/AB/R	19.01.01 WT/DS166/10
4. United States - Safeguard Measures on Imports of Fresh Chilled or Frozen Lamb Meat from New Zealand and Australia	19.11.99 New Zealand WT/DS177 Australia WT/DS178	21.12.00 WT/DS177/R WT/DS178/R	31.01.01 US WT/DS177/7 WT/DS178/8	16.05.01 WT/DS177/10 WT/DS178/11	01.05.01 WT/DS177/AB/R WT/DS178/AB/R	16.05.01 WT/DS177/10 WT/DS178/11
5. United States - Definitive Safeguard Measures on Imports of Circular Welded Carbon Quality Line Pipe from Korea	23.10.00 Korea WT/DS202	29.10.01 WT/DS202/R	19.11.01 US WT/DS202/9	08.03.02 WT/DS202/13	15.02.02 WT/DS202/AB/R	08.03.02 WT/DS202/13
6. Chile – Price Band System and Safeguard Measures Relating to Certain Agricultural Products	12.03.01 Argentina WT/DS207	03.05.02 WT/DS207/R	24.06.02 WT/DS207/5	23.10.02 WT/DS207/8	23.09.02 WT/DS207/AB/R	23.10.02 WT/DS207/8
7. Argentina – Definitive Safeguard Measure on Imports of Preserved Peaches	18.01.02 Chile WT/DS238	14.02.03 WT/DS238/R	N.A.	15.04.03 WT/DS238/5	N.A.	N.A.

	03.06.02	11.07.03	11.08.03 US	10.12.03	10.11.03	10.12.03
8. United States – Definitive Safeguard Measures on Imports of Certain Steel Products	EC WT/DS248	WT/DS248/R and Corr.1	WT/DS248/17	WT/DS248/20	WT/DS248/AB/R	WT/DS248/20
	14.06.02 Japan WT/DS249	WT/DS249/R and Corr.1	WT/DS249/11	WT/DS249/14	WT/DS249/AB/R	WT/DS249/14
	14.06.02 Korea WT/DS251	WT/DS251 and Corr.1	WT/DS251/12	WT/DS251/15	WT/DS251/AB/R	WT/DS251/15
	24.06.02 China WT/DS252	WT/DS252 and Corr.1	WT/DS252/10	WT/DS252/13	WT/DS252/AB/R	WT/DS252/13
	24.06.02 Switzerland WT/DS253	WT/DS253 and Corr.1	WT/DS253/10	WT/DS253/13	WT/DS253/AB/R	WT/DS253/13
	24.06.02 Norway WT/DS254	WT/DS254 and Corr.1	WT/DS254/10	WT/DS254/13	WT/DS254/AB/R	WT/DS254/13
	08.07.02 New Zealand WT/DS258	WT/DS258 and Corr.1	WT/DS258/14	WT/DS258/17	WT/DS258/AB/R	WT/DS258/17
	29.07.02 Brazil WT/DS259	WT/DS259 and Corr.1	WT/DS259/13	WT/DS259/16	WT/DS259/AB/R	WT/DS259/16

Appendix 3. "Transitional Product-Specific Safeguard Mechanism" in the China's WTO Accession Protocol[45]

16.   Transitional Product-Specific Safeguard Mechanism

1.   In cases where products of Chinese origin are being imported into the territory of any WTO Member in such increased quantities or under such conditions as to cause or threaten to cause market disruption to the domestic producers of like or directly competitive products, the WTO Member so affected may request consultations with China with a view to seeking a mutually satisfactory solution, including whether the affected WTO Member should pursue application of a measure under the Agreement on Safeguards. Any such request shall be notified immediately to the Committee on Safeguards.

2.   If, in the course of these bilateral consultations, it is agreed that imports of Chinese origin are such a cause and that action is necessary, China shall take such action as to prevent or remedy the market disruption. Any such action shall be notified immediately to the Committee on Safeguards.

3.   If consultations do not lead to an agreement between China and the WTO Member concerned within 60 days of the receipt of a request for consultations, the WTO Member affected shall be free, in respect of such products, to withdraw concessions or otherwise to limit imports only to the extent necessary to prevent or remedy such market disruption. Any such action shall be notified immediately to the Committee on Safeguards.

4.   Market disruption shall exist whenever imports of an article, like or directly competitive with an article produced by the domestic industry, are increasing rapidly, either absolutely or relatively, so as to be a significant cause of material injury, or threat of material injury to the domestic industry. In determining if market disruption exists, the affected WTO Member shall consider objective factors, including the volume of imports, the effect of imports on prices for like or directly competitive articles, and the effect of such imports on the domestic industry producing like or directly competitive products.

5.   Prior to application of a measure pursuant to paragraph 3, the WTO Member taking such action shall provide reasonable public notice to all interested parties and provide adequate opportunity for importers, exporters and other interested parties to submit their views and evidence

[45] WTO, WT/L/432 (dated Nov. 23, 2001).

on the appropriateness of the proposed measure and whether it would be in the public interest. The WTO Member shall provide written notice of the decision to apply a measure, including the reasons for such measure and its scope and duration.

6.   A WTO Member shall apply a measure pursuant to this Section only for such period of time as may be necessary to prevent or remedy the market disruption. If a measure is taken as a result of a relative increase in the level of imports, China has the right to suspend the application of substantially equivalent concessions or obligations under the GATT 1994 to the trade of the WTO Member applying the measure, if such measure remains in effect more than two years. However, if a measure is taken as a result of an absolute increase in imports, China has a right to suspend the application of substantially equivalent concessions or obligations under the GATT 1994 to the trade of the WTO Member applying the measure, if such measure remains in effect more than three years. Any such action by China shall be notified immediately to the Committee on Safeguards.

7.   In critical circumstances, where delay would cause damage which it would be difficult to repair, the WTO Member so affected may take a provisional safeguard measure pursuant to a preliminary determination that imports have caused or threatened to cause market disruption. In this case, notification of the measures taken to the Committee on Safeguards and a request for bilateral consultations shall be effected immediately thereafter. The duration of the provisional measure shall not exceed 200 days during which the pertinent requirements of paragraphs 1, 2 and 5 shall be met. The duration of any provisional measure shall be counted toward the period provided for under paragraph 6.

8.   If a WTO Member considers that an action taken under paragraphs 2, 3 or 7 causes or threatens to cause significant diversions of trade into its market, it may request consultations with China and/or the WTO Member concerned. Such consultations shall be held within 30 days after the request is notified to the Committee on Safeguards. If such consultations fail to lead to an agreement between China and the WTO Member or Members concerned within 60 days after the notification, the requesting WTO Member shall be free, in respect of such product, to withdraw concessions accorded to or otherwise limit imports from China, to the extent necessary to prevent or remedy such diversions. Such action shall be notified immediately to the Committee on Safeguards.

9.   Application of this Section shall be terminated 12 years after the date of accession.

Journal of International Economic Law 11(1), 107–133
doi:10.1093/jiel/jgm045.   Advance Access publication 1 February 2008

Chapter 6

FOE OR FRIEND OF GATT ARTICLE XXIV: DIVERSITY IN TRADE REMEDY RULES

Dukgeun Ahn *

ABSTRACT

While the WTO Member countries continue to increase their FTA arrangements with divergent frameworks, they have begun to adopt modified WTO trade remedy systems in FTAs. Although the content and degree of these modified systems may not be significant yet, they still set very important precedents, or 'seeds', for 'rule diversification' in the world trading system. Such modification typically aims to further liberalize mutual trade between FTA parties and thereby contribute to a freer world trading system. However, such rule diversification appears to be inconsistent with the mandate of Article XXIV of GATT by worsening economically inferior trade diversion. The reinterpretation of the legal obligations in Article XXIV commensurate with economically more reasonable structures implies that trade remedy rules in FTAs should be applied on a non-discriminatory basis. Moreover, an FTA safeguard measure must precede a WTO safeguard measure to ensure optimal competitive conditions among trading partners. In sum, the right channel for improving the current WTO trade remedy systems is not the FTA forums but the WTO negotiation.

I. INTRODUCTION

Whereas positive aspects of free trade agreements (hereinafter 'FTAs')[1] to promote more trade and investment have been well taken by policy makers as well as academics, negative aspects of FTAs particularly incurred by too much diversification in rules of origin systems, in addition to trade diversion effects, have also been raised concerning proliferation of what are basically

---

* Assistant Professor of International Trade Law and Policy; Graduate School of International Studies, Seoul National University. E-mail: dahn@snu.ac.kr. I am very grateful to constructive comments on the earlier draft by Professors Mitsuo Matsushita, Locknie Hsu and Alan Deardorff. I also appreciate helpful research assistance by Jooyoung Yang and Sherzod Shadikhodjaev.

[1] In recent years, the WTO Members use many different expressions basically to mean FTAs, such as strategic economic cooperation agreement (SECA), economic partnership agreement (EPA), strategic economic partnership agreement (SEPA), economic complementarity agreement (ECA), and so on. In this article, they are generally referred to as 'FTAs'.

Journal of International Economic Law Vol. 11 No. 1 © Oxford University Press 2008, all rights reserved

146

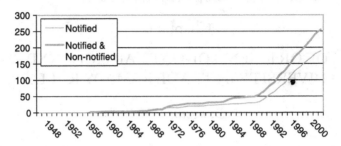

Figure 1.   Trend of FTAs: 1948–2003.

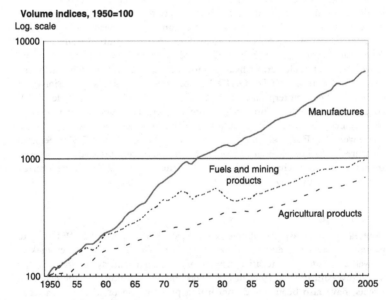

Figure 2.   Trend of sectoral trade: 1950–2005.

preferential trading arrangements.[2] These concerns have been assuaged by the paradoxical reality that an exponential increase of FTAs[3] since the 1990s—illustrated in Figure 1—has barely affected the total world trade, as shown in Figure 2.

A more recent FTA wave has, however, provoked more worrisome development. Aggressive FTA policies employed by Asian countries,

[2] See, for example, Peter Sutherland et al., *The Future of the WTO* (WTO, 2004) 19–28.
[3] WTO Secretariat, 'The Changing Landscape of RTAs' (WTO Discussion Paper, No. 8, 2003).

culminating in the Korea–US FTA, provoked even the European Union (EU) that practically abandoned FTAs since the late 1990s to reinitiate FTA negotiations, especially with Asian countries such as ASEAN, India and Korea.[4] A successful implementation of the EU's new FTA policy change would then instigate a chain reaction by other major countries such as Japan, China and the United States, and might lead to FTAs even among huge economies. In other words, unlike the situation so far, major trading countries may now begin a FTA race that can cause economically significant impacts to the world trading system.

On the other hand, many WTO Members often adopt interesting and experimental ideas in various elements of their recent FTAs. One of the most intriguing legal developments is the 'rule diversification' that emerges through the adoption of modified WTO trade remedy systems.[5] Although there have been some discussions among practitioners and academics as well as government delegations in Geneva about whether trade remedy measures may be permitted in FTAs,[6] this phenomenon of rule diversification is indeed unprecedented in the history of the GATT/WTO system.[7,8]

For example, the WTO Members have rarely tried to adopt different anti-dumping rules in FTA negotiations before the Doha Round negotiation in which rules negotiations to amend the current trade remedy systems

---

[4] 'Global Europe: Competing in the World – A Contribution to the EU's Growth and Jobs Strategy', Communication from the Commission to the Council, the European Parliament, the European Economic and Social Committee and the Committee of the Regions. http://trade.ec.europa.eu/doclib/html/130376.htm. (visited 10 May 2007). For critical assessment of the new EU trade policy, see Simon Evenett, 'Global Europe: An Initial Assessment of the European Commission's New Trade Policy', Aussenwirtschaft (December 2006), at 377–402 or Patrick Messerlin, 'Assessing the EC Trade Policy in Goods', Jan Tumlir Policy Essays 01/2007 (April 2007).

[5] This problem was already noted by Professor Jackson more than a decade ago. He opined that:

> Likewise, certain other trade policy laws and rules are not clearly addressed in the language of the GATT. For example, how does a safeguard or escape clause measure operate? Can a preferential arrangement give preferences to its preference parties in the application of an escape clause? Arguably, the answer should be yes, since the preferential group should be treated like a single trading entity. A similar argument, or problem, arises with regard to unfair trade rules (anti-dumping and countervailing duty rules), but a practice has developed of tolerating preferential agreements as long as they do not eliminate such unfair trade rules between the preference parties.

John H. Jackson, 'Perspectives on Regionalism in Trade Relations', 27 Law and Policy in International Business 873 (1996), at 876.

[6] For example, Estrella and Horlick argued that trade remedy measures must be abolished in FTAs. Their analysis is very enlightening, but not completely agreed by the view in this paper. See generally Angela T. Gobbi Estrella and Gary N. Horlick, 'Mandatory Abolition of Anti-dumping, Countervailing Duties and Safeguards in Customs Union and Free Trade Areas Constituted between WTO Members: Revisiting a Long-standing Discussion in Light of the Appellate Body's Turkey – Textiles Ruling', in L. Bartels and F. Ortino (eds), *Regional Trade Agreements and the WTO Legal System* (Oxford: Oxford University Press, 2006) 109–148.

[7] See generally Robert Teh et al., 'Trade Remedy Provisions in Regional Trade Agreements', (WTO Staff Working Paper, September 2007).

[8] WTO, *International Trade Statistics* (2006) at 26.

took one of the centre places.[9] But more FTAs, particularly involving Asian countries, have begun to adopt modified trade remedy rules that depart from the WTO systems.

FTA parties typically adopt modified WTO trade remedy systems in their FTAs in an effort to further facilitate trade between them and thereby contribute to a freer world trading system.[10] Despite such seemingly innocuous intents, however, such arrangements may cause serious economic problems by systemically inducing economically inferior trade diversion. This problem has already been manifested by many FTAs that exempt their parties from global—i.e. WTO—safeguard measures. For example, a selective application of WTO safeguard measures under the NAFTA invariably caused substantial trade diversion from other WTO Members to NAFTA parties so as to distort competitive conditions. This situation led to many WTO disputes,[11] although legal solution in the dispute settlement system was not fully satisfactory.[12]

The scholarly assessment of trade remedy rules—mostly of anti-dumping rules—has long proposed consistent legal systems to address problems in ensuring adequate competitive conditions between domestic and imported products.[13] The frequently suggested optimal solution has been to repeal anti-dumping rules and substitute them with competition rules that do not differentiate imported goods from domestic goods. In some sense, anti-dumping rules are discriminatory legal systems that do not respect the national treatment principle in terms of establishing competitive market conditions. However, we cannot conclude that even such a forceful solution to take competition policy approach always contributes to enhancing the world economic welfare if it is adopted only by subsets of WTO Members, not as a uniform standard. Or even the question whether such an approach

---

[9] For a more comprehensive analysis of restructuring the current WTO trade remedy systems, *see generally* M. Matsushita, D. Ahn and T. Chen, *The WTO Trade Remedy System: East Asian Perspectives* (London: Cameron May Publisher, 2005).

[10] For legal issues concerning coherent jurisprudence between the WTO and the RTAs, see Locknie Hsu, 'Applicability of WTO Law in Regional Trade Agreements: Identifying the Links', in L. Bartels and F. Ortino (eds), *Regional Trade Agreements and the WTO Legal System* (Oxford: Oxford University Press, 2006) 525–52.

[11] Among the NAFTA parties, the United States and Canada imposed six and one WTO safeguard measures, respectively. Four of the US measures were brought to the WTO dispute settlement system.

[12] For example, typically three year safeguard measures cannot be properly disciplined under the WTO dispute settlement system due to the period required for litigation that often takes almost three years including an implementation period. See Dukgeun Ahn, 'Restructuring the WTO Safeguard System', in M. Matsushita, D. Ahn and T. Chen (eds), *The WTO Trade Remedy System: East Asian Perspectives* (London: Cameron May Publisher, 2006) 11–31. See also William J. Davey, 'Implementation of the Results of WTO Trade', in M. Matsushita, D. Ahn and T. Chen (eds), *The WTO Trade Remedy System: East Asian Perspectives* (London: Cameron May Publisher, 2006) 32–61.

[13] For an aptly summarized overview, *see generally* Alan O. Sykes, 'Antidumping and Antitrust: What Problems Does Each Address?', in Robert Z. Lawrence (ed), *Brookings Trade Forum: 1998* (Washington: Brookings Institution Press, 1998) 1–43.

adopted in FTAs is consistent with the WTO disciplines remains unanswered. The drafting history of GATT Article XXIV does not provide any conclusive guideline on the question.[14]

This article argues that rule diversification in FTAs in terms of trade remedy systems is indeed legally inconsistent with Article XXIV requirements and economically inferior for global welfare. This conclusion is primarily based on the requirements under Article XXIV:5, instead of Article XXIV:8 which has been the focal point of discussion on the WTO consistency of FTAs. Part I summarizes the state-of-the-play of FTAs that adopt modified WTO trade remedy systems. Part II analyses the legal issues of rule diversification on the basis of Article XXIV. Part III explains economic problems incurred by modified trade remedy systems in FTAs. Part IV concludes.

II. EMERGING DIVERSITY IN TRADE REMEDY RULES

A. Anti-dumping systems for FTAs

Although most FTAs simply retain all the rights and obligations, without any change, under the WTO Anti-dumping Agreement, a few FTAs have incorporated special legal elements that are distinct from the WTO system.

Somewhat extreme cases categorically prohibit any anti-dumping measures. As the first example of this kind, Article M-01 of the Canada–Chile FTA enunciates reciprocal exemption of the application of anti-dumping laws, including the revocation of all the existing duties and the prohibition of new investigations. In recent years, EFTA advanced this approach strongly at least in terms of principles.[15] Article 16 of the EFTA-Singapore FTA stipulates that 'a Party shall not apply anti-dumping measures as provided for under the WTO Agreement on Implementation of Article VI of the GATT 1994 in relation to products originating in another Party'. Instead of anti-dumping actions, it proposed the use of necessary measures in the realm of competition policies. This approach was subsequently followed in the EFTA-Chile FTA. The competition policy approach adopted in these two FTAs—competition policy measures in lieu of anti-dumping measures to address alleged dumping problems—is noteworthy in that it is actually the first example in international trade agreements to employ competition policy solutions for dumping problems. The complete prohibition of anti-dumping measures between FTA signatories was also adopted by China for its 'Closer Economic Partnership Arrangement (CEPA)' with Hong Kong and Macao. However, CEPA merely banned anti-dumping measures as in the

---

[14] See, for example, Kerry Chase, 'Multilateralism Compromised: the Mysterious Origins of GATT Article XXIV', 5 (1) World Trade Review 1 (2006) 1–30.
[15] The European Free Trade Association (EFTA) includes Iceland, Liechtenstein, Norway and Switzerland.

Table 1. FTAs with Special Anti-dumping (AD) Rules

FTA (date of entry into force)	Special AD Rules	
	Prohibition of AD Action	Modification of AD Rules
EFTA-Singapore FTA (1 January 2003)	No AD measure allowed (Competition policy measures)	
EFTA-Chile FTA (1 December 2004)	No AD measure allowed (Competition policy measures)	
China-Hong Kong FTA (1 January 2004)	No AD measure allowed	
China-Macao FTA (1 January 2004)	No AD measure allowed	
Canada-Chile FTA (5 July 1997)	No AD measure allowed	
US-Israel FTA (19 August 1985)		Non-Cumulation
CAFTA-DR-US FTA		Non-Cumulation
Singapore-New Zealand FTA (1 January 2001)		- 5% of export price as *de minimis* margin for refund and review cases as well as new cases - 5% of import volume - 3-year sunset review
Singapore-Australia FTA (28 July 2003)		Lesser duty rule
Jordan-Singapore FTA (22 August 2005)		- 5% of export price as *de minimis* margin for new case - 5% of import volume - No third country dumping - 12-month period for injury determination - 3-year sunset review - Lesser duty rule - Prohibition of zeroing - No AD if SG imposed
Singapore-Korea FTA (1 March 2006)		- Lesser duty rule - Prohibition of zeroing
EFTA-Korea FTA (1 September 2006)		Lesser duty rule

Canada–Chile FTA, without providing an alternative solution such as competition policy measures (Table 1).

The United States and the European Union rarely touched anti-dumping provisions in their FTAs. A notable exception is the Central America–Dominican Republic–US FTA. Article 8.8 of the Central America–Dominican Republic–US FTA requires the United States to 'continue to treat each other Party as a "beneficiary country" for purposes of 19 U.S.C. §§ 1677(7)(G)(ii)(III) and 1677(7)(H) and any successor provisions', which means that in determining material injury for an anti-dumping action, the US International Trade Commission (ITC) shall not cumulatively assess the volume and effect of imports from any country designated as a beneficiary country under the Caribbean Basin Economic Recovery Act. This so-called 'non-cumulation' provision would substantially reduce the likelihood of injury determination because exportation from 'beneficiary countries' is assessed separately from that of other countries such as China and India in anti-dumping investigation.[16]

In contrast, Singapore appears to experiment with various legal elements in FTA anti-dumping systems. Article 9 of the Singapore–New Zealand FTA stipulates additional requirements to the WTO Anti-dumping Agreement 'in order to bring greater discipline to anti-dumping investigations and to minimize the opportunities to use anti-dumping in an arbitrary or protectionist manner'. Under the Singapore–New Zealand FTA, the *de minimis* dumping margin as a percentage of the export price was increased from 2% of the WTO Anti-dumping Agreement to 5% for both new investigations and review procedures. The maximum negligible volume of dumped imports was also raised from 3% of the WTO Anti-dumping Agreement to 5%. Furthermore, the sunset period was shortened to 3 years. In addition to such technical modification, Article 8.2 of the Singapore–Australia FTA mandates a 'lesser duty rule' which requires the party to impose a lower rate than a dumping margin if such a lesser duty would be adequate to remedy the injury to the domestic industry. The Jordan–Singapore FTA includes the most comprehensively modified anti-dumping system so far by including, *inter alia*, prohibition of zeroing and no third country dumping provided in Article 14 of the WTO Anti-dumping Agreement, in addition to all the elements described earlier. In fact, Article 2.8.1(h) of the Jordan–Singapore FTA stipulates a categorical prohibition of zeroing practices by providing that 'in the conduct of investigations and reviews, the margin of dumping and the resulting dumping duty based on such margin shall be calculated by strict price comparison on the basis of transaction to transaction, and weighted average to weighted average, and not weighted-average price and individual price'. Moreover, it provides that 'where weighted-average prices are used, such prices shall be calculated based on the entire period of investigation, and not any particular period therein'. It is particularly noteworthy that Article 2.8.3 of the Jordan–Singapore FTA forbids an anti-dumping investigation against a good that is subject to a safeguard measure.[17] Subsequently, Article 6.2 of the Singapore–Korea FTA adopted

---

[16] 'Non-cumulation' was first introduced by the US–Israel FTA. Although the text of the US–Israel FTA did not explicitly stipulate this exception, the non-cumulation requirement was included in Section 771(7)(G)(ii)(IV) of the US Tariff Act of 1930. See 19 U.S.C. 1676a.

[17] The parallel provision to ban a safeguard investigation for a good that is subject to an anti-dumping measure is also stipulated in Article 2.7.7 of the Jordan–Singapore FTA.

the lesser duty rule and the prohibition of zeroing.[18] The provision to prohibit zeroing practices was further simplified by enunciating that 'when anti-dumping margins are established on the weighted average basis, all individual margins, whether positive or negative, should be counted toward the average'.

The EFTA-Korea FTA also adopted the lesser duty rule. In addition, the EFTA-Korea FTA stipulates that parties 'shall endeavor to refrain from initiating anti-dumping procedures against each other' and consult 'with the other with a view to finding a mutually acceptable solution', but it does not mandate any specific additional legal requirements. In fact, the parties under the EFTA-Korea FTA shall review whether a need exists to maintain anti-dumping measures after 5 years of application. The usual approach of EFTA to replace anti-dumping measures with competition policy measures appears to be considered for adoption, *albeit* not immediately.

B. Countervailing systems for FTAs

Special countervailing systems adopted in relation to FTAs are much rarer. Even EFTA, which has recently adopted FTA rules to completely eliminate anti-dumping measures completely, has not adopted any new element to modify the WTO countervailing mechanism in their FTAs. As of July 2007, under Article 8 of the CEPA, only Hong Kong, Macao and China undertook not to apply countervailing measures to goods mutually imported and originated.[19] This arrangement under the CEPA is perfectly rational because all three entities are of the same country, eliminating the need to counteract their own subsidy programs. Other than the CEPA, there has been no FTA notified to the WTO that eliminates countervailing measures for FTA parties.

Countervailing actions that are designed to address distortion of competition by government subsidies are in fact completely different measures from anti-dumping actions that are intended to deal with private pricing behaviours. Consequently, even a competition policy solution to substitute anti-dumping actions that are economically preferred does not work for

---

[18] The 'zeroing' method has become practically prohibited through repeated rulings by the WTO panels and the Appellate Body. See WTO Panel and Appellate Body Report, *United States – Measures Relating to Zeroing and Sunset Reviews*, WT/DS322/R and WT/DS322/AB/R, adopted 23 January 2007; *United States – Laws, Regulations and Methodology for Calculating Dumping Margins ('Zeroing')*, WT/DS294/R, WT/DS294/AB/R, adopted 9 May 2006; *United States – Final Dumping Determination on Softwood Lumber from Canada*, WT/DS264/R, WT/DS264/AB/R, adopted 31 August 2004, WT/DS264/RW, WT/DS264/AB/RW, adopted 1 September 2006.

[19] The textual languages of the 'Closer Economic Partnership Arrangement' between China and Hong Kong and Macao are identical.

countervailing cases in which government subsidies arbitrarily distort competitive conditions. In other words, the seemingly contradictory approach by EFTA to maintain the WTO countervailing system in its FTAs is not actually unreasonable.

Nevertheless, it is difficult to understand why even FTAs which modify technical elements of anti-dumping investigations do not adopt fundamentally identical elements in practically identical parts of countervailing investigations. For example, the lesser duty rule, if adopted by a WTO Member, is in fact applied equally for anti-dumping and countervailing investigations in its domestic trade remedy system. However, the lesser duty rule has been explicitly codified only in the anti-dumping part, not in the countervailing part of FTAs. The lack of consistent procedures parallel to those of anti-dumping systems might be understood only as the result of arbitrary judgment of negotiators rather than by any rational explanation.

On the other hand, Article 2.9 of the EFTA-Korea FTA requires at least a 30-day period for mutual consultation before parties can initiate countervailing investigations. It is an additional requirement, *albeit* weak, to the WTO disciplines that merely require the notification of a decision to initiate an investigation. Similarly, Article 10.7 of the Korea–US FTA also requires a consultation opportunity preceding the initiation of an investigation.[20]

C. FTA safeguard mechanism

Unlike anti-dumping and countervailing systems, most FTAs adopt FTA-specific bilateral safeguard mechanisms to suspend a concession temporarily in case serious injury or threat thereof is caused to domestic industry. Although the exact natures of bilateral safeguard measures vary considerably depending upon FTAs, they share the common feature that the concession only under an FTA can be temporarily suspended against an FTA party. It should therefore be noted that the MFN tariff rates bound in the WTO become the maximum ceiling for bilateral FTA safeguard measures. In addition, many FTAs introduce sector-specific safeguard systems, typically for agricultural and textile industries.

On the other hand, following the NAFTA approach, increasingly more countries in recent years have sought to exempt the other FTA parties from

---

[20] The consultation requirement may be particularly weak in its binding nature with the United States where the procedural due process of trade remedy actions is rigorously enforced. For a more detailed discussion on the implication of the Korea–US FTA trade remedy systems, see generally Dukgeun Ahn, Analysis of Trade Remedy Systems in the Korea–US FTA (in Korean, 2007).

the application of global—i.e. WTO—safeguard actions. Article 802 of the NAFTA stipulates that:

> ...any Party taking an emergency action under Article XIX or any such agreement *shall* exclude imports of a good from each other Party from the action unless:
>
> (a) imports from a Party, considered individually, account for a substantial share of total imports; and
> (b) imports from a Party, considered individually, or in exceptional circumstances imports from Parties considered collectively, contribute importantly to the serious injury, or threat thereof, caused by imports.

The exclusion of FTA parties from the WTO safeguard coverage had been previously adopted in MERCOSUR, for which Article 98 of the Common Regulation stipulates that imports from member states of the customs union must be excluded from safeguard measures.[21] Fundamentally identical provisions were adopted in the Canada–Chile FTA.[22] These FTAs stipulate a 'duty' to exclude FTA parties from WTO safeguard actions if the pertinent legal requirements are satisfied.

A similar—but legally distinctive—approach to exclude FTA parties was adopted in other FTAs. For example, the Singapore–US FTA 'permits' a party taking a global safeguard measure to exclude imports of an originating good from the other party 'if such imports are not a substantial cause of serious injury or threat thereof'.[23] The textual language for exemption became weaker by providing that 'a Party taking a global safeguard measure *may* exclude imports of an originating good from the other Party'. By replacing 'shall' with 'may' in the relevant provision, these FTAs transform a 'duty' to exclude parties into a 'right' for parties to exempt the application. This system was subsequently adopted in many FTAs involving the United States, including the Australia–US FTA, the Central America–Dominican Republic–US FTA, the Korea–US FTA and so on. Table 2 shows that the US government appears to have adopted this provision almost as a template for its recent FTAs. In fact, Canada, Mexico and Israel were all excluded under such provisions when the US government imposed the global safeguard action on lamb meat, which led to a WTO dispute.[24] Israel and

---

[21] The Treaty of Asunción and the Common Regulation, adopted by Decision 17/96 of the Common Market Council.

[22] Article F-02, Canada–Chile Free Trade Agreement, http://www.dfait-maeci.gc.ca/tna-nac/cda-chile/chap-f26-en.asp. (visited 10 June 2007).

[23] Article 7.5, Singapore–US FTA, http://www.fta.gov.sg/fta/pdf/FTA_USSFTA_Agreement_Final. pdf. (visited 10 May 2007).

[24] WTO Panel Report, *US – Safeguard Measures on Imports of Fresh, Chilled or Frozen Lamb Meat from New Zealand and Australia*, WT/DS177, 178/R, adopted 16 May 2001, para. 2.8.

Table 2. FTAs with Special Safeguard (SG) Rules

FTA (date of entry into force)	Special SG Rules	
	Prohibition/Exclusion	Sectoral SG
MERCOSUR (29 November 1991)	Must exclude	
NAFTA (1 January 1994)	Shall exclude	Agriculture
Canada-Chile FTA (5 July 1997)	Shall exclude	
Jordan-Singapore FTA (22 August 2005)	May exclude (no SG if AD imposed)	
Thailand-Australia FTA (1 January 2005)	May exclude	- Agriculture
Thailand-New Zealand FTA (1 July 2005)	May exclude	- Agriculture
US-Israel FTA (1 September 1985)	May exclude	
US-Jordan FTA (17 December 2001)	May exclude	
US-Singapore FTA (1 January 2004)	May exclude	- Textiles
US-Australia FTA (1 January 2005)	May exclude	- Agriculture
CAFTA-DR-US FTA (not yet)	May exclude	- Agriculture - Textiles
Korea-US FTA (not yet)	May exclude	- Agriculture - Textiles
Singapore-New Zealand FTA (1 January 2001)	Prohibition of SG	
Singapore-Australia FTA (28 July 2003)	Prohibition of SG	

Jordan were similarly excluded from the global safeguard action related to the steel industry, which was also later contested in a WTO dispute.[25]

Singapore went further in its FTAs in terms of modifying the WTO safeguard system. Article 8 of the Singapore–New Zealand FTA categorically prohibits any safeguard measure within the meaning of the WTO Agreement on Safeguards. Article 9 of the Singapore–Australia FTA also similarly prohibits such WTO safeguard measures. In other words, unlike other FTAs that shall or may exclude a FTA party only under certain circumstances, these FTAs involving Singapore always exclude the FTA parties from WTO safeguard actions, irrespective of underlying economic situations.

There are various peculiar elements in different FTA safeguard systems. For example, Article 3.12 of the Korea–Chile FTA sets forth a special safeguard system for agricultural goods in case an import increase causes or threatens to cause serious injury or 'market disturbance'.[26] Although 'serious injury' and 'threat of serious injury' are defined in line with the WTO Safeguard Agreement, the concept of 'market disturbance' in the context of the safeguard system is not enunciated specifically in the FTA text and is completely unprecedented in the jurisdiction of both countries. The absence of a clear definition of the 'market disturbance' element for safeguard actions has raised concern about serious controversy in the actual application of

---

[25] WTO Panel Report, *US – Definitive Safeguard Measures on Import of Certain Steel Products,* WT/DS248, 249, 251, 252, 253, 254, 258, 259/R, adopted 10 December 2003, para. 1.19.

[26] This provision was reflected in the amendment of the 'Laws on Investigation of Unfair Trade and Safeguard' as Article 22.3 in Korea. Public Law 7093 (promulgated 20 January 2004).

the provision. However, this element was not yet elaborated by more concrete guidelines or criteria in either country.[27]

In the case of the Japan–Singapore FTA, Article 18.7 mandates a domestic judicial review procedure for safeguard actions, which is currently lacking in the WTO Safeguard Agreement. Article 2.7.5(b) of the Jordan–Singapore FTA also provides judicial review procedures for injury determination. Moreover, Article 2.7.7 of the Jordan–Singapore FTA stipulates that no bilateral safeguard investigation shall be initiated against a good that is the subject matter of an anti-dumping measure. This provision, however, does not explain how to coordinate exclusive application of anti-dumping measures with safeguard actions.[28]

The typical FTA bilateral safeguard system has shown two important departures—good and bad—from the WTO Safeguard Agreement.[29] First, a bilateral safeguard action can be taken normally based on a 'substantial' causation requirement.[30] This substantial causation requirement for safeguard actions appeared most notably in the NAFTA, and since then it has become a norm in most subsequent FTAs concluded not only by the United States but also by many other countries, where their domestic safeguard regulations require mere 'causation' pursuant to the WTO Safeguard Agreement instead of 'substantial causation'. This is indeed an important and desirable legal development because it is an indication that, WTO Members which are not subject to such a higher legal requirement, as in the United States and Canada whose domestic safeguard regulations mandate 'substantial' or 'principal' causation, have begun to adopt an economically more suitable legal element through FTAs. Secondly, bilateral safeguard systems do not generally include the 'facilitation of structural adjustment' requirement that must be a quintessential element necessary to maintain safeguard actions. It is contrasted with the WTO Safeguard Agreement, which explicitly mandates the application of a safeguard measure 'only to the extent necessary . . . to facilitate adjustment', although this legal requirement

---

[27] For example, in Korea, Article 22.3 of the Law on Investigation of Unfair Trade and Safeguard was elaborated by Article 22.3 of the Implementing Regulation (Presidential Order 18565, promulgated and entered into force 21 October 2004). However, the Implementing Regulation did not clarify the concept of 'market disturbance' either.

[28] It remains unclear whether a safeguard investigation will be reinitiated once an anti-dumping measure is expired or repealed while the safeguard measure is still enforced.

[29] Dukgeun Ahn, above n 12, at 17–19. See also Dukgeun Ahn, 'Trade Remedy System in East Asian Free Trade Agreements', in Y. Taniguchi, A. Yanovich and J. Bohanes (eds), *The WTO in the Twenty First Century: Dispute Settlement, Negotiations and Regionalism in Asia* (Cambridge: Cambridge University Press, 2007) 423–33.

[30] Yet, there are some FTAs that still incorporate a mere causation requirement instead of substantial causation. For example, Thailand has not adopted a substantial causation requirement. In any case, 'causation' issues have raised many controversial problems in the WTO jurisprudence. See Alan O. Sykes, *The WTO Agreement on Safeguards: A Commentary* (Oxford: Oxford University Press, 2006) 156–74; Alan O. Sykes, 'The Safeguards Mess: A Critique of Appellate Body Jurisprudence', 2 World Trade Review 261 (2003); Dukgeun Ahn, above n 12.

has been almost completely ignored in the WTO safeguard jurisprudence and practice.[31] Codification of legally inconsistent practices by formally deleting the 'facilitation of structural adjustment' requirement in FTA safeguard systems should be rectified to prevent further deterioration of the WTO safeguard mechanism.

III. LEGAL ISSUES UNDER GATT ARTICLE XXIV

The question of whether trade remedy systems are allowed by Article XXIV along with the listed provisions such as Articles XI, XII, XIII, XIV, XV and XX has been neither clearly answered nor decided by the GATT/WTO.[32] Nonetheless, the WTO Members have routinely adopted and sometimes modified the WTO trade remedy rules in their FTAs, leaving the permissibility question practically pointless. The legal boundary of Article XXIV has been scrutinized by many scholarly studies, but most analyses of Article XXIV have specifically addressed the implications for duties or import tariffs, which are not directly applicable to trade remedy rules.[33] In fact, the interpretation that the term 'duties' might encompass trade remedy measures cannot be supported by a more comprehensive consideration of GATT texts, especially the French and Spanish versions using the terms of 'droits de douane' and 'derechos de aduana', which are directly translated into 'customs duties'.[34]

On the other hand, the wording of 'other restrictive regulations of commerce' should be understood to embrace trade remedy measures that are typically imposed to restrict imports as a border measure.[35] In fact, the panel in *Turkey–Textiles* interpreted 'other regulations of commerce' very broadly to include any regulation having an impact on trade such as SPS, TBT and anti-dumping as well as environmental standards or export credit schemes.[36] A legal analysis of the provisions related to 'other restrictive regulations of commerce' seems to suggest the WTO inconsistency of diversification in terms of trade remedy rules as explained below.

---

[31] See Dukgeun Ahn, above n 12, at 21–2.

[32] WTO, TN/RL/W/8/Rev.1, paras. 73–7 (dated 1 August 2002). See also WTO, WT/REG/W/ 37, 18 (dated 2 March 2000).

[33] For example, WTO, *Analytical Index: Guide to GATT Law and Practice*, Vol. 2 (WTO, 1995), 800–07. See also Raj Bhala, *Modern GATT Law: A Treatise on the General Agreement on Tariffs and Trade* (London: Thomson Sweet and Maxwell, 2005), 566–614; John H. Jackson, *World Trade and the Law of GATT* (Indianapolis: Bobbs-Merrill, 1969), 575–623.

[34] A. Estrella and G. Horlick, above n 6, at 117–8.

[35] Ibid, at 118–21. See generally James H. Mathis, 'Regional Trade Agreements and Domestic Regulation: What Reach for 'Other Restrictive Regulations of Commerce'?, in L. Bartels and F. Ortino (eds), above n 6.

[36] WTO Panel Report, *Turkey – Restrictions on Imports of Textile and Clothing Products*, WT/DS34/ R, adopted 19 November 1999, para. 9.120.

A. Article XXIV:8

Article XXIV:8 stipulates the requirement for customs union and free-trade area as follows:

> 8. For the purposes of this Agreement:
>
> (a) A customs union shall be understood to mean the substitution of a single customs territory for two or more customs territories, so that
>
> > (i) duties and other restrictive regulations of commerce (except, where necessary, those permitted under Articles XI, XII, XIII, XIV, XV and XX) are eliminated with respect to substantially all the trade between the constituent territories of the union or at least with respect to substantially all the trade in products originating in such territories, and,
> >
> > (ii) subject to the provisions of paragraph 9, substantially the same duties and other regulations of commerce are applied by each of the members of the union to the trade of territories not included in the union;
>
> (b) A free-trade area shall be understood to mean a group of two or more customs territories in which the duties and other restrictive regulations of commerce (except, where necessary, those permitted under Articles XI, XII, XIII, XIV, XV and XX) are eliminated on substantially all the trade between the constituent territories in products originating in such territories.

Article XXIV:8 explicitly lists 'Articles XI, XII, XIII, XIV, XV and XX' as potential areas of exception for customs unions or FTAs. In contrast, other provisions—particularly Article VI and XIX, which provide trade remedy rules under GATT—are not included in the listed exception scope for duties and other restrictive regulations of commerce. Consequently, the question of whether a trade remedy measure might be maintained between parties of a customs union or FTA critically hinges on the exhaustiveness of the listed exception provisions in Article XXIV:8.

Despite unclear evidence from the negotiating history of Article XXIV, an overly narrow scope of listed provisions in the exception parenthesis of Article XXIV:8 seems to indicate that they are not an exhaustive list. For example, it would be inconceivable that all trade restrictions imposed on the basis of national security exceptions under Article XXI must be eliminated between FTA parties.[37] Moreover, because 'other restrictive regulations of commerce' including anti-dumping, countervailing and safeguard measures are to be eliminated with respect to 'substantially all',[38]

---

[37] Joost Pauwelyn, 'The Puzzle of WTO Safeguards and Regional Trade Agreements', 7 Journal of International Economic Law 109 (2004) at 126–7.

[38] There are two conflicting approaches to interpret 'substantially all the trade': quantitative and qualitative approach. See WTO, WT/REG/W/37, 21 (dated 2 March 2000). Despite the 'Understanding on the Interpretation of Article XXIV of GATT' which mentions the

not 'all' or 'completely all' the trade between parties,[39] the current practices to restrict imports under the trade remedy systems should be permitted by understanding that predominant parts of trade not subject to trade remedy actions between parties can still constitute 'substantially all the trade'.[40] In other words, although those listed provisions are wholly exempted from the liberalization requirement for 'substantially all the trade', the possibility of trade remedy actions between parties of customs union or free-trade areas that can be, by nature, used only under certain circumstances and also for a limited period of time would be regarded as the permitted realm of trade restriction even under customs unions or free-trade areas. The historical evidence related to the US–Canada FTA, which became the basis of Article XXIV text, also seems to suggest that the requirement to liberalize 'substantially all the trade', instead of total trade, was deliberately drafted to preserve anti-dumping and countervailing measures against Canadian goods.[41] In conclusion, the absence of Articles VI and XIX in the exception parenthesis might still be interpreted not to categorically prohibit trade remedy rules from customs unions or FTAs.

B. Article XXIV:5

Whereas Article XXIV:8 provides the definitions of a customs union and an FTA that imply the kind of measures permitted within the ambit of a regional trade agreement (hereinafter 'RTA'), Article XXIV:5 stipulates external requirements for an RTA which demand the consideration of an economic effect. Article XXIV:5 provides the following:

(a) with respect to a customs union, or an interim agreement leading to a formation of a customs union, the duties and other regulations of commerce imposed at the institution of any such union or interim agreement in respect of trade with contracting parties not parties to such union or agreement shall not on the whole be higher or more

---

exclusion of any major sector of trade as the diminution to the expansion of world trade, this issue has remained contentious. Ibid, at 21. On the other hand, the panel and the Appellate Body in the *Turkey–Textile* case agreed that the term 'substantially all' encompassed both quantitative and qualitative components. WTO Appellate Body Report, *Turkey – Restrictions on Imports of Textile and Clothing Products (Turkey – Textile)*, WT/DS34/AB/R, adopted 19 November 1999, para. 49.

[39] The Appellate Body in the *Turkey–Textile* case also explained that 'substantially all the trade' is not the same as all the trade and therefore Article XXIV:8(a)(i) offers 'some flexibility' to constituent members of a customs union when liberalizing their internal trade. Ibid, at para. 48.

[40] This view is also shared by other scholars. See, for example, Pauwelyn, above n 37, at 109. See also Won-Mog Choi, 'Regional Economic Integration in East Asia: Prospect and Jurisprudence', 6 Journal of International Economic Law 49 (2004), at 67–9.

[41] Kerry Chase, 'Multilateralism Compromised: The Mysterious Origins of GATT Article XXIV', 5 (1) World Trade Review 1 (2006), at 17.

restrictive than the general incidence of the duties and regulations of commerce applicable in the constituent territories prior to the formation of such union or the adoption of such interim agreement, as the case may be;

(b) with respect to a free-trade area, or an interim agreement leading to the formation of a free-trade area, the duties and other regulations of commerce maintained in each of the constituent territories and applicable at the formation of such free-trade area or the adoption of such interim agreement to the trade of contracting parties not included in such area or not parties to such agreement <u>shall not be</u> higher or <u>more restrictive</u> than the corresponding duties and other regulations of commerce existing in the same constituent territories prior to the formation of the free-trade area, or interim agreement as the case may be

This external requirement for RTAs, especially that other regulations of commerce shall not be more restrictive than those of pre-RTAs, embraces an economic concern that an RTA should not entail trade diversion effects. It is noteworthy that, although Article XXIV:4 also addresses the same aspect of the economic concern by stipulating that the purpose of RTAs 'should be to facilitate trade' between parties and 'not to raise barriers to the trade of other contracting parties', Article XXIV:5 stipulates a more direct and independent legal obligation.[42]

On the other hand, it is important to discern that mere trade diversion effects on balance may not make pertinent RTAs inconsistent with Article XXIV:5.[43] By the very nature of a preferential market access created by RTAs would trade diversion be unavoidable—in some cases, even to a considerable extent. In this regard, it is noted that Article XXIV:5 prescribes the different legal conditions for duties and other regulations of commerce: 'not higher' for the former and 'not more restrictive' for the latter. The requirement not to adopt higher post-FTA duties for non-party countries is easier to understand and implement because the application can be evidently verified through the numerical comparison. In other words, the market access condition in terms of tariffs set out in Article XXIV:5 can be satisfied when FTA parties do not increase their tariff levels as opposed to non-party members.

However, the requirement not to apply more restrictive regulations of commerce does demand *de facto* as well as *de jure* analysis. To put it

---

[42] In the first legal analysis to apply such an economic rationale, Professor Dam recommended a 'creative reinterpretation' of Article XXIV:4. Kenneth W. Dam, 'Regional Economic Arrangements and the GATT: the Legacy of a Misconception', 30 University of Chicago Law Review 615 (1963), at 633.

[43] James H. Mathis, *Regional Trade Agreements in the GATT/WTO: Article XXIV and the Internal Trade Requirement* (The Hague: Springer, 2002), 112.

differently, the legality of other regulations of commerce in respect of Article XXIV:5 might be determined not only by *ex ante* evaluation of structures of regulations but also by *ex post* assessment of trade effects. Nevertheless, whether this part of the legal obligations in Article XXIV:5 sanctions preferential trade remedy rules is not yet obvious.

In relation to the above inquiry, paragraph 2 of the *Understanding on the Interpretation of Article XXIV of the GATT 1994* (hereinafter '*Understanding on Article XXIV*') adopted by the Uruguay Round negotiation elaborates on Article XXIV:5 as follows:

> The evaluation under paragraph 5(a) of Article XXIV of the general incidence of the duties and other regulations of commerce applicable before and after the formation of a customs union shall in respect of duties and charges be based upon an overall assessment of weighted average tariff rates and of customs duties collected. This assessment shall be based on import statistics for a previous representative period to be supplied by the customs union, on a tariff-line basis and in values and quantities, broken down by WTO country of origin. The Secretariat shall compute the weighted average tariff rates and customs duties collected in accordance with the methodology used in the assessment of tariff offers in the Uruguay Round of Multilateral Trade Negotiations. For this purpose, the duties and charges to be taken into consideration shall be the applied rates of duty. It is recognized that for the purpose of the overall assessment of the incidence of other regulations of commerce for which quantification and aggregation are difficult, the examination of individual measures, regulations, products covered and trade flows affected may be required.

As emphasized in the above, the *Understanding on Article XXIV* countenances case-by-case assessment for 'other regulations of commerce', although it stipulates relatively articulated rules related to duties.[44] It does not, however, clarify specific criteria to examine each factor listed in the last sentence of the paragraph.

In a rare case that directly reflects the application of Article XXIV, the Appellate Body held that consistency with Article XXIV:5 requires an economic test to assess the effects of the resulting trade measures and policies of the new regional agreement:

> 54. With respect to "other regulations of commerce", Article XXIV:5(a) requires that those applied by the constituent members *after* the formation of the customs union "shall *not* on the whole be...*more restrictive* than the *general incidence*" of the regulations of commerce that were applied by each of the constituent members *before* the formation of the customs union. Paragraph 2 of the *Understanding on Article XXIV* explicitly recognizes that the quantification and aggregation of regulations of commerce other than

---

[44] For a more detailed analysis of the Understanding on Article XXIV, R. Bhala, above n 33, at 596–600.

duties may be difficult, and, therefore, states that "for the purpose of the overall assessment of the incidence of other regulations of commerce for which quantification and aggregation are difficult, the examination of individual measures, regulations, products covered and trade flows affected may be required."

55. We agree with the Panel that the terms of Article XXIV:5(a), as elaborated and clarified by paragraph 2 of the *Understanding on Article XXIV*, provide:

> ...that the effects of the resulting trade measures and policies of the new regional agreement shall not be more trade restrictive, overall, than were the constituent countries' previous trade policies.

and we also agree that this is:

> an "economic" test for assessing whether a specific customs union is compatible with Article XXIV.[45]

As quoted in the above ruling, the Appellate Body explained that Article XXIV:5 requires the evaluation of not merely the form but the effects of trade policy measures of the new RTAs. In particular, the Appellate Body emphasized the recommendation enunciated in the preamble of the *Understanding on Article XXIV*:

> 57. According to paragraph 4, the purpose of a customs union is "to facilitate trade" between the constituent members and "not to raise barriers to the trade" with third countries. This objective demands that a balance be struck by the constituent members of a customs union. A customs union should facilitate trade within the customs union, but it should *not* do so in a way that raises barriers to trade with third countries. We note that the *Understanding on Article XXIV* explicitly reaffirms this purpose of a customs union, and states that in the formation or enlargement of a customs union, the constituent members should "to the greatest possible extent avoid creating adverse affects on the trade of other Members". Paragraph 4 contains purposive, and not operative, language. It does not set forth a separate obligation itself but, rather, sets forth the overriding and pervasive purpose for Article XXIV which is manifested in operative language in the specific obligations that are found elsewhere in Article XXIV.[46]

Although the preambular language of the *Understanding on Article XXIV* does not stipulate binding legal duty, the recommendation to avoid creating adverse effects, to the greatest possible extent, on the trade of other Members sets out an important principle in interpreting and applying Article XXIV:5.

---

[45] WTO, above n 38, paras. 54–5.
[46] Ibid, at para. 57.

Therefore, based on the interpretation of the Appellate Body regarding Article XXIV:5, other regulations of commerce, including trade remedy rules, in FTAs should avoid adverse economic effects on other Member countries. This requirement provides an important implication for FTA negotiations. Despite innocuous intent by FTA parties to further liberalize or facilitate trade between them, preferential arrangement of trade remedy systems in FTAs would inevitably entail substantial trade diversion towards FTA parties.[47] Although non-discriminatory application of trade remedy rules would generally restore competitive conditions for exporters after the relevant measures are actually imposed, preferential application of trade remedy rules for FTA parties would substantially distort competitive conditions in favour of parties. In other words, preferential application of trade remedy rules would constitute a systemic distortion by creating a more trade-restrictive mechanism against non-party Members, which is inconsistent with the legal duty under Article XXIV:5. This interpretation of Article XXIV:5 would forbid FTA parties from creating any preferential arrangement in terms of trade remedy rules, including not just partial modification of the rules but also complete elimination of trade remedy actions between FTA parties which appears to have been a preferred solution.

As a case in contrast, suppose that an FTA includes trade remedy systems to the disadvantage of FTA parties as opposed to non-party Members. For example, suppose that a country currently applying a lesser duty rule concludes an FTA that forbids such a rule. Consequently, this country applies a lesser duty rule to all other WTO Members except for an FTA party. This arrangement is at least not inconsistent with Article XXIV:5 requirement because it is not 'more trade restrictive' to non-party Members. However, such an arrangement would in any case not be politically feasible during the FTA negotiation.

The critical difference between duties and other regulations of commerce in terms of legal obligations is that the former is typically the subject matter for negotiation to balance market access conditions whereas the latter tends to involve domestic regulatory reforms having an implication for competitive conditions. Therefore, a relatively more stringent obligation for other regulations of commerce might be understood as the system to ensure an equal competitive environment of a market in which market access arrangement is implemented.

In conclusion, under the mechanism of Article XXIV:5, the only legally viable solution for an FTA trade remedy system is either to adopt the WTO

---

[47] The discussion in the Committee on RTA also raised this point as early as 1998. Japan argued that an RTA adopting competition policy measures rather than anti-dumping measures would cause trade distorting effects. See WTO, WT/REG/W/28 (dated 28 July 1998).

trade remedy system *en bloc* or to apply trade remedy rules adopted by FTAs to all WTO Members so that FTA parties can still ensure non-discriminatory application of trade remedy rules. Only then would competitive conditions for other WTO Members remain to be no more trade restrictive after the conclusion of FTAs. The obligation of Article XXIV:5 to avoid trade distorting effects thus requires basically non-discriminatory application of trade remedy measures.

C. Non-discrimination requirement in AD/SCM agreement

Both the WTO Anti-dumping and Subsidy Agreement specify the non-discrimination principle. Article 9.2 of the AD Agreement requires that 'when an anti-dumping duty is *imposed* in respect of any product, such anti-dumping duty shall be *collected* in the appropriate amounts in each case on a non-discriminatory basis on imports of such product from all sources found to be dumped and causing injury'. This provision appears to prohibit discriminatory application of anti-dumping measures. Indeed, on the basis of this non-discrimination principle, some authorities refrained from imposing anti-dumping duties when they had convincing evidence that the domestic industry filed a selective application against certain countries while excluding other countries despite a *prima facie* case of injurious dumping.[48]

However, it should be noted that the non-discrimination principle in Article 9.2 of the Anti-dumping Agreement only applies to the collection, not the imposition, of anti-dumping duties. In fact, this article was inherited from Article 8.2 of the Tokyo Round Anti-dumping Code while the corresponding text of the Kennedy Round Code provided that 'such anti-dumping duty shall be *levied* in the appropriate amounts in each case on a non-discriminatory basis'. In a general procedure for an anti-dumping action, a dumping margin is first assessed and then an anti-dumping duty is imposed or levied. Only after the imposition of an anti-dumping duty would the duty be actually collected. Based on this procedure, a Member would be able to comply with Article 9.2 by non-discriminatorily collecting the anti-dumping duties even if the duties themselves are levied discriminatorily based on the preferential trade remedy rules.[49]

---

[48] Edwin Vermulst, *The WTO Anti-dumping Agreement: A Commentary* (Oxford: Oxford University Press, 2005), 173.

[49] The European Communities imposed anti-dumping duties on imports of hot-rolled coils originating in India, Taiwan and Serbia and Montenegro, but not on imports from Egypt, Slovakia and Turkey, although the investigation led to positive proposals. India brought a complaint against the European Communities based on discriminatory application of anti-dumping measures. The European Communities settled the case by terminating the anti-dumping measures for all pertinent countries. WTO, *European Communities – Anti-dumping Duties on Certain Flat Rolled Iron or Non-Alloy Steel Products from India*, WT/DS313/2 (dated 27 October 2004). This is the only case so far in which an actual discriminatory anti-dumping measure was challenged in the dispute settlement system.

In this regard, it is noteworthy that Article 19.3 of the SCM Agreement stipulates that 'when a countervailing duty is *imposed* in respect of any product, such a countervailing duty shall be *levied* in the appropriate amounts in each case on a non-discriminatory basis on imports of such product from all sources found to be subsidized and causing injury'. This provision was identically adopted from the Tokyo Round SCM Code.

This discrepancy between the Anti-dumping and Subsidy Agreement has never been a serious issue in the GATT/WTO system.[50] The intent of negotiators during the Tokyo Round to change the provision was not known, either. A practical implication from this change is that the US government could render preferential treatment in terms of an anti-dumping investigation for Israel by applying the non-cumulation provision and still comply with disciplines under the Anti-dumping Code. As already explained, no WTO Member has adopted preferential countervailing rules in FTAs. For that reason, it is necessary to loosen the legal requirement in the SCM Agreement. It might explain why Article 19.3 of the SCM Agreement still maintains a more stringent legal provision. It appears that this seemingly minor change in the WTO Anti-dumping Agreement might provide—intentionally or inadvertently—a legal cover to accommodate a potentially preferential and discriminatory application of anti-dumping measures.

D. Non-discrimination in safeguard agreement

Whether a WTO Member may exclude an FTA party from its WTO safeguard measures has been a focal point of controversy regarding the WTO safeguard system.[51] Despite the clear provision in Article 2.2 that safeguard measures shall be applied to a product being imported irrespective of its source, Article XXIV of GATT has been referred to as a possible justification to deviate from such a non-discrimination principle. In fact, footnote 1 of the WTO Safeguard Agreement provides that '[n]othing in this Agreement prejudges the interpretation of the relationship between Article XIX and paragraph 8 of Article XXIV of GATT 1994', suggesting that selective safeguard application was deliberately left unresolved during the Uruguay negotiation.

On the other hand, the following ruling of the Appellate Body in the Turkey–Textile case seems to indicate that selective or discriminatory

---

[50] There seems to be no formal record from the relevant committees of the GATT or the WTO of a discussion of this difference. This issue has not been raised in the Doha Rules negotiation, either.

[51] See, for example, J. Pauwelyn, above n 37, at 109–42; A. Sykes, above n 30, at 232–36.

safeguard application might not satisfy the requirements under Article XXIV[52]:

> 58. Accordingly, on the basis of this analysis of the text and the context of the chapeau of paragraph 5 of Article XXIV, we are of the view that Article XXIV may justify a measure which is inconsistent with certain other GATT provisions. However, in a case involving the formation of a customs union, this "defence" is available only when two conditions are fulfilled. First, the party claiming the benefit of this defence must demonstrate that the measure at issue is introduced upon the formation of a customs union that fully meets the requirements of sub-paragraphs 8(a) and 5(a) of Article XXIV. And, second, that party must demonstrate that the formation of that customs union would be prevented if it were not allowed to introduce the measure at issue. Again, *both* these conditions must be met to have the benefit of the defence under Article XXIV.

Therefore, any measure allegedly introduced for the formation of an RTA should satisfy both timing and necessity requirements. Even if the provision to exclude a FTA party from safeguard actions might arguably meet the timing requirement, it seems very unlikely for such a selective safeguard application to satisfy the necessity requirement elaborated by the Appellate Body.[53]

Moreover, as explained earlier, the interpretation of Article XXIV:5 particularly commensurate with an economic test emphasized by the Appellate Body also indicates that Article XXIV cannot be the basis of selective application of WTO safeguard measures. An adverse trade diversion effect induced by the preferential application of a measure is particularly severe in the case of safeguard measures. Consequently, exclusion of FTA parties from the scope of WTO safeguard actions would constitute a 'more trade restrictive' measure that violates Article XXIV:5.[54]

IV. ECONOMIC IMPLICATION OF DISCRIMINATORY TRADE REMEDY RULES

While preferential arrangement of trade remedy rules in FTAs typically aims to further facilitate trade between the constituent parties, it may aggravate already serious trade diversion problems.[55]

---

[52] WTO, above n 38, at para. 58.

[53] A. Sykes, above n 30, at 236.

[54] This conclusion disagrees with Pauwelyn's argument that exclusion of FTA parties should be possible in the current WTO system. However, he also indicated that the trade diversion effect occurring to non-party countries might tilt his conclusion on justifiability of selective safeguard application on the basis of Article XXIV:4 instead of Article XXIV:5. J. Pauwelyn, above n 37, at footnote 60.

[55] The balance between trade creation and trade diversion effects of RTAs has long been the subject of economic debates on efficiency and desirability of RTAs. See generally J. Bhagwati et al., *Trading Blocs: Alternative Approaches to Analyzing Preferential Trade Agreements* (Cambridge: MIT Press, 1999). Such economic consideration was also discussed in the

This problem has been widely recognized regarding safeguard measures, which has provoked serious controversy since the Tokyo Round negotiation.[56] The major problem of selective application of safeguard measures rests on the fact that such application of safeguard measures often results in substantial change of import sources instead of import volumes. As illustrated in the *US–Line Pipe* case, the exclusion of NAFTA parties from US safeguard measures resulted in import reduction mainly from Korea that was the historically largest exporter but, at the same time, significant increase of import from Mexico to leave overall import roughly unchanged.[57]

The current practice for selective safeguard measures by FTAs is especially devised and structured to create inefficient trade diversion. For example, NAFTA stipulates that imports of a good from each other Party are excluded from the action unless imports from a party, considered individually, account for a substantial share of total imports. Suppose that the United States has three different trading partners for a steel product in addition to Canada and Mexico. In the case that the US International Trade Commission finds that six trading partners are to be subjected to safeguard measures, whereas imports from Canada and Mexico are to be excluded since they do not account for a substantial share of total imports, the underlying economic reason may well be that producers in Canada and Mexico are relatively less efficient and competitive and thereby occupy only small shares of the total imports. In this situation, the selective application of safeguard measures to exclude Canada and Mexico from the import restriction merely shifts import sources from more efficient non-NAFTA countries to less-efficient NAFTA producers.[58]

To the contrary, when NAFTA parties are not excluded since they are indeed major import sources, the safeguard measures tend to address industry injury more reasonably by covering all imports—especially major

---

legal interpretation of Article XXIV in early GATT years. See, for example, Kenneth W. Dam, *The GATT: Law and International Economic Organization* (Chicago: University of Chicago Press, 1970) 274–95; J. Jackson, above n 33, 575–623.

[56] Gilbert R. Winham, *International Trade and the Tokyo Round Negotiation* (Princeton: Princeton University Press,1986) 197–200 and 240–7.

[57] Mexico actually became the largest exporter after the imposition of - indeed, exemption from - the safeguard measure. WTO Panel Report, *United States - Definitive Safeguard Measures on Imports of Circular Welded Carbon Quality Line Pipe from Korea*, WT/DS202/R, adopted 8 March 2002, para. 4.26. For a more general empirical evidence of trade diversion effects to non-FTA parties caused by selective safeguard actions, see Chad P. Bown and Rachel McCulloch, 'The WTO Agreement on Safeguards: An Empirical Analysis of Discriminatory Impact', in Michael G. Plummer (ed.), *Empirical Methods in International Trade: Essays in Honor of Mordechai Kreinin* (Cheltenham: Edward Elgar Publishing, 2004), 145–68.

[58] Until September 2007, the US government imposed six safeguard measures. Among them, except for only one case in which broom corn brooms from Mexico was not excluded, all five cases excluded imports from Canada and Mexico based on the NAFTA provisions. For the broom case, see WTO, G/SG/N/10/USA/1 (dated 6 December 1996).

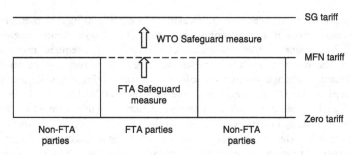

Figure 3. Sequential safeguard structure.

causes of injury. Another problem in this case is that an industry injury mainly incurred by FTA parties should be addressed by a FTA safeguard measure, not by a WTO safeguard measure whose MFN application requirement may restrict too much importation including economically innocuous imports from non-party Members. However, in the current NAFTA model, an FTA party basically has an option to choose between FTA and WTO safeguard measures. Considering the common structure of FTA safeguard measures that permit only the restoration to MFN tariff levels, an FTA party has little incentive to confine its safeguard protection by invoking an FTA safeguard mechanism in such a situation. It probably explains why there has been no case reported so far for the invocation of an FTA safeguard measure despite quite a few WTO safeguard measures.

Given such trade diversion or distortion effects by interplay of FTA and WTO safeguard systems, a more economically reasonable mechanism to maintain an FTA safeguard system by the WTO Members is to mandate an FTA safeguard action before a WTO safeguard action is permitted. When a domestic industry is seriously injured or threatened thereof by import increases, an FTA safeguard measure, if available, must be invoked first to restore an MFN competitive environment for importation. A WTO safeguard measure should be permitted only after an FTA safeguard action turns out to be ineffective to fully remedy industry injury problems. As illustrated in Figure 3, this sequential application of safeguard actions would be able to address industry injury caused by import increases more directly and reasonably through gradual constraints for importation. Furthermore, a sequential safeguard application that begins with an FTA safeguard action and follows with a WTO safeguard action would minimize potential trade diversion to respect legal obligations under Article XXIV:5.

A similar trade diversion problem also occurs in relation to anti-dumping systems as explained in Figure 4. Suppose that Country I imports a gadget from three WTO Members, A, B and C when the domestic market price is $100. Export prices and normal values for each Member are as shown in Figure 4, indicating that all exporters are currently engaged in dumping

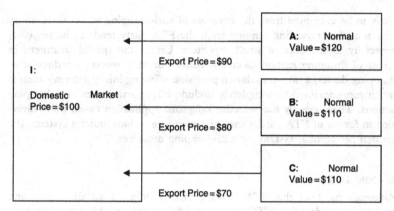

Figure 4. Trade diversion case by preferential anti-dumping action.

exportation. In a normal situation without applying a lesser duty rule, Country I would impose anti-dumping duties of $30, $30 and $40 for Country A, B and C, respectively, to make up for the dumping margins that are the difference between normal values and export prices. The competitive conditions among exporters are restored with anti-dumping duties that make normal values actual competing prices in Country I.

But, suppose that Countries I and A establish an FTA arrangement in which both countries agree on a lesser duty rule. In that case, Country I can impose the anti-dumping duty of only $10 to address the injury margin, not the dumping margin of $30, against Country A. So, the market price— including anti-dumping duty—for gadgets from A in Country I would be $100, whereas the prices for B and C be $110. Therefore, the preferential anti-dumping system under the FTA can also seriously distort competitive conditions among competitors, causing potentially substantial adverse effects on non-party countries. In other words, distortion, rather than restoration, of competitive conditions can induce substantial trade diversion. Considering the fact that competitive conditions among exporters critically hinge on relative competitive advantages, distortion caused by preferential trade remedy systems may have considerable economic implication in a real economy. The difference from the safeguard situation is that at least distortion caused in terms of dumping calculation tends to be random exclusively depending on the FTA arrangement rather than systemically aggravating economic inefficiency as in a FTA safeguard situation.

On the other hand, the non-cumulation provision currently adopted under the CAFTA-DR-US FTA may be regarded as a parallel provision of selective safeguard application in the anti-dumping system. When an import from an FTA party is separated from—i.e. not cumulated on—other countries' exportation for the purpose of injury determination, the FTA party is very likely to be exempted from the coverage of anti-dumping action since injury determination regarding imports from the FTA party tends to be negative, especially in the case of small exporters. Unlike the special treatment in terms of dumping margin calculation that normally works to reduce anti-dumping duties, a non-cumulation provision affecting injury determination is much more inclined to completely exclude FTA parties from anti-dumping actions. Then, exactly like selective safeguard application cases, trade diversion in favour of FTA parties may become more serious under a systemically created preferential system for anti-dumping measures.

V. CONCLUSION

Although most of the RTAs have primarily adopted all the rights and obligations under the WTO trade remedy system, modified models have begun to emerge in recent FTA negotiations. It is indeed noteworthy that such a 'rule diversification' in terms of trade remedy systems permeates into FTAs of some of the key players in the world trading system. Codification of such diversified rules at an international level might constitute important precedents for future trade negotiations and ultimately affect the development of the WTO trade remedy system.

A particularly disturbing aspect of the recent 'rule diversification' phenomenon is that FTA parties have a strong incentive to agree on preferential trade remedy rules because trade between parties will be further advantaged as opposed to non-party WTO Members. Furthermore, the less efficient or competitive is an FTA party compared to non-party WTO Members, the greater does the consequent adverse trade diversion effect tend to be. There are concerns that this problem may be utilized in future FTA negotiations as one of the major instruments to motivate negotiating partners. Therefore, rule diversification problems recently observed may have much more serious potential to spread over future FTA regimes. It appears that rule diversification in terms of trade remedy systems might be another channel to deepen a prisoner's dilemma situation for WTO Members facing FTA negotiations, which will result in a complex distorting mechanism only to worsen world economic welfare.[59]

The core problem of rule diversification lies in the creation of another method to wield a discriminatory authority which is structured to favour inefficient FTA parties at the expense of more efficient non-party WTO Members. Fortunately, actual trade diversion has not been substantially materialized on the basis of emerging preferential application of trade

---

[59] The risk of undermining trade rules founded on the MFN principle was forcefully raised even in some of very early analyses on the GATT system. For example, Professor Jackson wrote that '[p]erhaps no case is more revealing of the danger of preferential arrangements contrary to Most-Favored-Nation creeping into GATT through the ambiguity of Article XXIV'. J. Jackson, above n 33, 609.

remedy rules. A future risk, however, seems much more real when major exporting countries with keen interests for trade remedy systems including China, Japan and Korea are engaging actively in FTA negotiations even between themselves.

The implication of the analysis above makes us turn back to the WTO for addressing FTA trade remedy problems. The usual argument in favour of FTAs as opposed to the WTO in terms of market access appears to be forcefully applied to the trade remedy negotiation: FTA forums are preferred to experiment or adopt various reform proposals for WTO rules negotiations that seem too slow to generate tangible achievement in the near future.[60] Despite their innocuous intent to facilitate more intra-FTA trade, it is the WTO that should still be the place to undertake restructuring of the trade remedy rules for the world trading system unless any modified rules adopted through FTAs apply to all WTO Members on a non-discriminatory basis.

[60] It should be noted that even market access is not the area where RTA negotiations make significant improvement because market access for services as well as agricultural sectors has not been substantially enhanced beyond the WTO commitment levels under the most RTA arrangements.

Journal of International Economic Law 14(2), 329–368
doi:10.1093/jiel/jgr015

Chapter 7

COUNTERVAILING DUTY AGAINST CHINA: OPENING A PANDORA'S BOX IN THE WTO SYSTEM?

Dukgeun Ahn* and Jieun Lee**

ABSTRACT

In this article, we trace the jurisprudential history of the applicability of US countervailing duty (CVD) law to non-market economies (NMEs). We describe how, since the USA reversed its long-standing policy of not imposing CVDs on NMEs, concurrent application of antidumping (AD) duties and CVDs has become the country's major trade remedy action against China. Although the WTO panel rejected China's claim of WTO-inconsistency regarding the current US practices, the US Court of International Trade firmly ruled that the Department of Commerce's double counting of AD duties and CVDs against China violates domestic regulation. Finally, the WTO Appellate Body ruled that this 'double remedy' violates the rule to levy CVDs 'in the appropriate amounts' under Article 19.3 of the Agreement on Subsidies and Countervailing Measures. We will argue that, although the Appellate Body's ruling is praiseworthy in preventing an illogical practice, its legal reasoning may give rise to some doubts and controversy when the negotiating history of Article 19 is examined. We will also analyze key features of current double remedy practices in the USA and Canada.

I. INTRODUCTION

The recent global economic crisis poses unique challenges for the world trading system, especially for the Sino-American trade relationship. The USA and the People's Republic of China (China) are held most responsible for the massive global economic imbalances, which are thought to have bred the recent financial crisis itself. The position of the USA as the 'world's biggest spender and borrower' and China as the 'world's biggest saver and

*Associate Professor of International Trade Law and Policy, Graduate School of International Studies/Law School, Seoul National University; Visiting Fellow, Institute of International Economic Institute, Georgetown Law Center. E-mail: dahn@snu.ac.kr.
**Research Associate, Center for International Commerce and Finance, Seoul National University; Ford School of Public Policy, University of Michigan. E-mail: leejieun@umich.edu.
We are very grateful to useful comments by and support of by John H. Jackson, Christopher Parlin, Nohyoung Park, Sungjoon Cho, Julia Ya Qin, Mark Herlihy, Jennifer Hawkins, William J. Moon, and two anonymous referees.

173

330   *Journal of International Economic Law (JIEL) 14(2)*

lender' has continually created not only global trade asymmetry but also irritation of the US government.[1] Statistics show that US–China trade balances have been continually widening, specifically in the 2000s, until slight improvements were made in 2009.[2] However, even the latest turnover was due to reduced US imports rather than growth of its exports, and signs of even sluggish recovery seem clouded.

While the Obama administration pushes hard its $787 billion stimulus package and its recent 'National Export Initiative' to improve current conditions, it appears that the trade imbalances will be difficult to resolve without China's 'cooperation'.[3] In the midst of the recession, China surpassed Germany as the world's top exporter in 2009 and Prime Minister Wen Jiabao has become blunter in defending the Chinese currency, which has been at the center of US-China trade tensions.[4] These developments have brought forth strident calls from US Congress Members and economists to correct the alleged unfair trade practices by China and its currency manipulation.[5]

---

[1] One Hundred Eleventh Congress–First Session, *2009 Report to Congress of the US – China Economic and Security Review Commission* (Washinton DC, November 2009), at 3. For the recent account of US-Sino trade conflicts, see Gary Hufbauer and Jared Woollacott, *Trade Disputes between China and the United States: Growing Pains So Far, Worse Ahead?*, PIIE Working Paper Series 10–17 (December 2010).

[2] US Census Bureau, http://www.census.gov/foreign-trade/balance/c5700.html (visited 13 December 2010).

[3] See The American Recovery and Reinvestment Act of 2009 enacted by the One Hundred Eleventh US Congress in 13 February 2009. The Act followed other economic recovery legislations passed in the final year of the Bush presidency including the 'Economic Stimulus Act of 2008' and the 'Emergency Economic Stabilization Act of 2008' which created the 'Troubled Assets Relief Program'. The stimulus was intended to create jobs and promote investment and consumer spending during the recession. See also the 'Executive Order-National Export Initiative' issued on 11 March 2010, available at http://www.whitehouse.gov/the-press-office/executive-order-national-export-initiative (visited 20 January 2011).

[4] The emergence of China as the leading exporter in the world drew much public attention. See, e.g. Steven Mufson, 'China Surpasses Germany as World's Top Exporter', http://www.washingtonpost.com/wp-dyn/content/article/2010/01/10/AR2010011002647.html (visited 11 January 2010); Michael Wines, 'Chinese Leader Defends Currency and Policies', http://www.nytimes.com/2010/03/15/world/asia/15china.html (visited 14 March 2010); and BBC News, 'China Denies Currency Undervalued', http://news.bbc.co.uk/2/hi/8566597.stm (visited 14 March 2010).

[5] The US Congress has been pressuring the Obama administration to levy duties on Chinese imports if China does not revalue the renminbi. The Peterson Institute for International Economics (PIIE) estimates that the Chinese renminbi is undervalued by between 20% and 40%. Meanwhile, Paul Krugman, Nobel Prize winning economist, has been hitting hard on China's currency manipulation debate. See, e.g. Paul Krugman, 'Taking on China', http://www.nytimes.com/2010/03/15/opinion/15krugman.html (visited 14 March 2010); and Paul Krugman, 'Capital Export Opinion, Elasticity Pessimism, and the Renminbi (Wonkish)', http://krugman.blogs.nytimes.com/2010/03/16/capital-export-elasticity-pessimism-and-the-renminbi-wonkish (visited 16 March 2010). On the other hand, there are opposing views on taking legal actions against China based on foreign exchange policies. See, e.g. Robert Staiger and Alan Sykes, 'Currency Manipulation and World Trade', 9 World Trade Review 4, 583–627 (2010); and Simon Evenett (ed.), *The US-Sino Currency Dispute: New Insights from Politics, Economics and Law* (London: Centre for Economic Policy Research, 2010).

Various US efforts of directly pressuring China to revalue its currency, however, have not yet brought about any amicable solutions.

In this regard, one of the most notable trade remedy responses to China has been the US Department of Commerce's (DOC) reversal of its conventional policy of not applying the countervailing duty (CVD) law to non-market economies (NMEs).[6] This event shortly followed the outcry of the US Congress on China's currency manipulation and led to multiple trade remedy actions intended to slow down the firestorm of Chinese imports.[7]

Prior to this change, the USA, even as the most frequent user of countervail relief, did not approve of using CVDs against NME countries.[8] NMEs were entirely exempted from the coverage of the CVD law based on the theory that pervasive state control in these economies made it impossible to establish an effective benchmark against which the Department of Commerce could measure whether a particular government action created a countervailable subsidy. The normal practice of the DOC regarding transitional economies has been to not apply CVDs until the agency grants market economy status to those countries.[9] China, still classified as a NME, has

---

[6] The only statutory guideline for defining a non-market economy (NME) is provided in the Tariff Act of 1930, 19 USC § 1677(18), as amended (hereinafter, 'the Act'). This section, which appears in the context of an antidumping regulatory scheme, defines a non-market economy as follows:

> [A]ny foreign country that the administering authority determines does not operate on market principles of cost or pricing structures, so that sales of merchandise in such country do not reflect the fair value of the merchandise.

By making the determination a matter of discretion for the US administering authority, the statute grants a significant amount of flexibility to the US Department of Commerce (DOC). The decision made by the DOC remains effective until revoked by that authority and is excluded from judicial review.

The current list of countries designated as NMEs for purposes of the US trade remedy laws include Armenia, Azerbaijan, Belarus, Georgia, the Kyrgyz Republic, Moldova, the People's Republic of China, the Socialist Republic of Vietnam, Tajikistan, Turkmenistan and Uzbekistan.

[7] The US subprime mortgage crisis broke out on 2 April 2007, hallmarked by the bankruptcy of the New Century Financial Corporation, which used to be the second biggest US subprime mortgage company. It spread from the real estate market to the credit market, and proceeded to evolve into a global financial crisis. The US DOC's policy reversal soon followed on 9 April 2007, with its preliminary affirmative countervailing duty (CVD) determination on *Coated Free Sheet Paper* originating from China. See *Coated Free Sheet Paper from the People's Republic of China: Amended Preliminary Affirmative Countervailing Duty Determination*, 72 US Federal Register 17484 (Department of Commerce, 9 April 2007) (*Coated Free Sheet Paper case*).

[8] The United States is the most frequent user of countervailing actions in the World Trade Organization (WTO) system. Since the inception of the WTO until 30 June 2010, the United States has initiated a total of 104 CVD investigations. WTO, 'Countervailing Initiations: By Reporting Member 01/01/1995 – 30/06/2010', http://www.wto.org/english/tratop_e/scm_e/cvd_init_rep_member_e.pdf (visited 4 December 2010).

[9] In a CVD case involving exports from Hungary, the US DOC determined that subsidies provided by a transitional country, before its status changed to a market economy, are not subject to the US CVD law. See *Final Affirmative Countervailing Duty Determination: Sulfanilic Acid from Hungary*, 67 US Federal Register 60223 (Department of Commerce, 25 September 2002).

become the first target country against which US CVD measures have been applied, disregarding the nature of its economy.[10] The policy shift was significant and sweeping, and it brings about many questions.

The next section provides an overview of a jurisprudential history of the applicability of US CVD law to NME countries. Specifically, we discuss several backbone cases that ruled that CVD law did not apply to NMEs, and then we compare these cases with the *Coated Free Sheet Paper* case, which hallmarked the DOC's paradigm shift. Section Three examines the current state of CVD actions against China, primarily by the USA and Canada. Section Four highlights potential challenges of the US CVD actions and analyzes legal issues concerning the recent World Trade Organization (WTO) panel and the Appellate Body decisions.

II. JURISPRUDENTIAL HISTORY OF THE APPLICABILITY OF US CVD LAW TO NMES

The US statute allows CVDs to offset injurious subsidization and the country has become the heaviest user of countervail relief in the world trading system.[11] However, it had been the DOC's long-standing policy not to apply countervailing measures against NMEs. Only recently has the DOC reversed its policy to investigate and apply CVDs to NME countries.

A. Backbone cases for the non-application of US CVD law to NMEs

1. Textiles, apparel and related products from China
The first attempt to apply the CVD law against a NME country was undertaken in September 1983. The American Textile Manufacturers Institute, the Amalgamated Clothing and Textile Workers Union and the International Ladies' Garment Workers Union, on behalf of the US textile and clothing industries, filed a petition alleging subsidization of textiles and apparel

---

[10] In the antidumping case involving lined papers from China in August 2006, the DOC held the view that market forces in China are not yet sufficiently developed to permit the use of prices and costs in that country for purposes of the dumping analysis. See generally, *China's Status as a Non-Market Economy*, Memorandum (30 August 2006) in the lined paper investigation. This view was dramatically changed in March 2007 when the DOC found that 'market forces now determine the prices of more than 90 per cent of products traded in China' and these market forces are sufficiently developed to evaluate whether a particular alleged subsidy 'constitutes a distortion in the normal allocation of resources.' See, *Countervailing Duty Investigation of Coated Free Sheet Paper from the People's Republic of China – Whether the Analytical Elements of the Georgetown Steel Opinion are Applicable to China's Present-Day Economy*, Memorandum (29 March 2007) at 5.

[11] The US CVD authority is 19 USC § 1671(a). According to WTO statistics, from January 1, 1995 to 30 June 2009, the USA initiated 94 CVD investigations out of a total of 226 cases reported, and amongst those, ordered 57 measures out of the 113 effective cases worldwide. Statistics are available at http://www.wto.org/english/tratop_e/scm_e/cvd_init_rep_member_e.pdf and http://www.wto.org/english/tratop_e/scm_e/cvd_meas_rep_member_e.pdf (visited 23 January 2011).

exported from China.[12] However, the petition was withdrawn on the day the DOC was scheduled to issue its preliminary determination. As a result, the legal question of whether CVD law applies to NMEs was never formally addressed. Yet the attempt stirred the US government to take measures that would reduce its textile imports from China.[13]

2. Carbon steel wire rod from Czechoslovakia and Poland

On 23 November 1983, only two months after the textile industry's filing against China, four US steel manufacturers—Atlantic Steel Company, Continental Steel Company, Georgetown Steel Corporation and Raritan Steel Company—filed a CVD petition on behalf of the US industry producing carbon steel wire rod. Petitioners alleged that the manufacturers and exporters in Czechoslovakia and Poland received benefits which constituted 'bounties or grants' under the countervailing law.[14]

Since the earlier CVD investigation of textiles and apparel from China was terminated, the DOC had its 'first opportunity to determine preliminarily whether practices by a government of a so-called NME country confer countervailable benefits.'[15] The two main jurisdictional questions of the preliminary investigation were (i) whether section 303 of the Tariff Act of 1930 applied to NME countries and (ii) whether government activities in a NME conferred a 'bounty or grant' within the meaning of section 303. Regarding the former, the DOC preliminarily held that NME countries are not exempt *per se* from the CVD law. The final determination upheld its former ruling which was 'correctly addressed' based on a narrow reading of section 303, focusing on the phrase that the CVD law can be applied to '*any country*, dependency,

---

[12] See *Initiation of Countervailing Duty Investigations; Textiles, Apparel, and Related Products from the People's Republic of China*, 48 US Federal Register 46600 (Department of Commerce, 13 October 1983).

[13] The American textile industry withdrew its petition only after receiving assurance from the US government that it would take measures to reduce import. In effect, the American textile industry was considerably benefited from the mere filing of a CVD petition. See Michael G. Egge, 'The Threat of United States Countervailing Duty Liability to the Newly Emerging Market Economies in Eastern Europe: A Snake in the Garden?', 30 Virginia Journal of International Law 953 (1990) and Stanislaw J. Soltysinski, 'The US Import Relief Laws and Trade with Centrally Planned Economies', 3 Florida Journal of International Law 59 (1987), at 66. See also Alan F. Holmer and Judith H. Bello, 'US Trade Law and Policy Series #7: The Countervailing Duty Law's Applicability to Nonmarket Economies', 20 International Lawyer 319 (1986), at 322.

[14] See *Carbon Steel Wire Rod from Czechoslovakia; Preliminary Negative Countervailing Duty Determination*, 49 US Federal Register 6773 (Department of Commerce, 23 February 1984); *Carbon Steel Wire Rod from Czechoslovakia; Final Negative Countervailing Duty Determination*, 49 US Federal Register 19370 (Department of Commerce, 7 May 1984); *Carbon Steel Wire Rod from Poland; Preliminary Negative Countervailing Duty Determination*, 49 US Federal Register 6768 (Department of Commerce, 23 February 1984); and *Carbon Steel Wire Rod from Poland; Final Negative Countervailing Duty Determination*, 49 US Federal Register 19374 (Department of Commerce, 7 May 1984).

[15] See *Carbon Steel Wire Rod from Czechoslovakia; Preliminary Negative Countervailing Duty Determination*, 49 US Federal Register 6773-74 (Department of Commerce, 23 February 1984).

colony, province, or other political subdivision of government.'[16] Regarding the latter jurisdictional question, the DOC concluded that 'bounties or grants' within the meaning of section 303 could not be found in the two cases.[17] Whereas the preliminary determination limited the decision to the two particular cases of Czechoslovakia and Poland, the final determination reconsidered this question in a more general context.[18]

In the preliminary procedure, the DOC analyzed the programs in two stages: (i) whether the programs would confer a subsidy in a market economy and (ii) whether its first conclusion would be different for a NME country. Accordingly, the agency first reasoned that the multiple exchange rate systems, currency retention schemes, trade conversion coefficients for official exchange, tax exemption payments and price equalization mechanisms of Czechoslovakia and Poland do not confer bounties or grants either in market economies or in NMEs.[19] On such a basis, the DOC preliminarily determined that, while Congress did not essentially exempt NME countries from the CVD law, the alleged practices of Czechoslovakia and Poland did not constitute a provision of bounties or grants within the meaning of the CVD law.

In arriving at the final conclusion, the DOC sought more economic and definitional rationality of the existence of subsidies in a NME using a variety of sources, including Congressional guidance, and US governmental and academic sources. The DOC took the stand that government activities in a NME cannot confer a subsidy because a subsidy, by definition, means an act which distorts the operation of a market. It reasoned that it is theoretically and practically impossible to determine a subsidy in a NME country, which is subject to central planning rather than market forces. The DOC summarized the methodological problems it faced in these cases as follows:

> We believe a subsidy (or bounty or grant) is definitionally any action that distorts or subverts the market process and results in a misallocation of resources.... In NMEs, resources are not allocated by a market. With varying degrees of control, allocation is achieved by central planning. Without a market, it is obviously meaningless to look for a misallocation of resources caused by subsidies. There is no market process to distort or subvert.... It is a fundamental distinction–that in a NME system the government does not interfere in the market process but supplants it–that has led us to conclude that subsidies have no meaning outside the context of a market economy.[20]

---

[16] See *Carbon Steel Wire Rod from Czechoslovakia; Final Negative Countervailing Duty Determination*, 49 US Federal Register 19370-71 (Department of Commerce, 7 May 1984).
[17] Ibid.
[18] See *Carbon Steel Wire Rod from Poland; Final Negative Countervailing Duty Determination*, 49 US Federal Register 19374-75 (Department of Commerce, 7 May 1984).
[19] Amongst, trade conversion coefficients for official exchange and tax exemption programs for foreign trade earnings were programs specific to Czechoslovakia whereas the price equalization mechanism was that a program specific to Poland.
[20] See *Carbon Steel Wire*, above n 16, at 19372.

Based upon the legislative history of the CVD law and general international trade law, the DOC concluded that Congress 'never has confronted directly the question of whether the countervailing duty law applies to NME countries.'[21] Since Congress enacted the first generally applicable CVD law in section V of the Tariff Act of 1897, the statutory language of a 'bounty or grant' had remained substantially unaltered through several subsequent revisions. The growing importance of imports from NMEs had not changed the situation, and Congress had not taken any action to adapt the concept of a 'bounty or grant' to deal with the unique problems posed by imports from NMEs.

In 1974, and again in 1979, Congress undertook actions to address the problem of unfair trade practices with respect to imports from NME countries. Yet the option of applying the CVD law to NMEs was never raised. Rather, Congress turned to two other trade remedy measures for dealing with this problem. Specifically, in the Trade Act of 1974, Congress amended section 205 of the Antidumping Act of 1921 to establish rules to administer unfair competition from NME countries.[22] Congress also enacted section 406, a special 'market disruption' rule in the Trade Act of 1974, in order to protect US industries from trade harms caused by Communist countries.[23]

Likewise, Congress did not amend any CVD provisions in the Trade Agreement Act of 1979, in which Congress substantially revised the US CVD law. Although Article 15 of the very Act, implementing the Subsidies and Countervailing Code of the General Agreement of Tariffs and Trade (GATT), explicitly permitted to regulate unfairly priced imports from NME countries under either antidumping or countervailing duty legislation, Congress remained silent about the CVD track. Instead, Congress reenacted the special provision of the antidumping law governing NME country cases.

Accordingly, the Comptroller General of the DOC, in a study report to Congress, concluded that it is only 'remotely possible' to identify and classify subsidies in NMEs.[24] Academic guidance also advised that the CVD law could not be applied to NME countries. For instance, Professor John H. Barcelo III stated that 'if a nonmarket economy exporting country is involved, most of the analysis used thus far for both export and domestic subsidies, is entirely inapplicable.... Theoretically, any given sale may be subsidized or not, but since there is no market reference point, it is idle to speak in such terms.'[25]

---

[21] Ibid, at 19373.

[22] See 773(c) of the Tariff Act of 1930, 19 USC § 1677b(c) (1982).

[23] See 19 USC § 2436 (1974).

[24] See Comptroller General of the USA, *Report to the Congress of the United States: US Laws and Regulations Applicable to Imports from Nonmarket Economies Could Be Improved* (1981), at 32.

[25] John H. Barcelo, 'Subsidies and Countervailing Duties Analysis and a Proposal', 9 Law and Policy in International Business 779 (1977), at 850.

These reasonings led the DOC to finally conclude that, as a matter of law, section 303 was inapplicable to NMEs. Since the DOC determined both Czechoslovakia and Poland to be NME countries, it issued, effective 7 May 1984, final negative CVD determinations for the two countries.

3. *Potassium chloride from the German Democratic Republic and Soviet Union*
On 30 March 1984, shortly before the final determinations of the Czechoslovak and Polish cases, the DOC received petitions from Amax-Chemical, Incorporated and Kerr-McFee Chemical Corporation on behalf of the US industry producing potassium chloride (hereinafter, 'potash'), alleging illegal subsidization from the German Democratic Republic and Soviet Union. However, in light of its final negative determination in the *Carbon Steel Wire Rod* case, which concluded that bounties or grants, within the meaning of the CVD law, could not be found in NME countries, the DOC rescinded the potash investigations and dismissed the petitions.[26]

4. *Court decisions regarding the non-application of CVD law to NMEs*
(i) *Reversal by the US Court of International Trade*: Following the final negative determination and dismissal of the 1984 cases, the petitioners of the steel rod and potash industries sought review with the US Court of International Trade (CIT). The CIT consolidated the cases and reviewed the ruling of the DOC which concluded that, as a matter of law, subsidies cannot be found in NMEs. The CIT held that the CVD law 'covers countries with nonmarket economies in light of fact that government subsidies that are target of law may be found in nonmarket economies as well as in market economies.'[27] In its detailed opinion, the CIT addressed each of the four grounds on which the DOC had based its determination of non-applicability of countervailing procedures to NME countries.[28]

To begin with, in the view of the CIT, the DOC's position was 'self-contradictory'.[29] The DOC appeared to have recognized that the CVD law covers 'any country' and does not allow *per se* exemptions from the

---

[26] See *Potassium Chloride from the German Democratic Republic; Rescission of Initiation of Countervailing Duty Investigation and Dismissal of Petition*, 49 US Federal Register 23428 (Department of Commerce, 6 June 1984) and *Potassium Chloride from the Soviet Union; Rescission of Initiation of Countervailing Duty Investigation and Dismissal of Petition*, 49 US Federal Register 23428 (Department of Commerce, 6 June 1984).

[27] See *Continental Steel Co. v United States*, 9 C.I.T. 340, 614 F. Supp. 548 (30 July 1985).

[28] Recall that the four grounds refer to those specified in 2. *Carbon steel wire rod from Czechoslovakia and Poland* above: (a) the view that a subsidy cannot be conferred in a NME 'because subsidy, *by definition*, means an act which distorts the operation of a [free] *market*' (both italics in the original); (b) Congressional 'silence' on the issue and its apparent preference for other trade remedial procedures; (c) consensus of academic opinion as to the non-applicability of CVD law to NME countries; and (d) the International Trade Administration's (ITA) asserted broad discretion to determine the existence of subsidies.

[29] See *Continental Steel*, above n 27, at 342.

law for any political entity. However, the DOC went on to address its 'additional jurisdictional question', namely, whether or not government activities in a NME can confer a 'bounty or grant' within the meaning of the law. According to the Court, if such was truly a 'jurisdictional' question, a failure to meet the criteria would actually amount to a *per se* exemption from the law, and would be in conflict with the preceding statement that the law covers 'any country'.[30] The Court highlighted that the language of a statute must ordinarily be regarded as conclusive absent clear legislative intent to the contrary and thereby ruled that the language of section 303 is perfectly indifferent to the forms of an economy, holding that NME countries cannot be exempted from the countervailing law.[31] Furthermore, the CIT added that the usage of the broadest possible language 'clearly demonstrates to cover as many beneficial acts as possible.'[32]

Secondly, refuting congressional preference for other remedial measures, the CIT determined that section 406 of the Trade Act of 1947 was enacted as a separate remedy action for a separate circumstance.[33] Thus, the existence of alternative remedies would not alter the specialized nature of the CVD law. Moreover, the CIT pointed out that Article 15 of the Trade Agreements Act of 1979 'clearly gives [the USA] the choice of using subsidy law or antidumping law for imports from a country with a state-controlled economy' and that Congress was informed that NME countries participated in the preparation of the Trade Agreements Act of 1979.[34]

Thirdly, the CIT held that it could not be persuaded by the economic academia which voiced that governments of NME countries 'cannot show what amounts to favoritism towards the manufacture, production, or export of particular merchandise' and stated that such ideas 'violate common sense' and 'conflict with a rational construction of law'.[35]

Nowhere did the CIT object to the DOC's broad discretion in determining the applicability of CVD law to NMEs. Rather, the CIT argued that while the DOC gave the CVD law a 'grandiose, theoretical objective', it destroyed a significant part of its practical purpose to 'assure effective protection of domestic interests from foreign subsidies...' and it should rather 'enforce the law to the full extent of the agency's authority and ability.'[36]

---

[30] Ibid, at 342–43.
[31] Ibid, at 344. For more discussion on the Court's decision, refer to Congressional Research Service, *Trade Remedy Legislation: Applying Countervailing Action to Nonmarket Economy Countries* (31 January 2008), at 9.
[32] See *Continental Steel*, above n 27, at 344.
[33] See Barcelo, above n 25. This section, namely the safeguard provision, was passed to protect US industries from injurious market disruption due to sudden increases in imports from Communist countries.
[34] See *Continental Steel*, above n 27, at 349.
[35] Ibid, at 348.
[36] Ibid, at 347.

All the considerations above led the CIT, on 30 July 1985, to conclude that the DOC's determinations were contrary to law and to reverse the *Carbon Steel Wire Rod* cases of 1984.[37]

(ii) Reversal by the US Court of Appeals for the Federal Circuit: The DOC appealed the CIT decision to the Court of Appeals for the Federal Circuit.[38] Although the Court of Appeals dismissed the jurisdiction of the CIT based on the petitioner's procedural mistakes, it went on to rule that subsidization is a market phenomenon.[39] The Court of Appeals reasoned that the government of a NME 'subsidizes' in accordance with its central plan and not for purposes of unfair foreign market competition. Hence, it opined that the US countervailing law in question should not be applied to NME countries. Arguably, the *Georgetown Steel* decision was not premised on the assumption that a subsidy cannot exist in a NME, but rather, on the reasoning that a NME country does not intend to engage in 'unfair competition' by granting a subsidy.[40]

The Court of Appeals also reviewed, in detail, the legislative history and development of relevant trade remedy laws. It described the CIT's finding on the 1979 Act as a 'definite understanding by Congress that the CVD law covers countries with nonmarket economies' a 'non-sequitur', and stated that the CIT's decision is 'inconsistent with [the Court of Appeals'] analysis of the Congressional understanding and purpose in enacting the provisions in the 1974 and 1979 Acts dealing with the application of the antidumping duty law to NME's.'[41] The Court of Appeals stated that Congress decided the proper method for protecting the American industries against selling by

---

[37] Ibid, at 351.

[38] See *Georgetown Steel Co. v United States*, 801 F.2d. 1308 (18 September 1986).

[39] The Circuit Judge held that the steel companies did not invoke jurisdiction of the CIT when they mailed complaint with insufficient postage within thirty days of the filing of the summons and then re-mailed the complaint after the deadline. *Georgetown Steel* contended that the only jurisdictional prerequisite for invoking jurisdiction of the CIT was the filing of a summons within thirty days after the negative CVD determination, and that the CIT was authorized under its Rule 6(b) to waive the thirty-day limit for filing a complaint. However, the Court of Appeals refuted *Georgetown Steel's* argument based on the language of section 1516a(a)(2)(A) which requires both the filing of a summons and of a complaint on time and the legislative history of the provision.

[40] See Egge, above n 13. In his analysis, Egge summarizes the two schools of thought reflected in the *Georgetwon Steel* case, regarding the applicability of CVD law to NMEs. The idea was originally discussed in Gary Horlick and Shannon Shuman, 'Nonmarket Economy Trade and US Antidumping/Countervailing Duty Laws', 18 International Lawyer 807 (1984), at 829. The fundamental distinction between the two approaches is their differing conceptions of the legal definition and purpose of a countervailable subsidy. The first school defines a countervailable subsidy in terms of market distortion and therefore views the purpose of the CVD law as market-correction. Egge explains that the determination of the Court of Appeals is in line with this view. Meanwhile, the second school defines a countervailable subsidy in terms of preferentiality and views the purpose of the CVD law as protection of the domestic industry. This school of thought is characterized by Judge Watson's opinion in the CIT ruling.

[41] See *Georgetown Steel*, above n 38, at 1317.

NMEs at unreasonably low prices through the AD law, and thus it is 'up to Congress to provide any additional remedies it deems appropriate.'[42] The Court of Appeals ruled that it followed a precedent that 'recognized that the agency administering the CVD law [i.e., the DOC] has broad discretion in determining the existence of a 'bounty' or 'grant' under that law.'[43]

In conclusion, the US Court of Appeals, on 18 September 1986, reversed and reinstated the DOC's original determinations, thus affirming that the agency has the discretion to not apply the CVD law to NME countries.[44] It also reversed the CIT order insofar as it set aside the DOC's final actions regarding the potash cases.[45]

B. Shift in policy of CVD application in regards to China

1. Reversal by the Department of Commerce[46]

On 27 November 2006, the DOC announced its initiation of a CVD investigation on imports of coated free sheet paper (CFSP) from China. This was the first CVD investigation involving China since 1991.[47]

In the meantime, there had been some significant regulatory changes. The CVD regulations in *Georgetown Steel* were subject to 19 USC section 1303, based on section 303 of the Tariff Act of 1930. CVD actions are now governed by 19 USC section 1677, modified pursuant to the Uruguay Round Agreements Act of 1995.[48] The current CVD regulations are much more elaborate than the former, as they further incorporate the WTO Agreement on Subsidies and Countervailing Measures (SCM Agreement).

---

[42] Ibid., at 1318.

[43] Ibid.

[44] Ibid.

[45] Ibid.

[46] Note that Congressional pressure might be another important factor in the DOC's policy reversal. In the middle of the 2000s, Congress had pending several bills such as S.593(Collins)/H.R.1216(English) and H.R.3283(English), which would have required the application of a countervailing procedure to imports from non-market economy countries. Although these bills never became law, such Congressional efforts would have pressured the DOC to comply with the previous CIT ruling to apply CVDs to 'any country', including NMEs, ahead of any statutory changes.

[47] Since the conclusion of the wire rod and potash cases, the DOC had not initiated any CVD investigations of allegedly subsidized imports from NME countries with one special exception. On 13 November 1991, the DOC initiated a CVD investigation on *Ceiling and Oscillating Fans* imported from China. Petitioners claimed that, while China is a NME country, 'the PRC fan sector operates substantially pursuant to market principles and that the CVD law should apply'. However, in its final determination, the DOC concluded that 'the prices of several significant inputs are not market-determined' and the DOC issued the final negative determination. See *Final Negative Countervailing Duty Determinations: Oscillating and Ceiling Fans from the People's Republic of China*, 57 US Federal Register 24018 (Department of Commerce, 5 June 2002).

[48] Dana Watts, 'Fair's Fair: Why Congress should Amend US Antidumping and Countervailing Duty Laws to Prevent "Double Remedies"', 1(1) Trade Law and Development 145 (2009), at 155.

The initiation of the investigation required the DOC to review its long standing policy of not applying the CVD law to NME countries, such as China.[49] On 15 December 2006, the US International Trade Commission (ITC) preliminarily determined that 'there was a reasonable identification that a US domestic industry is materially injured or threatened with material injury' by reason of allegedly subsidized imports from China, thus referring the case back to the DOC for a preliminary determination. On the same day, the DOC issued a notice requesting comment on the applicability of the CVD law to imports from China.[50]

On 9 April 2007, the DOC announced its affirmative preliminary determination of the investigation.[51] The preliminary determination was primarily based on the DOC's analysis issued in March 2007 that discussed, in detail, the 'substantial difference' in economies at issue in *Georgetown Steel* and China's present-day economy.[52] Based on the new developments, the DOC concluded that it 'believe[s] that it is possible to determine whether the PRC Government has bestowed a benefit upon a producer (i.e., the subsidy can be identified and measured) and whether any such benefit is specific.'[53] The DOC determined that its approach in the *Georgetown Steel* litigation was inapposite to the investigation in hand and would not prevent the application of CVD law to imports from China. Preliminary estimates of the net countervailable duty ranged from 10.9 to 20.35%.[54] In the next phase of

---

[49] The DOC has classified China as a NME country since 1981. See *Final Determination at Less Than Fair Value: Natural Menthol from the People's Republic of China*, 46 US Federal Register 24614 (Department of Commerce, 1 May 1981). The DOC reaffirmed its determination in the context of an investigation on certain lined paper from China. See *The People's Republic of China Status as a Non-Market Economy*, Memorandum (15 May 2006). The agency conducted a more comprehensive analysis of the issue in an antidumping investigation of *Certain Lined Paper Products* from the PRC. See n 10 above.

[50] See *Application of the Countervailing Duty Law to Imports from the People's Republic of China: Request for Comment*, 71 US Federal Register 75507 (Department of Commerce, 15 December 2006). All issues raised in the case and rebuttal briefs by parties to this investigation are addressed in the Decision Memorandum to Stephen J. Claeys, Deputy Assistant Secretary for Import Administration, to David M. Spooner, Assistant Secretary for Import Administration. Refer to DOC, *Issues and Decision Memorandum for the Final Determination in the Countervailing Duty Investigation of Coated Free Sheet Paper from the People's Republic of China* (17 October 2007).

[51] See *Coated Free Sheet Paper from the People's Republic of China: Amended Preliminary Affirmative Countervailing Duty Determination*, 72 US Federal Register 17484 (Department of Commerce, 9 April 2007).

[52] The analysis elaborates the significant difference of China's economy from the Soviet-style economies at issue in *Georgetown Steel* based on its wages, prices, access to foreign currency, personal property rights, private entrepreneurship, foreign trading rights and allocation of financial resources. For details, see DOC, *Countervailing Duty Investigation of Coated Free Sheet Paper from the People's Republic of China–Whether the Analytical Elements of the Georgetown Steel Opinion are Applicable to China's Present-Day Economy*, Memorandum (29 March 2007).

[53] Ibid.

[54] See n 7 above.

the investigation, the DOC released its final affirmative countervailing duty with net countervailable subsidy rates, ranging from 7.40% to 44.25%.[55]

However, on 7 December 2007, the ITC announced its negative determination of injury in both the countervailing and antidumping investigations of CFSP.[56] Given that the ITC issued a final negative injury determination, the proceeding was terminated and all estimated duties deposited or securities posted as result of the investigation were refunded or cancelled. Nevertheless, the significance of this case lies in the DOC's reversal of its long-standing policy of the non-applicability of CVDs to NME countries and the applicability of the CVD laws to allegedly subsidized imports from China.

2. Decision by US Court of International Trade

In the decisions in the CFSP case, the DOC reversed its long-standing practice to exempt NMEs from the US CVD law on the basis of the inherent challenges in defining and measuring subsidies from a state-distorted market. The shift in a policy which stood for more than two decades could not be smooth. A contentious debate loomed over the revision. For instance, more than 47 comments, representing more than 50 industries and persons were filed in response to the DOC's notice requesting comments on the applicability of CVD law to imports from China.[57] Notwithstanding the adoption and practice of the new policy, the controversy has not yet ended. All decision memorandums regarding US CVD orders against Chinese imports contain at least one comment confronting the DOC's authority to apply the CVD law to China.[58]

---

[55] The net subsidy rate of 7.40% was determined to be applied to Gold East Paper Co., Ltd. and 'all others' while the rate of 44.25% was designated to Shandong Chenming Paper Holdings Ltd. The high rate of the latter can be explained by the application of the adverse facts available (AFA) in its final determination as Shandong Chenming failed to respond fully to the Department's questionnaires. Refer to *Coated Free Sheet Paper from the People's Republic of China: Final Affirmative Countervailing Duty Determination*, 72 US Federal Register 60645 (Department of Commerce, 25 October 2007) and the decision memo at above n 50.

[56] ITC, *Coated Free-Sheet Paper from China, Indonesia, and Korea* (Final), Publication 3695 (December 2007).

[57] Refer to *Request for Comment* of above n 50 and 'Application of Countervailing Duty Law to Imports from the People's Republic of China, Comments Received, 15 January 2007 (updated: 30 January 2007)' available at http:ia.ita.doc.gov/download/prc-cvd/cmts-011507/prc-cvd-comts-index.html (visited 11 November 2010). Among the 47 comments, 8 were against and 39 supported the policy shift.

[58] See, e.g. DOC, *Issues and Decision Memorandum for the Final Affirmative Countervailing Duty Determination: Certain New Pneumatic Off-the Road Tires from the People's Republic of China* (7 July 2008). Analyzes of comments include 'application of the CVD law to NMEs, including the PRC' and 'application of the CVD law to the PRC is consistent with the Administrative Procedure Act (APA).' Starting from late 2008, comments over the DOC's application of CVD law to China began to focus on its legal authority to apply the CVD law to China while simultaneously treating the PRC as a NME in parallel antidumping investigations.

Despite strong objections from respondents and importers, the DOC has set a very firm position. Referring to the 'country' provisions of sections 701(a), 771(5) and (5a) of the Tariff Act of 1930, the DOC argued that none of these limits its authority to determine a countervailable subsidy only from market economies. The DOC also brought attention to the 1984 *Carbon Steel Wire Rod* cases and the Federal Circuit's *Georgetown Steel* ruling that affirmed its 'broad discretion' in determining whether the CVD law applies to imports from a NME.

On the other hand, the Chinese paper manufacturers brought a suit to the CIT to enjoin the DOC investigation arguing that the Court of Appeals definitively prohibited the application of CVDs on products from NMEs. However, the CIT reaffirmed the DOC's 'broad discretion' and commented that the DOC's past decisions were reasonable based upon the facts of the case and not upon the NME factor *per se*.[59]

The DOC has argued that several Congressional actions express its understanding that the CVD law may be applied to China. For example, Congress authorized funding for the DOC to 'monitor compliance by the People's Republic of China with its commitments under the WTO, assist USA negotiators with the ongoing negotiations in the WTO, and defend USA antidumping and countervailing duty measures with respect to products of the People's Republic of China.'[60] Congress also approved the US-China bilateral agreement 'concerning the terms of China's eventual accession to the WTO' and ordered the US government to 'effectively monitor and enforce its rights' under the agreements.[61]

III. CVD ACTIONS AGAINST CHINA

After the CIT decision to reject the request to enjoin the DOC from proceeding, the DOC opened a floodgate of CVDs against China. In addition, more WTO members have been trying to use CVDs against China.

A. Countervailable subsidies under China's WTO Accession Protocol

As a necessary cost of the WTO accession, China has made unusual commitments, particularly in terms of its current trade practices.[62] All the China-specific rules were set out in both the text of China's WTO

---

[59] See *Government of the People's Republic of China v United States*, 483 F. Supp. 2d 1282 (29 March 2007). The Court states that 'the Georgetown Steel court only affirmed Commerce's decision not to apply countervailing duty law to the NMEs in question in that particular case and recognized the continuing "broad discretion" of the agency to determine whether to apply countervailing duty law to NMEs.'

[60] See 22 USC § 6943(a)(1).

[61] See 22 USC § 6901(8), 6941(5).

[62] See Qungjiang Kong, 'China's WTO Accession: Commitments and Implications', 3 Journal of International Economic Law 655 (2000).

Accession Protocol and the selected provisions of the *Report of the Working Party on the Accession of China* that were incorporated into the Accession Protocol, and that were made 'an integral part of the Agreement.'[63] Such specific commitments have become enforceable through the WTO dispute settlement procedure as part of a 'covered agreement.'[64]

Two specific trade remedy rules designed to protect the producers of other members from potential adverse effects of Chinese subsidies are worth noting. First, the Protocol makes subsidies to state-owned enterprises (SOEs) in China automatically specific under the SCM Agreement.[65] Second, section 15(b) of the Protocol authorizes the importing Member to use so-called 'NME methodologies' to identify and calculate Chinese subsidies. Conditions required to impose the use of countervailing measures are few.[66] The Protocol states:

> In proceedings under Parts II, III and V of the SCM Agreement, when addressing subsidies described in Articles 14(a), 14(b), 14(c) and 14(d), relevant provisions of the SCM Agreement shall apply; however, if there are special difficulties in that application, the importing WTO Member may then use methodologies for identifying and measuring the subsidy benefit which take into account the possibility that prevailing terms and conditions in China may not always be available as appropriate benchmarks. In applying such methodologies, where practicable, the importing WTO Member should adjust such prevailing terms and conditions before considering the use of terms and conditions prevailing outside China.[67]

Section 15(b) above, is the first and only WTO provision that explicitly authorizes the use of alternative benchmarks for a NME.[68] Importantly, in contrast with the transient antidumping provisions under section 15 and the product-specific safeguard provisions under section 16, this very provision is

[63] See WTO Working Party on the Accession of China, *Report of the Working Party on the Accession of China*, WT/ACC/CHN/49 (1 October 2001), at 29–31 and Part I, section 1 of WTO, *Accession of the People's Republic of China*, WT/L/432 (23 November 2001). The latter is based on the decision of *Protocol on the Accession of the People's Republic of China to the Marrakesh Agreement Establishing the World Trade Organization* (10 November 2001). For the general landscape of the China-specific rules, see Julia Ya Qin, '"WTO-Plus" Obligations and Their Implications for the World Trade Organization Legal System – An Appraisal of the China Accession Protocol', 37(3) Journal of World Trade 483 (2003).

[64] See Julia Ya Qin, 'WTO Regulation of Subsidies to State-Owned Enterprises (SOEs) – A Critical Appraisal of the China Accession Protocol', 7 Journal of International Economic Law 863 (2004).

[65] WTO, *Accession of the People's Republic of China*, WT/L/432, section 10.2 (23 November 2001).

[66] In fact, the lack of concrete criteria for countervailing measures is starkly contrasted with the case for antidumping measures. While paragraph 151 of the *Report of the Working Party on the Accession of China* (ibid) elaborates the conditions for WTO members to rely on non-market economy provisions, there is no similar clarification for CVDs.

[67] See WTO, above n 65, section 15(b).

[68] See Qin, above n 64, at 892.

344   *Journal of International Economic Law (JIEL)* 14(2)

Table 1.   CVD actions against China by WTO Members[a]

	2004	2005	2006	2007	2008	2009	2010	Total
Investigation Initiation	3 Canada(3)		2 Canada(1) USA(1)	8 Canada(1) USA(7)	11 Australia(2) Canada(3) S. Africa(1) USA(5)	13 Australia(1) Canada(1) India(1) USA(10)	5 Canada(1) EU(2) USA(2)	42
Measure		2 Canada(2)		1 Canada(1)	10 Canada(3) USA(7)	6 Canada(1) USA(5)	8 Australia(1) Canada(1) USA(6)	27

[a]The data are collected from the webpages of the WTO as well as each investigating authority. Since there was some inconsistency among the data, for example—the WTO notification versus the records of WTO members—we focused on the original records of the Member countries.

operates on a permanent basis, regardless of the nature of China's economy.[69] In this regard, countervailing measures against allegedly subsidized imports from China are expected to surge in anticipation of the expiration of alternative NME-specific trade remedies.

B. CVD measures against China in the WTO system

As of October 2010, a total of 27 countervailing measures were in force against China.[70] These consist of 18 cases imposed by the USA, another eight by Canada and a more recent one by Australia. Notably, this has been a very recent trend. Only since 2004, has China become a target of CVD investigations and only since 2005, have effective countervailing measures been put in place.[71]

Although only Australia, Canada and the USA have so far used actual CVDs against China, CVD investigations have been enacted by more members—such as India, South Africa and the EU. The EU decided to

[69] The Protocol notes that its special antidumping provision under section 15 shall expire 15 years after the date of China's accession (in 2016) while the product-specific safeguard measure under section 16 is to be terminated in 12 years (in 2013).

[70] WTO statistics updated by authors based on the online statistics database of the US DOC, Import Administration and of the Canada Border Services Agency (CBSA). The period of investigation in the current thesis spans from the beginning of 1995 to the end of October, 2010.

[71] See WTO, 'CV Initiations: By Exporting Country From 01/01/95 to 30/06/09', available at http://www.wto.org/english/tratop_e/scm_e/cvd_init_exp_country_e.pdf (visited 23 February 2011) and 'CV Measures: By Exporting Country From 01/01/95 to 30/06/09', available at http://www.wto.org/english/tratop_e/scm_e/cvd_meas_exp_country_e.pdf (visited 23 February 2011).
As shown in Appendix 2, there have been attempts by the Australian, Indian and South African trade authorities to countervail allegedly subsidized Chinese goods. While, the single Indian and South African cases were terminated, one of the Australian initiations became effective as of 14 April 2010.

Table 2. US CVD actions against China (2006–October 2010)

Case No.	Product	DOC Initiation	Order
C-570-906	Coated free sheet paper	27 November 2006	ITC Negative
C-570-911	Circular welded carbon quality steel pipe	5 July 2007	22 July 2008
C-570-915	Light-walled rectangular pipe and tube	24 July 2007	5 August 2008
C-570-917	Laminated woven sacks	25 July 2007	7 August 2008
C-570-926	Sodium nitrite	5 December 2007	27 August 2008
C-570-913	Certain new pneumatic off-the-road tires	7 August 2007	4 September 2008
C-570-923	Raw flexible magnets	18 October 2007	17 September 2008
C-570-921	Lightweight thermal paper	2 November 2007	24 November 2008
C-570-936	Circular welded carbon quality steel line pipe	28 April 2008	23 January 2009
C-570-931	Circular welded austenitic stainless pressure pipe	25 February 2008	19 March 2009
C-570-938	Citric acid and certain citrate salts	13 May 2008	29 May 2009
C-570-940	Certain tow-behind lawn groomers and certain parts thereof	21 July 2008	3 August 2009
C-570-942	Certain kitchen appliance shelving and racks	26 August 2008	14 September 2009
C-570-944	Certain oil country tubular goods	5 May 2009	20 January 2010
C-570-946	Pre-stressed concrete steel wire strand	23 June 2009	7 July 2010
C-570-963	Sodium and potassium phosphate salts	23 October 2009	22 July 2010
C-570-948	Steel grating	25 June 2009	23 July 2010
C-570-950	Wire decking	2 July 2009	ITC Negative
C-570-953	Narrow woven ribbons with woven selvedge	6 August 2009	1 September 2010
C-570-955	Magnesia carbon bricks	25 August 2009	21 September 2010
C-570-957	Seamless carbon and alloy steel standard line and pressure pipe	14 October 2009	
C-570-959	Coated paper suitable for high-quality print graphics using sheet-fed presses	20 October 2009	
C-570-961	Steel fasteners	22 October 2009	ITC (Prelim.) Negative
C-570-966	Drill pipe	27 January 2010	
C-570-968	Aluminum extrusions	27 April 2010	

Note: Cases listed by date of 'Order'.
Source: Import Administration, US Department of Commerce, *Antidumping and Countervailing Duty Case Information*, Retrieved from <http://ia.ita.doc.gov/stats/caselist.txt> and <http://ia.ita.doc.gov/stats/inv-initiations-2000-current.html>.

initiate its first CVD investigation against China in April 2010. While it was Canada that first initiated the countervailing investigations of China, the USA has emerged as the heaviest user.

As shown in Table 2, the 18 US countervailing measures in force against China have been active since 2008: seven cases have been in order since 2008, five since 2009, and six since 2010. Excluding three cases terminated due to ITC negative injury determinations, all other investigations initiated from 2007 to October 2010 produced affirmative actions.[72] On the other hand, it is noteworthy that the most recent termination of investigations was based on the preliminary negative determination on industry injury.

For Canada, as summarized in Table 3, two countervailing measures have been in action since 2005, one since 2007, three since 2008 and one each year since 2009 and 2010.[73] Eight countervailing measures are in force out of a total of nine investigations.[74]

It is also interesting that the two countries have only recently started taking countervailing measures against unfair trade practices of the Chinese government, even though China's WTO Accession Protocol in 2001 allowed importing members to impose CVDs against Chinese goods, regardless of the nature of its economy. The countervailing measures in force imposed by the USA and Canada are further discussed in the following sections.

C. US CVD orders against China

Although *Coated Free Sheet Paper* was eventually terminated due to the ITC's final negative determination, the DOC had finally opened the Pandora's box regarding the applicability of CVD law to NME countries. Since then, CVD investigations against China have proliferated.

Thirty-two countervailing investigations had been initiated against Chinese imports as of October 2010, leading to the 18 CVD measures shown in Table 2. This amounts to more than 80% of all those initiated since 2007.[75] The sudden surge in US countervailing initiations against China is remarkable considering the short period since CVD investigations were filed against the country.[76]

Based on the Harmonized Tariff Schedule of the USA (HTSUS), seven countervailing cases concern Chinese products outlined in section XV, three

---

[72] Refer to Appendix 3. As of 28 April 2010, the USA has initiated a total of 102 CVD cases since 1995. Amongst those, 25 cases target China including the 13 cases currently in force.

[73] Canada has evidently followed the USA practice not to use CVDs in cases where AD duties are imposed. See Gregory Bowman et al., *Trade Remedies in North America* (The Netherlands: Kluwer Law International, 2010), at 205–06.

[74] The only Canadian case eventually terminated is *Outdoors Barbeques* from China. See CBSA, *Anti-dumping & Countervailing Program–Statement of Reasons for Outdoor Barbeques Originating in or Exported from the People's Republic of China* (Ottawa, 3 December 2004), available at http://cbsa-asfc.gc.ca/sima-lmsi/i-e/ad1318/ad1318tsor-eng.html (visited 10 November 2010).

[75] After *Coated Free Sheet Paper* opened the possibility of determining countervailable subsidies from NME China, the DOC initiated 24 investigations regarding Chinese imports out of a total of 29 cases filed since 2007, which amounts to approximately 83% of all the recent investigations.

[76] This is likely to become the second major CVD surge by the USA, after the massive CVD action period of the early 1980s. For example, in 1982 alone, the USA initiated 123 CVD investigations. For a more detailed account on the early CVD surge period, see Michael Finger and Julio Nogues, 'International Control of Subsidies and Countervailing Duties', 1 The World Bank Economic Review 707 (1987).

Table 3. Canadian CVD measures against China (1995–current)

Case No.	Product	Initiation/Re-Initiation	CBSA preliminary	CBSA final	CITT affirmative
D-15-48	Laminate flooring	24 October 2004; Ex.12/17/2004 Re.10/23/2008	16 February/2005	17 May 2005	16 June 2005
D-15-49	Carbon steel screws (Fasteners)	28 April 2004 Re. 9/24/2009	10 September 2004	29 May 2009 9 December 2004 24 March 2010	7 January 2005
D-15-50	Copper pipe fitting	8 June 2006; Ex.8/17/2006 Re. 2/17/2007	20 October 2006	18 January 2007	19 February 2007
D-15-51	Seamless carbon or alloy steel oil and gas well casing	13 August 2007	9 November 2007	27 August 2008 7 February 2008	10 March 2008
D-15-52	Carbon steel welded pipe	23 January 2008	22 April 2008	21 July 2008	20 August 2008
D-15-53	Thermoelectric containers (coolers and warmers)	15 May 2008	13 August 2008	10 November 2008	11 December 2008
D-15-54	Aluminum extrusions	18 August 2008	17 November 2008	25 February 2009	24 March 2009
D-15-56	Certain oil country tubular goods	24 August 2009	26 November 2009	22 February 2010	23 March 2010

Notes: 'Ex.' stands for the date of extension and 'Re.' stands for the date of re-initiation. Cases listed by case number.
Source: Canada Border Services Agency, *Measures in Force: Goods Subject to Anti-dumping or Countervailing Duties*, http://cbsa-asfc.gc.ca/sima-lmsi/mif-mev-eng.html.

in section XVI, three in section VI, two in section XI and one each in sections VII, X and XIII.[77] As with other trade remedy actions, steel industries in China have been most heavily targeted by US CVD actions, followed by the chemicals sector and machinery sector. At least in terms of target industries so far, CVD actions against China do not seem to address any special industry injury problems, which is distinguishable from other trade remedy actions worldwide.

CVD margins of all individually investigated companies were calculated in accordance with section 705(c)(1)(B)(i)(I) of the Tariff Act of 1930. The 'all others' rates, designated to all non-individually determined firms, were derived as the weighted average of countervailable subsidy rates established for exporters and producers individually investigated, excluding any zero, *de minimis* countervailable subsidy rates and any rates based entirely on section 766 of the Act.[78] Despite a few cases that applied the simple average rather than the weighted average rate for 'all others' due to 'risks of disclosure of proprietary information', most rates were derived based on section 705(c)(5)(A)(i) of the Act.[79] Appendix 1 presents all the US CVD rates determined against subsidized Chinese imports.

While the difference between CVD rates applied to individual companies spans quite broadly from case to case, the general level of CVDs against China tends to be considerably high compared to CVDs against other countries. Notably, adverse facts available were more frequently used to result in much greater duty margins. For instance, in *Circular Welded Carbon Quality Steel Pipe*, a final countervailing duty amounting to 616.83% was ordered against Tianjin Shuangjie Steel Pipe Group Co., Ltd.; Tianjin Wa Song Imp.

---

[77] The description for each chapter may be found in the HTSUS, available at http://www.usitc. gov/tata/hts/bychapter/index.htm (visited 20 September 2010). The most updated revision took effect in 26 August 2010.

[78] Sections 776(a)(1) and (2) of the Tariff Act of 1930 provide that the Department of Commerce shall apply 'facts otherwise available' if, *inter alia*, necessary information is not on the record or an interested party or any person: (A) withholds information that has been requested; (B) fails to provide information within the deadlines established, or in the form and manner requested by the Department, subject to subsections (c)(1) and (e) of section 782 of the Act; (C) significantly impedes a proceeding; or (D) provides information that cannot be verified as provided by section 782(i) of the Act.

[79] A simple average rate was calculated for 'all others' in the cases of C-570-911, C-570-917, C-570-936 and C-570-938 due to risks of disclosure of proprietary information. See *Circular Welded Carbon Quality Steel Pipe from the People's Republic of China: Final Affirmative Countervailing Duty and Final Affirmative Determination of Critical Circumstances*, 73 US Federal Register 31969 (Department of Commerce, 5 June 2008); *Laminated Woven Sacks from the People's Republic of China: Final Affirmative Countervailing Duty Determination and Final Affirmative Determination, in Part, of Critical Circumstances*, 73 US Federal Register 35641 (Department of Commerce, 31 January 2008); *Circular Welded Carbon Quality Steel Line Pipe from the People's Republic of China: Final Affirmative Countervailing Determination*, 73 US Federal Register 70963 (Department of Commerce, 24 November 2008); and *Citric Acid and Certain Citrate Salts from the People's Republic of China: Final Affirmative Countervailing Duty Determination*, 74 US Federal Register 16837 (Department of Commerce, 13 April 2009).

& Exp. Co., Ltd.; and Tianjin Shuanglian Galvanizing Products Co, Ltd. (collectively, 'Shuangjie'). As an uncooperative firm, adverse facts available were applied to Shuangjie regarding all alleged subsidy programs. Consequently, a final CVD rate of approximately 617% was computed.

It is also noteworthy that the subsidy margins tend to significantly increase in the final determinations. Only in very recent cases did reduction of CVDs occur during final determinations. The sudden increases of CVDs at the final determination stage—for example, from 2.5 to 353% in *Laminated Woven Sacks* or from *de minimis* to 254% in *Magnesia Carbon Bricks*—raise concerns as to the stability and predictability of the US's trade remedy practice and system.[80]

In terms of subsidy programs determined to be countervailable, the most typical subsidy program provided by the central government was found to be fiscal benefits such as tax exemption or credits. As summarized in Appendix 2, this type of subsidy is followed by the provision of goods or services, such as land use rights or utilities. In contrast, the most popular provincial subsidy program turned out to be direct grants. While local governments in China seem to prefer indirect subsidization through their engagement in industry and trade promotion policies, the central government appears to be more direct in its subsidization of domestic firms.

Lastly, all US CVDs against China have been imposed simultaneously with antidumping duties. Considering the already exceptionally high level of CVDs, the duplicative trade remedy actions against China deserve more scrutiny in order to prevent unnecessary tension arising from political economy rather than legal legitimacy.

Aggressive CVD actions by the USA against China, especially those initiated in recent years, should be implemented cautiously, so as not to provoke unnecessary trade conflicts between major WTO members. The record so far, however, indicates arbitrary application of CVD actions and a great variance among duty rates.[81] The potential legal issues in the WTO system will be analyzed in a later section.

D. Canadian CVD orders against China

Unlike the US practices, Canadian CVD law and practice governed under the Special Import Measures Act (SIMA) has never barred or limited the application of CVDs on goods from NME countries entering Canadian

---

[80] The US DOC classifies duty rates less than 1% for developed countries or 2% for developing countries as *de minimis*. The 1% threshold is applied to China because the country is not yet designated as a developing country by the United States Trade Representative (USTR). See 'Comment 1' of the *Issues and Decision Memorandum for Final Determination in the Countervailing Duty Investigation of Certain Welded Austenitic Stainless Pressure Pipe from the People's Republic of China* (21 January 2009).

[81] The discriminative use of AFA in US CVD cases against China is elaborated in detail in ch. IV, section b.

borders. Under SIMA, the necessary criteria that define a 'subsidy' depend on whether a financial contribution by a state confers a benefit to the recipient and *not* on the nature of the economy.[82]

Canadian countervailing cases against China, however, were non-existent until 2004. The absence of such initiations was not due to impediments under the Canadian law. Rather, it was the reluctance of Canadian industries to file these cases against foreign governments, since it entails large legal expenses and practical difficulties. Generally, the antidumping relief is 'more expeditious, less expensive and more likely' than the 'slow, cumbersome, costly, and not entirely certain' countervail relief.[83]

Presumably, the change in Canada Border Services Agency's (CBSA) AD policy regarding China's market economy status in 2004 has triggered CVD actions against the country.[84] For dumping investigations, the CBSA abandoned its existing policy of a blanket categorization of China as a NME country in favor of a case-by-case sector examination under review.[85] Incidentally, the first CVD investigation against Chinese-made *Outdoor Barbeques* was initiated on 13 April 2004.[86] Eventually, the case was terminated due to the determination of insignificant amount of subsidies in accordance with paragraph 14(1)(b) of the SIMA.[87] However, after that case, eight more investigations were initiated and were all determined affirmative. By now, some of the early cases have expired or been reinitiated as shown in Table 3.[88]

---

[82] Special Imports Measures Act (SIMA), RSC 1984, c.25, s. 1, as amended, § 2(1)(i)(a)–(b).

[83] See Lawrence L. Herman, 'The China Factor: Canada's Trade Remedy Response to China's Economic Challenge', 33 Canada-US Law Journal 25 (2008), at 35.

[84] The CBSA and the Canadian International Trade Tribunal (Tribunal, CITT) are jointly responsible for administering the SIMA. The 'Anti-dumping and Countervailing Directorate' of the CBSA conducts investigations and determines whether goods imported into Canada are dumped or subsidized. The Tribunal is responsible for deciding whether the dumped or subsidized goods have caused injury or are threatening to cause injury to the Canadian industry, or have caused retardation of the establishment of an industry in Canada. The CBSA is analogous to the Import Administration of the US DOC whereas the CITT is that to the ITC of the United States.

[85] The policy change was formally promulgated by the CBSA in an important notice to stakeholders in June 2004.

[86] CBSA, *News Releases–The Canada Border Agency Imposes Provisional Duty on Outdoor Barbeques* (27 August 2004), available at www.cbsa-asfc.gc.ca/sima (visited 10 November 2010).

[87] SIMA, which came into force on 1 December 1984, incorporates in law Canada's rights and obligations in respect of antidumping and countervailing actions. The Act, as amended, incorporates the requirements of the North America Trade Agreement (NAFTA) and implements the relevant Agreements which resulted from the Uruguay Round of Multilateral Trade Negotiations signed on 15 April 1994 and which became effective on 1 January 1995.

[88] E.g. *Laminate Flooring* originating in or exported from China and France has an expiry date of 15 June 2010. See CBSA, *Dumping and Subsidizing Expiry – Laminate Flooring* issued on 30 September 2009. Meanwhile, *Certain Steel Fasteners* was re-initiated on 24 September 2009. See CBSA, *Notice of Conclusion of Re-Investigation – Certain Steel Fasteners* issued on 24 March 2010. Similarly, *Copper Fittings* from the USA, the Republic of Korea and China was re-investigated. See CBSA, *Notice of Conclusion of Re-Investigation – Copper Fittings* issued on 27 August 2008.

Table 4. Canadian CVDs against Chinese imports

Case No.	Product	CVD Payable	W.A. Margin
D-15-48	Laminate Flooring	3.54 RMB/m²	3
D-15-49	Carbon Steel Screws (Fasteners)	1.25 RMB/kg	31.53
D-15-50	Copper Pipe Fitting	17.73 RMB/kg	51
D-15-51	Seamless Carbon or Alloy Steel Oil and Gas Well Casing	3,381 RMB/MT	19
D-15-52	Carbon Steel Welded Pipe	5,280 RMB/MT	73
D-15-53	Thermoelectric Containers (Coolers and Warmers)	53.27 RMB/unit	9.9
D-15-54	Aluminum Extrusions	15.84 RMB/kg	47
D-15-56	Certain Oil Country Tubular Goods	4,070 RMB/MT	25.7
Average of weighted average margins			32.52

Note: 'W.A. Margins' stand for the weighted average subsidy margins determined in each case. Source: Canadian International Trade Tribunal, <http://www.citt.gc.ca/index_e.asp> and Canada Border Services Agency, *Measures in Force: Goods Subject to Anti-dumping or Countervailing Duties*, <http://cbsa-asfc.gc.ca/sima-lmsi/mif-mev-eng>.

Based on the Harmonized System classification numbers, Canada has six countervailing cases in order concerning Chinese products as outlined in section XV, and one case in each of the sections IX and XVI.[89] In other words, Canadian CVDs have been focused disproportionately on the steel industry.

Pursuant to paragraph 41(1)(a) of the SIMA, CBSA made final affirmative determinations of the eight goods in question and their amounts of counter-vailable subsidies in terms of Chinese Renminbi. Table 5 summarizes the amounts and weighted average countervailable subsidy margins determined for the exporters and producers investigated. As shown, the simple average of the eight weighted averages is about 33%. Similar to the US cases, the CBSA imposed punitive CVD rates in accordance with ministerial specification on companies that failed to fully comply or cooperate in the investigation process.[90] Nevertheless, Canadian CVD levels are generally much lower than that of the USA.

Similar to US CVD cases, Canadian CVDs against China are also always accompanied by antidumping duties. Although the levels of Canadian CVDs against China are generally lower than that of the USA, the double impos-ition of CVDs and antidumping duties raise concerns as to excessive trade protection as well as political conflicts between the governments.

[89] See n 77 above for descriptions of each HTSUS section and chapter.

[90] Ministerial specification is provided for in Article 29(1) of the SIMA. The Article 29(1) states that where the deputy minister is of the opinion that sufficient information has not been furnished or is not available for the determination of normal value and export price under sections 15–28, then these will be set by ministerial specification. See Jean Gabriel Castel, *The Canadian Law and Practice of International Trade: With Particular Emphasis on Exports and Imports of Goods and Services* (Toronto, Canada: Edmond Montgomery 1997).

Compared to the US CVD cases, Canadian CVDs against China have addressed provincial programs more frequently. Income tax reduction and credits appear to be the most typical kinds of provincial subsidy programs. Classification of individual countervailable subsidy programs challenged in each CVD case in force is presented in Appendix 3.

Finally, in contrast with the US practice, Canada considers China as a developing country in light of CVD investigations. CBSA normally refers to the 'Development Assistance Committee List of Official Development Assistance (ODA) Recipient' for guidance in determining a developing country.[91] China is currently listed as an ODA recipient and thereby treated as a developing country.[92]

IV. CHALLENGES FOR THE CVD LAW AND PRACTICE AGAINST CHINA

While the US and Canadian governments now impose CVD measures against China, they continue to face practical challenges in addressing Chinese subsidy programs.[93] For example, the USTR has pointed to the lack of transparency in China's subsidy regime, stating that 'Chinese subsidies are often the result of internal administrative measures and are not publicized.'[94] Only in 2006 did China first submit its long-overdue subsidies notification to the WTO's Subsidies Committee.[95] Yet other WTO members—in particular, the USA, which has been devoting significant efforts to monitor and investigate Chinese subsidy programs—identified significant omissions in this notification.[96] Besides, the USTR stressed that China's progress towards further liberalization began to slow down beginning

---

[91] The Organisation for Economic Co-operation and Development, DAC List of ODA Recipients as of 1 January 2006, the document is available at http://www.oecd.org/dataoecd/32/40/43540882.pdf (visited 15 January 2011).

[92] Certain Oil Country Tubular Goods Originating in or Exported from the People's Republic of China, CBSA, 4214-26(AM) AD/1385; 4218-27 CVD/125, 16 (8 September 2009).

[93] See General Accountability Office (GAO), *US – China Trade: Commerce Faces Practical and Legal Challenges in Applying Countervailing Duties* (Washington DC, 2005).

[94] See USTR, *National Trade Estimates Report* (Washington DC, March 2004), at 159.

[95] WTO Committee on Subsidies and Countervailing Measures, *New and Full Notification Pursuant to Article XVI:1 of the GATT 1994 and Article 25 of the SCM Agreement-People's Republic of China*, G/SCM/N/123/CHN (13 April 2006).

[96] Congress ordered the DOC to effectively monitor and to enforce its rights under 22 USC ch. 77(III)(B) § 6941(5). Despite China's reporting of its 87 subsidy programs, the USA reiterated its concerns as to the lack of provincial and local programs in China's subsidy notification and raised several other issues, including export-contingent subsidies, industrial subsidy policy administration, government assistance in the textiles and civil aerospace sectors and price controls on fuels and land administration. See USTR, *The 2010 Trade Policy Agenda and 2009 Annual Report of the President of the United States on the Trade Agreements Program* (Washington DC, 2010).

in 2006, despite its substantial adoption of market-oriented reforms in its early years of accession.[97]

Such problems have problematized CVD actions in response to alleged Chinese subsidy programs.[98] Moreover, growing tension concerning China's exchange rate policies has provoked more aggressive CVD actions, especially by the USA. This inevitably raises issues concerning the WTO's consistency.

A. Current practices and US court decisions for 'double remedy'

Both WTO rules and US laws require adjustments in combined duty rates to avoid double counting of export subsidies. Article VI:5 of the GATT specifies that no product can be subject to both antidumping and countervailing duties 'to compensate for the same situation of dumping or export subsidization.' The US law, parallel to this provision, requires the DOC to adjust antidumping duties in the event that CVDs are applied simultaneously to counter export subsidies on the same products.[99] More specifically, export prices are increased by the amount of CVDs imposed on the product to offset the export subsidy effect.[100] The simplified mechanism of this method is shown in Figure 1. Suppose that Country A provides $20 per unit subsidy to its own exporter, Company *a*, which charges $100 for the domestic market and $70 for exportation to the US market. When the DOC countervails the subsidy by $20 CVD, this amount would be added to the actual export price of $70 so that the dumping margin, or difference between the normal value and export price, is $10. The DOC explains that this practice avoids the imposition of double remedy in parallel trade remedy investigations involving imports from WTO Members that are designated as market economies.[101] In contrast, when there is a domestic subsidy that affects both the export price and normal value, the DOC does not make an adjustment to export prices. For example, if the normal value is also reduced

[97] See USTR, *The 2009 Trade Policy Agenda and 2009 Annual Report of the President of the United States on the Trade Agreements Program* (Washington DC, 2009), at 159.

[98] In recent years, the US frustration regarding China's exchange rate policies has provoked numerous CVD related congressional bills. For a more detailed account of the legality of such legislative actions, see Staiger and Sykes, above n 5; Dukgeun Ahn, 'Is the Chinese Exchange Rate Regime "WTO-legal"?', in Simon Evenett (ed.), *The US-Sino Currency Dispute: New Insights from Economics, Politics and Law* (London: CEPR, 2010), at 139–46.

[99] 19 USC § 1677a(c)(1)(C) and section 772(c)(1)(C) of the Tariff Act of 1930.

[100] However, domestic subsidies affecting both export price and normal value presumably by the same amount do not entail price adjustments.

[101] For recent adjustment practices, see, e.g. *Notice of Final Results of Antidumping Administrative Review: Low Enriched Uranium from France*, 69 US Federal Register 46501 (Department of Commerce, 3 August 2004); *Certain Cut-to-Length Carbon Steel Plate from Germany: Final Results of Antidumping Administrative Review*, 62 US Federal Register 18390 (Department of Commerce, 15 April 1997); and *Stainless Steel Wire Rod from the Republic of Korea: Final Results of Antidumping Duty Administrative Review*, 69 US Federal Register 19153 (Department of Commerce, 12 April 2004).

198

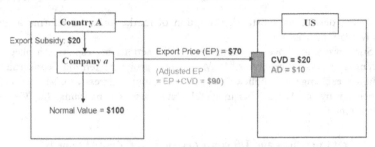

Figure 1.   CVD offset structure in dumping margin calculation: market economy.

to $80 by the subsidy in Figure 1, the dumping margin would be determined simply by comparing the normal value ($80) and the export price ($70).

But the DOC has not applied the same methodology for price adjustment when both CVD and AD duties are charged against non-market economies.[102] When the DOC addresses dumping problems by NMEs, it compares a subsidy-free constructed normal value with the subsidized export price to calculate the dumping margin. As a result, the difference reflects the price advantages that the exporting company has obtained from both export and domestic subsidies. Thus, in theory, antidumping duties derived in this way will already offset much of the benefits gained by both types of subsidies. Any additional CVD in this situation may create a double remedy for the alleged subsidy problems. Figure 2 shows a numerical example for how concurrent application of AD and CVD against NMEs may create double remedy problems with respect to domestic subsidies. In the dumping margin calculation, the DOC compares the constructed normal value that is calculated by using data from other market economies with the actual subsidized export price. Thus, in Figure 2, the dumping margin for NMEs would be $30. Accordingly, concurrent application of $20 CVD in this case would amount to a 'double remedy'.[103]

In case a NME provides an export subsidy that affects only export prices, GATT Article VI:5 mandates the choice between AD and CVD. This is

---

[102] On December 12, 2008, China filed an official request for the formation of a WTO panel to examine US antidumping and CVDs on certain Chinese products. Specifically, China's WTO case makes two types of challenges to the US AD and CVD investigations: 'as such' claims and 'as applied' claims. As part of its 'as such' claims, China argues that the combined application of CVD and NME AD methodology to China violates the most favored nation (MFN) treatment provisions of Article I of the GATT (1947). See *United States – Definitive Antidumping and Countervailing Duties on Certain Products from China: Request for the Establishment of a Panel by China*, WT/DS392/2 (12 December 2008).

[103] For a theoretical possibility of concurrent application of AD and CVD to resolve double remedy problems, see Brian D. Kelly, 'The Offsetting Duty Norm and the Simultaneous Application of Countervailing and Antidumping Duties', available at http://papers.ssrn. com/sol3/papers.cfm?abstract_id=1653631 (visited 12 November 2010).

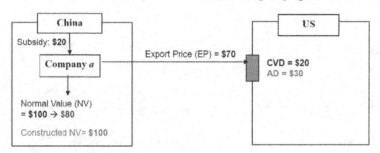

Figure 2. CVD offset structure in dumping margin calculation: non-market economy.

reasonable because either AD or CVD, but not both, can fully address subsidy impacts to an export price. If an export price is reduced by more than the subsidy amount—probably embracing dumping elements, AD would be enough to address the full subsidized and dumped price effects. In other words, if the export price is reduced by more than $20 due to the export subsidy of $20 in Figure 2 while the normal value remains $100, the dumping margin would cover both subsidy and dumping effects. On the other hand, if an export price is reduced by less than the subsidy amount, the CVD would be—actually more than—enough to counter the price effects. The CVD of $20 in Figure 2 should suffice to deal with any price effects of export subsidy that reduces the export price by less than $20.

The shift in the DOC's CVD policy starting from 2006 resulted in a surge of AD and CVD cases against China. As presented in Figure 3, US antidumping actions against China have shown a steady decline following a peak in the early 2000s, but then upturned with a sharp increase since 2007. After 2007, the trends of AD and CVD actions significantly correlate, illustrating the fact that all CVD measures in force were aligned with parallel antidumping actions. The introduction of countervailing measures clearly enhanced protective incentives to bring subsequent antidumping cases against China.[104] Considering that NME treatment of China under the WTO Accession Protocol expires in 2016, it is very likely that the US industries will continue to exploit the current trade remedy practices for the immediate time being.

As illustrated in Figure 1, no offset for CVDs in dumping margin calculation would lead to much higher antidumping duties. By pairing 'all others' CVD rates and 'PRC-wide' AD rates, Table 5 confirms this situation.[105]

---

[104] See Kenneth J. Pierce and Mathew R. Nicely, 'Transitioning to China's Market Economy Antidumping Treatment in 2016', available at http://www.abanet.org/intlaw/spring09/materials (visited 24 November 2010).

[105] There are many different rates for major exporters in these cases. So, for the sake of simplicity, 'all others' rates were chosen for the comparison.

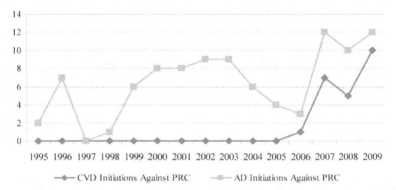

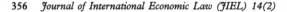

Figure 3. US CVD and AD measures in force against China (1995–31 December 2009). Source: Import Administration, US Department of Commerce, Antidumping and Countervailing Duty Case Information, <http://ia.ita.doc.gov/stats/caselist.txt> and <http://ia.ita.doc.gov/stats/inv-initiations-2000-current.html>.

Table 5. Simultaneous imposition of CVD and AD measures to the same Chinese imports

Case No.	CVD margin	Product	Case No.	AD margin
C-570-911	37.28	CWP	A-570-910	85.55
C-570-915	15.28	LWRP	A-570-914	264.64
C-570-917	226.85	LWS	A-570-916	91.73
C-570-926	169.01	Sodium Nitrite	A-570-925	190.74
C-570-913	5.62	OTR Tires	A-570-912	210.48
C-570-923	109.95	RFM	A-570-922	185.28
C-570-921	13.63	LWTP	A-570-920	115.29
C-570-936	35.67	Line Pipe	A-570-935	101.1
C-570-931	1.1	CWASPP	A-570-930	55.21
C-570-938	8.14	Citric Acid	A-570-937	156.87
C-570-940	13.3	Lawn Groomers	A-570-939	386.28
C-570-942	13.3	KASR	A-570-941	43.09
C-570-944	13.41	OCTG	A-570-943	99.14
C-570-946	27.64	PCSWS	A-570-945	193.55
C-570-948	62.46	Steel Grating	A-570-947	145.18
C-570-953	1.56	NWR with WS	A-570-952	247.65
C-570-955	24.24	MCB	A-570-954	236.00
C-570-963	109.11	S&PPS	A-570-962	95.40

Notes: 'CVD margins' are based on 'all others' rates whereas 'AD margins' are those of the 'PRC-wide' rates. Cases listed by date of 'Order'.
Source: Federal Register Notices.

Notably, the AD rates against China were, on average, roughly three times greater than the corresponding CVD rates when imposed simultaneously. Excluding *Laminated Woven Sacks*, AD rates were considerably higher than parallel CVD rates. This is in contrast with the previous perception that antidumping duties are likely to be reduced to account for the imposition of CVD measures against China.[106] Contrary to that perception, AD rates are far from being reduced. Moreover, the average AD/CVD ratio in these China cases remains considerably higher than that level derived for market economies. For example, based on data for market economies between 1995 and 2005, the average duty rate imposed in 36 CVD cases was about 13%, while the average AD rate imposed on NMEs was roughly double that, at about 26%.[107] In the subsidy cases regarding China, the CVD rates imposed on Chinese merchandise were notably high, but companion AD rates were even much higher.

Chinese respondents subject to *Pneumatic Off-the-Road Tires* challenged the DOC's NME treatment methodologies in their dumping margin calculations at the US CIT.[108] In a decision issued in September 2009, regarding *GPX International Corporation et al. v United States*, the CIT concluded that the DOC did not apply US law correctly and ordered the agency to revisit, and if necessary, recalculate the AD and CVD margins within ninety days. The most important aspect of the CIT decision in the *GPX* case may be its requirement that the DOC develop methodologies or new statutory tools to prevent double counting of subsidies if it applies AD and CVD duties simultaneously on imports of the same product, and to refrain from imposing CVDs on NME goods until it is prepared to address this problem.[109] The CIT also found that 'Commerce reasonably can do all of its remedying through the NME AD statute, as it likely accounts for any competitive advantages the exporter received that are measurable.'[110]

More significant decisions from the US CIT were issued in the second remand case. The US CIT ruled that the DOC must forego the imposition of CVDs on the NME products 'because its actions on remand clearly demonstrate its inability, at this time, to use improved methodologies to determine whether, and to what degree double counting occurs when NME antidumping remedies are imposed on the same good, or to otherwise comply with the unfair trade statutes in this regard.'[111] The DOC tried to comply with the US CIT decision by merely offsetting CVDs against NME AD after calculating the CVD and NME AD margins with regular methods. The US CIT, however, concluded that this offset method always leads to the unaltered NME AD margin, rendering concurrent CVD and AD investigations unnecessary. Perhaps more importantly, it ruled the method to be inconsistent with the US law by specifically permitting offsets only to export

---

[106] See GAO, *US – China Trade: Eliminating Nonmarket Economy Methodology Would Lower Antidumping Duties for Some Chinese Companies* (Washington DC, 10 January 2006).
[107] Ibid.
[108] See *GPX International Co. v United States*, Case No. 08-00285 (US Ct. Int'l Trade 2008).
[109] *GPX International Co. v United States*, 645 Fed Supp 2d. 1231 (US Ct. Int'l Trade 2009).
[110] Ibid, at 19.
[111] *GPX International Co. v United States*, 715 Fed Supp 2d. 1337 (US Ct. Int'l Trade 2010).

202

prices. Whether this decision can survive review by the Court of Appeals and congressional actions remains to be seen.

B. Consistency in the WTO system

Meanwhile, the Chinese government brought a case to the WTO, arguing that the failure of the USA to take action to avoid the double counting of duties that results from the combined application of the CVD and NME AD methodology is contrary to provisions of the AD Agreement and SCM Agreement, which limits the duties to 'appropriate amounts', as well as the most favored nation (MFN) treatment provision of Article I of the GATT. It is noteworthy that the DOC always takes offset procedures for CVDs in calculating dumping margins when dealing with market economies. The first litigation raised issue with the very first DOC decision to impose a CVD against China. However, this case was terminated as the ITC issued a negative injury determination.[112] In September 2008, China again raised the same issue concerning four CVDs imposed along with antidumping duties.[113] In October 2010, the Panel ruled that China did not establish the inconsistency of the imposition of 'double remedies' under, among others, SCM Agreement Articles 10, 19.3, 19.4 and 32.1, GATT Article VI:3 and GATT Article I:1.[114] Rejecting the Panel's 'rather mechanistic' reasoning[115], however, the Appellate Body in *US – AD CVD on China* ruled that the imposition of a double remedy is prohibited by Article 19.3 of the SCM Agreement.[116]

The Panel in *US – AD CVD on China* acknowledged that the concurrent imposition of ADs calculated under a NME methodology and of CVDs creates the potential of imposing a 'double remedy'.[117] However, the panel explained that CVDs are collected 'in the appropriate amounts' insofar as the amount collected does not exceed the amount of subsidy 'found to exist'. Since the imposition of AD duties calculated under a NME methodology has no impact on whether the amount of the concurrent CVD collected is

---

[112] *United States – Preliminary Anti-Dumping and Countervailing Duty Determinations on Coated Free Sheet Paper from China*, WT/DS368/1 (18 September 2007).

[113] WTO, *United States – Definitive Antidumping and Countervailing Duties on Certain Products from China: Request for the Establishment of a Panel by China*, WT/DS379/2 (12 December 2008).

[114] WTO Panel Report, *United States – Definitive Antidumping and Countervailing Duties on Certain Products from China (US – AD/CVD on China)*, WT/DS379/R, adopted 25 March 2011.

[115] WTO Appellate Body Report, *US – AD/CVD on China*, WT/DS379/AB/R, adopted 25 March 2011, para 567.

[116] Ibid, para 583. This article limits the scope of the analysis to the 'double remedy' issue, leaving other important legal issues such as 'public bodies' aside. For a more comprehensive legal analysis of the case, see Dukgeun Ahn, 'United States – Definitive Anti-Dumping and Countervailing Duties on Certain Products from China', 105(4) American Journal of International Law (forthcoming, 2011).

[117] WTO, above n 114, paras 14.69–14.70.

'appropriate' or not, the Panel ruled that Article 19.3 of the SCM Agreement does not address the question of double remedies. The Appellate Body viewed this panel interpretation as a 'willful isolation' of two agreements, explaining that '[i]t is counterintuitive to suggest that, while each agreement sets forth rules on the amounts of anti-dumping duties and countervailing duties that can be levied, there is no obstacle to the levying of a total amount of anti-dumping and countervailing duties which, if added together, would not be appropriate and would exceed the combined amounts of dumping and subsidization found.'[118] Thus, there was the fundamental difference in understanding of Article 19.3 in terms of whether the text provides the basis to link the two agreements on anti-dumping duties and countervailing duties.

On the other hand, a critical development in the drafting history relevant to the double remedy issue is the exclusion of Article 15 of the Tokyo Round Subsidies Code that explicitly required the choice between AD and CVD for addressing injuries caused by imports from NMEs. In fact, that provision did not draw any attention among the GATT contracting parties at that time, probably because no party ever used or was affected by it.[119] Consequently, Article 15 of the Tokyo Round Subsidies Code did not appear at the negotiation agenda and was removed even from the very first draft text of the SCM Agreement prepared in September 1990.[120] The Panel considered the existence of Article 15 of the Tokyo Round Subsidies Code to be 'significant'.[121] China argued that 'the circumstances surrounding the Uruguay Round negotiations strongly suggest that issues relating to these double remedies were no longer considered relevant at the time' because no contracting party had a practice of applying ADs concurrently with CVDs to NMEs and even the USA—the largest user of CVDs—had taken a clear position of not applying CVDs to imports from NMEs.[122] The USA countered by noting that the Tokyo Round Subsidies Code contained provisions that were virtually identical to Articles 19.3 and 19.4 of the SCM Agreement. In other words, the USA argued that 'had these provisions prohibited the imposition of double remedies, as China contends, there would have been no need to include in the same Code an express prohibition on concurrent anti-dumping and countervailing duty investigations.'[123]

[118] WTO, above n 115, para 572.
[119] For example, while more than 30 submissions on the SCM Agreement were made by the contracting parties during the Uruguay Round negotiation, none was made by a NME country.
[120] GATT, MTN.GNG/NG10/W/38/Rev.1 (4 September 1990). There appears to be no documentary evidence related to this part of the negotiating history. See WTO, above n 114, footnote 1025.
[121] WTO, above n 114, para 14.119.
[122] Ibid, para 14.85.
[123] Ibid, para 14.87.

The Panel 'consider[ed] it likely that the rationale for the inclusion of Article 15 of the Tokyo Round Subsidies Code was the potential for double remedies to result from the concurrent imposition of NME methodologies in calculating anti-dumping duties and of countervailing duties, or at least the recognition that the use of a NME methodology would capture price differences resulting from subsidies granted on the product subject to antidumping duties.'[124] Although the Panel did not provide explicit rulings about how to interpret the omission of Article 15 of the Code in the SCM Agreement, it ruled that the existence of Article 15 in the Code explicitly addressing the concurrent imposition of ADs and CVDs on NMEs should mean that Articles 19.3 and 19.4 of the SCM Agreement have no relevance for the question of the permissibility of double remedies.[125]

In relation to this issue, the Panel noted that the prohibition of double remedies under Article VI:5 of the GATT is limited only to export subsidies. Therefore, it was the Panel's view that while the double remedy with respect to export subsidies has been prohibited since the establishment of the GATT, the explicit elaboration for double remedy against NMEs was clearly changed during the Uruguay Round negotiation, implying that the drafters actually intended to broaden the scope of CVDs against NMEs.

Another relevant development is section 15 of China's Protocol of Accession, which permits CVDs against China.[126] Although section 15 does not directly address whether double remedy is allowed without any limitation, the Chinese government in the proceeding conceded that 'its Protocol of Accession permits the concurrent imposition of anti-dumping duties calculated under a NME methodology and of countervailing duties.'[127]

The Appellate Body categorically rejected this part of the panel finding. Ruling that the Tokyo Round Subsidies Code 'may, at most, form part of the circumstances of the conclusion of a treaty' under Article 32 of the Vienna Convention of the Law of the Treaties (VCLT) rather than an 'element of context' within the meaning of Article 31 of the VCLT, the Appellate Body did not consider it 'necessary to confirm the interpretation of Article 19.3 by relying on supplementary means of interpretation.'[128] Moreover, the Appellate Body explained that 'the absence of a provision like Article 15 of the Tokyo Round Subsidies Code in the SCM Agreement cannot be interpreted as indicating that Members intended to exclude from the scope of the SCM Agreement a different and narrower obligation, such as a prohibition on double remedies' because Article 15 'does more than merely

---

[124] Ibid, footnote 1026.
[125] Ibid, para 14.119.
[126] WTO, above n 65 (dated 23 November 2001).
[127] WTO, above n 114, footnote 1028.
[128] WTO, above n 115, paras 576–80.

prohibit double remedies in that it prohibits the concurrent application of anti-dumping and countervailing duties, regardless of whether they offset the same situation of subsidization'.

This ruling of the Appellate Body may raise some controversy because it is difficult to justify the interpretation of Article 15 as having a broader role than merely prohibiting double remedies. Considering the commonsensical understanding that the whole purpose of Article 15 was to prevent double remedies, the Appellate Body should have rendered a more convincing interpretation or explanation for deleting a directly relevant provision from the Tokyo Round Subsidies Code. Indeed, given the fact that overall disciplines under the SCM Agreement were significantly strengthened to regulate subsidy measures during the Uruguay Round negotiation, and that China—a major NME with huge trade potential—tried to join the GATT then, it may not be completely implausible to assume that CVD possibilities against NMEs were intentionally broadened, although this issue did not draw much attention among other—mostly inexperienced—contracting parties.

A more fundamental issue in the Appellate Body ruling is the legal interpretation of 'appropriateness' in SCM Article 19.3 to link the imposition of AD duties and CVDs. From the policy perspective, the Appellate Body set forth a desirable decision, in stating that 'it should not be possible to circumvent the rules in each agreement by taking measures under both agreements to counteract the same subsidization.'[129] However, the legal basis for the decision raises several controversial questions. For example, while the Appellate Body considers existence of the parallel expressions, 'in the appropriate amounts in each case', as evidence of the need to 'read the two agreements together', the 'appropriate amounts' expression in fact originated from the Kennedy Round Antidumping Code with which the matching Subsidies Code was not existent. Therefore, one can question whether the assumption that the parallel provisions in both agreements were designed to communicate with each other.

Moreover, the whole structure of Article 19 in the SCM Agreement may be viewed somewhat differently from the description provided by the Appellate Body. In fact, Article 19 of the SCM Agreement is a selected and modestly restructured provision from Article 4 of the Tokyo Round Subsidies Code. After laying out the general principle of CVD impositions in Article 19.1, the paragraphs that follow set forth the rules for subsequent stages of CVD imposition and collection. In other words, for the decision stage, Article 19.2 explains the full authority of an importing member for imposing CVDs—even stating that a lesser duty is 'desirable'. In the next stage of actual CVD imposition, Article 19.3 stipulates appropriateness and non-discrimination as the guiding principle. When a CVD is finally

[129] Ibid, para 572.

collected, Article 19.4 clarifies the maximum ceiling with the concrete criteria that 'the amount of the subsidy found to exist, [should be] calculated in terms of subsidization per unit of the subsidized and exported product'. It is noted that the maximum is set in terms of subsidy amount instead of price effect on exportation.

If we follow this reading of Article 19, the 'levying' rather than 'imposition' of CVDs 'in the appropriate amounts in each case' may be understood in a more specific and narrower context confined to CVD actions. As the USA adopts a retrospective system for levying or collecting CVDs, actual CVD amounts to be levied often differ from the initially imposed CVDs depending on the administrative review decisions. Thus, levying CVDs in the appropriate amount in each case may be understood to allow some variation in the final stage of CVD actions which constitutes the unique and most important feature of the US practices. The origin of this expression from the Kennedy Round Antidumping Code may render the above interpretation more persuasive. Even if this alternative interpretation is accepted, it may still be controversial whether such contextual or historical interpretations should prevail over perhaps a more literal approach by the Appellate Body, in tune arguably with the current WTO membership.

The following explanation of the Appellate Body on its interpretation of 'appropriateness' is also puzzling:

> In *EC – Salmon (Norway)*, the panel found that the appropriate amount of an anti-dumping duty 'must be an amount that results in offsetting or preventing dumping, when all other requirements for the imposition of anti-dumping duties have been fulfilled'. We consider that the panel's interpretation of Article 9.2 of the *Anti-Dumping Agreement* in *EC – Salmon (Norway)* is consistent with our interpretation of the phrase 'in the appropriate amounts' in Article 19.3 of the *SCM Agreement*, as prohibiting the imposition of double remedies, and with the notion that the two agreements should be read together in a consistent and coherent manner. In fact, applying the reasoning of the panel in *EC – Salmon (Norway)*, an appropriate amount of countervailing duty should be an amount that results in offsetting subsidization, with due regard being had to the concurrent application of anti-dumping duties on the same product that offset the same subsidization. (emphasis added)

The Panel in *EC – Salmon (Norway)* emphasized the determination of the appropriate AD amount within the context of the AD Agreement. It is not very clear how the panel's ruling in *EC – Salmon (Norway)* can be applied to the question of the concurrent application of ADs in determining appropriate amounts of CVDs.

The Appellate Body's ruling on appropriateness as a tool to link AD and CVD amounts filled another important gap in the porous textual language of the WTO Agreements, rectifying dangerously abusive trade remedy practices in the WTO system. Despite such contribution, the legal justification of the

Appellate Body ruling may create complications for future disputes due to the potentially overreaching implication of its legal interpretation.

V. CONCLUDING REMARKS

The USA has actually broadened the scope of CVD actions against NMEs by including Vietnam in 2009.[130] After a preliminary determination of 2–5% actionable subsidy rates for *Polyethylene Retail Carrier Bags*, in its final determination the DOC authorized rates ranging from 0.44 to 5.28%, except for one firm to which 52.56% was applied on the basis of adverse facts available in the final determination.[131] The US DOC practically applied the same methodology to this case as the one employed for other cases involving China.

Both China and Vietnam have been working through bilateral arrangements with many WTO members to resolve the AD problems caused by the NME provisions in the WTO Accession Protocol. Although several major WTO members, such as the USA, EU, Japan and Canada, refuse to treat China and Vietnam as market economies, many other WTO members, including Australia, New Zealand, Korea and ASEAN countries, have agreed to essentially repeal the NME treatment provisions. But US CVD actions against NMEs have opened a whole new possibility for the trade remedy actions, which pressures even the WTO Members abandoning NME provisions to consider CVDs for their aggrieved domestic industries. In this regard, it is noted that the number of WTO Members using countervailing measures has been constantly increasing since the inception of the WTO.[132]

This situation is disturbing since the WTO Members show a clear tendency toward bringing retaliatory actions against others when their subsidy policies are challenged. NMEs such as China and Vietnam may end up facing more politically controversial problems dealing with CVD actions based on the status of their economies, and not necessarily on particular trade policy measures. Moreover, another troubling problem is the possibility of using CVD actions against many other NMEs, some recently acceded to the WTO and still many others, such as Russia and Kazakhstan, in the

---

[130] See *Polyethylene Retail Carrier Bags from the Socialist Republic of Vietnam: Final Affirmative Countervailing Duty Determination*, 75 US Federal Register 16428 (Department of Commerce, 1 April 2010).

[131] Due to relatively high dumping margins of 52.3–76.11%, CVD actions were not taken seriously at least from the commercial point of view.

[132] By the end of 2009, the number of the WTO Members that imposed countervailing measures reached to 15, among the 20 Members that initiated countervailing investigations. http://www.wto.org/english/tratop_e/scm_e/cvd_meas_rep_member_e.pdf (visited 29 September 2010). Moreover, as of October 2009, 90 WTO Members notified their countervailing regulations to the WTO SCM Committee. This is in stark contrast with the GATT regime in which only contracting parties maintained countervailing regulations. See WTO, *Report of the Committee on Subsidies and Countervailing Measures*, G/L/906, adopted 26 October 2009.

process of WTO accession negotiations. Despite considerably articulated norms in the SCM Agreement, the authority of a WTO Member to impose CVDs against NMEs is completely contingent upon the discretionary judgment of whether a NME substantially differs from the former Soviet style economies or, generally speaking, whether the economic circumstances of a NME somehow render governmental functions as illegal subsidies that interfere with market competition. No better rule on this matter is expected in the foreseeable future in the WTO system. Although one of the most egregious problems of CVD actions against NMEs, i.e. the 'double remedy' issue was settled by the Appellate Body ruling, CVD actions would still become major trade policy measures against NMEs in the WTO system and continue to raise unprecedented complexity in legal jurisprudence.

While some improvements are expected to be made in due course, the perils of the prevailing order have many implications for future Sino-American trade relations and trade remedy practices against other transitional economies. Given the WTO Appellate Body decision to prohibit CVD actions against NMEs with the penalty of double remedy, many WTO Members need to articulate or refine their trade remedy actions. And yet numerous controversial legal challenges concerning CVD action against NMEs will be introduced into the WTO system through the newly opened door and will demand collective endeavor by the WTO membership to balance political compromises and the legal reality.

Appendix 1

Appendix 1. Rates and target industries in US CVDs against China

Case No.	Product	Sector	Producer/Exporter	Prelim.	Final	Order
C-570-911	CWP	XV	East Pipe	*0*	29.57	29.62
			Shuangjie[a]	264.98	615.92	616.83
			Kingland	16.59	44.86	44.93
			All others	16.59	37.22	37.28
C-570-915	LWRP	XV	(Kunshan)	*0.27*	2.17	2.17
			Qingdao[a]	77.85	200.58	200.58
			ZZPC	2.99	15.28	15.28
			All others	2.99	15.28	15.28
C-570-917	LWS	XI	SSJ[b]	2.57	352.82	352.82
			(Aifudi)	11.59	29.54	29.54
			Han Shing Chemical[a]	57.14	223.74	223.74
			Ningbo[b]	57.14	223.74	223.74
			Qilu[b]	57.14	304.4	304.4
			All others	2.57	226.85	226.85
C-570-926	Sodium Nitrite	VI	Shanxi Jiaocheng[a]	93.56	169.01	169.01
			Tianjin Soda Plant[a]	93.56	169.01	169.01
			All others	93.56	169.01	169.01

(continued)

Appendix 1. Continued

Case No.	Product	Sector	Producer/Exporter	Prelim.	Final	Order
C-570-913	OTR Tires	VII	Guizhou Tire	3.13	2.45	2.45
			Starbright	2.38	14	14
			TUTRIC[b]	6.59	6.85	6.85
			All others	4.44	5.62	5.62
C-570-923	RFM	XVI	Cixi[a]	70.41	109.95	109.95
			Polyflex[a]	70.41	109.95	109.95
			All others	70.41	109.95	109.95
C-570-921	LWTP	X	Hanhong	*0.57*	*0.57*	*0.57*
			Xiamen[a]	Pending	123.65	124.93
			Shenzhen Yuanming[a]	59.5	137.25	138.53
			MDCN[a]	59.5	123.65	124.93
			GG	5.68	13.17	13.63
			All others	5.68	13.17	13.63
C-570-936	Line Pipe	XV	Huludao Companies	18.89	35.63	31.29
			Liaoning Northern Steels	31.65	40.05	40.05
			All others	25.27	37.84	35.67
C-570-931	CWASPP	XV	Froch[a]	106.85	299.16	299.16
			Winner	1.47	1.1	1.1
			All others	1.47	1.1	1.1
C-570-938	Citric Acid	VI	Anhui BBCA[a]	97.72	118.95	118.95
			TTCA[b]	1.41	12.68	12.68
			Yixing Union	3.92	3.6	3.6
			All others	2.67	8.14	8.14
C-570-940	Lawn Groomers	XVI	Princeway	*0.95*	*0.56*	*0.56*
			Superpowers	2.77	13.3	13.3
			Qingdao Hundai[a]	254.52	264.98	264.98
			Qingdao Taifa[a]	254.52	264.98	264.98
			Qingdao EA[a]	254.52	264.98	264.98
			Maxchief Investments[a]	254.52	264.98	264.98
			World Factory[a]	254.52	264.98	264.98
			All others	2.77	13.3	13.3
C-570-942	KASR	XVI	Asber[a]	197.14	170.82	170.82
			Wire King	13.22	13.3	13.3
			Changzhou Yixiong[a]	162.87	149.91	149.91
			Foshan Winleader[a]	162.87	149.91	149.91
			Kingsun Enterprises[a]	162.87	149.91	149.91
			Zhongshan Iwatani[a]	162.87	149.91	149.91
			Yuyao Hanjun[a]	162.87	149.91	149.91
			All others	13.22	13.3	13.3
C-570-944	OCTG	XV	Changbao	24.33	11.98	12.46
			TPCO[b]	10.9	10.36	10.49
			Wuxi[b]	24.92	14.61	14.95
			Jianli	30.69	15.78	15.78
			All others	21.33	13.2	13.41
C-570-946	Prestressed Concrete Steel Wire Strand	XV	Xinhua	12.06	45.85	45.85
			Fasten	7.53	8.85	9.42
			Jiangyin	7.53	8.85	9.42
			All others	9.80	27.35	27.64
C-570-948	Steel Grating	XV	Ningbo	7.44	62.46	62.46
			All others	7.44	62.46	62.46
C-570-953	Narrow Woven Ribbons with Woven Selvedge	XI	Yama	0.29	1.56	1.56
			Changtai	118.68	117.95	117.95
			All others	59.49	1.56	1.56

(continued)

Appendix 1. Continued

Case No.	Product	Sector	Producer/Exporter	Prelim.	Final	Order
C-570-955	Magnesia Carbon Bricks	XIII	Mayerton	*de minimis*	253.87	253.87
			RHI	*de minimis*	24.24	24.24
			All others	*de minimis*	24.24	24.24
C-570-963	Sodium and Potassium Phosphate Salts	VI	Lianyungang	109.11	109.11	109.11
			Mianyang	109.11	109.11	109.11
			Shifang	109.11	109.11	109.11
			All others	109.11	109.11	109.11

Notes: 'Prelim.' stands for the preliminarily determined duty rates; 'Final' stands for that of final determinations; and 'Order' presents the actual subsidy margins that were levied to individual producers and exporters. Parenthesized 'Producers/Exporters' are the voluntary respondents while the italicized ones are uncooperative firms that were neither mandatory nor voluntary respondents in each case. Italicized duty margins represent zero or *de minimis* rates.
^aCases based on total AFA.
^bThe use of AFA in the countervailable subsidy margin determination.
Source: <http://ia.ita.doc.gov/stats/inv-initiations-2000-current.html>.

APPENDIX 2.

Subsidy program determined to be countervailable by US DOC

National programs

Section description / Section/Harmonized System code two digit / Case numbers (C-570-number)	Base metals and articles XV/73								Machinery XVI/84,85			Chemicals VI/28,29		Rubber VII/40	Paper X/48	Textile XI/63,58		Stone XIII/68,69	SUM
	911	915	931	936	944	946	948	963	923	940	942	926	938	913	921	917	953	955	
I. Provision of goods and services at less than adequate remuneration	x	x	x	x	x	x	x	x	x	x	x	x	x	x	x	x		x	16
II. Grants				x	x	x	x	x				x	x	x	x		x		9
III. Loans			x	x	x	x						x	x	x	x		x		9
IV. Income tax reduction and exemption programs		x	x	x	x	x		x	x	x	x	x	x	x	x	x	x	x	15
V. Other tax exemption programs												x		x	x				2
VI. Income tax credit and refund programs			x	x	x				x	x		x	x					x	7
VII. Indirect tax programs and import tariff programs			x		x		x	x	x	x		x	x	x	x	x	x	x	12
VIII. Debt forgiveness	x				x									x	x			x	4
Countervailable national subsidy programs by section	28								11			12		7	6	2	4	4	74

Provincial programs

Section description / Section/Harmonized System code two digit / Case numbers (C-570-number)	Base metals and articles XV/73								Machinery XVI/84,85			Chemicals VI/28,29		Rubber VII/40	Paper X/48	Textile XI/63,58		Stone XIII/68,69	SUM
	911	915	931	936	944	946	948	963	923	940	942	926	938	913	921	917	953	955	
I. Provision of goods and services at less than adequate remuneration				x			x	x	x	x		x	x	x					4
II. Grants	x				x	x	x	x	x	x		x	x		x	x		x	11
III. Loans	x								x	x		x	x						4
IV. Income tax reduction and exemption programs						x		x							x			x	6
V. Indirect tax programs and import tariff programs				x															1
Countervailable provincial subsidy programs by section	10								6			5		1	2	0	1	1	26

*Source: Data compiled from the Decision Memorandums of the thirteen effective US CVD cases against China.

*Note: Individual cases based upon total AFA are excluded.

APPENDIX 3.

Subsidy program determined to be countervailable by CBSA

National programs — Section/Harmonized System code two digit

Case numbers (D-15-number)	Base metals and articles XV/73,76						Machinery XVI/84	SUM
	56	52	51	50	49	54	53	
I. Provision of goods and services at less than adequate remuneration	x	x			x	x		4
II. Grants			x	x	x			3
III. Loans				x	x		x	3
IV. Income tax reduction and exemption programs								0
V. Other tax exemption programs								0
VI. Income tax credit and refund programs			x					1
VII. Indirect tax programs and import tariff programs								0
VIII. Debt forgiveness	x							1
Countervailable national subsidy programs by section	2	1	2	2	3	1	1	12

Provincial programs — Section/Harmonized System code two digit

Case numbers (D-15-number)	Base metals and articles XV/73,76						Machinery XVI/84	SUM
	56	52	51	50	49	54	53	
I. Provision of goods and services at less than adequate remuneration	x							1
II. Grants		x		x	x	x		4
III. Loans								0
IV. Income tax reduction and exemption programs	x	x	x	x	x	x	x	7
V. Other tax exemption programs				x				1
VI. Income tax credit and refund programs	x			x	x	x	x	5
VII. Indirect tax programs and import tariff programs	x		x	x		x		4
VIII. Debt forgiveness								0
Countervailable provincial subsidy programs by section	4	2	2	5	3	4	2	22

* Source: Statement of Reasons, CBSA.

* Note: D-15-49, 50 based on programs identified at initiation.

World Trade Review (2014), 13: 2, 267–279
© Dukgeun Ahn and Patrick Messerlin   doi:10.1017/S1474745614000020   First published online 12 March 2014

Chapter 8

United States – Anti-Dumping Measures on Certain Shrimp and Diamond Sawblades from China: never ending zeroing in the WTO?

DUKGEUN AHN*
Seoul National University
PATRICK MESSERLIN**
Sciences Po and Seoul National University

Abstract: Despite many legal rulings to clarify the WTO inconsistency of zeroing practices, in practically all aspects of antidumping proceedings, the United States declined to categorically rectify the illegal antidumping duties based on zeroing calculation methods. This dispute is merely example of a number of disputes where the US government had to exhaust the whole process for proper implementation of the WTO rulings under its domestic legal system. The US approach is starkly contrasted with the position taken by the European Union that categorically terminates zeroing practices pursuant to the WTO rulings. While the WTO system indeed recognizes individual Member's peculiar regulatory systems and policies during implementation phases, the current situation in which WTO Members must individually resort to the dispute settlement system in order to rectify the US zeroing practices raises a serious concern regarding the legitimacy and integrity of the WTO dispute settlement system. Maybe it is time for WTO Members to agree on better implementation mechanisms before more Members try to develop overly burdensome and complicated regulatory processes for compliance.

1. Introduction

Since a 'zeroing' dispute was first brought to the WTO dispute settlement system by the *EC–Bed Linen* (DS141) case in 1999, numerous relevant cases have followed to

* Email: dahn@snu.ac.kr
** Email: patrick.messerlin@free.fr
We are very grateful to insightful comments by Edwin Vermulst, Chad Bown, Petros Mavroidis and Sungjoon Cho, and participants in the European Union Institute Conference held in Florence during June 3-4, 2013. We also appreciate excellent research assistance by Wonkyu Shin, Minjung Kim and Hyoyoung Lee as well as the financial support from the National Research Foundation of Korea Grant funded by the Korean government (NRF-2011-330-B00063) and Seoul National University Asia Center (0448A-20130004).

267

broaden the scope of Appellate Body rulings.[1] Unlike the European Union, however, the United States has adopted a unique retrospective antidumping procedure and complicated implementation mechanisms to embrace adverse WTO rulings under the Uruguay Round Agreements Act (URAA). This peculiar antidumping system, combined with a dualistic legal system, made many WTO Members bring redundant complaints against the US government concerning essentially identical zeroing practices in order to rectify the existing illegal antidumping duty calculation method using zeroing methodologies.

The current dispute, *United States – Anti-Dumping Measures on Certain Shrimp and Diamond Sawblades from China* (DS422), is one of those cases where the US government simply exhausted the panel procedure to lose the case so that it could meet the URAA requirement to implement the WTO Dispute Settlement Body (DSB) recommendations. Accordingly, this case does not contribute to the zeroing jurisprudence by adding any significant legal ruling. Nevertheless, this dispute highlights systemic non-compliance problems in the WTO dispute settlement system. In particular, the starkly contrasted approaches by the United States and the European Union to incorporate WTO rulings on zeroing practices raise concerns regarding the structural delay and non-compliance problems, which were hardly anticipated at the inception of the WTO system. We would like to draw academic attention to this systemic problem in the WTO dispute settlement system and discuss the potential implications for the future of the world trading system.

The structure of this article is as follows. Section 2 explains the factual aspects of the dispute and rulings. Section 3 presents the case in the context of all WTO zeroing disputes. Systemic non-compliance problems and the consequent legal and policy issues will be discussed in Section 4. Section 5 addresses the remaining issues for zeroing practices in the WTO system.

2. Disputed issues and rulings

This dispute concerns the zeroing practices of the US Department of Commerce (DOC) in anti-dumping (AD) proceedings for shrimp and diamond sawblades imported from China. Based on the previous rulings on zeroing practices by the Appellate Body, China brought these disputes to the WTO dispute settlement system in order to rectify the existing AD duties.[2] The panel request made on 13 October 2011 led to the panel report which was adopted on 23 July 2012.

---

1 The controversy concerning legal decisions by the WTO panels and the Appellate Body has spawned a large number of academic studies, many of which were published in this journal. They include Bown and Sykes (2008); Crowley and Howse (2010); Grossman and Sykes (2006); Hoekman and Wauters (2011); Prusa and Vermulst (2009); Prusa and Vermulst (2011); Vandenbussche (2009).

2 The consultation request was submitted to the WTO DSB on 28 February 2011, WT/DS422/1 (dated 2 March 2011).

The European Union, Honduras, Japan, Korea, Thailand, and Vietnam joined as third parties in the panel proceeding.

In the AD investigation for shrimp, the US petitioners challenged exporters not only from China but also from Brazil, Ecuador, India, Thailand, and Vietnam. The dumping margins for Chinese exporters, however, were very high compared to those for other countries.[3] For example, the dumping margins for the exporters from Ecuador and Thailand were in the range of 2–4% and 5–6%, respectively. The highest dumping margins for India, Vietnam, and Brazil were about 13%, 25%, and 68%, respectively. But the major Chinese exporters were subject to AD margins which were higher than 90%, while the PRC-wide margin was determined to be 112.81%. More specific dumping margins for Chinese exporters are summarized in Table 1.

In any case, Ecuador (DS335), Thailand (DS324, 343) and Vietnam (DS404, 429) also brought separate WTO disputes concerning the same US zeroing practices.[4]

It is noted that around the time the consultation request was submitted to the WTO Dispute Settlement Body (DSB) the antidumping duties imposed on major Chinese exporters were already significantly reduced after the remand procedure. On the other hand, since China is treated as a non-market economy in the US AD investigation, India was selected as the surrogate country in this case, in consideration of India's comparable level of economic development to that of the PRC, India's significant production of frozen and canned warm-water shrimp, and the availability of India's data to value the factors of production. With respect to this shrimp AD investigation, China challenged the DOC on the use of the zeroing methodology in determining Allied, Yelin, and Red Garden's dumping margins and calculating the separate rate.

Figure 1 shows the trend of shrimp imports from the countries subject to the US AD investigations, illustrating a typical pattern for trade diversion among exporters. In the early 2000s, the imports from Thailand were dramatically replaced by the imports from China, India, and Vietnam. Then, AD actions against these exporters caused a significant negative impact on their exports to the US market. The fall in Thailand's exports relatively quickly recovered after the AD action, whereas China, India, and Brazil suffered for a longer period. However, by 2011, most of the plunges in imports from the major AD target countries generally recovered to the pre-AD period level. The recovery consequently led to the US countervailing duty actions against them in 2013.[5]

---

3 See 69 Federal Register 76910, 69 Federal Register 76913, 69 Federal Register 76916, 69 Federal Register 76918, 69 Federal Register 71005 (8 December 2004).

4 See a more detailed list in Table 3.

5 'Certain Frozen Warm Water Shrimp From the People's Republic of China, Ecuador, India, Indonesia, Malaysia, Thailand, and the Socialist Republic of Vietnam: Initiation of Countervailing Duty Investigations', 78 Federal Register 5416 (25 January 2013). This CVD action includes Indonesia and

In the AD investigation for diamond sawblades,[6] the DOC determined the dumping margins using zeroing methodologies for exports from China[7] and Korea.[8] On 24 November 2009, Korea brought a consultation request (DS402) to the WTO DSB. On 28 February 2011, China also brought a consultation request concerning the zeroing methodology in determining the dumping margin for one of the major exporters, AT&M (Table 2).

As shown in Figure 2, the imports of diamond sawblades from China had been rapidly increasing until around the time the AD investigations were initiated. Although the imports from China dropped subsequently for a few years due to the global financial crisis, it soon picked up the general trend of rapid increase – in contrast, despite its much smaller export volume.

When China brought this case to the WTO, the United States did not oppose China's arguments that the methodology applied by the DOC in the AD investigations was 'substantially identical in all legally relevant respects' to the methodology employed in *United States – Final Dumping Determination on Softwood Lumber from Canada* (DS264). In fact, the panel explained that this case presented a similar situation with a few previous disputes such as *US–Shrimp (Ecuador)* (DS335) and, subsequently, *US–Shrimp (Thailand)* (DS343), *US–Anti-Dumping Measures on PET Bags* (DS383), and *US–Zeroing (Korea)* (DS402).

Given that the United States did not rebut the arguments and the evidence submitted by China, the panel found that the United States acted inconsistently with Article 2.4.2 of the Anti-Dumping Agreement due to the DOC's use of zeroing in the calculation of the dumping margins for Allied, Yelin, and Red Garden in the shrimp investigation, and of the dumping margin for AT&M in the diamond sawblades investigation. In addition, the panel ruled that the calculation of the separate rate on the basis of these margins necessarily incorporated the WTO-inconsistent zeroing methodology.

3. Zeroing disputes in context

Considering many previous zeroing disputes in the GATT/WTO system, this dispute does not make any additional legal contribution to the relevant jurisprudence.[9] And yet, this case highlights the systemic problems of the WTO dispute settlement system in terms of implementation.

Malaysia, instead of Brazil whose exportation of shrimp to the United States almost disappeared due to the AD actions.

6 A diamond saw blade normally has a round shape with diamonds fixed on its edge for cutting hard or abrasive materials such as porcelain, ceramic, marble, brick, block, concrete, roof tile and asphalt.

7 71 Federal Register 29303 (22 May 2006).

8 71 Federal Register 29310 (22 May 2006). The weighted average dumping margins are 12.76% for Ehwa, 26.55% for Shinhan, 6.43% for Hyosung, and 16.39% for all others.

9 Regarding the concise overview of the zeroing jurisprudence, see Cho (2012); Vermulst and Ikenson (2007).

Table 1. Dumping margins for Chinese shrimp exporters

	Preliminary determination	Final determination (2004.12.8)	Amended final determination (2005.2.1)	Second amended final determination (2006.8.17)	Amended by remand decision (2011.4.26)	Amended by second remand decision (2011.5.24)
Allied	90.05%	84.93%	80.19%		Scope of AD revised to include dusted shrimp	5.07%
Yelin	98.34%	82.27%				8.45%
Red Garden	7.67%	27.89%				
Zhanjiang Guolian	0.04%	0.07% (de minimis)				
Separate rate	49.09%	55.23%	53.68%	11 exporters added		17.32%
PRC-wide rate	112.81%	112.81%				

Note: A separate rate was determined for each 35 exporters/producers who were not selected for individual examination but had established their independence from the government.

Table 2. Dumping margins for Chinese diamond sawblades exporters

	Preliminary determination	Final determination (2006.5.22)	Amended final determination (2006.6.22)
AT&M	0.11%	2.50%	2.82%
Bosun	16.34%	34.19%	35.51%
Hebei Jikai	10.07%	48.50%	
Separate rate	14.966%	20.72%	21.43%
PRC-wide rate	164.09%	164.09%	

Figure 1. US imports of certain frozen and canned warm water shrimp

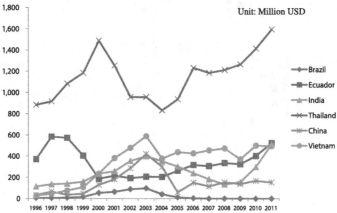

Note: This figure is based on HS 0306.13.0003–0024 and HS 1605.20.1010–1040 that are the subject of the AD actions.

Sources: Data have been compiled from tariff and trade data from the US Department of Commerce and the US International Trade Commission.

Broadly speaking, zeroing disputes may be categorized into two groups: one group for setting forth important legal principles concerning zeroing practices, 'principal cases' and the other group for rectifying the existing illegal AD duties based on rulings of principal cases, 'remedial cases'. Table 3 shows the zeroing disputes classified into the two categories.

The eight disputes listed in the 'Principal WTO Cases' category actually illustrate unprecedented legal controversy in the WTO system regarding the zeroing practice.[10] As discussed in previous analyses, four panel decisions directly attempted

10 *US – Provisional Anti-Dumping Measures on Import of Certain Softwood Lumber from Canada* (DS247) was not litigated.

Figure 2. US imports of diamond saw blades and parts

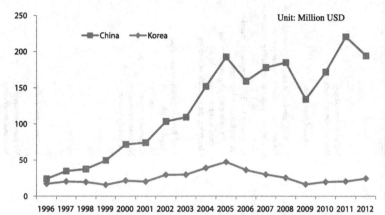

Note: This figure is based on HS 8202.39 and HS 8206.00 that are the subject of the AD actions.
Sources: Data have been compiled from tariff and trade data from the US Department of Commerce and the US International Trade Commission.

to reverse the Appellate Body rulings.[11] Moreover, predominant numbers of the WTO jurists, i.e., panelists and Appellate Body members, manifested the disagreement to the Appellate Body rulings. Despite all these controversies, the WTO dispute settlement system has repeatedly confirmed the illegality of zeroing practices in almost all aspects of the AD investigations.

Notwithstanding a host of the Appellate Body rulings, the fact that there are many subsequent 'remedial' disputes manifested structural problems in relation to the implementation of the WTO dispute settlement adjudications. Unlike other WTO Members that readily modify or change administrative actions such as by imposing AD duties pursuant to the WTO recommendations, the United States has continued to maintain its regulatory procedures to incorporate the WTO rulings.[12]

Under Section 129 of the Uruguay Round Agreements Act that stipulates 'Administrative Action Following WTO Panel Reports', the US Trade Representative (USTR) must consult with the DOC along with pertinent congressional committees so as to come up with an implementation plan, and may direct the

11 These cases are *US – Laws, Regulations and Methodology for Calculating Dumping Margins* (DS294), *US – Final Dumping Determination on Softwood Lumber from Canada (Art. 21.5)* (DS264), *US – Measures Relating to Zeroing and Sunset Reviews* (DS322), and *US – Final Anti-dumping Measures on Stainless Steel from Mexico* (DS344). Regarding legal disagreement between panels and the Appellate Body Members, see Lewis (2012).
12 See also Bown and Prusa (2010); Grimmett (2012); Nye (2009); Voon (2011).

Table 3. Classification of zeroing disputes

GATT case		
EC – Anti-dumping Duties on Audio Tapes in Cassettes Originating in Japan	ADP/136 (28.4.1995)	Unadopted
Principal WTO cases		
EC – Anti-dumping Duties on Imports of Cotton Type Bed Linen from India	DS141 (India)	No model zeroing
US – Sunset Review of Anti-dumping Duties on Corrosion-Resistant Carbon Steel Flat Products from Japan	DS244 (Japan)	No decision on zeroing
US – Provisional Anti-Dumping Measures on Import of Certain Softwood Lumber from Canada	DS247	No panel proceeding
US – Final Dumping Determination on Softwood Lumber from Canada	DS264 (Canada)	No W-W zeroing in original investigations
US – Laws, Regulations and Methodology for Calculating Dumping Margins	DS294 (EC)	No zeroing in administrative reviews
		Compliance panel & retaliation arbitration
US – Final Dumping Determination on Softwood Lumber from Canada (Art. 21.5)	DS264/RW (Canada)	No zeroing for T-T
US – Measures Relating to Zeroing and Sunset Reviews	DS322 (Japan)	No zeroing for T-T Compliance panel & retaliation arbitration
US – Final Anti-dumping Measures on Stainless Steel from Mexico	DS344 (Mexico)	Panel's ruling denying precedential effects was reversed by the AB
US – Continued Existence and Application of Zeroing Methodology	DS350 (EC)	Clarifying the illegality of zeroing
Remedial WTO cases		
EC – Anti-dumping Duties on Malleable Cast Iron Tube or Pipe Fittings from Brazil	DS219	Panel Report (PR)/Appellate Body Report (ABR)
US – Anti-dumping Duties on Silicon Metal from Brazil	DS239	No panel proceeding
US – Anti-dumping Measures on Cement from Mexico	DS281	No panel proceeding
US – Provisional Anti-dumping Measures on Shrimp from Thailand	DS324	No panel proceeding
US – Anti-dumping Determinations Regarding Stainless Steel from Mexico	DS325	No panel proceeding
US – Anti-dumping Measures on Shrimp from Ecuador	DS335	PR
US – Measures Relating to Shrimp from Thailand	DS343	PR/ABR
US – Anti-dumping Administrative Reviews and Other Measures Related to Imports of Certain Orange Juice from Brazil	DS382	PR
US – Anti-dumping Measures on Polyethylene Retail Carrier Bags from Thailand	DS383	PR
US – Use of Zeroing in Anti-dumping Measures Involving Products from Korea	DS402	PR
US – Anti-dumping Measures on Certain Shrimp from Vietnam	DS404	PR
US – Anti-dumping Measures on Corrosion-resistant Carbon Steel Flat Products from Korea	DS420	No panel proceeding
US – Anti-dumping Measures on Shrimp and Diamond Sawblades from China	DS422	PR
US – Anti-Dumping Measures on Imports of Stainless Steel Sheet and Strip in Coils from Italy	DS424	No panel proceeding
US – Anti-dumping Measures on Certain Shrimp from Vietnam	DS429	No panel proceeding

DOC to actually undertake it. In other words, implementation of an adverse WTO ruling is a two-step process. First, the USTR directs the DOC to make a new determination based on adverse WTO rulings. Second, the USTR may direct the DOC to implement the new determination.[13]

The United States has applied this regulatory procedure stringently by interpreting that the scope of the determination can be modified very narrowly. Thus, even after the panels and the Appellate Body ruled that the zeroing practices used in an AD investigation were not consistent with the WTO obligations, the implementation of the rulings was always confined to the specific AD investigation in respective disputes. This situation caused many other WTO Members to suffer from essentially the identical problems in the US AD actions and eventually led them to bring their own complaints to the WTO dispute settlement system, separately. The 15 remedial zeroing cases listed in Table 3 are the examples of such a kind.

4. Systemic non-compliance

In an effort to implement the WTO rulings, the DOC tried to change its zeroing methodology by adopting a new rule, *Antidumping Proceedings: Calculation of the Weighted Average Dumping Margin and Assessment Rate in Certain Antidumping Duty Proceedings (Proposed Modification for Reviews)*.[14] This new rule was finalized by the *Final Modification for Reviews* in February 2012.[15] The *Final Modification for Reviews* became effective and applicable to all reviews pending before the DOC for which the preliminary results were issued after 16 April 2012. This methodology would also be applicable to any reviews currently discontinued by the DOC if such reviews are continued after 16 April 2012 by reason of a court judgment. Pursuant to the *Final Modification for Reviews*, the DOC should calculate weighted-average margins of dumping and antidumping duty assessment rates without zeroing in annual administrative reviews and sunset reviews as well as in original investigations.

Although this regulatory reform resolved potential zeroing problems for AD investigations prospectively, the existing AD duties based on zeroing-laden determinations prior to the threshold timing under the *Final Modification for Reviews* had to be rectified pursuant to Section 129 of the Uruguay Round Agreements Act (URAA).[16] This implementation mechanism of the United States

---

13 See also Statement of Administrative Action, http://ia.ita.doc.gov/regs/uraa/saa-dr.html. H. Doc. No. 103–316, vol. 1, 103d Cong., 2nd Sess. (1994).

14 75 Federal Register 81533 (28 December 2010).

15 77 Federal Register 8101 (14 February 2012).

16 19 U.S.C. § 3538: Administrative action following WTO panel reports. Regarding the way the URAA applies, see J. J. Grimmett (2011), *World Trade Organization (WTO) Decisions and Their Effect in US Law*, Washington, DC: Congressional Research Service, 4 February 2011). One part of the URAA was

led to at least 11 'remedial' cases in the WTO dispute settlement system. In fact, this whole situation raises an unprecedented problem in the GATT/WTO system especially because most of those 'remedial' cases were brought by developing countries.

It is actually up to a WTO Member to decide on how it will implement the rulings of a panel or the Appellate Body. As is the case with the general tenet of public international law, each WTO Member enjoys a certain amount of discretion in implementing international norms in accordance with its own legal system. In particular, countries such as the United States that adopt dualism for embracing international law obligations into their domestic legal system would mandate more rigorous and burdensome procedures to implement international judicial decisions.

The US approach to the WTO rulings on zeroing is, however, contrasted to the approach of the European Union that also declines the direct effects of the WTO rulings. After losing the *EC–Bed Linen* (DS141) dispute concerning zeroing practices,[17] the European Union adopted the Council Regulation (EC) No 1515/2001.[18] Article 5 of this Regulation reads:

> The Community institutions may consider it appropriate to repeal, amend or adopt any other special measures with respect to measures taken under Regulation (EC) No 384/96 or Regulation (EC) No 2026/97, including measures which have not been the subject of dispute settlement under the DSU, in order to take account of the legal interpretations made in a report adopted by the DSB. In addition, the Community institutions should be able, where appropriate, to suspend or review such measures.

This Regulation leaves some room for EU freedom: it uses the discretionary terms 'may' and 'should', the decision is explicitly not retroactive, and it has to be implemented through a procedure (but this procedure involves the same EU bodies as those which decide the imposition of antidumping measures, with the same threshold of simple majority). It is also worth noting that, as is often in the EU case, this Regulation does not cover safeguards. That said, it remains to be seen whether this Regulation has essentially resolved the zeroing problem in the AD investigations of the European Union.[19] Therefore, the starkly contrasted situations of the United States and the European Union in implementing the WTO rulings on

challenged by Canada to the WTO dispute settlement system in *United States – Section 129(c)(1) of the Uruguay Round Agreements Act* (DS221). For the comprehensive analysis of the rulings, see Bagwell and Mavroidis (2005: 315–338).

17 WTO, *European Communities – Anti-Dumping Duties on Imports of Cotton-Type Bed Linen from India*, WT/DS141/R, WT/DS141/AB/R (adopted 12 March 2001).

18 Council Regulation (EC) No. 1515/2001 of 23 July 2001 on the measures that may be taken by the Community following a report adopted by the WTO Dispute Settlement Body concerning anti-dumping and anti-subsidy matters.

19 It does not mean that the European Union completely abandons the zeroing practices. The European Commission still applies zeroing practices in 'target dumping' situations that have not been addressed yet by the WTO dispute settlement system. See Section 5.

zeroing practices raise a fundamental issue in the systematic compliance mechanism at a time where the WTO has lost its centrality in terms of a trade forum for quite a long time.

In such circumstances, the United States' non-compliance on the zeroing issue is mutating from a frustrating problem into a systemic problem that is raised by a major and leading WTO Member – hence threatening the basic notion of 'fairness' of the WTO (Wauters, 2009). Such a situation raises the question of how the other WTO Members would feel entitled to react. Some proposals to amend the AD Agreement, for example in terms of monitoring, have already been tabled by ALI participants (Hoekman and Wauters, 2011; Vandenbussche, 2009). But they have been suggested at a time where the Doha Round was expected to address this issue. As a result, because the circumstances have changed, they seem today either too far-reaching or too limited to generate in the United States (Congress) a coalition of export interests strong enough to fight and win the compliance battle in Washington.

5. Remaining Issues

After a series of WTO disputes prohibiting zeroing methods in AD investigations, the last kind of zeroing practice to be legally addressed is the zeroing method applied in a target dumping situation. The European Commission has applied the zeroing methodology in allegedly target dumping cases,[20] which were repeatedly confirmed by the General Court.[21] In all these cases, the Commission's main argument has been the existence of 'significant' differences in export prices among different purchasers, regions, and time periods. But, the Commission has never defined the term 'significant', nor any other term such as region or period, and it has also systematically rejected the possibility to take into account the fact that such price patterns could be unintended. Combined together, these two points suggest that the zeroing method has still a bright future in the EU AD investigations. The DOC also applied target dumping concepts in recent AD investigations and calculated dumping margins based on zeroing methods. For example, in the AD investigation on 'Bottom Mount Combination Refrigerator-Freezer' from Korea, the DOC adopted a target dumping analysis and the zeroing method.[22]

20 See, e.g., Certain side-by-side refrigerators from Korea (2006) OJ L236/11 (definitive), Urea and ammonium nitrate solutions from Poland [2002] OJ L279/3 (review), Polyethylene terephthalate originating in India, Indonesia, Malaysia, the Republic of Korea, Thailand and Taiwan (2007) OJ L59/1 (definitive). For more detailed explanations of the EU practices on zeroing, see Edwin Vermulst, *EU Anti-Dumping Law and Practice*, 3rd edn, Sweet & Maxwell (forthcoming).

21 See, e.g., Case T 274–2, *Ritek, Prodisc v. Council*, judgment of 24 October 2006, Case T-167/07, *Far Eastern New Century Corp. v. Council*, judgment of 13 April 2011.

22 US DOC, Notice of Final Determination of Sales at Less Than Fair Value and Negative Critical Circumstances Determination: Bottom Mount Combination Refrigerator-Freezers From the Republic of Korea 77 Federal Register 17413.

In December 2012, the DOC again applied a target dumping analysis and the zeroing method in the AD investigation on 'Large Residential Washers' from Korea.[23] In this case, dumping margins were very high, 82.41% for Daewoo Electronics Corporation, 13.02% for LG Electronics, and 9.29% for Samsung Electronics. The Korean government recently indicated its intention to bring a complaint to the WTO DSB on this matter including zeroing methodology in target dumping investigations. This dispute would complete the legal gambit of zeroing practices in the WTO system. Moreover, the legal saga on zeroing practices would be one of the most significant judicial developments in the GATT/WTO jurisprudence, at least in terms of the trade remedy system.

Another issue is the diversity of trade remedy rules through the proliferation of FTAs.[24] For example, Article 6.2.3(a) of the Korea–Singapore FTA stipulates that 'when antidumping margins are established on the weighted average basis, all individual margins, whether positive or negative, should be counted toward the average'. In other words, zeroing practices are categorically prohibited for weighted average calculation methods. Considering many FTAs currently in negotiations among Asian countries that have been major targets of AD actions, it will be very likely that more Asian FTAs will adopt legal elements proposed in the Doha Round rules negotiation. On the other hand, the United States has insisted on maintaining zeroing practices at least in their markets.[25] In case this kind of rule diversification among FTA partners becomes more prevalent, FTAs may aggravate trade distortions caused by such legal elements as zeroing in the trade remedy system.

References

Ahn, D. (2008), 'Foe or Friend of GATT Article XXIV: Diversity in Trade Remedy Rules', *Journal of International Economic Law*, 11(1): 107–133.

Bagwell, K. and P. Mavroidis (2005), 'United States – Section 129(C)(1) of the Uruguay Round Agreements Act: Beating Around (the) Bush', in H. Horn and P. Mavroidis (eds.), *The American Law Institute Reporters' Studies on WTO Case Law: Legal and Economic Analysis*, Cambridge University Press, pp. 315–338.

Bown, C. P. and T. J. Prusa (2010), 'US Antidumping: Much Ado about Zeroing', World Bank Policy Research Working Paper No. 5352, The World Bank, Washington, DC.

Bown, C. P. and A. O. Sykes (2008), 'The Zeroing Issue: A Critical Analysis of Softwood V', *World Trade Review*, 7(1): 121–142.

Cho, S. (2012), 'No More Zeroing?: The United States Changes its Antidumping Policy to Comply with the WTO', *ASIL Insights*, 16(8).

Crowley, M. and R. Howse (2010), 'US – Stainless Steel (Mexico)', *World Trade Review*, 9(1): 117–150.

---

23 US DOC, Notice of Final Determination of Sales at Less Than Fair Value: Large Residential Washers From the Republic of Korea, 77 Federal Register 75988.

24 For the legal and economic issues on FTA trade remedy rules, see Ahn (2008).

25 See also the US proposal on zeroing in the Doha rules negotiation that insists amendments explicitly permitting zeroing practices. WTO, TN/RL/GEN/147 (27 June 2007).

Grimmett, J. J. (2011), 'World Trade Organization (WTO) Decisions and Their Effect in US Law', Congressional Research Service RL 22154 (4 February 2011).
—— (2012), 'WTO Dispute Settlement: Status of US Compliance in Pending Cases', Congressional Research Service RL32014 (23 April 2012).
Grossman, G. M. and A. O. Sykes (2006), 'European Communities – Anti-Dumping Duties on Imports of Cotton-Type Bed Linen from India: Recourse to Article 21.5 of the DSU by India', World Trade Review, 5(1): 133–148.
Hoekman, B. and J. Wauters (2011), 'US Compliance with WTO Rulings on Zeroing in Anti-Dumping', World Trade Review, 10(1): 5–43.
Lewis, M. (2012), 'Dissent as Dialectic: Horizontal and Vertical Disagreement in WTO Dispute Settlement', Stanford Journal of International Law, 48(1): 1–45.
Nye, W. W. (2009), 'The Implications of "Zeroing" for Enforcement of US Antidumping Laws', Journal of Economic Policy Reform, 12(4): 263–271.
Prusa, T. J. and E. Vermulst (2009), 'A One–Two Punch on Zeroing: US–Zeroing (EC) and US–Zeroing (Japan)', World Trade Review, 8(1): 187–241.
—— (2011), 'United States – Continued Existence and Application of Zeroing Methodology: The End of Zeroing?', World Trade Review, 10(1): 45–61.
Vandenbussche, H. (2009) 'United-States – Laws, Regulations and Methodology for Calculating Dumping Margins (Zeroing) (DS 294)', World Trade Review, 8(1): 255–257.
Vermulst, E. and D. Ikenson (2007), 'Zeroing under the WTO Anti-dumping Agreement: Where Do We Stand?', Global Trade and Customs Journal, 2(6): 231–242.
Vermulst, E. (forthcoming), EU Anti-Dumping Law and Practice, 3rd edn, Sweet & Maxwell.
Voon, T. (2011), 'Orange Juice, Shrimp, and the United States Response to Adverse WTO Rulings on Zeroing', ASIL Insights, 15(2).
Wauters, J. (2009), 'Comment 'United-States – Laws, Regulations and Methodology for Calculating Dumping Margins (Zeroing) (DS 294) and United-States – Measures Relating to Zeroing and Sunset Reviews (DS 322)', World Trade Review, 8(1): 243–253.

Chapter 9

WTO Appellate Body—countervailing duties—nonmarket economies—public bodies—double remedies—Agreement on Subsidies and Countervailing Measures

UNITED STATES—DEFINITIVE ANTI-DUMPING AND COUNTERVAILING DUTIES ON CERTAIN PRODUCTS FROM CHINA. WT/DS379/AB/R. *At* http://www.wto.org/english/tratop_e/dispu_e/cases_e/ds379_e.htm.
World Trade Organization Appellate Body, March 11, 2011 (adopted March 25, 2011).

In 2005 Canada became the first country to impose countervailing duties on Chinese products under the World Trade Organization (WTO) system,[1] which raised the whole new issue of the permissibility in WTO law of using such duties against nonmarket economies, particularly when the United States decided to join Canada by imposing its own countervailing duties against China. In so doing, the U.S. Department of Commerce suddenly reversed its longstanding policy not to use countervailing duties against nonmarket-economy countries—China is still treated as such for purposes of trade remedy actions—pursuant to the 1986 *Georgetown Steel* decision by the United States Court of Appeals for the Federal Circuit.[2] In response to the U.S. imposition of countervailing duties in all seven investigations initiated against China in 2007,[3] China brought the first four U.S. measures before the WTO dispute settlement system as soon as they were actually implemented in 2008.[4] China's complaint can be categorized broadly as comprising three issues: (1) how to define subsidies in the unique economic structure of China; (2) how to calculate countervailing duties; and (3) whether to permit the concurrent application of countervailing duties and antidumping duties against China's alleged subsidies—that is, a double remedy. As regards these three issues, the panel ruled that the Commerce Department had not been WTO inconsistent in determining that state-owned enterprises and state-owned commercial banks are public bodies; that the department's calculation of countervailing duties was largely WTO consistent; and that use of the double remedy did not violate the WTO Agreements. The Appellate Body reversed the panel on many crucial elements of these rulings, including the public-body determinations regarding state-owned enterprises and the findings on the U.S. imposition of double remedies.

While the legality of the U.S. measures against China was being contested in the WTO, countervailing duties had already become major trade barriers for China in the U.S. market.

---

[1] Dumping and Subsidizing—Finding and Reasons, Inquiry No. NQ-2004-005: Certain Fasteners (Can. Int'l Trade Trib. Jan. 7 & 21, 2005) & Inquiry No. NQ-2004-006: Laminate Flooring (Can. Int'l Trade Trib. June 16 & 30, 2005), 2005 CanLII 57594 & 57595 (CITT), *at* http://www.canlii.org/en/databases.html.

[2] Georgetown Steel Corp. v. United States, 801 F.2d 1308 (Fed. Cir. 1986).

[3] For a comprehensive review of countervailing duty actions brought by WTO members against China, see Dukgeun Ahn & Jieun Lee, *Countervailing Duty Against China: Opening a Pandora's Box in the WTO System?*, 14 J. INT'L ECON. L. 329 (2011).

[4] Panel Report, United States—Definitive Anti-dumping and Countervailing Duties on Certain Products from China, WT/DS379/R (adopted Mar. 25, 2011) [hereinafter Panel Report—*U.S. Anti-dumping and Countervailing Duties*], *modified by* Appellate Body Report, United States—Definitive Anti-dumping and Countervailing Duties on Certain Products from China, WT/DS379/AB/R (adopted Mar. 25, 2011) [hereinafter *U.S.—Anti-dumping and Countervailing Duties*]. The United States initiated nonmarket-economy dumping investigations regarding the same Chinese products simultaneously with the countervailing duty investigations. The documents of the WTO dispute settlement system and WTO and GATT legal texts cited in this case report are available online at http://www.wto.org/.

For example, in 2009 alone, the Commerce Department initiated ten additional countervailing duty investigations regarding Chinese products. Moreover, other WTO members, including the European Union, India, and South Africa, also imposed such measures against China.[5] These circumstances heightened the significance of the pending WTO rulings for China's current and future economic interests.

In its report of October 22, 2010, the panel, in considering the first issue raised by China's complaint, ruled that the Commerce Department had not acted inconsistently with Article 1.1(a)(1) of the WTO Agreement on Subsidies and Countervailing Measures (SCM Agreement),[6] which defines subsidies by public bodies, in determining that the state-owned enterprise producers of input and state-owned commercial banks are public bodies since they are controlled by the government mainly through majority ownership. The second issue deals more specifically with the calculation of subsidy benefits through the use of benchmarks under Article 14 for inputs produced by state-owned enterprises, government-provided land-use rights, and governmental provision of preferential loans. The panel ruled that since the government is the predominant supplier of products in China, in-country private prices are distorted and thus can be rejected as benchmarks. Similarly, since the government is the ultimate owner of all land in China, the panel concluded that an in-country benchmark for government-provided land-use rights should be rejected. Chinese interest rates were also rejected as a benchmark because of the predominant role of the government in the banking sector. Following these findings, the panel confirmed the WTO consistency of the benchmarks used by the Commerce Department, except for the average annual interest rates applied to dollar-denominated loans. Finally, with respect to the double-remedy issue, the panel ruled that the department had not violated the WTO Agreements, including Articles 19.3 and 19.4 of the SCM Agreement and Article VI of the General Agreement on Tariffs and Trade (GATT 1994), since they were essentially inapplicable in this case.[7]

The Appellate Body, in reversing the panel's rulings on the first issue, explained that a public body within the meaning of Article 1.1(a)(1) of the SCM Agreement must be "an entity that possesses, exercises or is vested with governmental authority" (para. 317). Although a government's meaningful control over an entity and its conduct may imply that the entity possesses and exercises governmental authority, the existence of mere formal links between an entity and government in the narrow sense is insufficient to establish the necessary possession of governmental authority. Thus, the Appellate Body concluded that "control of an entity by a

---

[5] The European Union imposed its first countervailing duty together with an antidumping duty against China in May 2011, which was after the WTO decision to ban double remedies. Council Implementing Regulation (EU) 452/2011 of 6 May 2011 Imposing a Definitive Anti-subsidy Duty on Imports of Coated Fine Paper Originating in the People's Republic of China, 2011 O.J. (L 128) 18; see also Council Implementing Regulation (EU) 451/2011 of 6 May 2011 Imposing a Definitive Anti-dumping Duty and Collecting Definitively the Provisional Duty Imposed on Imports of Coated Fine Paper Originating in the People's Republic of China, 2011 O.J. (L 128) 1.

[6] Agreement on Subsidies and Countervailing Measures, Apr. 15, 1994, Marrakesh Agreement Establishing the World Trade Organization, Annex 1A, 1869 UNTS 14 [hereinafter SCM Agreement].

[7] General Agreement on Tariffs and Trade 1994, Apr. 15, 1994, Marrakesh Agreement Establishing the World Trade Organization, Annex 1A, 1867 UNTS 190. Article VI of the GATT 1994 defines dumping and permissible countervailing duties but prohibits both antidumping and countervailing duties in the same situation, and Article 19.3 of the SCM Agreement, supra note 6, deals with nondiscrimination in the imposition of countervailing duties, and Article 19.4 prohibits such duties in excess of the subsidy found to exist.

229

government, in itself, is not sufficient to establish that an entity is a public body," and rejected the panel's interpretation (para. 320). On this basis, the Appellate Body found that the department's public-body determinations regarding state-owned enterprises in the four investigations at issue were inconsistent with Article 1.1(a)(1). But it affirmed the department's public-body determination regarding state-owned commercial banks.

As for the U.S. double remedies, the Appellate Body focused on Article 19.3 of the SCM Agreement, which requires that countervailing duties be levied "in the appropriate amounts in each case" on imports found to be subsidized and causing injury. It explained that the amount of a countervailing duty cannot be "appropriate" if that duty corresponds to the full amount of the subsidy and if antidumping duties, calculated on the basis of the same subsidization, are imposed concurrently to remove the same injury to the domestic industry (para. 582). The Appellate Body therefore reversed the panel's interpretation of Article 19.3 and the findings pursuant to that interpretation, concluding that the imposition of double remedies is inconsistent with Article 19.3 (para. 583).

****

In *U.S.—Anti-dumping and Countervailing Duties*, the WTO Appellate Body substantially filtered the broad scope of countervailing duty actions against China that was implied by the panel's rulings. The panel permitted countervailing duties against China, and thus even double remedies to target virtually the same subsidization on the premise that the imposition of countervailing duties is completely independent of antidumping actions. Moreover, the panel's ruling would have considerably expanded the potential scope of "subsidy" in the context of China in particular, and nonmarket economies in general, by interpreting the concept of a public body as contingent on governmental control driven by ownership share. As seen, the Appellate Body rejected these crucial parts of the panel's rulings.

First, the Appellate Body considerably limited the scope of the subsidy discipline under the SCM Agreement by ruling that a public body within the meaning of Article 1.1(a)(1) is not simply any entity controlled by a government by virtue of majority ownership. Rather, the Appellate Body emphasized that performance of governmental functions and the authority to perform such functions are core commonalities of governments and public bodies. In addition, the Appellate Body explained that "whether the functions or conduct [of an entity] are of a kind that are ordinarily classified as governmental in the legal order of the relevant Member may be a relevant consideration for determining whether or not a specific entity is a public body" (para. 297). Thus, the determination of what constitutes a public body embraces not only the characteristics of an entity itself but also a case-by-case examination of the legal order of the member concerned and the actual performance of governmental functions.

In its analysis of the "public body" concept, the Appellate Body addressed the issue of the applicability of public international law—more specifically, the Articles on Responsibility of States for Internationally Wrongful Acts of the International Law Commission (ILC)[8]—to interpreting the WTO regime. The panel had categorically rejected consideration of the ILC

---

[8] Articles on Responsibility of States for Internationally Wrongful Acts, *in* Report of the International Law Commission on the Work of Its Fifty-third Session, UN GAOR, 56th Sess., Supp. No. 10, at 43, UN Doc. A/56/10 (2001), *reprinted in* JAMES CRAWFORD, THE INTERNATIONAL LAW COMMISSION'S ARTICLES ON STATE RESPONSIBILITY: INTRODUCTION, TEXT AND COMMENTARIES (2002).

articles, insisting that they are not relevant to the interpretation of Article 1.1 of the SCM Agreement.[9] The panel recalled that in *Korea—Commercial Vessels*,[10] the panel had declined to rely on the ILC articles when presented with virtually the same question. In addition, the panel said that the rules of the SCM Agreement act as *lex specialis*, as opposed to the ILC articles.[11] The Appellate Body reversed this finding by ruling that while the treaty applied is the SCM Agreement, the attribution rules of the ILC articles are to be "taken into account" in interpreting the meaning of the terms of that treaty (para. 313). Citing the ILC articles as containing similar provisions to those of the WTO Agreement or by way of contrast with the provisions of the WTO Agreement means that the ILC articles are being "taken into account" in the sense of Article 31(3)(c) of the Vienna Convention on the Law of Treaties (Vienna Convention).[12] The Appellate Body thus confirmed its tendency to embrace the general principles and customary rules of international law.[13] Although this approach strengthened the integration of WTO jurisprudence into public international law, in future the ruling needs further elaboration of what should suffice as "taking into account" the relevant international law in the legal interpretation of the WTO Agreements.

Applying the above rationale to the Commerce Department's actual investigations, the Appellate Body upheld the panel's decision on state-owned commercial banks as public bodies and thus substantially increased the risk that Chinese companies having a financial relationship with such banks might incur countervailing duties. Moreover, the Appellate Body's rejection as public bodies of state-owned enterprises that produce steel, rubber, and petrochemical inputs was based on the department's failure to review the evidence properly and, instead, to rely principally on information about ownership. As a result, the Appellate Body did not rule out viewing state-owned enterprises as public bodies in countervailing duty investigations. That is, the Appellate Body's ruling addressed only the manner of the department's examination of state-owned enterprises rather than the legal nature of such enterprises per se. Accordingly, the Commerce Department would still be able to treat state-owned enterprises legitimately as public bodies by refining and clarifying its rationales in future investigations. This task, however, poses a greater challenge because governmental roles "in the legal order" of China tend to be more intrusive than in that of market-economy WTO members.

The unprecedented issue of the permissibility of countervailing duty actions against non-market economies, including China, highlights another legal conflict between panels and the Appellate Body in the WTO dispute settlement system.[14] In *U.S.—Anti-dumping and Countervailing Duties*, the disputing parties, as well as the panel and the Appellate Body, agreed that countervailing duties themselves are not prohibited against China pursuant to its accession

[9] Panel Report, U.S.—Anti-dumping and Countervailing Duties, paras. 8.90, 8.91.

[10] Panel Report, Korea—Measures Affecting Trade in Commercial Vessels, WT/DS273 (adopted Apr. 11, 2005).

[11] Panel Report, U.S.—Anti-dumping and Countervailing Duties, para. 8.90.

[12] Vienna Convention on the Law of Treaties, *opened for signature* May 23, 1969, 1155 UNTS 331.

[13] For the Appellate Body's approach to international law, see ISABELLE VAN DAMME, TREATY INTERPRETATION BY THE WTO APPELLATE BODY 355–74 (2009).

[14] Strikingly different legal interpretations between panels and the Appellate Body have often occurred in trade remedy cases dealing with, inter alia, zeroing practices in dumping investigations, "unforeseen developments" under GATT Article XIX, and the causation requirement for safeguard cases.

231

protocol.[15] They differed vastly, however, in terms of how these duties should be imposed against China. Although the panel accepted that the simultaneous imposition of countervailing duties and antidumping duties calculated under the nonmarket-economy methodology will be likely to result in offsetting any subsidy more than once, it ruled that the provisions of the WTO Agreements invoked by China, including Articles 10, 19.3, 19.4, and 32.1 of the SCM Agreement and Article VI:3 of the GATT 1994, do not provide the necessary legal basis for the double-remedy claims. In this regard, the panel stated that "Article 19.4 of the SCM Agreement is oblivious to any potential concurrent imposition of anti-dumping duties."[16] Furthermore, the panel considered it "significant" that the predecessor to the SCM Agreement— the Tokyo Round Subsidies Code[17]— contained an explicit provision addressing the concurrent application of antidumping duties using nonmarket-economy methodologies and countervailing duties to imports from nonmarket-economy countries.[18] The panel explained that the existence of Article 15 of the Tokyo Round Subsidies Code mandating that the importing member choose between antidumping and countervailing duties in adopting measures against subsidization by nonmarket economies supported its interpretation of Article 19.4 of the SCM Agreement as not addressing or encompassing the permissibility of double remedies.[19]

For its part, the Appellate Body considered as the main interpretative question the meaning of the phrase "in the appropriate amounts in each case" in Article 19.3 of the SCM Agreement. The Appellate Body's legal analysis focused on that provision and it considered Article 19.4 only as context relevant to the interpretation of Article 19.3 (para. 556 n.535). The key logic of the Appellate Body's ruling is aptly summarized by the following, which starkly contrasts with the panel's decision:

> It follows that a proper understanding of the "appropriate amounts" of countervailing duties in Article 19.3 of the *SCM Agreement* cannot be achieved without due regard to relevant provisions of [the Agreement on Implementation of Article VI of the General Agreement on Tariffs and Trade 1994, known as the Anti-dumping Agreement[20]] and recognition of the way in which the two legal regimes that these agreements set out, and the remedies which they authorize Members to impose, operate. To us, the requirement that any amounts be "appropriate" means, at a minimum, that investigating authorities may not, in fixing the appropriate amount of countervailing duties, simply ignore that antidumping duties have been imposed to offset the same subsidization. (Para. 571)

Thus, the Appellate Body concluded that "only if these provisions are read in wilful isolation from each other" can one profess to be in compliance with both antidumping and

---

[15] Protocol on the Accession of the People's Republic of China §15, WTO Doc. WT/L/432 (Nov. 23, 2001), 2182 UNTS 138; *see also* Panel Report, U.S.—Anti-dumping and Countervailing Duties, para. 14.121 n.1029.

[16] Panel Report, U.S.—Anti-dumping and Countervailing Duties, para. 14.112.

[17] Agreement on Interpretation and Application of Articles VI, XVI and XXIII of the General Agreement on Tariffs and Trade, Apr. 12, 1979, GATT B.I.S.D. (26th Supp.) at 51 (1979) [hereinafter Tokyo Subsidies Code].

[18] Panel Report, U.S.—Anti-dumping and Countervailing Duties, para. 14.119.

[19] *Id.*

[20] Agreement on Implementation of Article VI of the General Agreement on Tariffs and Trade 1994, Apr. 15, 1994, Marrakesh Agreement Establishing the World Trade Organization, Annex 1A, 1868 UNTS 201 [hereinafter Anti-dumping Agreement].

countervailing duty rules when double remedies are imposed (para. 572). The Appellate Body also rejected the panel's ruling that the explicit prohibition of a double remedy in Article VI:5 of the GATT 1994 is limited to export subsidies and that the WTO members therefore did not intend to prohibit double remedies for domestic subsidies.

Turning to Article 15 of the Tokyo Round Subsidies Code, which prohibited the concurrent application of antidumping and countervailing duties against nonmarket economies, the Appellate Body ruled that its provisions might be considered, at most, as the "circumstances of the conclusion of a treaty" under Article 32 of the Vienna Convention rather than "context" within the meaning of Article 31. Consequently, it did not consider it necessary to confirm the ruling on Article 19.3 of the SCM Agreement with such supplementary means of interpretation (paras. 579–80).

This ruling could present serious obstacles to WTO members seeking to impose countervailing duties against nonmarket economies such as China, Vietnam, and Russia. But it should be emphasized that the Appellate Body did not prohibit countervailing duties against nonmarket-economy countries altogether but, instead, double remedies caused by the concurrent application of antidumping duties to the same products. The Appellate Body explained that,

> [i]n principle, we agree with the statement by the Panel that double remedies would *likely* result from the concurrent application of anti-dumping duties calculated on the basis of [a nonmarket-economy] methodology and countervailing duties, but we are not convinced that double remedies *necessarily* result in every instance of such concurrent application of duties. This depends, rather, on whether and to what extent domestic subsidies have lowered the export price of a product, and on whether the investigating authority has taken the necessary corrective steps to adjust its methodology to take account of this factual situation. (Para. 599 (footnote omitted))

Thus, in theory, to the extent that antidumping duties calculated by the nonmarket-economy methodology and countervailing duties are properly adjusted to prevent double remedies, WTO members would be able to use both measures in a manner consistent with the WTO Agreements. However, given the current antidumping and countervailing duty practices of most WTO members, whether and how this sort of simultaneous application of duties would ever be feasible without violating Article 19.3 remains uncertain.[21]

Without doubt, the Appellate Body's decision in *U.S.—Anti-dumping and Countervailing Duties* has made a significant contribution to trade promotion in the WTO system by prohibiting potentially fatal trade remedy practices. Nevertheless, on legal analysis, the Appellate Body's interpretation of "appropriateness" in Article 19.3 of the SCM Agreement may raise some controversy. For example, while the Appellate Body considers the existence of the parallel expressions—"in the appropriate amounts in each case" in both the Anti-dumping and the SCM Agreements—as evidence of the need to read the two agreements together (para. 575), that phrase in fact originated in the Kennedy Round Anti-dumping Code, which was enacted

---

[21] On the theoretical possibility of concurrently applying antidumping and countervailing duties and avoiding the double-remedy problem of excess assessments, see Brian D. Kelly, *The Offsetting Duty Norm and the Simultaneous Application of Countervailing and Antidumping Duties* (Sept. 2010), *at* http://ssrn.com/abstract_id=1653631. But the practical feasibility of such cases is quite limited.

twelve years earlier than the Subsidies Code.[22] This fact raises doubt about the assumption that the parallel provisions in the two agreements were designed to communicate with each other.

Moreover, in contrast to the Appellate Body's interpretation, the whole structure of Article 19 may be viewed as a sequential process of countervailing duty actions. After laying out the general principle of such actions in Article 19.1, the paragraphs that follow set forth the substantive rules for subsequent stages of the imposition and collection of countervailing duties. For the decision stage, Article 19.2 explains the full authority of an importing member to impose a countervailing duty—even a lesser duty than the total subsidy is "desirable" if it would be adequate to remove the injury. In the next stage, Article 19.3 stipulates appropriateness and nondiscrimination as the guiding principles in imposing the countervailing duty. Finally, when a member actually collects (or "levies" in the terminology of the agreement) the duty, under Article 19.4 it must apply the concrete criterion that the amount of the subsidy found to exist should be calculated in terms of subsidization per unit of the subsidized and exported product. Note that the maximum duty is set in terms of the subsidy amount instead of the export price, and must not exceed the amount of the subsidy.

If one follows this reading of Article 19, levying rather than imposing a countervailing duty "in the appropriate amounts in each case" may be understood in a more specific and narrower context. For example, because the United States employs a retrospective system for levying, or collecting, countervailing duties, the actual amounts to be levied often differ from the initially imposed duty as a result of administrative review decisions. Thus, levying the duty in the appropriate amount in each case may be understood to allow for some variation in the final stage of countervailing duty actions, which constitutes the unique and most important feature of U.S. practice. However, even if this alternative interpretation is accepted, it may still be controversial whether such contextual interpretations should prevail over the perhaps more literal approach taken by the Appellate Body, arguably in tune with that of the current WTO membership. In addition, since the SCM Agreement lacks a parallel provision to Article 17.6 of the Anti-dumping Agreement, the Appellate Body is obliged to accept only one interpretation as correct, and may not choose to accept any one of the permissible interpretations.[23]

The Appellate Body's ruling in U.S.—Antidumping and Countervailing Duties has filled another important gap in the porous textual language of the WTO Agreements, rectifying dangerously abusive trade remedy practices in the WTO system. Nevertheless, this laudable effort raises the question whether it is the Appellate Body or the WTO members that should fill such lacunae in the WTO system.

DUKGEUN AHN
Seoul National University Law School

---

[22] Agreement on Implementation of Article VI of the General Agreement on Tariffs and Trade, Art. 8(b), June 30, 1967, GATT B.I.S.D. (15th Supp.) at 24, 31 (1968); Tokyo Subsidies Code, *supra* note 17, Art. 4(3), at 57.

[23] Under Article 17.6 of the Anti-dumping Agreement, *supra* note 20, dispute settlement panels "shall find the [importing country's] authorities' measure to be in conformity with the Agreement if it rests upon one of those permissible interpretations," i.e., interpretations of the agreement determined by the panel to be permissible.

Part Three

Interrelation between Trade and Finance

Journal of World Trade **34**(4): 1–35 2000.
© 2000 *Kluwer Law International. Printed in The Netherlands.*

Chapter 10
Linkages between International Financial and Trade Institutions

IMF, World Bank and WTO

Dukgeun AHN* [0]

I. INTRODUCTION

The intertwined relationship between international financial institutions such as the International Monetary Fund (IMF) or the International Bank for Reconstruction and Development (World Bank) and international trade institutions such as the General Agreement on Tariffs and Trade (GATT) and now the World Trade Organization (WTO) has become by far closer and more complex than ever.[1] Potential conflicts between their jurisdiction and operation have drawn much attention in recent years, mainly due to the formal establishment of international trade organization, or the WTO, and the resurgent roles of the IMF and the World Bank during the financial crisis in the late 1990s. When the roles of the IMF and the World Bank increased as a result of the recent financial and exchange crisis that swept over the substantial part of the world economy, the "new" Bretton Woods regime within which it now embraces the WTO has raised a concern on coherence and harmonization with respect to the areas of overlapping functions and mandates.

The need for a co-operative approach to the interface of trade and financial issues that would be governed by the separate regimes and organizations has long been recognized as essential and inevitable for maintaining a balanced world economic system. As the world economy becomes more globalized, the ubiquity of intertwined trade and financial issues in a certain international transaction or economic conduct tends to increase. For example, the exchange rate change that may be initiated as a part of the IMF reform programmes unequivocally affects the calculation of dumping margins and subsidy impacts which is viewed as the primary concern of the GATT/WTO.[2]

---

[0]   * Assistant Professor, School of Public Policy and Management, Korea Development Institute, Seoul, Korea; B.A., Seoul National University; Ph.D., University of Michigan; J.D., University of Michigan Law School. The author is currently advising the Ministry of Justice as special legal counsel on WTO and international trade laws. I am grateful to Professors John H. Jackson and Robert Howse for their insights and guidance on the subject discussed in this paper. This article has also benefited from useful comments by Professor Thomas Cottier.

    [1] The difference in the sizes of these institutions is still substantial. As of April 2000, the WTO Secretariat has 534 staffs and the total budget for year 2000 amounts to 125,386,460 SFR (about $ 75 million). See WTO, *Annual Report* (2000). The IMF has currently more than 2,000 working staffs and its administrative budget for the fiscal year 2000 is about $ 576 million. See IMF, *Annual Report* (1999). The World Bank has about 9,300 staffs and its administrative budget for 1999 was about $ 1,328 million. See World Bank, *Annual Report* (1999).

    [2] John H. Jackson, *Managing the Trading System: The World Trade Organization and the Post-Uruguay Round GATT Agenda*, in *Managing the World Economy: Fifty Years after Bretton Woods* (Peter B. Kenen ed., 1994), 131, 143.

Likewise, while many economic development strategies for developing countries that are funded mainly by the World Bank often try to utilize trade policies for the purpose of promoting exports or substituting imports or both, such subsidy policies affecting international trade may be prohibited by the Agreement on Subsidies and Countervailing Measures (hereinafter "SCM Agreement") under the auspice of the WTO.[3] As illustrated in several instances in the context of the recent IMF salvage programmes, certain elements of those programmes that tend to generate direct or indirect trade implication have been strongly opposed by other countries that allege the violation of the obligation under the WTO agreements.[4] At the same time, with intensified and broadened scope of the WTO, more of its jurisdiction seems to overreach into the territory in which monetary and financial institutions have conventionally exerted more or less exclusive jurisdiction. In fact, trade and financial elements in many international transactions have been so intertwined that their characterization as being either trade or financial becomes extremely difficult or even meaningless in many cases.

In this article, I present the broad overview of these institutions' coexistence since the Bretton Woods Conference mainly from the perspective of the trade institution and examine the relevant GATT/WTO cases in which the linkage issues between finance and trade were addressed. In addition, the role of the primary WTO organ that deals with financial matters, or the Committee on Balance-of-Payments Restrictions (hereinafter "BOP Committee"), is also examined in the context of WTO dispute settlement. More specifically, in section II, the historical review of coexistence of the IMF and the World Bank under the GATT system is presented. A brief history of the Bretton Woods system and legal provisions governing co-operation with other organizations in each institutional charter are reviewed. In section III, a recent and more formalized WTO agreement with the IMF and the World Bank for the purpose of assuring coherence is discussed. Section IV examines dispute panel decisions under the GATT and the WTO that addressed roles of the IMF and the BOP Committee in the WTO system. Section V provides proposals to be considered in future efforts to enhance the coherence among these organizations. The conclusion is given in section VI.

---

[3] Article 3.1 of the SCM Agreement prohibits both subsidies contingent, in law or in fact, upon export performance, and subsidies contingent upon the use of domestic over imported goods.
[4] For example, the European Communities raised a complaint against the Korean government concerning its work-out programme for the shipbuilding industry, alleging that the IMF financial assistance was channelled to that industry in order to subsidize it in violation of the SCM Agreement. In response to that argument, the Korean government explained that the IMF fund was merely deposited in the Federal Reserve Bank of New York to support exchange reserve and never actually transmitted to Korea.

II. HISTORICAL REVIEW OF COEXISTENCE UNDER THE GATT

A. BRIEF HISTORY ON THE BIRTH OF THE BRETTON WOODS SYSTEM AND THE GATT

After extensive co-operation and negotiation between the United States and the United Kingdom since mid-1941, the Bretton Woods Conference which was the first of the major international conferences to be convened for the purpose of establishing an international organization opened on 1 July 1944, at the Mount Washington Hotel in the remote town of Bretton Woods, New Hampshire.[5] Some 730 persons from 44 countries (most of the Allies of World War II) convened at the Conference to develop the new international monetary system.[6] The tremendous efforts by those delegates finally materialized when President Harry S. Truman signed the Bretton Woods Agreement Act on 31 July 1945, shortly after the Act obtained the congressional approval in the United States.[7]

While the international financial system was launched with two pillar institutions of the IMF and the World Bank, following the successful reconciliation at the Bretton Woods Conference, the multilateral effort to develop the international trade system was separately exerted. Following the 1943 Washington Seminar on commercial policy that discussed the initial planning of such an international trade system,[8] the US government produced, in December 1995, a detailed set of "Proposals" on which the negotiations for the "International Trade Organization" could be launched.[9] The Proposals called for the convening of a United Nations conference for the purpose of negotiating an international trade charter and for the establishment of the International Trade Organization (ITO).[10] In February 1946, the United Nations Economic and Social Council (ECOSOC) at its very first session established a Preparatory Committee with 18 countries to prepare the groundwork for a United Nations Conference on Trade and Employment and a draft Charter for consideration by the plenary Conference.[11] Over the next several months, the United States in consultation with the United Kingdom and Canada prepared a detailed draft trade charter elaborating the summary December 1945 Proposals.[12] The Preparatory Committee adopted this "suggested charter" as a basis for its discussion and the agenda for its first session held in Church House, London, during October and

---

[5] For a detailed account concerning the early history of the Bretton Woods Conference, see Richard N. Gardner, *Sterling-Dollar Diplomacy in Current Perspective* (New expanded edn, 1980) and Margaret G. de Vries, *The Bretton Woods Conference and the Birth of the International Monetary Fund*, in *The Bretton Woods-GATT System: Retrospect and Prospect After Fifty Years* (Orin Kirshner ed., 1996), p. 3.

[6] De Vries, as note 5, above, at p. 13.

[7] De Vries, as note 5, above, at p. 17.

[8] Gardner, as note 5, above, pp. 103–104. See also Robert E. Hudec, *The GATT Legal System and the World Trade Diplomacy* (2nd edn, 1990), p. 9.

[9] Proposals for Consideration by an International Conference on Trade and Employment, (U.S. Department of State Pub. No. 2411, Commercial Policy Series No. 79, 1945).

[10] Simon Reisman, *The Birth of a World Trading System: ITO and GATT*, in *The Bretton Woods-GATT System: Retrospect and Prospect After Fifty Years* (Orin Kirshner ed., 1996), pp. 82, 83.

[11] As note 10, above.

[12] As note 10, above.

4   JOURNAL OF WORLD TRADE

November of 1946.[13] The plenary Conference attended by some 54 countries, which
account for most of the 61 countries that made up the United Nations at the time,
opened at Havana on 21 November 1947.[14] The Final Act establishing the text of the
ITO Charter was signed on 24 March 1948.[15]

    Since the approval of the US Congress was required to authorize the US
government to accept the Havana Charter and to participate formally in the ITO, the
Havana Charter was submitted for congressional ratification in 1948. Due to several
reasons, including protectionist revival in domestic politics and dwindled support from
the business community, however, the Truman administration abandoned its efforts to
secure congressional approval of the Havana Charter by withdrawing it from the
legislative calendar in December 1950.[16] Considering the crucial economic power and
role of the United States in the world economy at that time, other countries could not
further this initiative in the absence of the participation of the United States that had
actually taken the principal initiative to develop the ITO Charter in the first place.[17]
Thereby, an international trade organization which was supposed to complement the
international financial and monetary institutions under the Bretton Woods system was
officially dead.

    Nevertheless, the tariff negotiation among the principal countries of the
Preparatory Committee at the second session lasting from 1 April to 30 October
1947 resulted in detailed tariff schedules for each participating country.[18] These
tariff schedules together with those articles of the draft charter that provided
substantive obligations to protect the integrity of the trade concessions constituted
an instrument titled the "General Agreement on Tariffs and Trade".[19] Although the
GATT included provisions on traditional trade issues such as national treatment,
quantitative restrictions, subsidies, antidumping, and countervailing duties, it did
not contain other provisions of the draft charter governing matters such as
employment, investment, restrictive business practices, and the organizational
provisions related to the ITO.[20] The GATT finally came into effect on 1 January
1948, pursuant to an ingenious instrument entitled the "Protocol of Provisional
Application".[21] This protocol enabled the United States to implement the GATT
pursuant to the powers delegated to the executive branch of government by the
1934 Reciprocal Trade Agreements Act, without mandating the congressional

---

    [13] As note 10, above.
    [14] John H. Jackson, *World Trade and the Law of GATT* (1969), p. 45.
    [15] United Nations Conference on Trade and Employment, Final Act and Related Document, E/Conf.2/78
(April 1948).
    [16] Raymond Vernon, *The U.S. Government at Bretton Woods and After*, in *The Bretton Woods-GATT System:
Retrospect and Prospect After Fifty Years* (Orin Kirshner ed., 1996), pp. 52, 58–61. See also William Diebold, Jr., *The
End of the I.T.O.* (1952) and Gardner, as note 5, above, pp. 348–380.
    [17] John H. Jackson, *The World Trading System: Law and Policy of International Economic Relations* (2nd edn,
1997), p. 38.
    [18] As note 10, above, at p. 84.
    [19] As note 10, above.
    [20] As note 10, above, at pp. 84–85.
    [21] See GATT, B.I.S.D. Vol. 1, 77 (1952); Vol. 2, 35 (1952).

approval.[22] Nevertheless, the GATT was intended to be merely a multilateral treaty rather than an organization. Therefore, multilateral decisions under the GATT are to be taken by the "CONTRACTING PARTIES acting jointly" and not by any organizational body.[23] Despite such flawed constitutional beginnings that had been termed "birth defects",[24] the GATT has subsequently played the most important role to bolster and develop the world trading system since World War II, filling the vacuum created as a result of the failure of the ITO.[25]

B. COEXISTENCE OF THE BRETTON WOODS SYSTEM AND THE GATT

In August 1948, the Interim Commission for the ITO prepared a "Revised Draft of Provisional Working Arrangements between the ITO and the IMF" in which broad provisions concerning mutual observer status and consultation requirement were given.[26] In September 1948, the Interim Commission for the ITO completed an agreement on "Relations between ITO and IMF" that stipulated a consultation obligation with each other, co-ordinated policies, and institutional framework necessary to assure policy co-ordination such as reciprocal representation and joint committees.[27] But, when the ITO failed to be established, a formal agreement between trade and monetary organizations was no longer considered necessary.

There were, however, continuous efforts to address the financial and balance-of-payment issues under the auspices of the GATT. Notably, in 1979, the Consultative Group of Eighteen and its mandates were formulated to facilitate, *inter alia*, the international adjustment process and the co-ordination between the GATT and the IMF.[28] In its 1983 Report, the Consultative Group of Eighteen concluded that:

> "In the context of improved GATT/IMF cooperation, the GATT contribution could be to ensure that the Fund was made aware of trade policy problems for the purposes of discussion with its members and was also able to take better account of the trading environment confronting them. ... The most effective contribution the GATT could make to the resolution of trade and financial problems would be the energetic pursuit of its normal activities—the identification of trade problems, efforts to define solutions and help in implementing them."[29]

---

[22] Jackson, as note 14, above, pp. 60–63.

[23] Jackson, as note 14, above, pp. 126–132.

[24] John H. Jackson, *The World Trade Organization: Constitution and Jurisprudence* (Royal Institute of International Affairs, 1998), p. 15.

[25] For the principles and functions of the GATT system, see generally Jackson, as note 17, above. See also Robert E. Hudec, *Enforcing International Trade Law: The Evolution of the Modern GATT Legal System* (1993); Kenneth W. Dam, *The GATT: Law and International Economic Organization* (1970); Oliver Long, *Law and its Limitations in the GATT Multilateral Trade System* (1987) and Robert Howse, *The World Trading System: Critical Perspectives on the World Economy* (1998).

[26] U.N. Doc. ICITO/EC.2/2/Add.2, Rev.1 (dated on 14 August 1948).

[27] U.N. Doc. ICITO/EC.2/SC.3/6 (dated on 4 September 1948).

[28] GATT, B.I.S.D. (26th Supp., 1980), at p. 289. The membership of the Group in 1980 consisted of eight industrial countries and 10 developing countries, i.e., Argentina, Australia, Brazil, Canada, Egypt, European Communities and their Member States, Hungary, India, Japan, Malaysia for ASEAN, Nigeria, Norway for the Nordic Countries, Pakistan, Peru, Spain, Switzerland, United States and Zaire. GATT, B.I.S.D. (26th Supp., 1980) at pp. 289–290.

[29] As note 28, above, at p. 99.

6   JOURNAL OF WORLD TRADE

In other words, the mutual relationship between the GATT and the IMF was viewed as being rather independent and sustainable exclusively by pursuing their "normal activities".

When ministers determined to launch the Uruguay Round at Punta del Este in 1986, the Functioning of the GATT System (hereinafter "FOGS") negotiating group was directed to develop agreements, *inter alia*, "to increase the contribution of the GATT to achieving greater coherence in global economic policy-making through strengthening its relationship with other international organizations responsible for monetary and financial matters."[30] Pursuant to this mandate, the FOGS negotiating group worked to develop a scheme that promoted greater coherence between the GATT and financial institutions, i.e., the IMF and the World Bank. These efforts, however, could not create a separate agreement to address the interface issues between those institutions. While most developed countries proposed a more formalized co-operation scheme, many developing countries were opposed to that idea mainly due to the possibility of cross-conditionality between the three institutions.[31]

Despite the absence of rigorous agreements or rules that spelled out a co-operation mechanism, the world economic system bolstered separately by the financial institutions under the Bretton Woods system and the trade regime under the GATT have not experienced any particular incident that cause acute conflict between the regimes of those institutions. Such relatively stable, if not harmonious, coexistence of them seems to have been sustained mainly by the limited scope of the GATT. Whereas the main focus of the IMF is macro-economic policies to sustain stability in the international financial system and the major function of the World Bank is long-term lending for economic development, the GATT is primarily concerned with sector-specific trade policies.[32] In addition, a relatively weak institutional status of the GATT and consequent flexibility of the GATT operation also contributed to the avoidance of any serious discord with regimes under the IMF and the World Bank. However, the jurisdictions of these institutions have increasingly not been established in accordance with those fundamental missions.[33]

The provisions that establish co-operation mechanisms for each institution prior to the WTO system are examined below.

---

[30] *Ministerial Declaration on the Uruguay Round, Declaration of September 20, 1986*, GATT, B.I.S.D. (33rd Supp., 1987), at p. 19.

[31] Robert A. Weaver & Delphine A. Abellard, *The Functioning of the GATT System*, in *The GATT Uruguay Round: A Negotiating History (1986–1992)*, (Terence P. Stewart ed., 1993), pp. 1891, 1942.

[32] Frieder Roessler, *The Relationship Between the World Trade Order and the International Monetary System*, in *The New GATT Round of Multilateral Trade Negotiations: Legal and Economic Problems* (Petersmann & Hilf eds., 2nd edn, 1991), p. 363.

[33] The mandates for each institution are briefly summarized in the GATT document: GATT, MTN.GNG/NG14/W/6 (9 June 1987).

1.   *Trade Concern in the IMF*

The IMF is mainly an international organization that administers the international monetary system, whose area of responsibility and jurisdiction is the balance-of-payments of the Member States and the stability of their currencies. Although the IMF began as an organization to manage a global macro-economic policy regime with a specified system of rules about fixed exchange rates, it currently implements two primary functions:
- conducting research and providing advice on macro-economic policies mainly for less developed countries; and
- making a loan at a time of balance-of-payments crisis.[34]

Nevertheless, the concerns on international trade are indeed specified in the language that presents the purposes of the IMF. The Articles of Agreement of the IMF (hereinafter "IMF Agreement") stipulate, in Article I, that one of the purposes of the IMF is:

> "[to] facilitate the expansion and balanced growth of international trade, and to contribute thereby to the promotion and maintenance of high levels of employment and real income and to the development of the productive resources of all members as primary objectives of economic policy."[35]

It is noted that the IMF Agreement does not contain a comparable requirement for consultation with the GATT. This is because the IMF Agreement was adopted before the GATT was formulated. Therefore, the text of the IMF Agreement lacks articulated co-operation provisions with the GATT. Instead, Article X of the IMF Agreement, entitled "Relations with Other International Organizations", summarily provides that "the Fund shall cooperate within the terms of this Agreement with any general international organization and with public international organizations having specialized responsibilities in related fields".

2.   *Organizational Co-operation in the World Bank*

The Articles of Agreement for the World Bank (hereinafter "World Bank Agreement") set out, in Article I, one of the purposes of the Bank "[t]o promote the long-range balanced growth of international trade ... by encouraging international investment".[36] Although there is no GATT provision that formulates an institutional relationship with the World Bank parallel to that with the IMF,[37] the World Bank Agreement has a mandate for co-operation with other international organizations that

---

[34] David Vines, *The WTO in Relation to the Fund and the Bank: Competencies, Agendas, and Linkages*, in *The WTO as an International Organization* (Anne O. Krueger ed., 1998), pp. 59, 63.
[35] The Articles of Agreement of the International Monetary Fund, Art. I, reprinted in Jackson *et al.*, *Documents Supplement to Legal Problems of International Economic Relations* (3rd edn, 1995), p. 451.
[36] The Articles of Agreement for the World Bank, Art. I (iii).
[37] See Section II.B.3. below.

are similar to the one for the IMF.[38] For example, Article V, Section 8 of the World Bank Agreement provides that:

> "(a) The Bank, within the terms of this Agreement, shall cooperate with any general international organization and with public international organizations having specialized responsibilities in related fields. Any arrangements for such cooperation which would involve a modification of any provision of this Agreement may be effected only after amendment to this Agreement under Article VIII.

> (b) In making decisions on applications for loans or guarantees relating to matters directly within the competence of any international organization of the types specified in the preceding paragraph and participated in primarily by members of the Bank, the Bank shall give consideration to the views and recommendations of such organization."

The requirement under subsection (b) might raise a question on coherence between the World Bank and the GATT. In fact, many World Bank loans and guarantees were aimed to develop certain industry sectors as well as public infrastructure for less developed or developing countries. Alternatively, a government that received World Bank development loans implemented economic development programmes centred on target industries whose outputs were in competition with foreign products, either in domestic markets when intended to protect domestic "infant" industries, or in foreign markets when a domestic market is insufficient to accommodate its desired production level. Such economic development policies involving industry targeting strategy, however, might constitute either export promotion subsidies or import substitution subsidies. Under the GATT, Article XVI addresses subsidies that might distort international trade, and export promotion subsidies were squarely prohibited after the Tokyo Round.[39] Despite this potential conflict between economic development programmes assisted by the World Bank and legal obligations under the GATT, it had not caused any serious problem under the GATT regimes mainly because Article 14 of the Tokyo Round Subsidy Code exempted developing countries that were the primary beneficiaries of the Bank programmes from the Code obligations.

3.   IMF and World Bank in the GATT

The role of the IMF in the context of the GATT is mainly played in relation to balance-of-payment (BOP) matters. The basic relationship of the IMF to the GATT is established by Article XV:2 as follows:

> "In all cases in which the CONTRACTING PARTIES are called upon to consider or deal with problems concerning monetary reserves, balances of payments or foreign exchange arrangements, they shall consult fully with the International Monetary Fund. In such

---

[38] GATT, MTN.GNG/NG14/W/6 (dated on 9 June 1987), at p. 6.
[39] GATT, Agreement on Interpretation and Application of Articles VI, XVI and XXIII of the General Agreement on Tariffs and Trade (hereinafter "Tokyo Round Subsidy Code"), *The Text of the Tokyo Round Agreements* (1986), p. 51.

consultations, the CONTRACTING PARTIES shall accept all findings of statistical and other facts presented by the Fund relating to foreign exchange, monetary reserves and balances of payments, and shall accept the determination of the Fund as to whether action by a contracting party in exchange matters is in accordance with the Articles of Agreement of the International Monetary Fund, or with the terms of a special exchange agreement between that contracting party and the CONTRACTING PARTIES. The CONTRACTING PARTIES in reaching their final decision in cases involving the criteria set forth in paragraph 2(a) of Article XII or in paragraph 9 of Article XVIII, shall accept the determination of the Fund as to what constitutes a serious decline in the contracting party's monetary reserves, a very low level of its monetary reserves or a reasonable rate of increase in its monetary reserves, and as to the financial aspects of other matters covered in consultation in such cases."[40]

Thus, when a country tries to impose import restrictions by invoking Article XII or Article XVIII:B of the GATT to safeguard the balance of payments, the IMF may play an important role in determining whether those import measures are justified under the given BOP situation.[41]

Concerning the relationship between the IMF and the GATT stipulated in Article XV, there are several points that should be noted. First, the role of the IMF is limited to providing "findings of statistical and other facts", i.e., technical information and determination on compliance with the IMF Agreement, rather than any interpretation on relevant GATT articles.[42] Second, although the finding and determination by the IMF on statistical and factual matters related to the BOP status would not be contradicted, the final decision on whether BOP measures are justified under relevant GATT articles rests on the CONTRACTING PARTIES.[43] Third, whereas the division of work between the IMF and the GATT was regarded to be "based on the technical nature of government measures rather than on the effect of these measures on international trade and finance" in the early years of the GATT,[44] the Committee on Balance-of-Payments Restrictions (hereinafter "BOP Committee") in 1981 concluded that a government measure, monetary in form and yet with trade effects, could be considered a trade measure taken for BOP purposes.[45] In other words, the determination of whether a government measure is a trade action or exchange action hinges on the actual effects of that measure, rather than arbitrary demarcation of a technical nature.

Another important GATT provision that deals with the integrated area of trade and finance is Article XII governing restrictions to safeguard the balance of payments. In the early years of the GATT, the BOP exception was used primarily to cover many quantitative import restrictions. Since the introduction of the floating exchange rate

---

[40] World Trade Organization, *The Results of the Uruguay Round of Multilateral Trade Negotiations: The Legal Texts* (1994), p. 507.

[41] For discussion on problems of BOP measures allowed under Articles XII and XVIII:B, see Richard Eglin, *Surveillance of Balance-of-payments Measures in the GATT*, (March 1987) 10 World Econ. 1, pp. 1–5.

[42] GATT, B.I.S.D. (27th Supp., 1981), at p. 149.

[43] World Trade Organization, *Analytical Index: Guide to GATT Law and Practice* (6th edn, 1995), p. 431.

[44] GATT, B.I.S.D. (3rd Supp., 1955), at pp. 170, 196.

[45] WTO, as note 40, above, pp. 435–436.

system in 1973,[46] however, Article XII has been rarely used.[47] In fact, the Declaration on Trade Measures Taken for Balance-of-Payments Purposes, adopted in 1979, recognized that "restrictive trade measures are in general an inefficient means to restore balance-of-payments equilibrium" and that "developed contracting parties should avoid the imposition of restrictive trade measures for balance-of-payments purposes to the maximum extent possible".[48] Thus, under the current monetary system of flexible exchange rates which replaced the par-value system and subsequently the central rate system, the IMF has a much weaker basis to perform the advisory function stipulated by Article XV, namely to determine the reserve need of the import restrictions for the GATT.[49] This, in turn, implies that the BOP Committee would not be able to perform properly the legal function of determining whether or not BOP measures are consistent with Article XII or XVIII:B.[50]

On the other hand, the interrelationship between the World Bank and the GATT is formulated in Part IV of the GATT that addresses issues related to trade and development. Since the role of the World Bank in assisting economic development for less developed countries was fully acknowledged when Part VI of the GATT was drafted in 1965,[51] the text of Part VI of the GATT clearly recognized the importance of collaboration between the World Bank and the GATT. For example, Article XXXVI of the GATT provides, in relevant parts, that:

> "6. Because of the chronic deficiency in the export proceeds and other foreign exchange earnings of less-developed contracting parties, there are important inter-relationships between trade and financial assistance to development. There is, therefore, need for close and continuing collaboration between the CONTRACTING PARTIES and the international lending agencies so that they can contribute most effectively to alleviating the burdens these less-developed contracting parties assume in the interest of their economic development.

> 7. There is need for appropriate collaboration between the CONTRACTING PARTIES, other intergovernmental bodies and the organs and agencies of the United Nations system, whose activities relate to the trade and economic development of less-developed countries."[52]

In other words, the text of Article XXXVI acknowledges the need for "close and continuing" and "appropriate collaboration" between the GATT and the World Bank. This provision, however, does not articulate concrete procedures or substantive obligations between the two institutions.

In addition, Article XXXVIII concerning joint action provides, in pertinent parts, that:

---

[46] Nowadays, countries employ various exchange regimes such as fixed, crawling peg, managed float and free float. See, e.g., K. Michael Finger & Ludger Schuknecht, *Trade, Finance and Financial Crises* (1999), p. 16.

[47] Roessler, as note 32, above, p. 372. Concerning the relationship between the GATT and the IMF on the issues of specific duties and floating exchange rates, see GATT, B.I.S.D. (27th Supp., 1980), at p. 149.

[48] GATT, B.I.S.D. (26th Supp., 1978), at p. 205.

[49] Roessler, as note 32, above, p. 379.

[50] Roessler, as note 32, above.

[51] The protocol amending the GATT to add Part VI was completed on 8 February 1965 and entered into force on 27 June 1966. GATT, B.I.S.D. (13th Supp., 1965), at p. 2.

[52] WTO, as note 40, above, at p. 534.

"2. In particular, the CONTRACTING PARTIES shall:

...

> (c) collaborate in analysing the development plans and policies of individual less-developed contracting parties and in examining trade and aid relationships with a view to devising concrete measures to promote the development of export potential and to facilitate access to export markets for the products of the industries thus developed and, in this connexion, seek appropriate collaboration with governments and international organizations, and in particular with organizations having competence in relation to financial assistance for economic development, in systematic studies of trade and aid relationships in individual less-developed contracting parties aimed at obtaining a clear analysis of export potential, market prospects and any further action that may be required."[53]

Article XXXVIII:2(c) indicates that the drafters of the GATT indeed envisaged the potential conflict of regimes when "financial assistance for economic development" was utilized to "devis[e] concrete measures to promote the development of export potential and to facilitate access to export markets for the products of industries thus developed". Thereby, they mandated collaboration in this regard. However, commitments stated in the general language of Article XXXVIII do not sufficiently illustrate how such co-operation should be implemented in the face of regime conflicts between economic development and promotion of free trade.

III. WTO AGREEMENTS WITH THE IMF AND THE WORLD BANK

A. WTO AGREEMENTS AND GATT 1994

When the establishment of a new international trade organization was envisioned in the course of the Uruguay Round negotiation, the longstanding question of how the trade regime should be arranged to assure the coherence with the Bretton Woods system drew the attention of the contracting parties. This issue, however, could not generate a separate and rigorous agreement that addresses concerns raised under the GATT system.

In the Marrakesh Declaration of April 15, 1994 which announced the completion of the Uruguay Round negotiation, ministers of contracting parties agreed to confirm "their resolution to strive for greater global coherence of policies in the fields of trade, money and finance, including cooperation between the WTO, the IMF and the World Bank for that purpose".[54] In addition, Article III of the Agreement Establishing the World Trade Organization (hereinafter "WTO Agreement") stipulated, in paragraph 5, that "[w]ith a view to achieving greater coherence in global economic policy-making, the WTO shall cooperate, as appropriate, with the International Monetary Fund and with the International Bank for Reconstruction and Development and its affiliated agencies."[55] This mandate was further elaborated in the Declaration on

---

[53] WTO, as note 40, above, at p. 537.
[54] WTO, as note 40, above, at p. iv.
[55] WTO, as note 40, above, at p. 7.

the Contribution of the World Trade Organization to Achieving Greater Coherence in Global Economic Policymaking (hereinafter "Coherence Declaration").[56] For example, paragraph 5 of the Declaration provides that:

> "5. The interlinkages between the different aspects of economic policy require that the international institutions with responsibilities in each of these areas follow consistent and mutually supportive policies. The World Trade Organization should therefore pursue and develop cooperation with the international organizations responsible for monetary and financial matters, while respecting the mandate, the confidentiality requirements and the necessary autonomy in decision-making procedures of each institution, and avoiding the imposition on governments of cross-conditionality or additional conditions. Ministers further invite the Director-General of the WTO to review with the Managing Director of the International Monetary Fund and the President of the World Bank, the implications of the WTO's responsibilities for its cooperation with the Bretton Woods institutions, as well as the forms such cooperation might take, with a view to achieving greater coherence in global economic policymaking."[57]

Thus, at the time the WTO was established as the new international trade organization to supplement the Bretton Woods institutions in 1995, it was merely mandated to "pursue and develop" further co-operation, rather than follow any settled rules on co-operative relationship. It was only in November 1996 that the separate WTO agreements with the IMF and the World Bank were actually prepared.[58]

Even if the institution of GATT is now over,[59] the substantive obligations (and some of the procedural obligations) of GATT continue with the text of GATT 1994 as part of Annex 1A of the WTO Agreement.[60] Thus, the discussion *supra* regarding the GATT is still valid under the context of the WTO.

B. GENERAL AGREEMENT ON TRADE IN SERVICES

The General Agreement on Trade in Services (hereinafter "GATS"), Annex 1B of the WTO Agreement, includes several provisions that address the relationship between the WTO and the IMF. For example, Article XI:2 of GATS addressing the issue of payments and transfers, provides that:

> "2. Nothing in this Agreement shall affect the rights and obligations of the members of the International Monetary Fund under the Articles of Agreement of the Fund, including the use of exchange actions which are in conformity with the Articles of Agreement, provided that a Member shall not impose restrictions on any capital transactions inconsistently with its specific commitments regarding such transactions, except under Article XII or at the request of the Fund."[61]

---

[56] WTO, as note 40, above, at pp. 442–443.
[57] WTO, as note 40, above, at p. 443.
[58] See section III.C. above.
[59] To facilitate the transition from the GATT to WTO system, the legal instruments under the GATT system were terminated one year after the date of entry into force of the WTO Agreement. GATT, B.I.S.D. (41st Supp., 1997), at p. 6.
[60] Jackson, as note 14, above, at p. 48.
[61] WTO, as note 40, above, at p. 337.

In addition, Article XII:2(b) of GATS requires that restrictions to safeguard the balance of payments be consistent with the IMF Agreement. Article XII:5(e) provides that, in consultation with the BOP Committee with respect to BOP safeguard measures:

> "all findings of statistical and other facts presented by the International Monetary Fund relating to foreign exchange, monetary reserves and balance of payments, shall be accepted and conclusions shall be based on the assessment by the Fund of the balance-of-payments and the external financial situation of the consulting Member."

This provision almost duplicates the languages in Article XV:2 of GATT. That is because there is not much difference between GATT and GATS in application of BOP safeguard measures and thereby the importance of the role of the IMF in relation to adoption of BOP safeguard measures is similarly recognized in GATS.

On the other hand, Article XXVI of the GATS on the relationship with other international organizations provides that:

> "The General Council shall make appropriate arrangements for consultation and cooperation with the United Nations and its specialized agencies as well as with other intergovernmental organizations concerned with services."[62]

Thus, the WTO is again mandated by GATS to establish proper arrangements for co-operative relationship with the IMF.

C. AGREEMENTS BETWEEN THE IMF/WORLD BANK AND THE WTO

In the meeting on 11 July 1995, the General Council of the WTO required the Director-General to develop draft agreements for co-operation with the IMF and the World Bank pursuant to the Coherence Declaration.[63] The mandates by the General Council included, *inter alia*, the formalization of the provisional arrangement with the IMF, mutual grant of observer status to the other organization, access to the other's documentation and database, and maintenance of necessary confidentiality.[64] It was also noted that the Members accepted "with reluctance" the participation of the IMF and the World Bank as observers in the Dispute Settlement Body of the WTO.[65]

In November 1996, the General Council formally approved the "WTO Agreements with the Fund and the Bank".[66] Those agreements, however, had to be signed to enter into force. Thus, the Agreement with the IMF was signed at the Singapore Ministerial Conference in December 1996 and that with the World Bank was finally signed in late April 1997.[67]

---

[62] WTO, as note 40, above, at p. 348.
[63] WTO, WT/GC/M/5 (17 August 1995), pp. 6–8.
[64] As note 63, above, p. 7.
[65] As note 63, above.
[66] WTO, WT/L/195 (18 November 1996). This document was previously issued as WT/GC/W/43 (4 November 1996).
[67] WTO, WT/GC/W/68 (13 November 1997), p. 1.

The "Agreement between the International Monetary Fund and the World Trade Organization"[68] (hereinafter "Agreement between IMF and WTO") was formulated in a somewhat more detailed fashion than the "Agreement between the International Bank for Reconstruction and Development, the International Development Association and the World Trade Organization"[69] (hereinafter "Agreement between World Bank and WTO"). The total 17 paragraphs of the former encompass most of the 13 paragraphs of the latter. Since the two agreements are almost identical in substance except for a bit more elaborated prescription in the Agreement between the IMF and WTO, the subsequent discussion is centred on the Agreement between the IMF and WTO.

In the preamble of the agreement, "the close collaborative relationship existing over the past several decades between the Fund and the CONTRACTING PARTIES to the General Agreement on Tariffs and Trade, and the importance of continuing and strengthening such a relationship between the Fund and the WTO" are explicitly recognized. The preamble also recognizes "the increasing linkages between the various aspects of economic policymaking that fall within the respective mandates of the International Monetary Fund and the World Trade Organization, and the call in the Marrakesh Agreement for greater coherence among economic policies internationally." Moreover, by specifically having regard to relevant articles, the agreement ensures that it should be considered in conjunction with those articles.[70]

The content of the agreement essentially provides for the mutual granting of observer status to the secretariats or staffs of the other institutions at relevant meetings; and consultation between the secretariats and staffs of the institutions concerning the matters of mutual interest that are basically trade policy related issues.[71] For example, paragraph 3 provides that the IMF shall inform the WTO of any decisions approving restrictions on payments or transfers or discriminatory currency arrangements. In paragraph 4, the IMF also agrees to participate in consultations in the WTO BOP Committee and the existing procedures for the IMF participation shall continue and may be adapted as appropriate.

Paragraph 5 provides the WTO Secretariat with a standing invitation to ordinary meetings of the IMF's Executive Board when general and regional trade policy issues are discussed or discussions of the World Economic Outlook (WEO) involve a significant trade content. It also provides for the possibility of *ad hoc* invitations to the WTO Secretariat to send an observer to Executive Board meetings when the consultations between two organizations conclude that a matter is of particular common interest to both institutions.[72] In March 1997, pursuant to this provision, the

---

[68] As note 57, above, Annex I, at p. 2.
[69] As note 57, above, Annex II, at p. 8.
[70] Those articles include the Coherence Declaration, Articles XV:1, XV:2, XV:3, XII, XVIII of GATT 1994 and Articles XI, XII and XXVI of GATS.
[71] Vines, as note 34, above, p. 78.
[72] WTO, WT/L/195 (18 November 1996), at p. 16.

WTO secretariats attended an IMF Executive Board meeting, for the first time, as an observer on the discussion of the WEO.[73]

Paragraph 6 provides a member of the IMF's staff who would attend as an observer with a standing invitation to the meetings of the Ministerial Conference, General Council, Trade Policy Review Body, the three sectoral councils, Committee on Trade and Development, Committee on Regional Trade Agreements, Committee on Trade-Related Investment Measures, Committee on Trade and the Environment and their subsidiary bodies, and to the Dispute Settlement Body where matters of jurisdictional relevance to the IMF are to be among those considered.[74] However, the Committee on Budget, Finance and Administration, dispute settlement panels, and the Dispute Settlement Body with no jurisdictional relevance to the IMF are specifically excluded.[75] In this case, the phrase "dispute settlement panels" includes panels, arbitrators and the Appellate Body established under the WTO Dispute Settlement Understanding (hereinafter "DSU"), the Textiles Monitoring Body established under the WTO Agreement on Textiles and Clothing, the Permanent Group of Experts established under the WTO Agreement on Subsidies and Countervailing Measures, panels appointed by the independent entity established pursuant to the WTO Agreement on Preshipment Inspection and any other bodies with restricted membership constituted for the settlement of disputes.[76] The WTO dispute settlement panels are also excluded from the stipulation that requires written communication on matters of mutual interest in paragraph 8. Nonetheless, paragraph 8 provides that the IMF shall inform in writing the relevant WTO body (including dispute settlement panels) considering exchange measures within the IMF's jurisdiction whether such measures are consistent with the IMF Agreement. Thus, it is noteworthy that the WTO dispute settlement panels are not subject to the provisions of mutual consultation requirement although the IMF may be mandated to inform those panels whether exchange measures are consistent with obligations under the IMF's jurisdiction. When the IMF provides such information to dispute settlement panels, it will have official status in the proceedings and thus may be recorded in panel reports.[77] On the other hand, the "Agreed Commentary" attached to the Agreement between the IMF and WTO explains that "the scope of such communication is limited to jurisdictional matters and would not include views on policy matters".[78]

Paragraph 10 requires the IMF and the WTO to consult with each other concerning issues of possible inconsistency between measures under discussion with a common member and that member's obligations under the other organization's

[73] WTO, WT/GC/W/68 (13 November 1997), para. 6. Similarly, in July 1997, the WTO Secretariat was an observer, for the first time, at the World Bank's Executive Board, for the discussion of the World Bank paper on Global Economic Prospects. WTO, WT/GC/W/68 (13 November 1997), para. 9.

[74] WTO, WT/L/195 (18 November 1996), at p. 17.

[75] As note 74, above.

[76] As note 74, above, pp. 17–18.

[77] As note 74, above, p. 19.

[78] As note 74, above.

charter. The feedback from the other organization on an inconsistency issue, however, would not constitute an authoritative statement of the views of the organization with primary jurisdiction and thus would not be binding.[79]

The IMF documents, such as staff reports and related background staff papers on Article IV consultations, concerning the use of IMF resources on common members and IMF members seeking accession to the WTO, would be provided to the WTO Secretariat for the confidential use after five working days following circulation of those documents to Executive Directors of the IMF, but before discussion by the Executive Board.[80] This provision reflects the WTO Secretariat's need to receive those documents earlier than allowed under the IMF's policy. But, the provision of those documents by the IMF is subject to the consent of the members that are involved.[81] Likewise, the WTO is also required to promptly provide the IMF with Trade Policy Review Reports, summary records and reports of Councils, Bodies and Committees, and reports of WTO Members.[82] It is noted that this provision does not require the member's consent and thus in this respect is not reciprocal.

The agreement itself shall be reviewed upon the request of either party and may be amended by mutual agreement.[83] By written notice to the other organization, the agreement may be terminated six months after the receipt of such notice.[84] The necessary confidentiality in co-operating with the IMF shall be respected, as provided in paragraphs 13, by ensuring that "any information communicated under the agreement be used only within the limits specified by the other party".

This agreement is meaningful in that it is the first formalized instrument by the WTO and the IMF to address the coherence issue in the operation within their jurisdictions. Despite the success to materialize co-operative efforts, the degree of co-operative arrangement is not sufficient to address problems that have been experienced under the WTO system.[85]

IV. IMF AND BOP COMMITTEE IN WTO DISPUTE SETTLEMENT

The issue of BOP disequilibria is essential among the operational matters concerning coherence.[86] As explained in the previous section, Article XV provides that the CONTRACTING PARTIES, or now the WTO,[87] shall consult fully with the IMF with regard to exchange questions such as monetary reserves, balances of payments or foreign exchange arrangements. This provision is typically invoked in the

---

[79] As note 74, above, p. 20.
[80] As note 74, above.
[81] Agreement between IMF and WTO, para. 11.
[82] As note 81, above, para. 12.
[83] As note 81, above, para. 15.
[84] As note 81, above, para. 16.
[85] See section IV.C. below.
[86] WTO, WT/GC/13 (19 October 1998), para. 17.
[87] The references to the CONTRACTING PARTIES acting jointly in Article XV shall be deemed to be references to the WTO. GATT 1994, Art.2(b). WTO, as note 40, above, p. 22.

context of Article XVIII when a Member country tries to justify its policy measures on the ground of balance-of-payment difficulties because the determination of financial difficulties is generally considered within the jurisdiction of the IMF.

On the other hand, the GATT and now the WTO also prepared the BOP Committee within their institutional ambit and this BOP Committee has a primary authority to consult and make a decision on BOP-related matters of Member countries. It thus raises a question of proper division and scope of works concerning BOP-related problems, particularly within the context of dispute settlement between Member countries. In other words, when the WTO dispute settlement system deals with BOP-related matters of its Member countries, it faces a complicated question of how a dispute settlement panel should allocate the jurisdictional authority to the IMF and the BOP Committee or make a deference to those organizations' decisions. So far, the GATT/WTO dispute settlement panels made limited rulings on this issue and the review of them follows below.

A.   RELEVANT GATT/WTO DISPUTE SETTLEMENT CASES

Concerning the issue of co-ordination between a panel and the BOP Committee in the dispute settlement, there are two notable cases, *Republic of Korea—Restrictions on Imports of Beef Complaint by the United States* (hereinafter "*Korea—Beef*")[88] and *India—Quantitative Restrictions on Imports of Agricultural, Textile and Industrial Products* (hereinafter "*India—Quantitative Restrictions*").[89] The former is the case adopted under the dispute settlement system of GATT and the latter under the WTO.

India—Quantitative Restrictions also discussed the role of the IMF in WTO dispute settlement. In addition, the Appellate Body in *Argentina—Measures Affecting Imports of Footwear, Textiles, Apparel and Other Items* (hereinafter "*Argentina—Textiles*") briefly examined the Agreement between IMF and WTO in the context of WTO dispute settlement.[90]

B.   BOP COMMITTEE AND DISPUTE SETTLEMENT PANEL

In *Korea—Beef*, the United States and Australia brought the complaints concerning Korea's beef import restrictions to the GATT in 1988, alleging the violation of Article XI:1.[91] Korea invoked Article XVIII:B to justify its import restrictions on the grounds that the ordinary dispute settlement procedure under Article XXIII cannot be employed due to the existence of special review procedures stipulated in Articles XVIII:12(b) and

---

[88] GATT, BISD 36S/268 (adopted on 7 November 1989).
[89] WTO, WT/DS90/R, WT/DS90/AB/R (adopted on 22 September 1999).
[90] WTO, WT/DS56/AB/R (adopted 22 April 1998).
[91] GATT, as note 88, above, paras. 1–4.

XVIII:12(d)[92] and that its BOP restrictions had never been disapproved by the BOP Committee.[93]

With respect to the procedural aspects of Article XVIII, the panel ruled that, despite the special procedures provided in Article XVIII:B, recourse to Article XXIII was allowed for the current case.[94] The panel held, in pertinent parts, that:

> "In comparison, the wording of Article XXIII was all-embracing; it provided for dispute settlement procedures applicable to all relevant articles of the General Agreement, including Article XVIII:B in this case. Recourse to Article XXIII procedures could be had by all contracting parties. However, the Panel noted that in GATT practice there were differences with respect to the procedures of Article XXIII and Article XVIII:B. The former provided for the detailed examination of individual measures by a panel of independent experts whereas the latter provided for a general review of the country's balance-of-payments situation by a committee of government representatives. ...[95]

> Indeed, either procedure, that of Article XVIII:12(d) or Article XXIII, could have been pursued by the parties in this dispute. But as far as this Panel was concerned, the parties had chosen to proceed under Article XXIII."[96]

Thus, the panel concluded that whether a dispute concerning BOP matters should be dealt with under Article XVIII or Article XXIII is a matter of choice by the parties and, in *Korea—Beef*, it made a ruling on the case since both parties agreed to the establishment of the panel or utilization of Article XXIII procedure.

Concerning the justification for restrictions under Article XVIII:B, the panel concluded that (noting the information provided by the IMF) "there was a need for the prompt establishment of a timetable for the phasing-out of Korea's balance-of-payments restrictions on beef".[97] In this case, the panel noted the BOP Committee's opinion that "[t]he prevailing view expressed in the Committee was that the current situation and outlook for the balance of payments was such that import restrictions could no longer be justified under Article XVIII:B".[98] This conclusion was, in fact, supported by the information furnished by the IMF.[99] Hence, the panel in this case did not have to deal with any contradictory decision by the IMF and the BOP Committee. This panel report was adopted on 7 November 1989, after Korea blocked adoption of the report for six months.[100]

---

[92] GATT, as note 88, above, paras. 43–70.
[93] GATT, as note 88, above, paras. 71–98.
[94] GATT, as note 88, above, paras. 116–119.
[95] GATT, as note 88, above, para. 118.
[96] GATT, as note 88, above, para. 119.
[97] GATT, as note 88, above, para. 123.
[98] GATT, as note 88, above, para. 122.
[99] For example, "Recent Economic Developments" of May 1988 published by the IMF reported that the external current account registered surpluses of $ 5 billion in 1986 (5 percent of GNP) and $ 10 billion (8 percent of GNP) in 1987 and the external debt declined from $ 47 billion (56 percent of GNP) to $ 36 billion (30 percent of GNP)—at para. 84.
[100] Hudec, as note 25, above, p. 563.

Since the WTO came into being in 1995, its dispute settlement system has been extensively utilized by its Member countries.[101] Under the newly established WTO dispute settlement procedure, the question of compatibility and competence among the IMF, the WTO BOP Committee and a WTO dispute settlement panel in cases involving Article XVIII have been scrutinized in *India—Quantitative Restrictions*, in which various quantitative restrictions imposed by India were found to be in violation of the WTO agreements and were not justified under the BOP exception of Article XVIII:B.[102] In this case, quantitative restrictions maintained by India since 1957 under Article XVIII:B were challenged by the United States,[103] especially noting the IMF's view that, as of January 1997, "India's current monetary reserves were not inadequate and that there was no threat of a serious decline in India's monetary reserves".[104] In contrast to the *Korea—Beef* case, the BOP Committee in this case, despite continuous attempts by the United States, could not reach a consensus on a Committee recommendation to the General Council until the June 1997 consultation.[105]

India therefore claimed that "the BOP Committee and the General Council have the exclusive authority to determine whether a time-schedule for the removal of import restrictions is consistent with Article XVIII:11 of the GATT".[106] India emphasized the fact that, in *Korea—Beef*, the panel did not initiate a *de novo* review of the BOP justification for Korea's import restrictions.[107] Rather, the panel took the prevailing view of the BOP Committee that the BOP measure was no longer justified under Article XVIII:B. Thus, India argued that allowing a panel's competence in this case:

> "could result in frustrating the ability of the Committee to exercise its responsibility in the future. A single member could frustrate a consensus on approving the legal status of the import restrictions of a Member invoking Article XVIII:B in the future and then take recourse to dispute settlement on the basis that the legal status of the import restrictions remained in doubt."[108]

In response to India's arguments, the panel delved into the question of its competency to review BOP justification of measures taken under Article XVIII:B.

---

[101] As of 18 April 2000, 192 complaints have been notified and 34 Appellate Body and panel reports were adopted. Among them, 32 cases have been settled or inactive. So far, the developed country Members made 139 consultation requests on 109 distinct matters while the developing country Members made 43 requests on 37 matters. The rest of 10 requests were made by both developed and developing country Members. WTO, *Overview of the State-of-play of WTO Disputes* <http://www.wto.org/wto/dispute/dispute.htm>. For the statistical review of WTO dispute settlement cases, see Y. Park & B. Eggers, *WTO Dispute Settlement 1995–1999: A Statistical Analysis*, 3 J. Int'l Econ. L. 193 (2000).

[102] WTO, as note 89, above.

[103] Import restrictions on Almonds by India under Article XVIII:B were challenged by the United States in 1987 and the same issue of whether BOP justification could be investigated under Article XXIII was contested. This complaint, however, was withdrawn due to settlement on 8 June 1988. Hudec, as note 25, above, pp. 548–549.

[104] WTO, WT/DS90/R, para. 5.7.

[105] As note 104, above, paras. 2.1–2.7.

[106] As note 104, above, para. 3.69.

[107] As note 104, above, para. 3.134.

[108] As note 104, above, para. 3.135.

When the panel reached the conclusion that a panel established under the Article XXIII is competent to adjudicate BOP-related matters taken under Article XVIII:B, it laid out several important decisions on related issues.

First, examining the ordinary meaning of the terms and context of footnote 1 of the Understanding on Balance-of-Payments Provisions of the General Agreement on Tariffs and Trade 1994,[109] the panel concluded that Article XXIII provision may be invoked to address the question of "justification" as well as "application" of restrictive import measures taken for BOP purposes. In response to India's argument that only the consistency of BOP measures with other WTO agreements, not the question of BOP justification, can be examined by a panel,[110] the panel stated that "in a practical sense, the consideration of the application of a measure must necessarily embrace its justification" since "[t]he notion of application includes both the mode of application and the level of application."[111]

Second, whereas Article XVIII:B allows a Member to institute BOP measures without any prior approval by a WTO body,[112] that Member may not claim "a right to maintain its balance-of-payments measures until the General Council advises it to modify them under Article XVIII:12 or establishes a time-period for their removal under paragraph 13 of the 1994 Understanding."[113]

Third, dispute settlement-like procedures provided in Article XVIII:12 (c) and (d) are not the exclusive means to determine the justification of BOP measures under Article XVIII:B.[114] That is, justification of BOP measures may be covered by the general dispute settlement system of the WTO which is based on Article XXIII of the GATT 1994 and the DSU.

Fourth, the panel ruled that it may consider even "specialized or more generally 'non-legal' matters" since it can consult, if appropriate, with experts and seek information and technical advice under Article 13 of the DSU.[115] Thus, it did not accept India's argument that the task of determining the legal status of politically delicate issues was assigned "not to panels but to specialized bodies acting under particular procedures".[116]

Fifth, the panel concluded that even if it has the competence to determine the justification of BOP measures, the BOP Committee procedures still play a significant role in dealing with BOP issues and thus Article XVIII:B and related WTO provisions would not be rendered redundant or inutile.[117] It noted that "dispute settlement procedures and the BOP Committee consultation procedures differ in nature, scope, timing and type of outcome".[118]

[109] WTO, as note 40, above, p. 27.
[110] WTO, as note 104, above, para. 5.56.
[111] WTO, as note 104, above, para. 5.60.
[112] WTO, as note 104, above, para. 5.77.
[113] WTO, as note 104, above, para. 5.80.
[114] WTO, as note 104, above, para. 5.85.
[115] WTO, as note 104, above, para. 5.87.
[116] WTO, as note 104, above, para. 5.86.
[117] WTO, as note 104, above, paras. 5.90–5.91.
[118] WTO, as note 104, above, paras. 5.90.

Sixth, the panel concluded that potential conflicts either between a panel report and the BOP Committee decision or between panels are not likely to occur.[119] In this regard, the panel stated that "the arguments raised by India concerning any potential conflict do not seem to outweigh the drawbacks which could result from the absence of availability of dispute settlement procedures to deal with balance-of-payments measures taken under Article XVIII:B."[120]

India made an appeal to the Appellate Body on this issue, alleging that while a panel can examine whether a BOP measure is applied in a manner that is consistent with the WTO agreements, it is not allowed to review the overall justification under Article XVIII:B.[121] The Appellate Body, upholding the panel's relevant decisions, concluded that "if panels refrained from reviewing the justification of balance-of-payments restrictions, they would diminish the explicit procedural rights of Members under Article XXIII and footnote 1 to the BOP Understanding, as well as their substantive rights under Article XVIII:11."[122] Therefore, the Appellate Body summarily held that "[m]ore generally, ... the dispute settlement provisions of the GATT 1994, as elaborated and applied by the DSU, can be invoked with respect to *any matters* relating to balance-of-payments restrictions"[123] (emphasis added). In other words, the Appellate Body substantially broadened the scope of the competence of a panel to "any matter relating to" BOP restrictions, even if it noted that the panel did not conclude that the panel's competence to review justification of BOP restrictions is unlimited.[124]

The rulings by the panel and the Appellate Body on the competence of a panel concerning BOP measures in *India—Quantitative Restrictions* would clearly strengthen the compulsory jurisdiction and mandatory nature of WTO panel proceedings.[125] However, those rulings without further articulation may raise policy concerns about the institutional balance of the WTO or, more specifically, the proper role of the WTO BOP Committee. For example, in *India—Quantitative Restrictions*, the BOP Committee could not reach a consensus on India's proposed schedule to eliminate its quantitative restrictions in spite of continuous consultations from November 1994 to June 1997.[126] But, by taking this matter to the DSB, the United States could obtain the panel and the Appellate Body decision that were adopted on 22 September 1999,[127] and thereby gained legally binding powers on India under the general principles of

---

[119] WTO, as note 104, above, paras. 5.92–5.95.
[120] WTO, as note 104, above, para. 5.97.
[121] WTO, WT/DS90/AB/R, para. 89.
[122] As note 121, above, para. 102.
[123] As note 121, above, para. 109.
[124] As note 121, above, para. 82.
[125] For detailed accounts on the WTO dispute settlement system, see Ernst-Ulrich Petersmann, *The GATT/WTO Dispute Settlement System: International Law, International Organizations and Dispute Settlement* (1997) and David Palmeter & Petros C. Mavroidis, *Dispute Settlement in the World Trade Organization: Practice and Procedure* (1999).
[126] WTO, as note 104, above, at paras. 2.1–2.7.
[127] See WTO, *Dispute Settlement Body Annual Report (1999)*, WT/DSB/16 and WT/DSB/16/Add.1 (22 October 1999).

public international law. It means that the United States could resolve this case somewhat promptly by resorting to the dispute settlement system, rather than by proceeding through Article XVIII:B procedures under the auspices of the BOP Committee.

Generally, a WTO committee is open to all Member countries that indicate their wish to serve on it and thus typically comprises many Member countries with divergent interests.[128] For example, the Committee on Trade and Development has a wide membership that covers almost all of WTO Members,[129] and the BOP Committee currently has 40 members.[130] Since the WTO and its committees still follow the consensus practice of the GATT for decision-making,[131] it is often very difficult for them to reach a consensus agreement, especially for controversial issues including BOP-related measures, considering their structural diversity in the composition of the membership. Therefore, with such structural drawback of a WTO Committee, a Member country is more likely to take a controversial issue to a dispute settlement panel, if allowed, rather than to try to get a consensus decision in the relevant committee that may demand much more time and effort. Moreover, the absolute right of a Member to establish panels, i.e., no possibility to block panel establishment under the WTO dispute settlement procedures, would serve to make Article XXIII procedures a clear priority relative to any multilateral channel such as a procedure within the BOP Committee in dealing with disputable issues. Although a broad jurisprudence of the WTO dispute settlement system plays a significant role in developing a rule-oriented world trading system, the possibility that Members entirely resort to a dispute settlement panel for "any matter relating to BOP restrictions", even immature issues in that, for example, political sensitivity of the issues requires more prudent and multilateral decision, raises concern on balanced maintenance of the system that was crafted by the multilateral agreement of all Member countries during the Uruguay Round. To put it differently, the dispute settlement procedures under Article XXIII may practically replace the procedures under Article XVIII although the panel in *India—Quantitative Restrictions* "do not conclude that panels can substitute themselves for the BOP Committee, making the Committee procedure redundant and depriving Members of their rights under Article XVIII:B procedures."[132]

Therefore, in order to avoid unintended absorption of the BOP Committee functions by dispute settlement panels, there must be a procedural clarification on what kind of procedures must be taken before parties in dispute are able to invoke the dispute settlement mechanism under Article XXIII. Accordingly, later rulings or

---

[128] The WTO has 136 Member countries, upon the recent accession of Jordan on 11 April 2000. WTO, WT/INF/6/Rev.7 (21 March 2000).

[129] World Trade Organization, *Guide to the Uruguay Round Agreements* (1999), p. 8.

[130] In this count, "European Communities and Member States" is considered one member. See WT/BOP/INF/6 (16 July 1997) and WT/BOP/INF/6/Corr.1 (24 July 1997).

[131] WTO Agreement, Art. IX. WTO, as note 40, above, p. 11. See generally Mary E. Footer, *The Role of Consensus in GATT/WTO Decision-Making*, 17 Nw. J. Int'l L. & Bus. 653 (1996–97).

[132] WTO, as note 104, above, para. 5.114.

guidance elaborated by panels and the Appellate Body on this issue would be useful to sustain the institutional balance of the WTO system. Otherwise, considering the Appellate Body's explicit ruling to allow Article XXIII dispute settlement procedures for any matters relating to BOP restrictions, the problem of mooting the Article XVIII procedures within the BOP Committee does not seem merely theoretical.

C. IMF IN WTO DISPUTE SETTLEMENT

In *Argentina—Textiles*, the United States challenged, *inter alia*, Argentina's measures imposing a statistical tax of 3 percent *ad valorem* on imports from all sources other than MERCOSUR countries.[133] Argentina argued that the statistical tax was part of a package of fiscal commitments undertaken by the agreement between Argentina and the IMF and thereby beyond the framework of a possible bilateral trade dispute.[134] In other words, Argentina raised a question of a conflict of cross-conditionality, i.e., the situation in which "the continued implementation of its IMF commitments could place it in a position incompatible with its obligation under the WTO".[135] This issue, however, was not squarely addressed in the panel report. The panel stated, in the "Interim Review" section of the panel report, that it has no reason to address this issue because there is no evidence that the IMF requested Argentina to impose a statistical tax that would violate the provisions of the WTO agreements.[136]

The Appellate Body concluded, upholding the relevant part of the panel report, that:

"We also agree with the Panel that there is nothing in the Agreement Between the IMF and the WTO, the Declaration on the Relationship of the WTO with the IMF or the Declaration on Coherence which justifies a conclusion that a Member's commitments to the IMF shall prevail over its obligations under Article VIII of the GATT 1994. ...[137]

The Agreement Between the IMF and the WTO, however, does not modify, add to or diminish the rights and obligations of Members under the WTO Agreement, nor does it modify individual States' commitments to the IMF. It does not provide any substantive rules concerning the resolution of possible conflicts between obligations of a Member under the WTO Agreement and obligations under the Articles of Agreement of the IMF or any agreement with the IMF."[138]

In other words, the Appellate Body reaffirmed the panel's decision that, at least regarding Article VIII, no WTO agreement justifies conflicting IMF operation. It implies that there is still no mechanism or agreement to honour the IMF functions within the WTO system and thereby an IMF programme that has elements in conflict

---

[133] WTO, WT/DS56/R, paras. 2.19–2.21. MERCOSUR, or Southern Common Market, currently includes Argentina, Brazil, Paraguay and Uruguay.
[134] As note 133, above, paras. 3.276–3.296.
[135] As note 133, above, para. 3.277.
[136] As note 133, above, para. 5.3.
[137] WTO, as note 90, above, para. 70.
[138] WTO, as note 90, above, para. 72.

with the WTO agreements may be trumped when such a programme is contested by the WTO dispute settlement system. Moreover, the Appellate Body opined that the recent Agreement between the IMF and WTO provides for merely "specific means of administrative cooperation",[139] but not any substantive rules to address the potential conflicts between obligations under the IMF and WTO agreements.

Therefore, this issue should be timely addressed before substantial operation and functions of both institutions are seriously handicapped. Probably one of the possible alternatives to acknowledge the IMF functions in the WTO system is to grant a provisional waiver of WTO obligations to a Member country subject to an IMF programme for a specified period of time depending on the nature of urgency.

With respect to the role of the IMF in a panel proceeding, in *India—Quantitative Restrictions*, the United States argued that the determination of the IMF concerning BOP and reserve situations should be accepted as dispositive.[140] On the other hand, India argued that only the BOP Committee and the General Council, not the IMF, should make the final decision on the need and adequacy of BOP measures, merely taking into account the factual finding by the IMF on financial aspects of the BOP matters.[141] The panel declined to make a specific ruling on this issue, i.e., "the extent to which Article XV:2 may require panels to consult with the IMF or consider as dispositive specific determinations of the IMF".[142] Instead of taking such delicate issue, the panel simply held that since it was allowed to seek relevant information or expert opinion under Article 13.1 of the DSU, it chose to consult with the IMF. Then, on the basis of the position supported by the IMF, the Reserve Bank of India and three of the four alternative methods of assessing reserve adequacy cited by India, it found that India's reserves were not inadequate.[143] On this part of the panel's ruling, the Appellate Body held that the panel made an objective assessment of the matter as required by Article 11 of the DSU.[144]

The above ruling implies that the determination by the IMF on BOP situations would not be considered dispositive *per se* because that would in fact violate the mandate for a panel to do an objective assessment of the factual matters. But then, does it imply that a panel should or can treat the determination by the IMF just like several other factors that can be disregarded by its own discretion? As the panel noted, the IMF is "obviously a highly relevant source of information" concerning BOP issues, "as a recognized body with extensive expertise in these matters".[145] In *India—Quantitative Restrictions*, the IMF's assessment on the BOP situation of India was supported by most other evidence including even that of the Reserve Bank of India. Thus, basically, there was no need to weigh conflicting evidence on this issue. But what if a panel should

[139] WTO, as note 90, above, para. 71.
[140] WTO, as note 90, above, para. 3.310.
[141] WTO, as note 90, above, paras. 3.323–3.325 and 3.329.
[142] WTO, as note 90, above, para. 5.13.
[143] WTO, as note 90, above, paras. 5.175–5.176.
[144] WTO, as note 121, above, paras. 146–152.
[145] WTO, as note 104, above, para. 5.12.

deal with starkly conflicting views on a BOP situation between the IMF and a panel or other experts or, more likely, a party in dispute?

Considering the expertise and role of the IMF in the world economic system, a better way to balance the inputs by the IMF on BOP-related issues may be to consider the determination by the IMF a *prima facie* case. Thus, as far as the BOP-related issues are concerned, the determination by the IMF establishes a rebuttable presumption that a BOP measure is, or is not, justified pursuant to the IMF determination. The opposing party to the IMF determination would then have a burden of proof to refute the presumption with regard to the justification of BOP measures.

In fact, this approach is similarly taken in the context of applying the Agreement on the Application of Sanitary and Phytosanitary Measures, especially Article 3.2.[146] The Appellate Body ruled that, in *European Communities—Measures Concerning Meat and Meat Products (Hormones)*, an SPS measure conforming to an international standard would establish "a presumption (albeit a rebuttable one) that it is consistent with the relevant provisions of the SPS Agreement and of the GATT 1994".[147] To the extent that the IMF maintains its expertise and responsibility to control BOP-related matters of its Member countries, the recognition of a rebuttable presumption on the basis of the IMF determination would better serve the organizational purposes that aim to establish specialized jurisdictions pursuant to their own mandates on the one hand and co-operative relationship between their operations on the other.

V. ANCILLARY PROPOSALS ON CONGRUENCE

Although the WTO has already been in place for more than five years, the framework for co-operation and coherence among the IMF, the World Bank and the WTO has yet to be completed and fully established. Now, after the failure in the Seattle Ministerial Conference to launch a new trade round, the WTO Member countries are more eager to prepare for the next trade round that is expected to begin sooner or later. Some commentators even view the current circumstances in international monetary regimes ripe for the next multilateral trade round.[148] When they are given such an opportunity, the WTO Member countries should address, in full scale, the following issues that had been noted throughout the GATT practice.

First, there should be a clear rule to recognize trade liberalization undertaken as parts of IMF or World Bank programmes in subsequent multilateral trade negotiations under the aegis of WTO or WTO accession proceedings. In fact, the interrelationship between trade liberalization as the outcome of GATT/WTO negotiations and unilateral trade reforms as part of IMF or World Bank programmes has been noted as

---

[146] WTO, as note 40, above, p. 71.
[147] WTO, WT/DS26, DS48/AB/R (adopted on 13 February 1998), para. 170.
[148] C. Fred Bergsten, *The International Monetary Scene and the Next WTO Negotiations*, in *Launching New Global Trade Talks: An Action Agenda* (Jeffrey J. Schott ed., 1998), p. 39.

an important example of common policy issues among those institutions.[149] The FOGS negotiating group had also shown much interest in this issue during the Uruguay Round negotiation.[150]

So far, the multilateral trade negotiations have been conducted in discrete forums lasting several years. Since those multilateral negotiation outcomes have often been the collection of results from individual bilateral negotiations, each country tends to withhold or postpone any additional or unilateral liberalization in order to maintain a "bargaining chip" for subsequent trade negotiation. Thus, despite the economic lesson that unilateral trade liberalization benefits domestic welfare or even despite domestic economic necessity to liberalize their own market, many Member countries have been reluctant to pursue autonomous trade liberalization initiatives and rather have adopted or maintained unnecessarily protective trade policies on the grounds of political consideration. In fact, trade liberalization is often a high, if not top, priority for IMF stabilization programmes or World Bank development loan programmes. Such political concern for trade negotiation may, however, lead a country to avoid unilateral liberalization and thereby adversely influence an efficient implementation of those programmes. Therefore, a mechanism to "credit" such liberalization, particularly those adopted as parts of IMF or World Bank programmes, in future trade negotiations should be established in the context of the WTO to facilitate trade liberalization for developing countries. In addition, in order to assure such mechanism, the trade reform and liberalization must be permanent in character and in conformity with the GATT obligations, i.e., "GATTable" in nature.[151]

Second, GATT/WTO provisions to deal with BOP measures should be modified. It is well acknowledged in economics that trade policy measures are inappropriate instruments to address balance-of-payments problems arising from inadequate macro-economic policies, particularly under a flexible exchange rate system.[152] Nevertheless, Article XII and Section B of Article XVIII of the GATT 1947 permit the otherwise prohibited quantitative restrictions to be imposed for balance-of-payments reasons. Unfortunately, the current GATT/WTO agreement still encompasses these provisions without modification or amendment of them.

The potential problems in relation to these provisions are twofold:
 – the lack of concrete mechanisms by which the co-operation between the primary financial organization, or the IMF, and the WTO should be undertaken; and
 – the insufficient capacity of the WTO dispute settlement system to deal with these kinds of issues.

---

[149] WTO, WT/GC/13 (19 October 1998), para. 15.
[150] GATT, MTN.GNG/NG14/W/35 (20 September 1989), para. 32.
[151] As note 150, above.
[152] See generally Eglin, as note 41, above. See also Paul R. Krugman & Maurice Obstfeld, *International Economics: Theory and Policy* (4th edn, 1997); Richard E. Caves *et al.*, *World Trade and Payments: An Introduction* (8th edn, 1998); and Peter B. Kenen, *The International Economy* (3rd edn, 1994).

In dealing with these problems, the coherent decision-making and assessment on balance-of-payment problems should be first assured to have consistent solution proposals. Yet, in cases where a dispute actually reaches a panel of the WTO dispute settlement system, there is still no clear rule regarding how much deference should be granted to what kind of expertise in the functions of the IMF. The current text of the DSU that simply allows a panel to seek information and technical advice from a body that it deems appropriate is far from an easy guideline for relevant parties as well as panels to determine these crucial issues.[153] Therefore, at least, a more concretely formulated scheme to assure the coherent assessment on the balance-of-payment problems should be developed, unless provisions to allow BOP measures are altogether eradicated.

Third, co-operation between the IMF, the World Bank and the WTO must not result in cross-conditionality nor compound the complexities of conditionality.[154] It is conceivable that attempts to enhance co-operation among those organizations may lead to cross-institutional conditionality for the purpose of increasing coherence.[155] As indicated *supra* in section III, the three organizations are mindful of the need to avoid imposing on their members anything that could be interpreted as a form of cross-conditionality. But, there is much concern that some developed countries with a substantially greater power under the weighted voting system in the IMF and the World Bank, compared to one-nation-one-vote system under the WTO, may try to leverage that power to "punish" or "influence" other WTO Member countries if they violate the WTO agreements.[156] This risk seems especially real for developing countries that have experienced the recent financial crisis and thereby have been subject to various reform programmes of the IMF or the World Bank or both thereof. Those developing countries would not be in an easy situation to resist pressure from the IMF and the World Bank to alter or influence their trade policy measures as part of restructuring programmes. Therefore, unless a more rigorously designed framework to assure a harmonized outcome is established, the current trade and financial regimes based on different institutions should be particularly careful to avoid any such cross-institutional conditionality. Otherwise, the consensual development of an international trade system sustained by equal voting rights and consensus practice may be substantially undermined by different regimes that formally permit the consideration of economic realities of their Member States. In other words, co-operation among these organizations should be conducted in such a way that fully respects the separate mandates and decision-making processes of the three organizations.

---

[153] DSU, Article 13.1. WTO, as note 40, above, p. 416.
[154] WTO, WT/GC/W/140 (3 February 1999), p. 2. For the general discussion on conditionality of the IMF, see John Williamson, *IMF Conditionality* (1983).
[155] T.N. Srinivasan, *Developing Countries and the Multilateral Trading System: From the GATT to the Uruguay Round and the Future* (1998), p. 96.
[156] As note 155, above.

Finally, the Trade Policy Review Mechanism (hereinafter "TPRM") of the WTO may be utilized with respect to financial aspects of the Member countries, so as to provide more informed *ex ante* guidance or assessment on BOP situations.[157] Although some trade policy reviews contain selected information on financial areas of Member countries, most of them do not squarely deal with such matters because the primary objective of the TPRM is defined to examine the impact of a Member's trade policies and practices on the multilateral trading system.[158] But, reviews of BOP-related matters can be included insofar as they have trade implication and the recognition of this possibility is implied in paragraph E of Trade Policy Review Mechanism, Annex 3 of the WTO Agreement, that provides harmonious administrative arrangement with BOP Committee procedures.[159]

A trade policy review of a particular Member country is currently to be presented to the Trade Policy Review Body that is indeed the General Council of the WTO. Therefore, the review and incorporation of financial matters, especially BOP-related situations, in the trade policy review for the Member countries would create a multilateral opportunity to filter the IMF inputs on BOP-related matters. Such preliminary non-binding reviews within the WTO system may be more efficiently utilized by Member countries and other WTO organs including dispute settlement panels.

VI. CONCLUSION

The coexistence of the international trade system buttressed by the GATT and international financial system represented by the IMF and the World Bank has not been seriously challenged during the past five decades. Such a relatively peaceful coexistence in turn leads to, despite the importance of establishing co-operative mechanisms among those institutions, relatively little academic research regarding this issue as well as few institutional outcomes. In the early 1980s when the debt problem of some developing countries deteriorated dramatically, there were some multilateral efforts to address these issues.[160] This question seemed to regain its paramount importance with the formal establishment of the WTO and against the backdrop of the financial and exchange crises that have affected many developing and transition economies in recent years.

Traditionally, the most conspicuous area of interrelationship between those institutions has been trade restriction for balance-of-payments reasons. But, in a world of floating exchange rates, this can be no longer a legitimate focus of interrelationship because the exchange rate is supposed to shift and cause automatic adjustment in the

---

[157] For the detailed account of the WTO TPRM, see generally Donald B. Keesing, "The Improving Trade Policy Reviews in the World Trade Organization", *Policy Analyses in International Economics* (Institute for International Economics, 1998), p. 52.

[158] WTO, as note 40, above, p. 434.

[159] WTO, as note 40, above, p. 436.

[160] See, e.g., GATT, CG.18/W/74 (26 April 1983).

balance of trade and payments.[161] Moreover, the nature of the recent international economic relationship which involves more intertwined trade and financial elements requires a careful assessment and examination of the interface issue of coherence among those institutions, especially as the WTO rapidly establishes its own jurisdiction on the basis of its formal status as an international organization.

The current arrangement between the IMF/World Bank and the WTO discussed *supra* has shown some advance in this endeavour. Considering the importance of the issue and the changed circumstances in the world economic system, however, the coherence issue among these organizations should be addressed more squarely either in a separate forum with the IMF/World Bank or in a new trade negotiation under the aegis of the WTO. It is hoped that the present review and discussion can initiate more in-depth research and contemplation for this agenda.

Annex I

Agreement between the International Monetary Fund and the World Trade Organization

Preamble

CONSIDERING the growing interactions between economic policies pursued by individual countries arising from the globalization of markets;

RECOGNIZING the increasing linkages between the various aspects of economic policymaking that fall within the respective mandates of the International Monetary Fund ("Fund") and the World Trade Organization ("WTO"), and the call in the Marrakesh Agreement for greater coherence among economic policies internationally;

RECOGNIZING the close collaborative relationship existing over the past several decades between the Fund and the CONTRACTING PARTIES to the General Agreement on Tariffs and Trade, and the importance of continuing and strengthening such a relationship between the Fund and the WTO;

HAVING REGARD to Article X of the Fund's Articles of Agreement, which provides that "the Fund shall cooperate within the terms of this Agreement with any general international organization and with public international organizations having specialized responsibility in related fields";

HAVING REGARD to Article III.5 of the Marrakesh Agreement Establishing the World Trade Organization, which provides that "with a view to achieving greater coherence in global economic policymaking, the WTO shall cooperate, as appropriate, with the International Monetary Fund";

HAVING REGARD to the Declarations in the Marrakesh Agreement on the Contribution of the World Trade Organization to Achieving Greater Coherence in Global Economic Policymaking and on the Relationship of the WTO with the Fund, and to the provisions of Article XV:1, XV:2, XV:3 and Articles XII and XVIII of the General Agreement on Tariffs and Trade 1994 (GATT 1994) and of Articles XI, XII, and XXVI of the General

---

[161] Jackson, as note 14, above, pp. 242–243.

Agreement on Trade in Services (GATS) concerning cooperation and consultation, including on exchange and trade matters;

The Fund and the WTO *agree* as follows:

Paragraph 1

The Fund and the WTO shall cooperate in the discharge of their respective mandates in accordance with the provisions of this Agreement.

Paragraph 2

The Fund and the WTO shall consult with each other with a view to achieving greater coherence in global economic policymaking.

Paragraph 3

The Fund shall inform the WTO of any decisions approving restrictions on the making of payments or transfers for current international transactions, decisions approving discriminatory currency arrangements or multiple currency practices, and decisions requesting a Fund member to exercise controls to prevent a large or sustained outflow of capital.

Paragraph 4

The Fund agrees to participate in consultations carried out by the WTO Committee on Balance-of-Payments Restrictions on measures taken by a WTO member to safeguard its balance of payments. For these consultations, existing procedures for Fund participation shall continue and may be adapted as appropriate in accordance with paragraph 14 below.

Paragraph 5

The Fund shall invite the WTO Secretariat to send an observer to the ordinary meetings of the Executive Board of the Fund on general and regional trade policy issues, including the formulation of Fund policies on trade matters, and to discussions of the World Economic Outlook (WEO) when there is a significant trade content. In addition, when consultations between the Fund's staff and the WTO Secretariat lead to the conclusion that matters of particular common interest to both organizations will be under discussion at other meetings of the Executive Board, including country-specific matters, or at meetings of the Committee on Liaison with the WTO, the Managing Director shall recommend that the WTO Secretariat be invited to send an observer to such meetings.

Paragraph 6

The WTO shall invite the Fund to send a member of its staff as an observer to the meetings of the Ministerial Conference, General Council, Trade Policy Review Body, the three sectoral councils, Committee on Trade and Development, Committee on Regional Trade Agreements, Committee on Trade-Related Investment Measures, and Committee on Trade and the

Environment and their subsidiary bodies (excluding the Committee on Budget, Finance and Administration, the Dispute Settlement Body, and dispute settlement panels). The WTO shall invite the Fund to send a member of its staff as an observer to meetings of the WTO Dispute Settlement Body where matters of jurisdictional relevance to the Fund are to be considered. The WTO shall also invite the Fund to send a member of its staff to other meetings of the Dispute Settlement Body as well as of other WTO bodies for which attendance is not provided above (excluding the Committee on Budget, Finance and Administration, and dispute settlement panels), when the WTO, after consultation between the WTO Secretariat and the staff of the Fund, finds that such a presence would be of particular common interest to both organizations.

Paragraph 7

The Fund and the WTO shall make available to each other in advance the agendas, and relevant documents, for the meetings to which they are invited pursuant to the terms of this Agreement. In addition, the Fund shall make available to the WTO Secretariat the agendas of the Executive Board meetings at the time of their circulation in the Fund, and the WTO shall make available to the Fund the agendas of the Dispute Settlement Body at the time of their circulation in the WTO.

Paragraph 8

Each organization may communicate its views in writing on matters of mutual interest to the other organization or any of its organs or bodies (excluding the WTO's dispute settlement panels) and such views shall become part of the official record of such organs and bodies. The Fund shall inform in writing the relevant WTO body (including dispute settlement panels) considering exchange measures within the Fund's jurisdiction whether such measures are consistent with the Articles of Agreement of the Fund.

Paragraph 9

For the purpose of this Agreement, the Director-General of the WTO and the Managing Director of the Fund shall ensure cooperation between the staffs of the two institutions and, to that end, shall agree on appropriate procedures for collaboration, including access to databases, and exchanges of views on jurisdictional and policy issues.

Paragraph 10

The Fund's staff shall consult with the WTO Secretariat on issues of possible inconsistency between measures under discussion with a common member and that member's obligations under the WTO Agreement. The WTO Secretariat shall consult with the Fund's staff on issues of possible inconsistency between measures under discussion with a common member and that member's obligations under the Fund's Articles of Agreement.

Paragraph 11

The Fund shall provide the WTO, promptly after circulation to the Executive Board, for the confidential use of its Secretariat, with staff reports and related background staff papers on

Article IV consultations and on use of Fund resources on common members and on Fund members seeking accession to the WTO, subject to the consent of the member.

Paragraph 12

The WTO shall provide the Fund, for the confidential use of its management and staff, with Trade Policy Review Reports, summary records and reports of Councils, Bodies and Committees, and reports of WTO Members to these organs.

Paragraph 13

Each party to this Agreement shall ensure that any information communicated under this Agreement shall be used only within the limits specified by the other party.

Paragraph 14

The Director-General of the WTO and the Managing Director of the Fund shall be responsible for the implementation of this Agreement and, to that effect, shall make such arrangements as they deem appropriate.

Paragraph 15

This Agreement shall be reviewed upon the request of either party and may be amended by mutual agreement.

Paragraph 16

This Agreement may be terminated by either party by written notice to the other and, unless otherwise agreed by the parties, shall terminate six months after receipt of such notice.

Paragraph 17

Following approval by the General Council of the WTO and the Executive Board of the Fund, this Agreement shall enter into force on the date of its signature.

To be added at time of signature:

Signed at _____ on _____ in duplicate

For the World Trade Organization,   For the International Monetary Fund,

Director-General   Managing Director

ANNEX II

AGREEMENT BETWEEN THE INTERNATIONAL BANK FOR RECONSTRUCTION AND DEVELOPMENT, THE INTERNATIONAL DEVELOPMENT ASSOCIATION AND THE WORLD TRADE ORGANIZATION

AGREEMENT, dated_____,_____,_____, between the INTERNATIONAL BANK FOR RECONSTRUCTION AND DEVELOPMENT, the INTERNATIONAL DEVELOPMENT ASSOCIATION (hereinafter collectively referred to as the World Bank) and the WORLD TRADE ORGANIZATION (hereinafter referred to as WTO).

Preamble

CONSIDERING the growing interactions between economic policies pursued by individual countries arising from the globalization of markets;

RECOGNIZING the increasing interlinkages between various aspects of economic policymaking that fall within the respective mandates of the World Bank and the WTO and the call in the Marrakesh Agreement for greater coherence among economic policies internationally;

RECOGNIZING the close collaborative relationship existing over the past several decades between the World Bank and the CONTRACTING PARTIES to the General Agreement on Tariffs and Trade, and the importance of continuing and strengthening such a relationship between the World Bank and the WTO;

HAVING REGARD to Article V, Section 8(a) of the Articles of Agreement of the International Bank for Reconstruction and Development, which provides that the Bank "shall cooperate with any general international organization and with public international organizations having specialized responsibilities in related fields",

HAVING REGARD to the Declaration on the Contribution of the World Trade Organization to Achieving Greater Coherence in Global Economic Policymaking, and to Article III.5 of the Marrakesh Agreement Establishing the World Trade Organization, which provides that "with a view to achieving greater coherence in global economic policymaking, the WTO shall cooperate, as appropriate, with the International Monetary Fund and with the International Bank for Reconstruction and Development and its affiliated agencies".

The World Bank and the WTO *agree* as follows:

Paragraph 1

The World Bank and the WTO shall cooperate in the discharge of their respective mandates in accordance with the provisions of this Agreement.

Paragraph 2

The World Bank and the WTO shall consult with each other with a view to achieving greater coherence in global economic policymaking.

Paragraph 3

The World Bank agrees that the WTO be granted observer status at the Annual Meetings of its Board of Governors. The WTO agrees that the World Bank be granted observer status at meetings of its Ministerial Conference.

Paragraph 4

The World Bank shall invite the WTO Secretariat to send an observer to the meetings of the Executive Directors of the World Bank on general and regional trade policy issues, including the formulation of World Bank policies on trade matters. In addition, when consultations between the World Bank's staff and the WTO Secretariat lead to a conclusion that matters of particular common interest to both organizations will be under discussion at other meetings of the Executive Directors, including country specific matters, the President of the World Bank shall recommend that the WTO Secretariat be invited to send an observer to such meetings.

Paragraph 5

The WTO shall invite the World Bank to send a member of its staff as an observer to the meetings of the General Council, Trade Policy Review Body, the three sectoral councils, Committee on Trade and Development, Committee on Regional Trade Agreements, Committee on Trade-Related Investment Measures, and Committee on Trade and Environment and their subsidiary bodies (excluding the Dispute Settlement Body, the Committee on Budget, Finance and Administration and dispute settlement panels). The WTO shall invite the World Bank to send a member of its staff as an observer to meetings of other WTO bodies for which attendance is not provided above (excluding the Committee on Budget, Finance and Administration and dispute settlement panels) where the World Bank and the WTO expect that particular matters of common interest to both organizations will be under discussion.

Paragraph 6

The World Bank and the WTO shall make available to each other in advance the agenda, and relevant documents, for the meetings to which they are invited pursuant to the terms of this Agreement. In addition, the World Bank shall make available to the WTO Secretariat agendas of meetings of the Executive Directors at the time of their circulation in the World Bank, and the WTO shall make available to the World Bank the agendas of other bodies at the time of their circulation in the WTO.

Paragraph 7

For the purposes of this Agreement, the Director-General of the WTO and the President of the World Bank shall ensure cooperation between the staffs of the two institutions who, to that end, as appropriate, shall share access to databases, undertake joint research and technical cooperation activities and exchange views on policy issues.

Paragraph 8

The WTO Secretariat and the World Bank staff shall consult and exchange views on all matters of mutual interest with the view to ensuring the adoption of consistent and mutually supportive policies. To that end, they shall keep each other regularly informed of their programmes and activities in matters related to international trade.

Paragraph 9

Subject to such limitations as may be necessary for safeguarding of confidential material, the WTO and the World Bank shall arrange the timely exchange of information, reports and other documents of mutual interest.

Paragraph 10

Each party to this Agreement shall ensure that any information communicated under this Agreement shall be used only within the limits specified by the other party.

Paragraph 11

The Director-General of the WTO and the President of the World Bank shall be responsible for the implementation of this Agreement and, to that effect, shall make such arrangements as they deem appropriate.

Paragraph 12

This Agreement shall be reviewed upon the request of either party and may be amended by mutual agreement.

Paragraph 13

This Agreement may be terminated by either party by written notice to the other and unless otherwise agreed by the parties, shall terminate six months after receipt of such notice.

This Agreement shall enter into force on the date of its signature.

Signed at _____ on _____ in duplicate.

For the World Trade Organization,   For the World Bank,

Director-General   President

Chapter 11

WTO DISCIPLINES UNDER THE IMF PROGRAM: CONGRUENCE OR CONFLICT?

Dukgeun Ahn*

I. STRUCTURE OF IMF PROGRAMS AND SOURCE OF PROBLEMS

The importance of interrelationship and linkage between globalized economies was forcefully illustrated during the recent financial crises of 1997-1998 that swept some Asian and Latin American countries. In addition to demonstrating interconnectivity of individual economies, the recovering process from such economic calamity has raised an interesting question from another dimension of international economic relations: coherence of international organizations, especially international financial institutions and international trade organization. The delicate issue of congruence between legal obligations under the WTO and policy measures adopted under the IMF program has become much more real, rather than theoretical, and imminent to be addressed as a series of trade disputes concerning such issue have been submitted to the WTO dispute settlement system.[1]

In principle, the answer for the question of how the WTO should treat policy measures adopted under the IMF programs is simple and clear. There is no exception to WTO obligations for policy measures

---

* Director, WTO & Trade Strategy Center; KDI School of Public Policy and Management, KOREA. I am very grateful to useful comments and insights on an earlier draft by James Durling, Debra Steger and participants at the 2003 Symposium on the WTO and East Asia. I also acknowledge excellent research assistance by Hyunjeong Kim.
[1] This issue was first raised by *Argentina – Measures Affecting Imports of Footwear, Textiles, Apparel and Other Items*, WT/DS56/R (adopted on Apr. 22, 1998; hereinafter '*Argentina – Footwear*'). Various measures adopted by the Korean government during the financial crisis of 1997-1998 have recently become a focal point for trade disputes with the United States and the European Communities. The consequent WTO cases include *Korea – Measures Affecting Trade in Commercial Vessels* (DS273), *US – Countervailing Duty Investigation on Dynamic Random Access Memory Semiconductors (DRAMS) from Korea* (DS/296), and *EC – Countervailing Measures on Dynamic Random Access Memory Chips from Korea* (DS/299).

25

regardless of whether they are employed as parts of adjustment measures or IMF conditionality.[2] This principle was basically affirmed by the Appellate Body in its ruling for the *Argentina – Footwear* case.[3] The Appellate Body clarified that nothing justified a conclusion that a Member's commitments to the IMF shall prevail over its obligations under GATT 1994.[4] In other words, any measure taken as a part of either IMF conditionality or overall adjustment measures should comply with pertinent WTO disciplines. In fact, IMF conditionality had rarely stipulated an implementation of trade policy measures that contradicted with WTO – or, previously GATT.

Although this principle may be conveniently enunciated, the actual application of it demands more complicated consideration. A country that receives financing under an IMF program typically undertakes three kinds of reform or adjustment policies, some of which are specifically mandated as IMF conditionality: financial restructuring measures, corporate restructuring measures and economic liberalization measures – especially, for foreign exchange and trade.

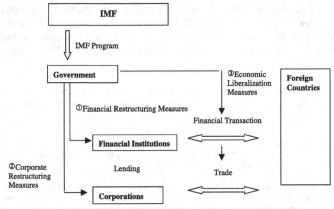

Figure 1. Structure of IMF Programs

[2] For a detailed account of distinction between IMF conditionality and adjustment measures committed by a government seeking the Fund financing, *see* Deborah Siegel, "Legal Aspects of the IMF/WTO Relationship: The Fund's Articles of Agreement and the WTO Agreements", 96 *American Journal of International Law* 561 (2002), 573-575.

[3] *See generally* Dukgeun Ahn, "Linkages between International Financial and Trade Institutions – IMF, World Bank and WTO", 34 *Journal of World Trade* 1 (2000), 23-25.

[4] WTO, WT/DS56/AB/R (adopted on Apr. 22, 1998), para.70. In fact, the Appellate Body ruling is more specific by focusing on Article VIII of the GATT 1994 as opposed to import surcharges of the Argentine government. But, the logic in that case can plausibly be applied to a broader context of IMF programs versus WTO obligations.

Since a standard condition for continued receipt of IMF financing requires countries to refrain from imposing import restrictions or to further import liberalization, trade policy measures taken as parts of formal IMF programs would rarely cause direct contradiction with WTO agreements.

More controversial problems, however, occur through seemingly incidental channel or nexus of financial institutions and corporations. Normally, financial institutions such as banks engage in divergent lending activities with corporations, which are considered to be governed by a market mechanism. When a government under an IMF program undertakes various adjustment measures or IMF conditionality, it typically embraces restructuring measures for not just financial sectors but also corporate sectors. These restructuring measures inevitably invite more active and visible roles of governments in both financial and corporate sectors. These increased roles of governments during the IMF program are now subject to considerably strengthened disciplines of the WTO Agreement on Subsidies and Countervailing Measures. Without considering such peculiar circumstances, substantial parts of governmental roles during the IMF program may be regarded as government 'directed' or even 'entrusted' activities that are inconsistent with subsidy disciplines, in case corporations are engaged in competition with imported products or at export markets. The possibility for WTO Members to raise such complaints, even more successfully, would rise as the degree of financial crisis gets more severe, because exports from countries under the IMF programs would increase more with larger exchange rate depreciation.[5] This structural part of problems concerning the IMF program deserves more attention and sensible resolution by the WTO Members to enhance congruence and coherence between two pillars of the world economic system. More specific examples based on the Korean experience will be discussed below.

II. Trade Liberalization by the Korean Government under the IMF Program

Korea's economic liberalization policies undertaken pursuant to the mandates under the IMF program consist of mainly three parts: foreign

---

[5] The magnitude of the exchange rate volatility during the financial crisis is truly immense. For example, the Korean won was depreciated to an almost half value within a 4 month period from October 1997. *See* Dukgeun Ahn, "Korea in the GATT/WTO Dispute Settlement System: Legal Battle for Economic Development", 6 *Journal of International Economic Law* 597 (2003), 621.

exchange liberalization, capital account liberalization, and trade liberalization. Firstly, an exchange rate policy adopted freely flexible exchange rate systems by abolishing daily exchange rate bands. The Korean government implemented the first stage of foreign exchange liberalization on April 1, 1999 by liberalizing foreign currency transaction of companies and financial institutions. The second stage implementation was initiated on January 1, 2001 by permitting foreign currency transaction of individuals. Secondly, capital account liberalization policies include, *inter alia*, eliminating restriction for foreigners' access to domestic money market instruments and corporate bond markets, permitting foreign financial institutions to participate in mergers and acquisitions of domestic financial institutions, and increasing the ceilings on aggregate foreigners' ownership of listed Korean shares. Thirdly, trade policies adopted further liberalization measures such as termination of the Import Diversification Program and abolition of trade related subsidies.

Despite substantial difficulties to address precipitous reduction of foreign exchange reserve, the Korean government committed to continue trade liberalization under the IMF program. In that regard, the Korean government agreed not to make purchases under the Stand-By Arrangement with the IMF that would increase the IMF's holdings of Korea's currency subject to repurchase beyond 25% of quota, if Korea imposes or intensifies import restrictions for balance of payments reasons at any time during the period of the Stand-By Arrangement.[6]

Moreover, as a part of the comprehensive economic policy program for structural reforms, the Korean government agreed to set, at the time of the first full review, a timetable in line with WTO commitments to eliminate trade-related subsidies, restrictive import licensing and the import diversification program. It also committed to streamline and improve the transparency of the import certification procedures.[7] At the letter of intent dated December 24, 1997, the Korean government confirmed its intent to accelerate import liberalization and eliminate trade-related subsidies. To facilitate further liberalization, it categorized three types of trade measures: trade-related subsidies, import liberalization and financial services liberalization.

With regard to trade-related subsidies, the Korean government agreed to abolish three subsidies that were due to be terminated by the

---

[6] Stand-By Arrangement (dated Dec. 3, 1997), para. 3(e)(iv).
[7] Korea-Memorandum on the Economic Program (dated Dec. 3, 1997), para. 30.

end of 1998 under the purview of the WTO and delete one administrative subsidy program.

Abolition of Trade-Related Subsidies

The first subsidy repealed under the IMF program was tax concession for "Reserves for Export Losses" to compensate for the loss of export businesses under Article 16 of the Tax Exemption and Reduction Control Law.[8] The reserves set aside to compensate for its losses by a resident or a domestic corporation, running a business earning foreign currency, had been counted as a loss when calculating the taxable income within a certain limit (that of an amount equivalent to 1% of its foreign currency receipts or 50% of its income, whichever is less). The amount allocated to such reserves was added back to the resident's or corporation's gains in three-year instalments from the year after the year in which the reserves were counted as a loss, but in the case of export businesses, starting two years after the year in which the reserves were counted as a loss. This tax concession was granted since March 3, 1973. The second subsidy abolished was tax concession for "Reserves for Overseas Market Development" under Article 17 of the Tax Exemption and Reduction Control Law that aimed to promote the overseas market development of a business earning foreign currency. Reserves set aside for overseas market development had been treated as a loss when calculating the taxable income in the same manner as the reserves for export losses. This tax benefit was maintained since July 31, 1969. The third subsidy eliminated was tax concession for "Tax Credit for Investment in Facilities" to encourage investment in facilities for small and medium enterprises or for developing technology and manpower under the Tax Exemption and Reduction Control Law. Under this tax program, various tax credits were provided for investment in facilities for small and medium enterprises, facilities for technology and manpower, housing for employees. Also, tax credits were granted for businesses moving to a provincial area and business conversion or reorganization. This tax concession started from December 30, 1970 and subsequently expanded in 1976, 1985 and 1990. Another program was abolished by the approval of the National Assembly.

Import Liberalization: Termination of Import Diversification Program

Despite the accession to the GATT in 1967, the Korean government maintained various import restraints primarily due to its balance-of-

---

[8] WTO, G/SCMN/25/KOR (dated July 23, 1997).

payment problems. The chronic foreign debt problems aggravated by the heavy chemical industry promotion policy starting from 1973 and the first oil shock in 1974 in fact strengthened import restrictions. It was only in 1977 when the total value of exportation exceeded $10 billion that a serious effort to liberalize importation was undertaken.[9] In 1978, three major import liberalization measures were implemented in May, July and September.

In May 1978, as a safeguard mechanism for major import liberalization, the Korean government effectively applied the Import Diversification Program that was first introduced concerning 7 product items in 1977.[10] Subsequently, the Executive Order of the Trade Transaction Act was amended to include Article 21:3 that stipulated discretionary import restriction of products from countries with which Korea had trade deficits.[11] The legal foundation for the Import Diversification Program was later replaced with Article 19.2 of the Foreign Trade Act.[12] Article 35.5 of the Executive Order of the Foreign Trade Act provided a more specific legal support for the Programme that was employed to address country specific trade imbalance.[13]

The Import Diversification Program basically targeted the imports from Japan. After the liberation from colonial governance in 1945, Korea resumed economic relationship with Japan since 1965. Bilateral trade with Japan, however, caused huge trade deficits for Korea that often intensified political tension rooted on a former colonial history. The Import Diversification Program was, therefore, devised from the inception to address potentially too dependent trade structure on Japanese imports. When Korea experienced the largest trade deficit with Saudi Arabia in 1982, the Import Diversification Program was modified in 1983 to apply to the country with the largest trade surplus "in the past five years". This amendment was solely to single out Japan as the potential target for the system. As a result, products from countries other than Japan had never been subject to the Import Diversification Program.

---

[9] The overall trade balance in 1977 was still in deficit at some $764 million.

[10] Public Notice by the Ministry of Commerce and Industry, No. 78-8.

[11] Executive Order of the Trade Transaction Act (Presidential Decree No.10057, Nov. 1, 1980), Art.21:3, para.2.4.

[12] Public Law No. 3895 (Enacted on Dec. 31, 1986; entered into force on July 1, 1987).

[13] Executive Order of the Foreign Trade Act (Presidential Decree No.12191, June 30, 1987).

Table 1. Number of Items Subject to the Import Diversification Program

Year	Number of Items			Liberalization Rate
	CCCN 4 level	CCCN 8 level	CCCN 10 level	
1980	195			69.3
1982	209	913		76.6
1984	168	590		84.9
1986	159	414		91.5
1988			344	94.8
1990			268	96.3
1991			258	97.2
1992			258	97.7
1993			258	98.1
1994			230	98.6
1995			204	99.0
1996			162	99.3
1997			127	99.9
1998			88	99.9

Source: Ministry of Commerce and Industry
Note: The increase of the number of the items subject to the Import Diversification Program is due to the amendment of HS code on January 1, 1990.

Although the Import Diversification Program began with 7 product items in 1977, it soon included 100 additional items by May 1978 and 107 more items by the end of 1978. But, the problem of the Import Diversification Program was already raised when the application to intermediary products and machinery harmed competitiveness of domestic production. Accordingly, the product coverage under the Import Diversification Program was focused on final consumer products, rather than intermediary products that were used in subsequent manufacturing process. The Korean Government allowed various exceptions to the Import Diversification Program. These have been granted for production facilities, parts and components in connection with the Foreign Investors Industrial Parks; sample products for domestic production; and materials for producing exports. In addition, the Import Diversification Program also covered divergent products for which import substitution policies were undertaken. This function of the Import Diversification Program, however, was not as crucial as the role to address unbalanced trade deficits.

The product coverage was continuously increased until 1981[14] and then gradually reduced to phase out by June 1999. The Import

---

[14] The product coverage in 1981 on the basis of the CCCN 8-digit reached about 924 items.

Diversification Program was formally terminated when the last 16 product items including VCR, mobile phones, colour televisions, automobiles, and camera were removed from the list.

The Japanese government had requested repeatedly to repeal the Import Diversification Program, alleging the violation of GATT obligation particularly, under Articles I, XI and XIII. Since the Korean government disinvoked Article XVIII:B for its import restrictive measures in 1990[15], the legitimacy of the Import Diversification Program under GATT obligations was indeed questionable. But, the Japanese government never brought a formal complaint on the Program to the GATT dispute settlement system. Instead, the Japanese government relied on a more political and diplomatic channel, for example, by raising the issue at the ministerial level.

Table 2. Liberalization Schedule of the Import Diversification Program under the IMF Program

Items to Be Liberalized (113 Items as of Dec. 18, 1997)	Due Date
25	Dec. 30, 1997
40	July 31, 1998
32	Dec. 31, 1998
16	June 30, 1999

As an effort to improve bilateral economic relations and also to cope with a new trading system established by the Uruguay Round negotiation, the Korean government decided to reduce the product coverage of 258 items by half during the five year period beginning in 1994.[16] The long term plan for the Import Diversification Program prepared in December 1993 left open for future works the reform plan for 1999 and thereafter.

But, with the accession to the OECD in 1996, Korea agreed to eliminate the Import Diversification Program by the end of 1999. The OECD accession negotiation took place between November 1995 and July 1996 had seven evaluation sectors and four policy review areas. As one of policy review area, trade issue was discussed and the Import Diversification Program was scheduled to phase out by the end of 1999.

---

[15] Ahn, *supra* note 5, 603-606.
[16] MITI, 1999 Report on the WTO Consistency of Trade Policies by Major Trading Partners 55 (1999).

In addition, at the end of 1997 when the Korean government reached an agreement with the IMF on economic reform programs to receive financial supports, it committed to repeal the Import Diversification Program by the end of June 1999. After the Korean government reached a stand-by arrangement with the IMF in an effort to overcome a financial crisis on December 3, 1997, 11 "Letters of Intents" were exchanged to elaborate the structural reform programs in the course of restructuring and recovery process. By the Letter of Intent dated December 18, 1997, the Korean government committed to accelerate the phase-out of the Import Diversification Program by June 1999, six months earlier than the due date committed to the WTO. Pursuant to this agreement, the Korean government removed 25 items by the end of 1997, 40 items by the end of July 1998, 32 items by the end of 1998, and finally the remaining 16 items – primarily in industrial machinery, electrical and electronic equipment, and automotive sectors – by the end of June 1999. As part of a restructuring program committed to the IMF, the Korean government successfully implemented the scheduled liberalization, as indicated in Table 2, or the complete phase-out of the Import Diversification Program.

Financial Service Liberalization

The Korean government committed to bind under the WTO the liberalization of financial services as agreed with the OECD. This commitment was announced in the WTO Financial Services Committee on January 30, 1998. On January 19, 1999, The Korean government submitted the revised services offer consistent with the OECD commitments to the WTO.

III.   GOVERNMENTAL ROLE IN THE CORPORATE RESTRUCTURING PROGRAM

Corporate restructuring program aimed to support economically viable but distressed companies reform their business operations and management, and financially restructure their liabilities to restore corporate financial sustainability. The fundamental objectives of corporate restructuring programs undertaken by the Korean government were established at the meeting on January 13, 1998 between the President-elect and the CEOs of top five *chaebols*. To achieve those objectives, the government focused on systemic reforms to facilitate corporate restructuring while actual restructuring was conducted on the basis of voluntary agreements between companies and pertinent creditor financial institutions. The Korean government tried to ensure that all individual corporate restructuring was voluntary and market oriented, since the governmental intervention in such processes could aggravate distrust of the markets and relevant economic circumstances for the companies.

This corporate restructuring policy was in fact the adoption of the so-called "London Approach" under which corporate restructuring has been conducted by voluntary agreements between corporations and creditor financial institutions with active mediation of the Bank of England.[17] The corporate restructuring program implemented under the London Approach normally contains three elements: voluntary restructuring procedures led by creditor financial institutions on the basis of market oriented principles, loss sharing among interested parties not to unduly undermine particular parties' financial health, and utilization of corporate workout programs as a primary method of restructuring. Corporate workout programs had been implemented pursuant to the principles of loss minimization, fairness and justice, expeditiousness and cost minimization. The Korean government indeed encouraged banks to set up voluntary creditor committees to assess the need and modality of corporate debt restructuring. Subsequently, in order to provide an overall framework of principles and procedures for voluntary corporate workouts, the Financial Supervisory Corporation (FSC) provided guidelines on the Corporate Restructuring Agreement that was to set a structure for negotiations between creditors and debtors, and on creation and operation of the Corporate Restructuring Coordination Committee that was established to resolve inter-creditor disputes. The FSC monitored workouts conducted under the Corporate Restructuring Agreement to ascertain consistency with the issued guidelines.

The corporate restructuring programs were later more directly and concretely addressed by the Structural Adjustment Loan (SAL) of the World Bank.[18] Under the SAL, the Korean government agreed to extend policy support for corporate restructuring by, *inter alia*, curtailing emergency loans, facilitating use of debt/equity conversion to address excessive leverage among *chaebol* affiliates, reducing cross guarantees, removing tax disincentives for mergers and acquisitions, debt restructuring and asset dispositions as a means of corporate restructuring, improving procedures and coordination for court-supervised insolvency.

---

[17] For more detailed explanations on the London Approach, *see*, for example, Pen Kent, 'Corporate Workouts – A UK Perspective', *International Insolvency Review* (1997).

[18] Korea-World Bank SAL II, Policy Matrix on Corporate Restructuring (dated July 23, 1998).

Moreover, the Korean government accelerated implementation of corporate restructuring by pursuing inter-creditor agreements on corporations to be restructured, seeking a timely exit strategy for non-viable corporations, identifying additional non-viable corporations, initiating resolution of corporations that were not under corporate supervision but received emergency loans, expediting resolution of corporations under court supervision in which the Korean government was a major shareholder, developing an ability to anticipate corporate default or insolvency, promoting self-restructuring by the top five *chaebols*. These corporate restructuring policies were further elaborated by the Corporate and Financial Sector Restructuring Loan agreed between the Korean government and the World Bank on November 18, 1999. These series of corporate restructuring programs did accomplish substantial reforms for a Korean corporate sector, most notably dismantling the Daewoo group.

IV. ALTERNATIVE SOLUTIONS

The exchange rate fluctuation during the financial crisis alone can cause trade disputes, particularly concerning antidumping measures.[19] By arbitrary segregation of investigation periods, price difference between normal values and export prices calculated in terms of dollar that is in turn transformed into antidumping duties may appear to be considerable. There is another risk of trade remedy actions based on governmental functions that should be inevitable and essential in the course of implementing IMF programs to overcome financial crises. Legitimate governmental roles in an economic emergency situation may be perceived as unjustified market intervention or interruption if considered entirely detached from the contextual economic circumstances. A more fundamental problem is that the risk of entailing trade disputes gets higher when the degree of a financial crisis is more severe because precipitous exchange rate depreciation tends to promote more exportation and trade liberalization policies embedded in the IMF program also induce more import competition.

What should then be the optimal solution for this inter-linkage problem? There may be three different approaches to this problem. Firstly, the WTO would not make any special consideration or exception to policy measures adopted, formally or informally, as parts of IMF programs. In

[19] For example, *United States - Anti-Dumping Measures on Stainless Steel Plate in Coils and Stainless Steel Sheet and Strip from Korea* (WT/DS179/R, adopted on Feb. 1, 2001).

other words, the WTO agreements may be applied in its entirety to a country or policy measures subject to IMF programs in the same manner as for other policy measures or WTO Members. This approach may, however, substantially undermine the effectiveness of policy measures under the IMF programs when trading partners counter with trade remedy actions. Moreover, such a bifurcated approach would cause unnecessarily adverse political repercussion against the IMF as well as the WTO.

Secondly, the IMF and the WTO can endeavor to enhance *ex ante* direct consultation so that they can ensure WTO consistency of policy measures proposed under the IMF programs. In fact, the Trade Policy Division of the Policy Development and Review Department in the IMF has conducted *ex ante* checking of WTO legality for IMF supported programs.[20] The WTO may also augment its institutional functions in this regard, for example by strengthening the Trade Policy Review Mechanism to review WTO consistency of any proposed policy measures under the IMF programs. This approach, however, is not free from structural problems, either. On the one hand, unlike the IMF conditionality that stipulates implementation *per se* of specific actions and no liability to consequential effects of those measures, WTO consistency of policy measures is typically determined by actual consequences of the implemented measures that depend on intricate market mechanisms. The WTO rules accommodating *de facto* standard, therefore, make such *ex ante* assessment of consistency or legality very vulnerable to future challenges. On the other hand, although the WTO may invoke its own institutional review procedure or a consultation process with the IMF, the nature of the WTO obligations seriously undermines the effectiveness of outcomes therefrom. This is because, under the WTO system, duties and obligations for a Member occur not against the WTO, but against other Members.[21] In other words, institutional cooperation between the IMF and the WTO would have an intrinsic limitation for fully resolving WTO inconsistency problems of IMF programs.

Thirdly, the WTO may provide a provisional and limited waiver of WTO obligations to a Member subject to an IMF program, at least during the period for which the IMF programs are enforced.[22] This waiver would be limited in that only certain trade remedy actions, especially antidumping and countervailing measures, and subsidy challenges to the

---

[20] Siegel, *supra* note 2, 575.
[21] It is contrasted with the IMF for which Member countries have specific legal duties for various actions. *See generally* Siegel, *supra* note 2.
[22] This approach was first proposed by Ahn, *supra* note 5, 24.

WTO are inhibited against a Member subject to an IMF program. Instead, safeguard actions may still be permitted for other Members that suffer from serious injury or threat thereof. Whereas there is too much risk of misplacing wrongdoings by exporters or exporting governments during the IMF program, it would not affect a safeguard mechanism that primarily hinges on domestic industry situations instead of actions by exporters or exporting governments. To the contrary, the concern by other Members on import surges from a country subject to IMF programs should be addressed by the WTO safeguard mechanisms that embraced elaborated disciplines such as compensation, retaliation and non-discriminatory application of measures.

V.   CONCLUDING REMARKS

The economic impacts of the financial crisis to the Korean economy are truly tremendous. The Korean government played an important role under the IMF rescue program to overcome the unprecedented crisis in all aspects of economic policies. Although the crisis was triggered mainly by severe problems in the financial sector, the trade area was considerably affected by ensued volatile fluctuation of foreign exchange rate and also played a key role to deal with serious economic distress with the help of the IMF. The Korean government's strong policy commitment for persistent trade liberalization despite a markedly deteriorated foreign reserve situation would shed some light on policy consideration for WTO Members.

Corporate restructuring programs undertaken as parts of the IMF program might have an effect on international trade, as certain trading partners raised concerns especially in the context of the WTO Subsidy Agreement[23], since restructured corporations under the IMF program might subsequently be engaged in import or export competition. Most, if not all, parts of these economic policy measures were, however, devised to promote import liberalization or domestic market competition, rather than market operation. The governmental role was in fact vital, not to interfere but to improve market competition that, in turn, contributed to recover from the financial distress. It was meticulously prepared and monitored by the IMF to ensure proper implementation of the

---

[23] The United States had also closely monitored the Korean government's roles in financial and corporate restructuring programs. See, for example, USTR, *Subsidies Enforcement Annual Report to the Congress* (February 1999), 7-8.

commitments under the Stand-By Arrangement. From the outset of implementing the IMF program, the recipient governments are normally mindful of potential issues in the context of the WTO Agreements and emphasized voluntary and market-oriented nature of the policy measures. A categorical rejection of the legitimacy of the these governments' roles under the IMF program would, therefore, deserve a more careful scrutiny.

Chapter 12

Is the Chinese exchange-rate regime "WTO-legal"?

Dukgeun Ahn
Seoul National University

How might the US take action through the WTO over China's alleged currency manipulation? This paper analyses three potential legal issues: legality of exchange-rate policy under the GATT rules, legality under the subsidy rules and feasibility of non-violation complaints. It concludes that any WTO resolution will be difficult to achieve because the organisation is not designed to deal with alleged exchange-rate manipulation.

Introduction

Pegging an exchange rate to other key currency is not *per se* illegal nor irrational.[1] But, in the case of China, the unprecedented level of current account surplus and dollar accumulation supported by alleged "exchange rate misalignment" or "protracted large-scale intervention in one direction in exchange markets" have provoked huge controversy over the legality under the international treaty obligation, especially the WTO and the IMF. Although the IMF seems to have a more direct jurisdiction over this exchange-rate related matter, massive trade consequences of exchange-rate policies compellingly demand remedial trade measures under the auspices of the WTO that has more effective enforcement mechanisms.

Here I analyse three potential legal issues focusing on the WTO Agreements: legality of exchange-rate policy under the GATT rules, legality under the subsidy rules and feasibility of non-violation complaints. I argue that although the current Chinese exchange rate regime may be found to be inconsistent with the GATT provision, it will be still very difficult to address the problems concerning exchange-rate regime in the WTO system. That is not because the Chinese system is complicated but primarily because the WTO rules are not devised to deal with alleged exchange-rate manipulation.

Frustrating the intent of WTO or IMF?

Generally speaking, the application of Article XV of GATT that stipulates rules on exchange arrangements to current WTO Members requires special caution because the underlying international financial system has been critically changed. When

---

1 Currently, 79 IMF members adopt pegging exchange rate arrangements. China is one of eight members that adopt the crawling peg arrangement anchored on the dollar pursuant to the IMF classification.

139

VOX

Research-based policy analysis and commentary from leading economists

Article XV was first devised, the IMF meticulously implemented the fixed exchange rate system. In contrast, a majority of WTO members, especially developed country members, adopt the floating exchange-rate arrangement. Nevertheless, Article XV has significant relevance to the exchange-rate policy issues in the current context.

Article XV of GATT requires cooperation with the IMF regarding a broad range of exchange questions such as monetary reserves, balance of payments or foreign exchange arrangements. For example, Article XV(2) provides that "in all cases" in which the WTO considers or deals with problems concerning foreign exchange arrangements, the WTO "shall consult fully" with the IMF. Moreover, in such consultations, the WTO "shall accept all findings" of statistical and other facts presented by the IMF relating to foreign exchange, as well as determination of the IMF as to whether action by a WTO Member in exchange matters is in accordance with the Articles of Agreement of the IMF.[2]

In addition to the consultation requirement in Article XV(2), Article XV(4) provides more substantive obligation for WTO Members as follows:

> Contracting parties shall not, by exchange action, frustrate the intent of the provisions of this Agreement, nor, by trade action, the intent of the provisions of the Articles of Agreement of the IMF.

Addenda of Article XV(4) provides that

> The word "frustrate" is intended to indicate, for example, that infringements of the letter of any Article of this Agreement by exchange action shall not be regarded as a violation of that Article if, in practice, there is no appreciable departure from the intent of the Article.

So, the key question from Article XV is whether China, by exchange action, frustrates the intent of GATT provisions.[3] This leads to three legal issues:

- Is China's current exchange-rate policy tantamount to "exchange action"?,
- What is the intent of the pertinent GATT provisions?
- Is that intent frustrated?

Some commentators argue that "exchange action" in Article XV(4) should be narrowly interpreted to cover liberalisation of payments or convertibility (see Koops 2010 and Denters 2003). They point out that "exchange action" should be different from "exchange-rate action". However, at the time of drafting GATT, currency par value manipulation was well known measure to protect domestic markets. Therefore, in GATT drafting, the US delegates "felt constrained to include some protection against them in the tariff agreement, even though the IMF articles contained some

---

2 The legal issues concerning the IMF rules are not the scope of this paper. Those issues are addressed in Seigel (2002).

3 Some have argued that China's exchange-rate policy should be regarded as "trade action" since it had significant implication and effect for trade. But, considering the general practice to divide works of the GATT and the IMF based on the technical nature of government measures rather than on the effect of these measures, China's exchange-rate policy must be regarded as exchange action (see WTO 1995).

similar provisions." (Jackson 1969). It implies that exchange action could well encompass the exchange-rate policy of WTO Members to fix its currency value at a certain level. Moreover, what the US government is complaining about is not the adoption of crawling peg system *per se*, but rather "maintaining" the current exchange rate for a prolonged period of time despite huge trade and financial consequences. This specific governmental policy choice can be understood as "exchange action", although adoption of crawling peg system may not be qualified for deliberate and specific nature connoted from "exchange *action*".

Second, the intent of GATT provisions is indeed hard to know. The "intent" may or may not be an "objective". The preamble of GATT is often discussed to draw "intent" of GATT, although the subsequent analysis seems to focus on broad economic goals mentioned therein. Or it is assumed that the intent of GATT must be obviously trade liberalisation or even balanced trade. For example, some argue that intent of GATT should be "balanced trade among its members on a multilateral basis" (see Hufbauer et al. 2006 for a critical analysis). However, instead of aiming to achieve economic goals such as raising living standards or full employment, "intent" of GATT provisions may be interpreted to embrace more "legal" aspects. For example, the intent of GATT provisions may be to stipulate articulated rule of conducts for commercial transaction so that the bargained competitive conditions for members' markets are not arbitrarily disturbed. If the intent of the GATT provisions is understood this way, the focus of the analysis will be more on structure and design of GATT rather than economic or trade performance. Actually, the goal or objective of the GATT system may be to achieve better economic performance through free trade, whereas the intent to devise elaborated GATT provisions may be to establish a more rule oriented system in which bargained competitive conditions among members will not be arbitrarily or unjustifiably disturbed.

Lastly, what constitutes "frustration" of the intent of GATT provisions? In fact, the expression "shall not frustrate the intent" is exceptional not only in GATT/WTO law, but also in public international law. But, if the above understanding for the intent is adopted, prolonged arbitrary misalignment of exchange rates can be seen to frustrate it since the exchange action deliberately employed by the Chinese government resulted in appreciable departure from what would have happened otherwise.

It was also argued that Addenda to Article XV(4) demands specific GATT article to be frustrated in an important way (Hufbauer et al. 2006). But, this argument ignored that Addenda present only examples, not the definitive explanation.

On the other hand, Article XV(9a) provides that "nothing in this Agreement shall preclude the use by a contracting party of exchange controls or exchange restrictions in accordance with the Articles of Agreement of the IMF." The scope of measures dealt in this article is limited, certainly not covering China's exchange-rate policy. Historically, exchange controls or restrictions related to convertibility were permitted by specific decisions of the IMF as special measures to address balance of payment problems of its members. So, "exchange controls or exchange restrictions" in accordance with the Articles of Agreement of the IMF would mean more specific exchange policies adopted pursuant to the IMF decision. A grand scale exchange-rate policy to fix its currency value is not covered by Article XV(9) exception clause.

Although this interpretation of Article XV may be one possible way to legally challenge China's exchange-rate policy, it raises another controversial issue in terms

VOX

Research-based policy analysis and commentary from leading economists

of enforcement. In case China does not comply with the recommendation by the WTO Dispute Settlement Body, the retaliation becomes prohibitively difficult or impractical due to the technical problems of injury calculation. What should be the proper exchange rate not to frustrate the intent of the GATT provisions raises the whole new sets of questions and legal issues. There is no consensus even on whether the IMF can and should deal with those questions.

Illegal subsidy?

Economically speaking, an undervalued exchange rate works as an import tax and an export subsidy. So, it is natural that the WTO Agreement on Subsidies and Countervailing Duties (SCM Agreement) is invoked to address trade problems caused by devalued exchange rates.

The most important legal element under the SCM Agreement is that the measure at issue - in this case, China's exchange-rate policy - must be a subsidy under Article 1. In order for China's exchange-rate policy to be regarded as subsidy, the following criteria must be met:

- there must be financial contribution by a government,

- benefit is conferred, and

- the subsidy must be specific. Financial contribution is made by direct transfer of funds, foregone government revenues, the provision or purchase of goods or services other than general infrastructure, or payment to a funding mechanism.

The first obstacle to invoke the SCM Agreement in relation to exchange rate policies is to prove financial contribution. Although it is argued that China's exchange-rate policy somehow provides financial contribution, those arguments are not tenable. For example, some argue that exchange of currency at an undervalued rate can be seen as direct transfer of funds and foregone government revue. This is, however, partial consideration of the full market situation. The same exchange rate applies to not only exporters, but also all other people and products. It means that unlike normal financial contribution situation which absolutely improve financial states of recipients, the manipulation of exchange rate affects relative prices of traders and thereby balances off gains.

Next, it is very difficult to argue that China's exchange-rate policy satisfies specificity requirement by affecting only a small number of enterprises or industries. It is often argued that China's exchange-rate policy is a prohibited export subsidy that is deemed to be specific. Although undervalued exchange rates crucially promote exportation, it is untenable to argue that China's exchange-rate policy is a subsidy contingent upon export performance. The fact that the fairly detailed illustrative list for export subsidy in Annex I does not mention this well known - probably the most important - contributing factor for export promotion indicates the boundary of export subsidy envisioned for multilateral disciplines.

Lastly, whether benefit is conferred critically hinges on market elasticity and production structure. Since market prices tend to adjust to exchange-rate regimes, benefits may not be readily conferred (see Staigner and Sykes 2008 for a rigorous analysis). This issue may be more controversial relative to the above legal elements of a subsidy. But, in any case, it will be very difficult to demonstrate that China's exchange-rate policy is a measure to be disciplined under the SCM Agreement simply because it has export promoting effects.

Non-violation complaints

Alternatively, a WTO member can raise a "non-violation" complaint in Article XXIII(1b) if any benefit accruing to it directly or indirectly from the GATT is nullified or impaired or the attainment of any objective of the GATT is impeded by any measure of another member, "whether or not it conflicts with the GATT provisions". Since there is no explicit violation of GATT, a WTO member losing the dispute based on a non-violation complaint has no obligation to withdraw the measure at issue but still must make a mutually satisfactory adjustment that may include compensation arrangement (see WTO, Understanding on Rules and Procedures Governing the Settlement of Disputes (DSU), Article 26.1.).

Although a non-violation complaint appears to be intriguing in the textual languages especially for complainants whose violation claims are not robust, the WTO jurisprudence has established the rigorous legal elements that must be demonstrated by a complainant:

- application of a measure by a WTO Member;
- a benefit accruing under the relevant agreement; and
- nullification or impairment of the benefit as the result of the application of the measure (WTO 1998).

A benefit accruing under the relevant agreement is typically that of legitimate expectations of improved market-access opportunities arising out of and at the time of relevant tariff concessions (WTO 1998). In the case of China's exchange-rate policy, it will be unattainable to demonstrate that other WTO Members cannot legitimately expect China to maintain basically the same exchange-rate policy as that retained prior to the WTO accession. Accordingly, it is unlikely that a non-violation complaint can be successfully raised in the case of China's exchange-rate policy.

Policy recommendation

As shown above, addressing China's exchange-rate policy with WTO rules will be formidable although it may not be completely impossible. This issue appears to be a kind of "political question" in the WTO system, rather than a legal problem to be judged by the dispute settlement system. Therefore, the litigation of this issue cannot produce proper solutions. Accordingly, the US and China should find other more "politically" attuned forum, such as G20 meeting, more suitable to resolve this conflict.

Difficulty of WTO rules in dealing with China's exchange-rate policy, however, has already caused considerable problems in the world trading system. Frustration on the WTO rules has inevitably led to more antidumping and countervailing duties, and

VOX

Research-based policy analysis and commentary from leading economists

recently even transitional product specific safeguard measure from the US side. It has provoked many retaliatory trade remedy actions by China against the US products (see Evenett 2010). This situation highlights the need of more cooperation among G20 states whose roles are crucial to contain the protectionist sentiment.

References

Bhala, Raj (2008), "Virtues, the Chinese Yuan, and the American Trade Empire", *Hong Kong Law Journal*, Vol. 38, 183-253.

China Currency Coalition (2004), The Section 301 Petition, September,

Denters, Erik (2003), "Manipulation of Exchange Rates in International Law: The Chinese Yuan", ASIL Insights, November.

Hufbauer, Gary C, Yee Wong, and Ketki Seth (2006), 'US-China Trade Disputes: Rising Tide, Rising Stakes', *Policy Analyses in International Economics 78*, Peterson Institute for International Economics.

Jackson, John H (1969), *World Trade and the Law of GATT*, Michie Company.

Koops, Catharina (2010), "Manipulating the WTO? The Possibilities for Challenging Undervalued Currencies under WTO Rules", Amsterdam Center for International Law Research Paper Series.

Mattoo, Aaditya and Arvind Subramanian (2008), "Currency Undervaluation and Sovereign Wealth Funds: A New Role for the World Trade Organization", World Bank Policy Research Paper 4668, July.

Mercurio, Bryan C (2009), "Is China a 'Currency Manipulator'? The Legitimacy of China's Exchange Regime Under the Current International Legal Framework", *The International Lawyer*, 43(3):1257-1300

Sanford, Jonathan E (2008), "Currency Manipulation: The IMF and WTO", CRS Report for Congress, May 8, RS22658.

Siegel, Deborah E (2002), "Legal Aspects of the IMF/WTO Relationship: The Fund's Articles of Agreement and the WTO Agreements", *The American Journal of International Law*, 96(3), July.

Simon J. Evenett (ed.) (2010), *Will Stabilisation Limit Protectionism? The 4th GTA Report*, CEPR.

Staiger, Robert W and Alan O Sykes (2008), "Currency Manipulation' and World Trade", Stanford Law and Economics Olin Working Paper 363, 13 June .

Zimmerman, Claus D (2008), "Jurisdictional Competition Between the IMF and the WTO and Its Impact on the Prevention of Monetary Protectionism", SIEL Working Paper, 16/08, June 26, 2008.

WTO (1994), "Understanding on Rules and Procedures Governing the Settlement of Disputes (DSU)", Article 26.1.

WTO (1995), Analytical Index: Guide to GATT Law and Practice, Vol. 1.

WTO (1998), Japan - Measures Affecting Consumer Photographic Film and Paper (WT/DS44/R, adopted April 22, 1998), Para. 10.41.

Chapter 13

Book Review: International Law in Financial Regulation and Monetary Affairs

International Law in Financial Regulation and Monetary Affairs. Edited by Thomas Cottier, John H. Jackson, and Rosa M. Lastra. Oxford, New York: Oxford University Press, 2012. Pp. xiv, 455. Index. $105, £60, cloth.

Serious academic efforts to reconsider the legitimacy and integrity of international financial systems followed in the wake of the 1997–98 Asian financial crisis, which originated in developing economies but threatened global financial stability. Scholars and practitioners identified a host of structural problems in the international financial markets that hampered rational and efficient operations, and offered a variety of reform proposals—albeit mostly from a strictly economics perspective.[1] Only a few legal studies tackled the fundamental issues of the international financial

system, such as externality problems of regulatory discrepancy, systemic gaps between domestic regulations and international markets, and, most importantly, the lack of effective multilateral treaties.[2] And in 2007–09, before any significant reform measures were incorporated into the international financial system, the world economy experienced an even greater crisis; the structural problems of international financial markets, the result of weak regulatory frameworks, were made well apparent. The question confronting the world economy is no longer whether the international financial system demands "hard" law; instead, we need to determine how international economic law can be brought to bear on increasingly fluid financial and monetary affairs.

The twenty-two articles in *International Law in Financial Regulation and Monetary Affairs* were originally published in the September 2010 special issue of the *Journal of International Economic Law.* Both the special issue and this book were edited by Thomas Cottier of the University of Bern, John Jackson of the Georgetown University Law Center, and Rosa Lastra of the Centre for Commercial Law Studies, Queen Mary, University of London.

In 1998, writing the lead article of that journal's inaugural issue, Jackson as editor-in-chief envisioned "a very high probability that the international community will turn toward the formation and designing of a treaty-based multilateral institution which could enable it appropriately and efficiently to respond to the problems of such regulation," and he presented a series of legal issues that needed to be considered when designing international institutions.[3] Many of those same issues are addressed in the essays presented in the book under review, with leading legal scholars

as a component of the right to an adequate standard of living, Raquel Rolnik–Mission to Maldives, UN Doc. A/HRC/13/20/Add.3 (Jan. 11, 2010).

[20] Human Rights Council, Human Rights and the Environment, UN Doc. A/HRC/RES/19/10 (Mar. 22, 2012). The present reviewer was appointed to the position in July 2012 and submitted his first report the following December. Report of the Independent Expert on the issue of human rights obligations relating to the enjoyment of a safe, clean, healthy and sustainable environment, John H. Knox, UN Doc. A/HRC/22/43 (Dec. 24, 2012).

[1] See, for example, the works listed by the Group of Thirty, *at* http://www.group30.org/publications. shtml, and also the *Report of the Commission of Experts of the President of the United Nations General Assembly on Reforms of the International Monetary and Financial System* (2009) ("Stiglitz Commission Report") *at* http://

www.un.org/ga/econcrisissummit/docs/FinalReport_ CoE.pdf.

[2] *See, e.g.,* THE REGULATION OF INTERNATIONAL FINANCIAL MARKETS: PERSPECTIVES FOR REFORM (Rainer Grote & Thilo Marauhn eds., 2006); GLOBAL GOVERNANCE OF FINANCIAL SYSTEMS: THE INTERNATIONAL REGULATION OF SYSTEMIC RISK (Kern Alexander, Rahul Dhumale & John Eatwell eds., 2006).

[3] John H. Jackson, *Global Economics and International Economic Law,* 1 J. INT'L ECON L. 1, 21–23 (1998).

presenting comprehensive prescriptions and policies for strengthening the international financial system.

The book comprises five parts. As background for the analyses presented in parts II to V, part I analyzes the nature and causes of the 2007–09 financial crisis. Part II probes the architecture of, and conceptual issues relating to, the international financial system, ranging from systemic differences between the international law of trade and finance, to the peculiar historical development of the international monetary system, and to the growing predominance of soft law for international finance. This part sets forth principles for a new architecture to enhance financial stability, and the "Santiago Principles" for sovereign wealth funds[4] are discussed as a current example of international financial standard-setting processes. Part III delves into more specific issues to be tackled in developing and applying international law for international financial markets. Problems relating to multilayered governance, borders, transparency, and regulatory competition and subsidiarity are scrutinized, as is international financial law's potential contribution to addressing situations in which governmental regulation has altogether failed. Included here are proposals involving organizational design, and the principles and directions for capital and securities regulation reforms are also presented. Part IV explores the implications of global trade rules such as the nondiscrimination obligation, prudential standards, and World Trade Organization (WTO) disciplines on subsidies and services. Also addressed are the interconnections among competition, state aid policies, and financial taxes in international financial law. Part V deals with the potential role of international law in monetary affairs, the need for international surveillance of monetary policies, and the regulatory authority of the International Monetary Fund (IMF). Part VI presents an insightful concluding chapter by Cottier and Lastra—a critical addition in view of the decision to publish the original special issue as a book.

[4] International Working Group of Sovereign Wealth Funds, *Generally Accepted Principles and Practices—Santiago Principles* (2008), *at* http://www.iwg-swf.org/pubs/gapplist.htm.

As R. Michael Gadbaw explains in his essay, "Systemic Regulation of Global Trade and Finance: A Tale of Two Systems," the legal frameworks regulating global trade and global finance—the two central pillars of international economic law—are strikingly different despite their common origin in the Bretton Woods system. Modern international trade law originated with the General Agreement on Tariffs and Trade, compromised by all its inherent weaknesses, or "birth defects." But trade law then significantly matured with the establishment of the WTO, including the enforcement of WTO agreements through an effective dispute settlement system. By contrast, modern international financial law arose originated in the fulcrum defined by the IMF and the World Bank, but its rigorous legal rules based on the gold standard and fixed exchange rates have given way to a corpus of soft law comprising best practices, regulatory reports, and memorandums of understanding, with two of the primary goals being greater information sharing and cooperation, all to generate better compliance. As Gadbaw notes:

> The WTO became a member-driven, rule-oriented, unitary, comprehensive and nearly universal system where the obligations run *horizontally* from members to other members, decisions are made by consensus, and obligations are interpreted and enforced through a dispute settlement system with a highly developed judicial function having the power to determine violations and authorize sanctions. The international financial regulatory system became a fragmented, complex, multi-tiered, multi-dimensional, resource-oriented system that accommodates the different domains and regulatory prerogatives of finance officials, central bankers, and bank regulators as well as the private financial community by creating a variety of different organizations from treaty-based to intergovernmental to cooperative arrangements among functional regulators. (pp. 41–42) (footnote omitted)

The asymmetrical evolution, systemic deficiency, and instability of international financial and trade law were much in evidence during the 2007–09 global financial crisis. In this context, Andreas F. Lowenfeld reviews the institutional evolution and dwindling roles of the IMF, effectively highlighting the systemic limitations of current regulatory structures. Lowenfeld thus answers, in part, a question raised by Gadbaw (which can also be understood as the central question in the entire volume)—namely, whether "greater convergence" is needed "in the global regulatory regimes governing trade and finance" (p. 51). Chris Brummer examines the reason for predominance of "soft law" in international financial systems and calls for "more robust monitoring of regulatory rules" and "institutional innovations" to enhance legitimacy (p. 112). In practice, conventional recourse to soft law in financial markets has resulted from the mismatch between the treaty-based powers exercised by governmental administrative bodies and the much stronger powers of domestic financial and banking organizations that are in charge of financial affairs— organizations that are typically protected from governmental interference in order to ensure their political neutrality and independence in making financial policy decisions. This situation seems to require more serious academic efforts from both the international and domestic/constitutional law perspectives.

As a theoretical foundation for developing international law applicable to financial systems, Rolf Weber posits a global coherence in which multilayered governance is used to maintain financial stability, and in which the trust and integrity of financial markets and actors play a central role. He suggests that "the allocation of regulatory responsibilities to the different layers of governance should be based on the (geographic) scope of the underlying financial activities and the importance of the regulatory objectives by reference to the common core values" (p.170). Joseph Norton presents the Santiago Principles for sovereign wealth funds—a set of twenty-four principles and practices addressing, inter alia, legal and institutional governance, accountability arrangements, investment policies, and risk management—which he sees as the product of an "initially unplanned and largely disjointed pattern of incipient 'multi-level global governance' among major national and regional actors" (p. 126).

Luis Garicano and Rosa Lastra elaborate seven regulatory principles that should be considered as principles of multilevel governance. Among other things, they support the following: further integration in the supervision of banking, securities, and insurance; systemic supervision under the purview of the central bank; limited reliance by the macro-supervisor (that is, the overarching regulatory authority) on self-regulation; and hierarchical structure of international supervision. Christine Kaufmann and Rolf Weber suggest a three-dimensional, rule-based approach to transparency in financial regulation. As a precondition for building confidence, they separate the notion of transparency into three parts: the constitutional dimension, which defines procedures and institutions for regulating financial markets; the substantive dimension, which establishes the values and objectives of financial regulations; and the accountability dimension, which is an essential element for rebuilding confidence in the financial system.

But other factors also come into play. Because of the intrinsically transnational character of financial products and markets, the main purpose of coordinating international financial regulation is not necessarily to "level the playing field" or to promote equal competition. Christian Tietje and Matthias Lehmann emphasize that an internationally harmonized financial system may potentially undermine the efficiency of financial markets and increase the probability of a global crisis. The crucial task of international financial law is therefore to find the "right balance" (p. 149) between global harmonization and regulatory competition. Joel Trachtman explains why international financial stability is a public good and why it is so important for international financial law to overcome externality problems. He argues that globalization, technological advance, financial innovation, and economic growth inevitably increase the need for stronger international financial law. Steve Charnovitz addresses how international financial law could address the failure of governmental regulation, and concludes that international financial law needs to be responsive to the problems not only of market failure but also of government failure.

On the more practical level, Hal Scott focuses a central problem underlying the global financial crisis—namely, the systemic risk inherent in inadequate or failed capital regulation. With respect to limits on leverage (in particular, the Basel methodology), Scott discusses the weaknesses of the reform plans prepared by the Committee on Capital Markets Regulation in May 2009[5] and argues for more use of market discipline in calibrating and regulating capital requirements. Although securities markets may not play a fundamental causal role in financial crises, they typically work as a mechanism for spreading the contagion of financial shocks and crises. That said, Donald Langevoort argues that focusing on the existing institutional aspects of securities regulation would enhance international cooperation and regulatory convergence.

Other areas of international economic law—especially in relation to trade, competition, and taxation—highlight elements of international financial law and the ways in which it has developed. Cottier and Markus Krajewski argue that the cornerstone principle of nondiscrimination in WTO law is absent in the international financial system due to the different legal relationships and different functions embodied in the financial and trading systems. Unlike the WTO system, the international financial system employs a more diverse and less legalistic set of rules, and aims to secure financial stability instead of market liberalization. They suggest that global minimal prudential standards should be adopted and then applied in a nondiscriminatory manner to international financial institutions. They also make an intriguing proposal based on the Reference Paper on Telecommunications,[6] which incorporates additional commitments into the WTO's General Agreement on Trade in Services (GATS). In particular, they suggest using the same approach to incorporate supplementary rules and policies for competition and regulation—especially pruden-

tial standards—into the WTO's legal framework for financial services under GATS. This approach has the advantage of being more flexible, less cumbersome, and easier to implement and enforce. Panagiotis Delimatsis and Pierre Sauvé argue, however, that the recent financial crisis would likely hinder efforts to negotiate market liberalization in financial services, especially at the WTO (as opposed to preferential trade agreements). They also argue that the financial crisis and subsequent policy responses of many developed countries increased the likelihood that the scope and application of international trade and investment standards will be determined through binding dispute settlement, if even then;[7] the massive post-crisis subsidies to the financial services industry are still largely unchallenged under GATS. In this context, Gary Horlick and Peggy Clarke discuss the limitations of the current WTO subsidy disciplines to address government intervention in financial markets. They support the use of non-actionable services subsidies—for example, in relation to logistics services, capital markets, and communication services—to advance the economic development of the least-developed countries, though persuading WTO members to agree may present a difficult challenge. Kern Alexander argues that financial taxes should become an integral component of prudential regulatory regimes and should be used, when necessary, to pay for the social costs of financial crises.

The termination of the gold standard and fixed exchange rates left room for legal (and governmental) interventions on monetary issues such as the money supply, interest rates, and exchange rates. Ernst Baltensperger and Cottier examine the role of international law in monetary affairs from the perspective that the global monetary system is a product of globally competing monetary monopolies and sovereign rights. They argue that nondiscrimination and conditional most-favored-nation treatment should be incorporated into policymaking and the future architecture of the international monetary system. Gary

[5] The Global Financial Crisis: A Plan for Regulatory Reform (2009), at http://capmktsreg.org/2009/05/the-global-financial-crisis-a-plan-for-regulatory-reform/.

[6] World Trade Organization, Negotiating Group on Telecommunications, Telecommunications Services: Reference Paper (Apr. 24, 1996), at http://www.wto.org/english/tratop_e/serv_e/telecom_e/tel23_e.htm.

[7] The interface between financial market developments and GATS has drawn more academic attention in recent years. See, e.g., Panagiotis Delimatsis, Transparent Financial Innovation in a Post-crisis Environment, 16 J. INT'L ECON L. 159 (2013).

Hufbauer and Daniel Danxia Xie suggest that the monetary framework be expanded to take explicit account of financial stability as a policy objective for central banks.

What to do now? Echoing Einstein's words that "[w]e can't solve problems by using the same kind of thinking we used when we created them," Cottier and Lastra argue in their concluding chapter for a "bolder approach" (p. 421) to rectify the current soft law–based international financial system. If they are correct, then future efforts should focus more directly on the design of an institutional framework that can embrace the legal insights presented in *International Law in Financial Regulation and Monetary Affairs*. The Bretton Woods system, originally perceived as a trinity of institutions—the IMF, International Bank for Reconstruction and Development, and International Trade Organization—could barely survive the demise of the ITO, even with the resulting expansion of the General Agreement on Tariffs and Trade. Although the WTO significantly improved the scope and role of international trade law, the post–Bretton Woods system of the twenty-first century may need a more coherent and newly augmented trinity of the WTO, World Bank, and potentially a World Financial Organization that would provide a "rule-oriented" system, modeled on the WTO, to supplant the IMF. If such an effort were undertaken, the scholarly contributions of the book under review would prove invaluable.

The 2007–09 financial crisis spawned a large body of work (as listed in the book's bibliography) that explores the theoretical underpinnings of, and possible institutional reforms needed by, the international financial system. The essays in *International Law in Financial Regulation and Monetary Affairs* not only build upon that scholarship but present significant new analyses and proposals that deserve careful attention by scholars and financial regulators alike.

DUKGEUN AHN
Seoul National University

Part Four

Legal and Economic Analysis of Free Trade Agreements

Chapter 14

DISPUTE SETTLEMENT SYSTEMS IN ASIAN FTAS: ISSUES AND PROBLEMS

*Dukgeun Ahn**

ABSTRACT

Asian countries have actively engaged in global FTA races and led rule development in terms of FTA negotiations. While proliferating FTAs raise concern for growing inconsistency problems between the WTO and FTAs, this paper shows diverging approaches in Asian FTAs in relation to dispute settlement systems that are the core element of the legal basis for FTAs. Broadly speaking, many Asian FTAs adopt a "WTO type" dispute settlement system. Asian FTAs involving the United States, however, have invariably employed the "NAFTA type" dispute settlement system that puts more emphasis on prompt implementation by unilateral retaliation, monetary settlement, and numerical limit for special disputes typically concerning labor and the environment. Since more Asian countries are negotiating FTAs with the United States, this divergent approach toward dispute settlement systems in FTA should be thoughtfully realigned to ensure a coherent development between WTO and FTA systems.

KEYWORDS: *FTA, Dispute Settlement System, implementation*

* Professor of International Trade Law and Policy, Seoul National University; Commissioner, Korea Trade Commission; Member, National Economic Advisory Council, Korea. I am very grateful to Professors Patrick Messerlin, Asif Qureshi, Mitsuo Matsushita, Bryan Mercurio and Chang-fa Lo for constructive comments and encouragement regarding this study. I also acknowledge the research support by the National Research Foundation of Korea Grant (NRF-2011-330-B00063) and Seoul National University Asia Center (0448A-20130004). The author can be reached at dahn@snu.ac.kr.

I. INTRODUCTION

Asian countries have actively engaged in global FTA races and thereby expect to play more significant roles in promoting global trade as well as developing world trade rules. In this regard, it is important to review how Asian countries establish the core element of the FTA system: "dispute settlement mechanism". Since Asian countries have consistently increased their involvement in the WTO dispute settlement system, dispute settlement systems adopted in Asian FTAs can provide important insights for the approach or practices to be taken in future WTO development. Considering the fact that most Asian FTAs are classified as adopting "quasi-judicial" dispute settlement systems, the practices of Asian FTAs are particularly useful to assess directions of judicial developments.[1] In addition, previous experience in FTA negotiations may also shed light on current grand scale FTA negotiations that many Asian countries are engaged in.

An interesting point to be noted is that some Asian FTAs seem to adopt contradictory approaches in dispute settlement systems. How to establish coherent dispute settlement systems in the WTO system may become another stumbling block in subsequent FTA negotiations.

II. FTA DISPUTE SETTLEMENT SYSTEMS IN ASIA

A. Exclusive Jurisdiction

Most Asian FTAs provide exclusive jurisdiction for the FTA to prevent conflict of law problems.[2] A typical example is Article 139 of the Japan-Singapore FTA that stipulates: "once the complaining Party has requested the establishment of an arbitral tribunal under this Chapter or a panel under Article 6 of the Understanding on Rules and Procedures Governing the Settlement of Disputes, in Annex 2 to the WTO Agreement with respect to a particular dispute, the arbitral tribunal or panel selected shall be used to the exclusion of the other procedure for that particular dispute." Following this model, most Asian FTAs adopt exclusive jurisdictional provisions.

In this regard, it is noted that Article 139.3 of the Japan–Singapore FTA includes the following provision: "However, this does not apply if substantially separate and distinct rights or obligations under different international agreements are in dispute." Legally speaking, this provision

---

[1] For a comprehensive classification of FTA dispute settlement systems, *see generally* Claude Chase et al., *Mapping of Dispute Settlement Mechanisms in Regional Trade Agreements: Innovative or Variations on a Theme?* (WTO, Staff Working Paper ERSD-2013-07, 2013).

[2] Conflict of law problems concerning FTAs and the WTO have drawn much academic interests. *See generally* Tim Graewert, *Conflicting Laws and Jurisdictions in the Dispute Settlement Process of Regional Trade Agreements and the WTO*, 1(2) CONTEMP. ASIA ARB. J. 287 (2008).

is merely a restatement of public international law principles with respect to jurisdictional overlap. More interestingly, Article 139.4 of the FTA stipulates that: "Paragraph 3 above shall not apply where the Parties expressly agree to the use of more than one dispute settlement procedure in respect of a particular dispute." In other words, Japan and Singapore explicitly agreed to duplicative jurisdiction between the FTA and the WTO by formal agreement. This provision, however, was not adopted by subsequent FTAs, including those by Japan and by other Asian countries.

B. Scope of Disputes

The scope of application for FTA dispute settlement procedures is generally given loosely as "the avoidance and the settlement of disputes between the parties regarding the interpretation or application" of FTAs. Article 133 of the Japan–India FTA, Article 204 of the Japan–Peru FTA, Article 116 of the Japan–Vietnam FTA, Article 184 of the China–New Zealand FTA, Article 141 of the China–Costa Rica FTA, and Article 14.2 of the Korea–EU FTA all show such cases. Since this provision only covers the "interpretation and application" of FTAs, it is understood that the dispute settlement system addresses merely so-called "violation" claims.

On the other hand, some FTAs try to elaborate the scope of the application by covering both violation claims and "inaction" claims. For example, Article 22.4 of the KORUS FTA provides that the FTA dispute settlement system applies whenever a party considers that a measure of the other party is inconsistent with the FTA obligations or the "other party has failed to carry out" its FTA obligations. The "inaction" claims, however, are not familiar to Asian countries that still have limited experience in the international judicial systems, including the WTO dispute settlement system. In fact, the WTO dispute settlement system does not allow "inaction claims", whereas it still includes "situation claims", in addition to violation and non-violation claims. The lack of prior experience and practices to apply "inaction claims" in the world trading system makes it difficult to anticipate how this legal claim may affect FTA jurisprudence. Nevertheless, the implications of this legal claim should be more seriously addressed in future FTA negotiations by Asian countries such as TPP, RCEP, and China–Japan–Korea FTA.

In addition, Article 22.4 of the KORUS FTA also covers non-violation claims by stipulating a benefit the party could reasonably have expected to accrue, but is being nullified or impaired as a result of a measure that is not inconsistent with the FTA obligations. Non-violation claims are also typically included in other FTAs involving the United States. It is also noted that non-violation claims in FTAs normally stipulate certain limits or exceptions. For example, the exceptions for the non-violation claims in the

KORUS FTA are provided for cross-border trade in services and intellectual property rights "if the measure is subject to an exception under Article 23.1 (General Exception)". In addition, Footnote 1 of Chapter 22 of the KORUS FTA provides that neither party will invoke FTA dispute settlement procedures with respect to a measure affecting benefits under Chapter Eighteen (Intellectual Property Rights) during any period for which WTO Members have agreed not to initiate non-violation complaints under the TRIPS Agreement. This model was adopted in Article 14.2 of the Korea–India FTA, although the scope of the non-violation claims was limited to trade in goods, rules of origins, and trade in services. In this regard, it is noteworthy that Article 23.2 of the Korea–Peru FTA accepts violation claims and inaction claims, but not non-violation claims.

C. Panel and Appellate Procedure

Asian FTAs do employ the general panel procedures that are routinely adopted for recent FTAs. For example, each FTA party appoints one panelist from their own nation on the roster and "shall agree on a third panelist" who will chair arbitral panels. The deliberations of arbitral tribunals shall be normally confidential. Unlike the WTO panel procedure that permits dissenting opinions if necessary, some FTAs such as the Korea–EU FTA specifically prohibit the publication of dissenting opinions.[3]

In order to promote dispute resolution without litigation, parties are allowed to terminate panel proceedings at any time by joint agreement. Unlike the WTO dispute settlement system, FTA dispute settlement systems do not normally have an appeal proceeding. Rare exceptions are MERCOSUR and ASEAN. The ASEAN appellate review system, closely resembling the WTO dispute settlement system, was introduced by the 2004 "ASEAN Protocol on Enhanced Dispute Settlement Mechanism"; but it has not yet been invoked. Whether this model will be adopted in the RCEP negotiations, in which ASEAN is playing a key role, remains to be seen.

The timeframes for FTA dispute settlement are normally shorter than WTO dispute settlement procedures. Many FTAs stipulate 30 to 60 days for consultation and 90 to 120 days for issuing panel reports after panel establishment. This timeline for dispute settlement has been adopted by many Asian FTAs such as: Korea–EU, China–New Zealand, Japan–

---

[3] Although the WTO Dispute Settlement Understanding does not explicitly mention the permissibility of dissenting opinions, it has become a well-established practice to include dissenting opinions when panelists may not consensually agree on the reasoning of the ruling as well as on the rulings themselves. Many FTAs that provide no specific provision on dissenting opinions are likely to follow the WTO practices.

Singapore, and India–Korea. A longer timeframe, however, is typically adopted in FTAs involving the United States. For example, the KORUS FTA stipulates 225 days for issuing a panel report after panel establishment. But, this timeline may be further delayed by pre-panel procedures and the panelist selection process.

Although most of the procedural elements are substantially standardized across FTAs, and Asian FTAs do not show significant deviations from normal practices, increasing diversity in Asian FTAs may raise a concern regarding the consistent development of dispute settlement systems.

D. Implementation

While Asian FTAs do follow general practices for dispute settlement procedures, they show divergent approaches for the process regarding implementation stages. Broadly speaking, many FTAs in Asia try to adopt the established practices under the WTO system. Parties will first attempt to resolve non-implementation by compensation arrangement and then resort to the arbitral panel concerning failure to comply with the ruling, the appropriate implementation period, and the level of suspension regarding obligation. But some FTAs, such as the Korea–US FTA and China's recent FTAs, adopt a "NAFTA" type implementation procedure. They allow complaining parties to engage in retaliation without compliance panel decisions and also leave the rectifying tasks for "over-retaliation" to responding parties.

1. "WTO Type" Implementation. — Despite the controversial legal texts of the WTO DSU and no formal decisions yet to amend it, WTO members have established reasonable practices for sequencing problems. In case of non-compliance by the respondents, complainants should apply for a compliance panel to determine whether the implementing measure is consistent with the DSB rulings. The complainant will only be authorized to suspend the concessions when the compliance panel rules the respondent failed to fully comply with the DSB recommendations.

A majority of Asian FTAs adopt these established WTO practices for implementation stages. For example, Article 14 of the Korea–EU FTA provides that if there is disagreement on the reasonable period of time to comply with the ruling, the complaining party will make the request to the original panel to determine the length of the period. Moreover, where there is disagreement as to the existence of compliance measures or consistency of such measures with compliance commitments, the complaining party may request in writing for the original panel to rule on the matter.

If the responding party fails to notify compliance measures taken before the expiry of the implementation period, or if the compliance panel rules it was the failure of the responding party to implement the rulings, th en the complaining party shall be entitled to suspend the obligations. It is noted that in suspending obligations, the complaining party may choose to increase its tariff rates to the level applied to other WTO members. The volume of trade will be determined in such a way that the volume of trade multiplied by the increase of the tariff rates equals the value of the nullification or impairment caused by the violation.[4]

This type of implementation process has been adopted in, *inter alia*, the Japan–India FTA, the China–Singapore FTA, the China–New Zealand FTA and the Korea–India FTA. It is noteworthy that the China–New Zealand FTA stipulates the reliance on the WTO system for FTA panel selection. Article 189.4 stipulates that if any member of the arbitral tribunal has not been designated or appointed within 30 days after the establishment of a tribunal, either party may request that the Director-General of the WTO designate a member within 30 days of that request. Moreover, Article 189.5 provides that all arbitrators comply with the WTO Rules of Conduct for DSU. Whether the WTO Director-General may or can be involved in the panel selection process for the China–New Zealand FTA should be cons idered, although it is very unlikely.

2. "NAFTA Type" Implementation. — Unlike WTO practices, the US government emphasized the retaliatory function to expedite implementation in case of non-compliance. This approach was codified in Chapter 20 of NAFTA. Article 2019.1 of NAFTA provides that if a panel determines that a measure is inconsistent with the legal obligations of NAFTA or causes nullification or impairment, and the responding party cannot agree on a mutually satisfactory resolution, a complaining party may suspend the application of benefits of equivalent effect. On the written request of a responding party, a panel will be established to determine whether the level of benefits suspended by a complaining party is manifestly excessive.

This "NAFTA type" process for implementation phases was adopted in the US–Australia FTA. Article 21.11 provides that if the parties are unable to agree on compensation within 30 days of negotiations or the complaining party considers that the responding party has failed to observe the terms of the compensation or settlement agreement, the complaining party may at any time provide written notice to suspend the application of benefits of equivalent effect. If the responding party considers that the level of benefits proposed to be suspended is manifestly excessive or if it has eliminated the non-conformity or the nullification or impairment, it may request the panel to be reconvened to consider the matter. If the panel determines that the level of benefits proposed to be suspended is manifestly

---

[4] Free trade Agreement between the European Union and its Member States and the Republic of Korea, E.U.-S. Kor., art. 14.11, ¶3, Oct. 15, 2009, 2011 O.J. (L 127) 6.

excessive, then it shall determine the level of benefits it considers to be of equivalent effect. This non-implementation provision was adopted in the Korea–US FTA ("KORUS FTA") without any modification. Article 22.13.2 of the KORUS FTA is essentially the same as the provision in the US–Australia FTA.

The interesting element of the "NAFTA type" FTA dispute settlement system is the mechanism of using monetary payment for settling disputes. The complaining party may not suspend benefits if the responding party provides written notice to the complaining party that it will pay an annual monetary assessment. Beginning no later than ten days after the responding party provides written notice, the parties shall consult with a view to reaching agreement on the amount of the assessment. If the parties are unable to reach an agreement within 30 days after consultations begin, the amount of the assessment shall be set at a level, in U.S. dollars, equal to 50 % of the level of the benefits the panel has determined to be of equivalent effect or, if the panel has not determined the level, 50 % of the level that the complaining party has proposed to suspend. Unless the Joint Committee decides otherwise, a monetary assessment shall be paid to the complaining party in U.S. currency, or in an equivalent amount of local currency, in equal, quarterly installments. If the responding party fails to pay a monetary assessment, the complaining party may suspend the application of benefits. If the responding party considers that it has eliminated the non-conformity or the nullification or impairment that the panel has found, it may refer the matter to the panel. If the panel decides that the responding party has eliminated the nonconformity or the nullification or impairment, the complaining party shall promptly reinstate any benefits it has suspended and the responding party shall no longer be required to pay any monetary assessment. This monetary settlement system has been adopted in identical formats by many recent FTAs, including US–Australia and KORUS.

It is also noted that in the case of labor or environmental disputes, "NAFTA type" FTAs set a limit for monetary compensation.[5] For example, in Article 22.16.2 of the US–Chile FTA, the amount of the annual monetary assessment cannot exceed $15 million adjusted for inflation.[6] This was also adopted with slight modification in subsequent FTAs such as US–Singapore, US–Australia, US–Morocco, and US–Bahrain. Since the labor and environment chapters were added after the original negotiation

---

[5] NAFTA itself does not provide any specific limit for monetary assessment in relation to suspension of benefits for labor or environmental disputes.

[6] Annex 19-A of the FTA provides an inflation adjustment formula for monetary assessment. An annual monetary assessment imposed before December 31, 2005 shall not exceed 15 million U.S. dollars. But, beginning January 1, 2006, the 15 million U.S. dollars annual cap shall be adjusted for inflation in accordance with specific calculation methods stipulated in paragraphs 3 through 5.

was concluded, in the case of the KORUS FTA this special provision was not included. Instead, both parties reaffirmed to resort to dispute settlement "only in cases with merit where trade or investment effects can be established."[7]

Considering the fact that this special "NAFTA type" FTA dispute settlement system was also adopted in CAFTA-DR,[8] which embraced multiple parties, it is very likely that the current model may be the basis of the Trans-Pacific Partnership ("TPP") Agreement. Although many major parties of TPP already accepted the "NAFTA type" dispute settlement system, it may cause serious controversy among some parties that are unfamiliar to such monetary settlement mechanisms for international trade dispute resolution.

E. Private Rights

As adopted in Article 22.16 of the KORUS FTA, neither party of the FTA provides for a right of action under its law against the other party on the ground that a measure of the other party is inconsistent with FTA obligations. The implementing legislation for the KORUS FTA prohibit non-US nationals from challenging any action or inaction by a US federal, state, or local agency on the ground that the action or inaction is inconsistent with the KORUS FTA. This provision to limit a private right in legal proceedings in relation to FTA parties is invariably adopted in Asian FTAs.

F. Secretariat Support

It is in fact recognized by WTO Members and experts that the WTO legal secretariats have played crucial roles in supporting and developing WTO jurisprudence.[9] Despite such consensual understanding, very few FTAs provide secretariat support for managing dispute settlement systems. It is indeed puzzling why so few FTAs pay little attention to this crucial infrastructure practice for implementing FTA systems. Analyzing often enormous amount of documentary submissions, managing oral hearings, fact finding, and handling expert opinions, in addition to holding panel deliberations, are all likely to raise daunting challenges for panelists to

---

[7] Letter from Susan C. Schwab, United States Trade Representative, Office of the United States Trade Representative, to Hyun Chong Kim, Minister for Trade, Ministry for Trade of South Korea (June 30, 2007).

[8] The FTA between the Dominican Republic, Central America and the United States.

[9] The role of the WTO legal secretariats was taken seriously even at the very early stage of the WTO dispute settlement system. *See generally* Robert Hudec, *The New WTO Dispute Settlement Procedure: An Overview of the First Three Years*, 8 MINN. J. GLOBAL TRADE 1 (1999).

delay dispute settlement procedures much too frequently.

Like most other FTAs, Asian FTAs do not normally require the establishment of legal secretariats. The exceptions are FTAs involving the United States that "designate[s] an office that shall be responsible for providing administrative assistance to panels". This provision is included, for example, in the Singapore–US FTA and the KORUS FTA. However, it merely stipulates that each party "shall" designate an office for administrative assistance. Many issues such as what roles this office is supposed to undertake, whether and how two offices from each party should cooperate, and when their assistance should be given, in addition to other issues, are not addressed and are not even mentioned as future topics for further elaboration.

In this regard, it is noted that the Korea–EU FTA does not include any provision regarding institutional support for dispute settlement procedures.

III. FROM CONTRADICTION TO COHERENCE

As explained in the previous section, there are two lines of dispute settlement systems adopted in Asian FTAs. Given that the Trans-Pacific Partnership Agreement ("TPP") is driven by the United States and the Regional Comprehensive Economic Partnership ("RECP") is centered on ASEAN, there will be controversy over which model should be followed in future negotiations. In particular, since almost half of the participants in TPP and RCEP overlap, the divergent approaches of Asian FTAs may cause inconsistency in judicial processes for international trade disputes. In addition, ASEAN adopted the "Protocol on Enhanced Dispute Settlement Mechanism" in 2004 that also includes peculiar elements such as appellate review and funding for the dispute settlement mechanism.[10]

Recent phenomena of duplicative FTA competition raises unprecedented problems for dispute settlement. For example, if China and Korea have a trade dispute concerning an antidumping measure, the two countries may have practically four different judicial alternatives to settle the dispute: the dispute settlement system under the China–Korea FTA, the China–Japan–Korea FTA, the RCEP, and the WTO. This is not a unique situation merely for China and Korea. Many ASEAN countries are currently engaged in multiple FTAs — and will be engaged in more FTAs — with the same trading partners.

Therefore, divergent approaches for dispute settlement in different FTAs increases forum shopping problems. Moreover, the absence of

---

[10] To date, the only other FTA that includes an appellate review system is MERCOSUR's Permanent Tribunal of Review, which was established by the Protocol of Olivos entering into force in 2004.

appellate review, the lack of legal secretariats to support dispute settlement, and the panel selection rule to appoint their own nationals in FTAs may aggravate inconsistent jurisdictional problems. Ironically, the incompetency of many FTAs to actually handle the dispute settlement process alleviates the potential contradictory or inconsistent jurisdictional development among the FTAs. But gradual improvement of legal capacity and more dispute settlement experience under the WTO system will soon make Asian countries better utilized to actively and strategically engage in FTA dispute settlement systems.

On the other hand, there are structural drawbacks to the FTA dispute settlement system that are related to implementation stages. In the case of retaliation by a complaining party, the party is normally allowed to raise FTA tariffs up to the MFN level applicable to other WTO members. This makes the utility of FTA dispute settlement systems significantly reduced from the perspective of the complaining party. Therefore, whenever a party has an alternative to bring a dispute, it will prefer the WTO to FTAs, since the retaliation possibility under the WTO dispute settlement system appears much more effective in ensuring compliance by the responding party. In other words, although FTA specific issues are to be addressed by FTA dispute settlement systems, any overlapping areas or legal issues are more likely to be handled by the WTO dispute settlement system. This draws more attention to the WTO dispute settlement system, as more divergent FTA dispute settlement systems are created.

In reality, it will be very difficult, if not impossible, for FTAs to uniformly harmonize legal rules and practices, especially considering the vastly different economic and legal situations of FTA parties. Thus, it seems inevitable to find a more diverse variety of FTA rules, including dispute settlement systems. That may not, however, mean actual diversity in jurisprudence regarding the world trading system. To the contrary, significantly articulated jurisprudence of the WTO dispute settlement system based on an unprecedented level of utilization may become a much more important forum to resolve international trade disputes, compared to the weak institutional framework of FTA dispute settlement systems.

Accordingly, one of the practical solutions for inconsistent development of FTA dispute settlement systems and consequent jurisprudence may be to further develop the WTO dispute settlement system by rectifying drawbacks and improving procedural rules. To put it differently, we may expect more disputes brought by Asian members to the WTO dispute settlement system when they are exposed to more diverse FTA options, due to the inferior institutional capacities of FTA dispute settlement systems. When the WTO dispute settlement system improves the ir implementation mechanism and legitimacy, its role for the world trading system will be elevated by practically resolving jurisdictional and jurisprudential conflicts between the WTO and FTAs.[11]

IV. CONCLUSION

The legal elements of FTAs have shown growing diversity particularly in recent years. In this regard, the experiences of Asian countries deserve more attention, because they often lead to regulatory developments as important precedents for subsequent FTAs, and at the same time they become focal points for causing regulatory contradiction. For example, Asian countries such as Singapore and Korea have undertaken interesting legal experiments by incorporating modified trade remedy rules in FTAs.[12] This is understandable, since these countries have demanded such amendments in Doha rules negotiations and have perceived FTAs as a good test bed for introducing new legal models. Moreover, in reality, it see ms unlikely for parties to invoke or use modified FTA trade remedy systems.

To the contrary, the phenomena of rule diversity regarding FTA dispute settlement systems has been imposed by "NAFTA type" FTAs, even if there is no particular consensus or interest to insist on such diverging models. The development of different rules and subsequent practices through FTAs should draw more serious attention by academics as well as practitioners to prevent or alleviate the inconsistency problems of the WTO system. This study hopes to invite subsequent researchers to find better systems for the many remaining legal issues in Asian FTA negotiations that are currently in progress.

---

[11] It is in line with the proposal by Henry Gao & C. L. Lim. *See generally* Henry Gao & C. L. Lim, *Saving the WTO from the Risk of Irrelevance: The WTO Dispute Settlement Mechanism as a "Common Good" for RTA Disputes,* 11(4) J. INT'L. ECON. L. 899 (2008).

[12] *See generally* Dukgeun Ahn, *Foe or Friend of GATT Article XXIV: Diversity in Trade Remedy Rules,* 11(1) J. INT'L. ECON. L. 107 (2008).

REFERENCES

Articles

Ahn, Dukgeun (2008), *Foe or Friend of GATT Article XXIV: Diversity in Trade Remedy Rules*, 11 JOURNAL OF INTERNATIONAL ECONOMIC LAW 107.

Gao, Henry & C. L. Lim (2008), *Saving the WTO from the Risk of Irrelevance: the WTO Dispute Settlement Mechanism as a "Common Good" for RTA Disputes*, 11 JOURNAL OF INTERNATIONAL ECONOMIC LAW 899.

Graewert, Tim (2008), *Conflicting Laws and Jurisdictions in the Dispute Settlement Process of Regional Trade Agreements and the WTO*, 1 CONTEMPORARY ASIA ARBITRATION JOURNAL 287.

Hudec, Robert (1999), *The New WTO Dispute Settlement Procedure: An Overview of the First Three Years*, 8 MINNESOTA JOURNAL OF GLOBAL TRADE 1.

Treaty

Free trade Agreement between the European Union and its Member States and the Republic of Korea, E.U.–S. Kor., October 15, 2009, 2011 O.J. (L 127) 6.

Working Papers and Other Sources

Chase, Claude *et al.*, *Mapping of Dispute Settlement Mechanisms in Regional Trade Agreements: Innovative or Variations on a Theme?* (WTO, Staff Working Paper ERSD-2013-07, 2013).

Letter from Susan C. Schwab, United States Trade Representative, Office of the United States Trade Representative, to Hyun Chong Kim, Minister for Trade, Ministry for Trade of South Korea (June 30, 2007).

Appendix. Comparison of Key Dispute Settlement Provisions of KORUS and KOREU FTAs

KORUS FTA	KOREU FTA
Article 22.4: Scope of Application	Article 14.2 Scope
(a) a measure of the other Party is inconsistent with its obligations under this Agreement; (b) the other Party has otherwise failed to carry out its obligations under this Agreement; or (c) a benefit the Party could reasonably have expected to accrue to it under Chapter ... is being nullified or impaired as a result of a measure that is not inconsistent with this Agreement, except ... if the measure is subject to an exception under Article 23.1 (General Exceptions).	This Chapter applies to any dispute concerning the interpretation and application of the provisions of this Agreement unless otherwise provided.
Article 22.12: Implementation Of The Final Report	Article 14.8 Compliance with the arbitration panel ruling
2. If, in its final report, the panel determines that a Party has not conformed with its obligations under this Agreement or that a Party's measure is causing nullification or impairment in the sense of Article 22.4(c), the resolution, whenever possible, shall be to eliminate the non-conformity or the nullification or impairment.	Each Party shall take any measure necessary to comply in good faith with the arbitration panel ruling, and the Parties will endeavour to agree on the period of time to comply with the ruling.
Article 22.13: Non-Implementation	Article 14.10 Review of any measure taken to comply with the arbitration panel ruling
1. If . . . the Parties are unable to reach agreement on a resolution pursuant to Article 22.12.1 within 45 days . . . , the Party complained against shall enter into negotiations with the complaining Party with a view to developing mutually acceptable compensation.	1. The Party complained against shall notify the complaining Party and the Trade Committee, before the end of a reasonable period of time, of any measure that it has taken to comply with the arbitration panel ruling.

2. If the Parties: (a) are unable to agree on compensation within 30 days after the period for developing such compensation has begun; or (b) have agreed on compensation or on a resolution pursuant to Article 22.12.1 and the complaining Party considers that the Party complained against has failed to observe the terms of the agreement, the complaining Party may at any time thereafter provide written notice to the Party complained against that it intends to suspend the application to the Party complained against of benefits of equivalent effect. The notice shall specify the level of benefits that the complaining Party proposes to suspend. Subject to paragraph 5, the complaining Party may begin suspending benefits 30 days after the *later* of the date on which it provides notice to the other Party under this paragraph or the panel issues its determination under paragraph 3, as the case may be.	2. Where there is disagreement between the Parties as to the existence of a measure or consistency with the provisions referred to in Article 14.2 of any measure notified under paragraph 1, the *complaining Party* may request in writing the original arbitration panel to rule on the matter. Such request shall identify the specific measure at issue and it shall explain how such measure is incompatible with the provisions referred to in Article 14.2. The arbitration panel shall issue its ruling within 45 days of the date of the submission of the request.
3. If the *Party complained against* considers that: (a) the level of benefits that the complaining Party has proposed to be suspended is manifestly excessive; or (b) it has eliminated the non-conformity or the nullification or impairment that the panel has found, it may . . . request that the panel be reconvened to consider the matter.	Article 14.11 Temporary remedies in case of non-compliance

5. The complaining Party may not suspend benefits if, within 30 days after it provides written notice of intent to suspend benefits or, if the panel is reconvened under paragraph 3, within 20 days after the panel provides its determination, the Party complained against provides written notice to the other Party that it will pay an annual monetary assessment. The Parties shall consult, beginning no later than ten days after the Party complained against provides notice, with a view to reaching agreement on the amount of the assessment. If the Parties are unable to reach an agreement within 30 days after consultations begin, the amount of the assessment shall be set at a level, in U.S. dollars, equal to 50 % of the level of the benefits the panel has determined under paragraph 3 to be of equivalent effect or, if the panel has not determined the level, 50 % of the level that the complaining Party has proposed to suspend under paragraph 2.	1. If the Party complained against fails to notify any measure taken to comply with the arbitration panel ruling before the expiry of the reasonable period of time, or if the arbitration panel rules that no measure taken to comply exists or that the measure notified under Article 14.10.1 is inconsistent with that Party's obligations under the provisions referred to in Article 14.2, the Party complained against shall, if so requested by the complaining Party, present an offer for temporary compensation.
6. Unless the Joint Committee decides otherwise, a monetary assessment shall be paid to the complaining Party in U.S. currency, or in an equivalent amount of Korean currency, in equal, quarterly installments beginning 60 days after the Party complained against gives notice that it intends to pay an assessment. Where the circumstances warrant, the Joint Committee may decide that an assessment shall be paid into a fund established by the Joint Committee and expended at the direction of the Joint Committee for appropriate initiatives to facilitate trade between the Parties, including by further reducing unreasonable trade barriers or by assisting a Party in	2. If no agreement on compensation is reached within 30 days of the end of the reasonable period of time or of the issuance of the arbitration panel ruling under Article 14.10 that no measure taken to comply exists or the measure notified under Article 14.10.1 is inconsistent with the provisions referred to in Article 14.2, the complaining Party shall be entitled, upon notification to the Party complained against and to the Trade Committee, to suspend obligations arising from any provision referred to in Article 14.2 at a level equivalent to the nullification or impairment caused by the violation. The notification

carrying out its obligations under this Agreement.	shall specify the level of obligations that the complaining Party intends to suspend. The complaining Party may implement the suspension 10 days after the date of the notification, unless the Party complained against has requested arbitration under paragraph 4.
7. If the Party complained against fails to pay a monetary assessment, the complaining Party may suspend the application to the Party complained against of benefits in accordance with paragraph 4.	3. In suspending obligations, the complaining Party may choose to increase its tariff rates to the level applied to other WTO Members on a volume of trade to be determined in such a way that the volume of trade multiplied by the increase of the tariff rates equals the value of the nullification or impairment caused by the violation.
	4. If the Party complained against considers that the level of suspension is not equivalent to the nullification or impairment caused by the violation, it may request in writing the original arbitration panel to rule on the matter. Such request shall be notified to the complaining Party and to the Trade Committee before the expiry of the 10 day period referred to in paragraph 2. The original arbitration panel shall issue its ruling on the level of the suspension of obligations to the Parties and to the Trade Committee within 30 days of the date of the submission of the request. Obligations shall not be suspended

	until the original arbitration panel has issued its ruling, and any suspension shall be consistent with the arbitration panel ruling.
	6. The suspension of obligations shall be temporary and apply only until any measure found to be inconsistent with the provisions referred to in Article 14.2 has been withdrawn or amended so as to bring it into conformity with those provisions, as established under Article 14.12, or until the Parties have agreed to settle the dispute.
Article 22.14: Compliance Review	Article 14.12 Review of any measure taken to comply after the suspension of obligations
1. Without prejudice to the procedures set out in Article 22.13.3, if the *Party complained against* considers that it has eliminated the non-conformity or the nullification or impairment that the panel has found, it may refer the matter to the panel by providing written notice to the complaining Party. The panel shall reconvene as soon as possible after delivery of the request and shall issue its report on the matter within 90 days after the Party complained against provides notice.	1. The Party complained against shall notify the complaining Party and the Trade Committee of any measure it has taken to comply with the ruling of the arbitration panel and of its request for the termination of the suspension of obligations applied by the complaining Party.

2. If the panel decides that the Party complained against has eliminated the non-conformity or the nullification or impairment, the complaining Party shall promptly reinstate any benefits it has suspended under Article 22.13, and the Party complained against shall no longer be required to pay any monetary assessment it has agreed to pay under Article 22.13.5.	2. If the Parties do not reach an agreement on the compatibility of the notified measure with the provisions referred to in Article 14.2 within 30 days of the date of the notification, the *complaining Party* shall request in writing the original arbitration panel to rule on the matter. Such request shall be notified to the Party complained against and to the Trade Committee. The arbitration panel ruling shall be issued to the Parties and to the Trade Committee within 45 days of the date of the submission of the request. If the arbitration panel rules that any measure taken to comply is in conformity with the provisions referred to in Article 14.2, the suspension of obligations shall be terminated.

Chapter 15

Analysis of Anti-dumping Use in Free Trade Agreements

Dukgeun AHN and Wonkyu SHIN[*]

Proliferating free trade agreements (FTAs) in recent years may have conflicting effects on anti-dumping (AD) uses among FTA parties. On the one hand, an FTA may increase a country's AD activities to protect its domestic industries from the increased import flows from other parties. On the other hand, an FTA supposedly helps reduce the use of AD measures to accomplish the purpose of free trade. Which effects prevail can shed important lights on the question of whether an FTA can be a stumbling block or a building block.

This article examines the effects of FTAs on AD activities based on comprehensive empirical analysis. Using longitudinal data of major AD user countries from 1995 to 2009, we found that there is clearly an inverse relationship between an FTA and AD activities. This finding represents the user's tendency to trigger less AD filings against FTA membership, regardless of facing more imports from FTA partners. This article also captured dynamic FTA effects based on a series of distribution of time dummies. The estimation results from the dynamic model show that the FTA enactment year clearly has significant effect, suggesting substantial reduction of AD investigations in that year.

1. INTRODUCTION

Proliferating free trade agreements (FTAs) since the 1990s have provoked heated discussion on whether they have contributed to facilitating more trade or aggravating discriminatory trade diversion. The general observation is that although FTAs may have significant trade effects on certain trading partners, the overall impact to the global trading system appears to be insignificant or less impressive than expected. Apart from this macro-level question on the relationship between global trade and FTAs, there are not many studies on the micro-level question of how FTA parties behave against each other, in particular whether FTA parties use anti-dumping (AD) measures more or less frequently against the other parties. Considering the fact that AD measures are still one of the major trade barriers in the world trading system, the effect of FTAs on AD uses can provide an important implication to FTA policies or trade policy implementation in general.

The empirical intuition raises conflicting possibilities for potential impacts of FTA on AD activities between FTA parties. On the one hand, an FTA may increase a country's AD activities to protect its domestic industries from the increased import flows from the other parties. After repealing most of the trade barriers and eliminating tariffs, AD measures become practically the only legitimate tool to address industry injuries related to import

---

[*] Dukgeun Ahn is a Professor of International Trade Law and Policy, Graduate School of International Studies/Law School, Seoul National University. Email: <dahn@snu.ac.kr>. Wonkyu Shin is a Research Associate in the Center for International Commerce and Finance, Graduate School of International Studies, Seoul National University. Email: <wkshin@snu.ac.kr>. We are grateful to Professors Chongsup Kim and Yeongseop Rhee for their helpful comments. We are also indebted to Wonhee Lee for research assistance.

Ahn, Dukgeun & Wonkyu Shin. 'Analysis of Anti-dumping Use in Free Trade Agreements'. *Journal of World Trade* 45, no. 2 (2011): 431–456
© 2011 Kluwer Law International BV, The Netherlands

increases. On the other hand, an FTA supposedly helps reduce the use of AD measures to accomplish the purpose of free trade. Regardless of the legal consistency of trade remedy actions against FTA parties, FTA parties may abstain from using trade barriers – including AD measures – basically to promote more trade with FTA parties. When we consider the recent phenomena of FTA parties modifying trade remedy rules in the context of FTAs, the latter possibility gets even more compelling.[1]

This article tries to examine this theoretical question by conducting an empirical test to quantify the effects of FTA on AD activity. Since our dependent variable is the count data – that is, the number of AD investigations – we used the negative binomial regression techniques (I, II) in order to come to a more robust estimation. Based on the most updated World Trade Organization (WTO) database of AD investigation activities between FTA parties from 1995 to 2009, the overall trend shows gradual decrease in the AD uses between FTA parties. In addition to analysing the overall trend, this article also analysed the twelve major AD users – that is, Argentina, Australia, Brazil, Canada, China, European Union (EU),[2] India, Korea, Mexico, South Africa, Turkey, and the United States – individually to examine comparative characteristics.

We overview the developments of FTAs and AD uses in the current world trading system in section 2 and raise a research question by conceptualizing the relationship between FTA and AD in section 3. In sections 4 and 5, empirical tests to answer the question are elaborated by adopting various methods such as simple data analysis and negative binomial regression estimation. Section 6 concludes with policy implications.

Figure 1. RTA[3] Trend in the World Trading System

Source: Calculated using WTO RTA database, <http://rtais.wto.org/UI/Public MaintainRTAHome.aspx>.

---

[1] For a more detailed legal and economic analysis on rule diversification by FTAs, see Dukgeun Ahn, 'Foe or Friend of GATT Article XXIV: Diversity in Trade Remedy Rules', *Journal of International Economic Law* 11 (2008), 107–133. Trade remedy provisions in FTAs are compiled in Robert Teh et al., 'Trade Remedy Provisions in Regional Trade Agreements', in *Regional Rules in the Global Trading System*, ed. A. Estevadeordal (Cambridge Univ. Press, 2009), 166–249.

[2] The EU is counted as one country even if it has currently twenty-seven Member States because an anti-dumping action is taken collectively by the European Commission.

[3] The term RTAs is used to refer to various types of Regional Trading Arrangements including preferential trade agreements, free trade agreements (FTAs), customs unions (CU), strategic economic cooperation agreements (SECA), and economic partnership agreements (EPA).

2.   OVERVIEW OF FTAs AND AD ACTIONS IN THE WTO SYSTEM

2.1.   FTA DEVELOPMENT IN THE WTO SYSTEM

Aside from the long-held debate in academic and policy circles since the 1990s on whether FTAs are building blocks or stumbling blocks for the multilateral trading system, the surge in FTAs has continued unabated since the early 1990s.[4]

Of these RTAs, FTAs for goods and services account for a predominant portion of about 90%, while customs unions account for less than 10%. As shown in Figure 1, RTAs have proliferated ironically since the inception of the WTO, and almost 200 RTAs are in force as of December 2010.[5]

It seems that the trend of FTAs would continue to increase as the WTO system remains stuck in the deadlock of the Doha Development Agenda and WTO members try to fill in the gap of multilateral trade process by FTAs. Since no country is willing to bear the opportunity cost that may come from lagging behind in the FTA race, the proliferation of FTAs is unlikely to decline soon. In this regard, it is particularly alarming to observe strategic FTA interactions by major countries such as the United States, the EU, and China.

2.2.   AD DEVELOPMENT IN THE WTO SYSTEM

There have been significant developments in the use of AD policies over the last two decades. First, there was the considerable increase in the total number of AD investigations filed worldwide. For example, the average annual number of AD investigation initiations was 207 during the GATT period of 1985–1994, while in 1995–2004, the annual average reached about 265.[6] Second, the number of AD-using countries has substantially increased since developing countries utilize very actively the WTO trade remedy systems.

As shown in Figure 2, AD investigations do not show an exponentially increasing trend although the general frequency of investigations is higher than that of the GATT period. Instead, the overall trend of AD investigations clearly shows the counter-cyclical movement that the increases of AD investigations during the early and the late 2000s have coincided with global economic recession.

As shown in Table 1, it is noted that new AD users – primarily developing countries such as Argentina, Brazil, China, India, Mexico, and Turkey – have become remarkably active and been responsible for much of the growth of AD activities in the WTO system. This situation is starkly contrasted with the GATT period in which trade remedy measures are almost exclusively utilized by the United States, the EU Canada, and Australia.[7] Since

---

[4] See Jagdish Bhagwati & Arvind Panagariya, 'Preferential Trading Areas and Multilateralism – Strangers, Friends, or Foes?', in *The Economics of Preferential Trade Agreement*, eds J. Bhagwati & A. Panagariya (AEI Press, 1996), 1–78.

[5] See <http://rtais.wto.org/UI/PublicAllRTAList.aspx>, (visited 3 Jan. 2011). Among 198 RTAs notified to the GATT/WTO and in force as of December 2010, 167 RTAs were notified under Art. XXIV of the GATT 1947 or GATT 1994, 29 under the Enabling Clause, and 69 under Art. V of the GATS.

[6] See Chad P. Bown, 'The WTO and Antidumping in Developing Countries', *Economics and Politics* 20, no. 2 (2008), 255–288.

[7] The use of trade remedy measures by developing countries is more prominent in the case of safeguard actions. See, generally, Dukgeun Ahn, 'Restructuring the WTO Safeguard System', in *The WTO Trade Remedy System: East Asian Perspectives*, eds M. Matsushita, D. Ahn & T. Chen (Cameron May, 2006).

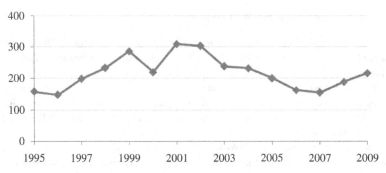

Figure 2. The Trend of AD Investigations in the WTO System

Source: 'Annual Reports of the Committee on AD Practices'.

the WTO was established, developing countries have continued to increase AD uses reaching 71% of the total share during the latter half of the 2000s, while the share of developed countries in terms of AD uses has significantly decreased as illustrated in Figure 3. In fact, this observation illustrated that developing countries did not generally reduce their AD uses during the global economic crisis period of the late 2000s in which developed countries tried to standstill or minimize AD actions in order to support the recovery of global trade.[8]

3.   THE RELATIONSHIP BETWEEN FTAs AND AD ACTIVITIES

Whether trade remedy actions should be permitted in FTAs has drawn much attention among WTO members as well as scholars.[9] There was no clear answer based on drafting history or formal decisions yet in the GATT/WTO system about how to interpret Article XXIV:8 of GATT.

A group in favour of a literal approach points to the definition of an FTA in Article XXIV:8 that 'a free-trade area shall be understood to mean a group of two or more customs territories in which the duties and other restrictive regulations of commerce (except, where necessary, those permitted under Articles XI, XII, XIII, XIV, XV and XX) are eliminated on substantially all the trade'. They argue that even the balance of payment related exceptions enunciated in the parenthesis should be permitted limitedly 'where

---

[8] Despite political commitments in the G-20 or the WTO in relation to global economic crisis, many developed countries still adopted numerous trade barriers. See the 'Reports by Global Trade Alert', <www.globaltradealert.org/tensions_contained_8th_gta_report>, (visited 20 Dec. 2010). However, as far as AD is concerned, the developed countries as a whole appeared to contain themselves in order to avoid excessive trade conflicts.

[9] For more comprehensive overviews on this issue, see James Mathis, *Regional Trade Agreements in the GATT/WTO: Article XXIV and the Internal Trade Requirement* (TMC Asser Press, 2002).

Table 1. Top Twelve AD Users in the WTO System

Rank	1995–1999 Country	AD	2000–2004 Country	AD	2005–2009 Country	AD	1995–2009 Country	AD
1	EU	164	India	244	India	171	India	498
2	United States	136	United States	223	EU	104	United States	429
3	Argentina	89	EU	133	China	81	EU	401
4	Australia	89	Argentina	104	Argentina	79	Argentina	267
5	South Africa	89	Canada	78	United States	70	Australia	201
6	India	83	Australia	77	Turkey	64	South Africa	172
7	Brazil	56	Brazil	60	Brazil	56	Brazil	170
8	Canada	50	South Africa	48	Australia	35	Canada	150
9	Mexico	46	Turkey	48	South Africa	35	Turkey	126
10	Korea	37	Mexico	41	Pakistan	29	China	120
11	New Zealand	28	China	39	Korea	29	Korea	105
12	Venezuela	23	Korea	39	Canada	22	Mexico	88

Source: 'Annual Reports of the Committee on AD Practices' sorted by authors.
Note: The above statistics are based on AD initiations.

Figure 3. Trend of AD Use by the Developing and the Developed Countries

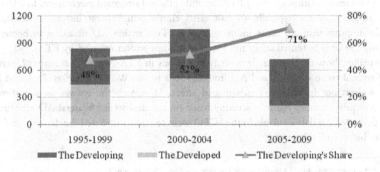

Source: Calculated using 'Annual Reports of the Committee on AD Practices'.

necessary'. Accordingly, there is no room for trade remedy measures to be allowed in this structure of FTAs.

The other group in support of trade remedy measures in FTAs argues that those provisions in the parenthesis should not be understood as the exhaustive list since many other obvious exceptions such as national security and general exception are not explicitly mentioned. Moreover, duties and other restrictive regulations of commerce are to be eliminated only on 'substantially all the trade' not 'all the trade'. In other words, selective trade limitation based on legitimate trade remedy measures should be embraced by the purview of Article XXIV:8.

While the legal issue concerning trade remedy measures, particularly AD measures, has not been clearly settled, WTO members have adopted a variety of 'FTA-customized' trade remedy systems.[10] A majority of FTAs still adopt the WTO trade remedy system without any change. However, some FTAs entirely prohibit trade remedy measures between parties. In addition, recent FTAs adopt increasingly more customized trade remedy systems that modify procedural or substantive elements of the WTO trade remedy rules. Table 2 categorized AD provisions in FTAs.

The EU, as an economic union, does not allow AD measures among Member States although the EU approves new member countries to resort to AD temporarily during their transitional periods into full EU membership in accordance with the Treaty of Rome. Likewise, FTAs between Canada-Chile, Australia-New Zealand,[11] EFTA-Chile, and EFTA-Singapore categorically prohibit AD activities between FTA parties, notwithstanding countervailing or safeguard measure are still allowed in their FTAs. On the other hand, other FTAs try to modify WTO AD rules. For example, Jordan-Singapore FTA stipulates mandatory lesser duty requirement, a 5% de minimis rule, the prohibition of the zeroing method, a three-year sunset review period, and so on.

These modified FTA provisions basically aim to reduce AD actions between FTA parties. Despite such intent, an FTA may increase the need for AD activities to protect its domestic industries from the increased import flows from other parties. For most countries, AD measures remain practically the only tool to address industry injuries related to import increases. Although many FTAs include bilateral safeguard mechanisms to address import surge, they are typically to halt tariff elimination process instead of limiting particular imports that can cause industry injuries. That makes AD measures to become practically the only potential safety net for import competition induced by FTAs.

In reality, how do those trade remedy provisions in FTAs work? A cursory observation of overall trend of FTAs and AD investigations in the WTO system as illustrated in Figure 4 does not indicate any meaningful effect. However, the answer to the above question requires a more rigorous scrutiny based on the data set for bilateral AD activities. This article used the data available in the WTO website and constructed the data set for AD activities between FTA parties.

---

[10] For a more detailed legal analysis on rule diversity, see Ahn, 2008, *supra* n. 1.

[11] The Australia-New Zealand FTA was agreed in 1988. In Art. 4 of its Protocol, they declared that anti-dumping actions were inappropriate for free trade in goods under the accelerated implementation agreed in the Agreement.

Table 2. AD Provisions in Selected FTAs

AD Disallowed	AD Allowed With Specific Provisions		No Specific Provisions
Canada-Chile	Andean Community	EFTA-Croatia	AFTA
CER	Australia-Singapore	EFTA-FYROM	ALADI
China-Hong	Australia-Thailand	EFTA-Israel	Australia-US
Kong	CACM	EFTA-Jordan	Canada-Israel
China-Macao	Canada-Costa Rica	EFTA-Morocco	CEMAC
EC	CARICOM	EFTA-Palestine	EC-Andorra
		Authority	
EEA	COMESA	EFTA-Tunisia	EC-OCT
EFTA	EC-Algeria	EFTA-Turkey	GCC
EFTA-Chile	EC-Chile	Group of Three	Japan-Singapore
EFTA-Singapore	EC-Croatia	Korea-Chile	Mexico-Chile
	EC-Egypt	MERCOSUR	Mexico-Japan
	EC-Faroe Islands	Mexico-EFTA	US-Bahrain
	EC-FYROM	Mexico-Israel	US-CAFTA &
	EC-Israel	Mexico-Nicaragua	Dom. Republic
	EC-Jordan	Mexico-Northern	US-Chile
	EC-Lebanon	Triangle	US-Israel
	EC-Mexico	Mexico-Uruguay	US-Jordan
	EC-Morocco	NAFTA	US-Morocco
	EC-Palestine	New Zealand	US-Singapore
	Authority	Singapore	
	EC-South Africa	SADC	
	EC-Switzerland-	SAFTA	
	Liechtenstein	SPARTECA	
	EC-Syria	Turkey-Israel	
	EC-Tunisia	UEMOA	
	EC-Turkey		

Source: WTO; Teh et al. (2007).

Figure 4. The Superficial (Non-)Relationship between FTAs and AD Investigations

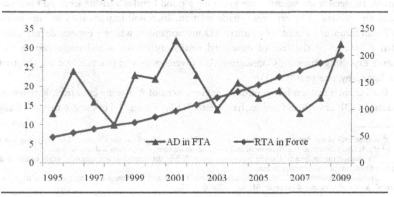

Source: Calculated using 'Annual Reports of the Committee on AD Practices'.

Detailed data on AD investigations, initiated by WTO member countries against which countries and when, was obtained from the 'Annual Reports of the Committee on Anti-dumping Practices to General Council'[12] for the period of 1 July 1994 to 30 June 2009. In the econometric analysis using pooled data, we examined the effects of FTAs on AD investigations of the twelve major AD user countries.[13] This pooled data analysis enables us to analyse the above question appropriately because the twelve main AD users have coincided mostly with active FTA negotiating countries.

4.   ANALYTICAL FRAMEWORKS FOR EMPIRICAL MODEL

4.1.   AD ACTIVITIES BETWEEN FTA PARTIES

The yearly trend of AD investigations since 1995 shows a slight downward movement, although this inverse relationship was not significant. AD investigations against FTA parties have not been a significant portion of overall AD actions. As shown in Figure 5, the AD investigations against FTA parties have remained generally around 10% of the total AD actions. It is interesting to note that AD investigations against FTA parties have shown exactly the opposite trend to the overall AD investigations in Figure 2. As shown in Figure 5, AD investigations against FTA parties had declined until 2001 during which the overall AD actions had constantly increased. In addition, while the overall AD actions decreased after 2001, the AD investigations against FTA parties continued to increase until 2005 when the trend was reversed.

4.2.   ECONOMETRIC MODEL

4.2.1.   *Description of Variables*

The overall trend shown in the previous section should be tested with other control variables to analyse specifically how much the FTA factor affects AD activities.

Trade volumes of FTA parties – especially, imports – and macroeconomic factors such as GDP growth rate and exchange rate are often included to empirically examine AD activities. Bilateral trade volumes are generally a good control variable since AD activities are directly influenced by reciprocal trade relation. Increased imports tend to raise incentives for an importing country to initiate AD investigations, whereas exports decrease such tendency because of the fear of unwanted retaliatory measures and trade dispute with lucrative exporting markets. Considering AD investigations in practice, we use the trade value lagged by one year $(t - 1)$.

For variables that explain economic environment of AD-using countries, Knetter and Prusa used GDP growth and real exchange rate (RER) effects.[14] They argue that AD filings

---

[12] Article 18.5 of the Agreement provides that: 'Each Member shall inform the Committee of any changes in its laws and regulations relevant to this Agreement and in the administration of such laws and regulations'.

[13] We limited the analysis to the top twelve countries. While the limitation was arbitrary, other countries are insignificant in terms of trade remedy actions.

[14] Michael M. Knetter & T.J. Prusa, 'Macroeconomic Factors and Antidumping Filings: Evidence from Four Countries', *Journal of International Economics* 61, no. 1 (2003), 1–17.

Figure 5. Yearly Trend of AD Investigations against FTA Parties

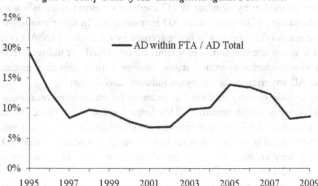

Source: 'Annual Reports of the Committee on AD Practices'.

of a country increase in years after experiencing lower GDP growth. Lower GDP growth makes it more likely that investigating authorities find an industry injury to filed AD cases. They also showed that an appreciation of the RER led to a higher number of AD case filings for their sample countries. The relationship between AD activities and macroeconomic factors – particularly, GDP growth and exchange rate – has been confirmed by subsequent studies. Using the semi-annual data of US AD actions from 1980 to 1998, Feinburg showed that RER and economic growth rate are significant variables to AD investigations.[15] In the case of AD activities by developing countries such as Argentina, Brazil, India, and South Africa, Hallworth and Pirachal analysed the number of AD actions and related macroeconomic factors, suggesting that an economic growth rate and an RER of reporting countries are significant factors in their tests.[16]

In our analysis, however, an RER was not used since bilateral imports and exports are included as control variables and thereby an RER could be redundant with these variables.[17] In fact, an exchange rate effect is more desirable to be used in the disaggregated time series data analysis and in the case specific studies.[18] GDP growth rates are calculated by the average of three years.

---

[15] R.M. Feinburg, 'U.S. Anti-dumping Enforcement and Macroeconomic Indicators Revisited: Do Petitioners Learn?', *Review of World Economics* 141 (2005), 612–622.

[16] Taro Hallworth & Matloob Piracha, 'Macroeconomic Fluctuations and Anti-dumping Filings: Evidence from a New Generation of Protectionist Countries', *Journal of World Trade* 40, no. 3 (2006), 407–417.

[17] Nevertheless, the regression result including RER instead of export is given in Appendix 3 to compare the difference in econometric analysis.

[18] The RER is related to price competitiveness of domestic producers and their imports/exports; however, whether producers file a petition for an AD investigation would be determined by the net effect of currency fluctuation. For instance, appreciation of domestic currency might cause more imports from abroad or boost exports of final goods with lower production costs incurred with the weaker foreign currency. Since our model focusing on a broad relationship between AD and FTA is neither for industrial level nor sector-specific analysis, we used bilateral trade as control variables with year effects controlled.

328

440   JOURNAL OF WORLD TRADE

In addition, our model incorporated the total number of AD actions that partner countries were accused of by all other WTO member countries as an indicator of partner countries' vulnerability of exportation to AD investigations. In other words, the larger the number is, the greater the tendency of being accused by other countries' AD investigations. This variable may capture the impact of various factors directly or indirectly related to AD filings, such as non-market economy status, business relationship in a particular sector, dumping and AD experiences in a relevant industry, and the like.

We also include country dummies in order to fix unobserved remaining individual characteristics varying across countries. This helps control the residual country-specific characteristics such as the level of economic development, a country's unique political situation, and historical or cultural features in relation to AD actions. Since AD investigations are usually very volatile over time, year dummies are included in all specifications of our regression model to control for any change in trends over time.

The dependent variable and the control variables are summarized in Table 3.

4.2.2. Model Specification

To examine the impact of FTAs on AD investigations with control variables explained above, we consider the following regression model:

$$AD_{ijt} = \alpha + \alpha_i + \alpha_j + \beta_2 lnIM_{ijt} + \beta_3 lnEX_{ijt} + \beta_4 GRGDP_{it} + \beta_5 AD_{Partner_{jt}} + \beta_6 FTA_{ijt} + \delta Year_{dum_t} + \mu_{ijt}$$

The AD_{ijt} denotes the number of AD investigations by country i against an import source j in year t. The FTA_{ijt} is a dummy variable indicating whether i and j are members of the

Table 3. Summary Description of Variables

Name	Explanation	Remarks	Source
AD	The number of AD investigation initiated by reporting country.	Bilateral data	WTO
Partner_AD	The total number of initiated AD investigation against partner country.	Partner country's data	WTO
LnIM	Logarithm of imports from partner (one year lagged, $t-1$).	Bilateral data	UN COMTRADE
LnEX	Logarithm of exports to partner (one year lagged, $t-1$).	Bilateral data	
GRRGDP	Growth rate of real GDP (mean of three years of gross domestic production).	Reporting countries' data	IMF
FTA	When FTA enter into force (dummy).	Once FTA is enacted = 1, otherwise 0	WTO

Table 4. Summary Statistics for Data

Variables	Mean	Maximum	Minimum	Standard Deviation	Observations
AD	0.109	18.00	0.00	0.599	32,120
PARTNER_AD	1.019	78.00	0.00	4.070	32,120
LNIM $(t-1)$	15.454	26.60	0.00	5.609	32,120
LNEX $(t-1)$	16.472	26.64	0.00	4.832	32,120
GRR_GDP	3.568	11.13	-10.26	3.294	32,120
FTA	0.061	1.00	0.00	0.240	32,120
FTA $(t-2)$	0.005	1.00	0.00	0.074	32,120
FTA $(t-1)$	0.006	1.00	0.00	0.077	32,120
FTA (t_0)	0.006	1.00	0.00	0.078	32,120
FTA $(t+1)$	0.007	1.00	0.00	0.083	32,120
FTA $(t+2)$	0.006	1.00	0.00	0.079	32,120
FTA $(t+3)$	0.006	1.00	0.00	0.077	32,120
FTA $(t+4)$	0.005	1.00	0.00	0.073	32,120
FTA $(t+5)$	0.005	1.00	0.00	0.072	32,120

same FTA in effect in the given year t, and the $\delta Year_{dum_i}$ represents period specific effects while α_i and α_j indicate country fixed dummies.

Our dependent variable is the reported number of AD investigations initiated by WTO member countries. In other words, this dependent variable is a count variable which takes on non-negative integer values. In such case, ordinary least squares (OLS) models might not provide the best overall fit for the values of the explanatory variables since the dependent variable is not continuous and does not have a normal distribution. While OLS models assume normality as the standard distributional assumption, a count variable cannot have a normal distribution due to the discontinuity of values. Moreover, when it takes on only a few values, its distribution becomes very different from a normal distribution. Instead, the nominal distribution for count data is typically the Poisson or negative binomial distribution.[19]

On the other hand, the Poisson distribution is subject to the restriction that the variance of the dependent variable is equal to the mean of the dependent variable. It has long been recognized that the Poisson distributional assumption has serious difficulty in its applicability to real practice while the negative binomial distribution assumption has a better applicability by allowing the variance to differ from the mean. Since our data show considerable dispersion inconsistent with the Poisson restriction, we adopted the negative binomial distribution.[20] In particular, for a more accurate and robust estimation, we used

---

[19] Jeffrey M. Wooldridge, 'Quasi-likelihood Methods for Count Data, Ch. 8', in *Handbook of Applied Econometrics*, eds M. Hashem Pesaran & P. Schmidt (Massachusetts: Blackwell, 1997).

[20] The test for the Poisson restriction is based on an auxiliary regression. After the test regressions, with derived variance parameter, we can compute variance parameters for each negative binomial pseudo-maximum likelihood (NB PML) estimator. In this analysis, our tests suggest the presence of over-dispersion and that the estimated coefficient is

negative binomial quasi-maximum likelihood estimation (NB QMLE) introduced by Gourieroux et al. using the estimate of $\hat{\eta}^2$ from Cameron and Trivedi tests.[21]

The data set contains the number of AD investigations as a dependent variable and various macroeconomic variables for the period from 1995 to 2009. Because the number of AD investigations initiated varies from year to year and from country to country, the number of observations varies each year under the assumption that each bilateral sample is case-specific and independent from one another.[22] Table 4 presents summary statistics for the data employed in the estimation.

5. EMPIRICAL RESULTS

Table 5 summarizes the results of NB QMLE regression.[23] More detailed econometric results that analyse country-specific data are provided in Appendix 2.

The FTA dummies representing the FTA deterrent effects on AD investigations are significantly negative (-) in the NB QLME model, as shown in columns (A) and (C). The results indicate, for instance, that subsequent to FTA enactment, the number of AD investigations initiated against FTA partners considerably dropped – by approximately 79% (C) or 109% (A), all else being equal.[24] It is noted that while all major AD-using countries follow the general pattern to reduce AD investigations against FTA parties, Argentina and Mexico actually increase the AD actions against FTA parties. In that sense, it is also noted that the result for Brazil, another Latin American country, showed the positive sign but was statistically insignificant. It is not clear whether this result can be generalized as a region-specific characteristic. However, the fact that two major AD users in Latin America showed the tendency to increase AD investigations against FTA parties demands more attention from policy makers as well as rigorous scrutiny by academics.

On the other hand, countries such as China, India, and Turkey show significant negative effects of FTAs on AD investigations, possibly implying that the AD actions in those countries are strongly influenced by overall trade policies. The political commitment to facilitate more trade with FTA parties in those countries may dominate policy decisions on whether selective trade constraints based on trade remedy actions should be utilized against FTA parties. In any case, the finding seems to suggest that considering China, India, and Turkey are all very active countries in AD actions in recent years, FTAs can become more attractive policy tools to address trade remedy problems in those countries.

---

significantly positive with the t-statistic of the coefficient highly significant, indicating the rejection of the Poisson restriction A.C. Cameron & P.K. Trivedi, 'Econometric Models Based on Count Data: Comparison and Applications of Some Estimators and Tests', *Journal of Applied Econometrics* 1, no. 1 (1986), 29–53; A.C. Cameron & P.K. Trivedi, 'Regression-Based Tests for Overdispersion in the Poisson Model', *Journal of Econometrics* 46, no. 3 (1990), 347–364. Refer to the appendix for more details of this issue.

[21] C. Gourieroux, A. Monfort & C. Trognon. 'Pseudo-maximum Likelihood Methods: Applications to Poisson Models', *Econometrica* 52 (1984), 701–720; Cameron & Trivedi, *supra* n. 20.

[22] In fact, it is common that more than one partner country is involved with one AD investigation and reporting countries initiated AD investigations one or more times for a year.

[23] The Poisson regression estimation showed that the signs of the coefficients on variables are consistent with this result, although the values of the coefficients are different.

[24] When the conditional mean function contains a dummy variable, the marginal effect could be calculated in the given maximum likelihood (ML) estimates 'δ'. The details are explained in the appendix.

Table 5. FTA Deterrent Effects on the AD Investigation

Dependent Variable (Number of AD)	NB QMLE Regression			
	(A)	(B)	(C)	(D)
Constant	−10.70***	−10.55***	−12.61***	−12.20***
	(0.273)	(0.269)	(1.051)	(1.042)
Partner_AD	0.112***	0.113***	0.141***	0.146***
	(0.007)	(0.007)	(0.013)	(0.013)
LnIM $(t − 1)$ (imports)	0.214***	0.211***	0.226***	0.222***
	(0.018)	(0.018)	(0.034)	(0.034)
LnEX $(t − 1)$ (exports)	0.168***	0.164***	0.222***	0.207***
	(0.021)	(0.021)	(0.038)	(0.037)
GRRGDP $(t − 3–t)$	0.152***	0.156***	0.025*	0.026*
	(0.009)	(0.009)	(0.014)	(0.014)
FTA	−0.736***		−0.580***	
	(0.108)		(0.140)	
FTA $(t − 2)$		0.555**		0.513*
		(0.266)		(0.311)
FTA $(t − 1)$		−0.694**		−0.543
		(0.348)		(0.384)
FTA (t_0) (year in force)		−0.819**		−0.638*
		(0.363)		(0.399)
FTA $(t + 1)$		−0.766**		−0.590*
		(0.304)		(0.346)
FTA $(t + 2)$		−0.487		−0.502
		(0.296)		(0.359)
FTA $(t + 3)$		−0.639*		−0.286
		(0.338)		(0.393)
FTA $(t + 4)$		−1.056***		−0.877**
		(0.358)		(0.401)
FTA $(t + 5)$		−1.126***		−0.991**
		(0.374)		(0.420)
Country fixed effect[25]	No	No	Yes	Yes
Number of observations	32,120	32,120	31,770	31,770
Fixed variance parameters (α)	4.538	4.465	5.169	5.416
	(0.043)	(0.043)	(0.032)	(0.033)
Log likelihood	−7,444.11	−7,443.64	−6,441.51	−6,466.17

Note: * denotes statistical significance at the 10% level, ** at the 5% level, and *** at the 1% level. Robust standard errors are in parenthesis. Period effect is considered in all models. The result is based on NB I, which has a variance that is proportional to the mean, that is, $(1 + \alpha)\lambda$. Refer to the appendix regarding the issues of QML parameter (α), a measure of over-diversion, used for estimations.

[25] Unconditional ML by estimating negative binomial regression models that include dummy variables for all individuals are considered as a true fixed effects regression model. See Paul D. Allison, 'Fixed Effects Regression Models', in *The Fixed Effects Models for Count Data* (2009), 49–69 and Joseph M. Hilbe, *Negative Binomial Regression* (Cambridge Univ. Press, 2007), 199–203.

To examine dynamic FTA effects, additional specifications are introduced by dividing the FTA dummy into FTA dummies of different years as in columns (B) and (D). Dummy variables of $t - 2$ through $t + 5$ are designed to capture the FTA deterrent effects on AD activities along with time variance. For example, the dummy variable t_0 takes the value of 1, if the current year is the first year that the FTA between countries comes into force; otherwise, it is zero. Likewise, $t + $ 'n' takes the value of 1 if t is the 'nth' year after FTA's entry into force; otherwise, it is zero.[26]

The results of Table 5 reveal a statistically significant and negative relationship between the number of AD investigations and FTA $(t - 2$–$t + 5)$ except for FTA $(t - 2)$.[27] The estimate on FTA (t_0) implies that FTAs would reduce AD investigations against the named parties by about 89–115% in the year the FTA enters into force. At FTA $(t + 1)$, one year after the FTA's entry into force, AD investigations decrease by 80–115%, compared with other years of FTA implementation. However, by looking at the result of the FTA effects in dynamic dimension, we can find an interesting result associated with our hypothesis. For the result of FTA (t_0), an incentive to serve the purpose of FTA, facilitating freer trade and maintaining good foreign relations with the parties, prevails over an incentive for protecting domestic industries driven mostly by internal politics. If the initiation of AD investigations itself has a chilling effect on bilateral trade, as empirically supported by Prusa and other scholars, it seems that two governments do not wish to cast a chill over a trade relationship that has just upgraded with a strong economical tie.[28] Ironically, this result implies that investigating authorities of major AD-using countries maintain substantial discretion for AD investigations although the WTO system aims to strengthen the rule-based mechanism for controversial trade remedy systems, especially AD actions.

On post-FTA $(t + 2, t + 3 \ldots)$, as imports normally grow due to the FTA with the actual elimination of the tariffs and non-tariff barriers, AD petitions by industries that are competing with foreign exporting companies are likely to rise. During this period, governments may need to compromise between domestic and foreign politics since the economic and political pressures from domestic industries might not be left ignored. The coefficient signs of FTA $(t + 2)$ and FTA $(t + 3)$ in Table 5 indeed give a hint on that. The coefficients are losing statistical significance, indicating that, to some extent, the negative relationship between FTAs and AD investigations is considerably diluted after two or three following years of the FTA's entry into force.

---

[26] Note that FTAs enacted before 1994 – WTO system is invalid – are counted as $t + 1$ (one year after FTA enactment) from 1995. Since the inception of the WTO system, new rules of AD and FTA are applied. Thus, setting aside the question of data unavailability, it is better to fix the data set in this way for a consistent analysis.

[27] It is interesting to note that the coefficient of FTA $(t - 2)$ came out to be positive. It might be explained that those countries several years prior to FTA enactment used to be targets for AD use against each other since many FTAs were created among intensive trading partners formed naturally by the benefits of regional approximation.

[28] T.J. Prusa, 'On the Spread and Impact of Anti-dumping', *Canadian Journal of Economics* 34, no. 3 (2001), 591–611; T.J. Prusa, 'Anti-dumping: A Growing Problem in International Trade', *The World Economy* 28, no. 5 (2005), 683–700.

Interestingly, the coefficients for $t + 4$ and $t + 5$ in both models are statistically significant and shows negative signs again, implying that FTA $(t + 4)$ and FTA $(t + 5)$ decrease AD investigations by about 140–187% and 169–208%, respectively. This means that the FTA enactment ultimately leads to a reduction in AD investigations. In other words, when market liberalization by FTAs that provide typically three- to five-year transition periods becomes almost completed, trade remedy actions against FTA parties tend to eventually decrease despite somewhat vague tendency during the transition period. As a result, substantial deterrent effects of FTAs on AD investigations not only do exist but also become stronger after the typical FTA adjustment period.

Macroeconomic variables reflected the typical features that might lead to AD investigations. As expected, the coefficients for 'Partner_AD' as a good indication of a country's vulnerability to AD uses from other countries and 'LnIM' (imports from partners) have positive signs with great significance. The positive coefficient of 'Partner_AD' indicates that a country tends to initiate more AD investigations when the exporting countries are exposed to more AD investigations. In other words, importing countries become more aware of dumping possibilities from a certain country when AD investigations are initiated against exportation from that country. This effect, however, appears to be much less significant than the effect of import increase that is the most direct factor for AD actions.

On the other hand, the coefficients of exports and the growth rate of GDP turned out to be positive, which seems contradictory to previous literature. As shown in Appendix 2, the regression by individual countries showed that in the case of some Latin American countries such as Argentina and Mexico, their three-year average $(t - 3–t)$ of GDP growth rates was negatively related with AD filings. However, the GDP growth rate and AD activities showed a positive relationship at a significant level mostly in developed countries such as Australia, Canada, EC, United States, and Korea. This peculiarity may be explained at least partly by recent international initiatives of G-20 that includes all of the countries in our data. These countries committed themselves to gradual reduction of trade barriers including AD measures. The overall downward trend of AD actions since the early 2000s might be the result of these political initiatives. In fact, some researchers in their recent papers found that GDP growth rates as a macroeconomic factor turned out to be either insignificant or sometimes positively related with AD investigations.[29] Moreover, it is possible that protection-seeking activities and political voices from marginalized industries could be even stronger and thereby their AD petition might be easily heard during times of economic growth. In other words, as GDP growth leads to more import and export growth, it is more likely that AD petitions requesting protection from the sectors relatively more aggrieved could be greater than before. Actually, AD investigations are mostly initiated in the marginalized sector decoupled with economic growth.

---

[29] For example, see Mustapha Sadni-Jallab, R. Sandretto & M. Gbakou. 'Antidumping Procedures and Macro-economic Factors: A Comparison between the United States and the European Union', *Global Economy Journal* 6, no. 3 (2006): Art. 5, Bown, *supra* n. 6, and Michael Moore & Maurizio Zanardi, 'Trade Liberalization and Antidumping: Is There a Substitution Effect?', Working Papers ECARES no. 024 (2008).

The positive coefficients of exports also appear for many major AD-using countries at a significant level. The positive correlation between exports and AD actions may be due to growing trends of retaliatory AD actions. More exportation tends to cause more AD actions from importing countries and in turn invokes more AD investigations by exporting countries. It seems clear that countries are no longer seriously limited or intimidated by the size of export markets against which they initiate AD investigations. In fact, the United States, the EU, China, India, and Korea show a tendency to increase AD investigations when they have more exportation. It seems that those countries have more widely diversified their trading partners through the WTO and FTAs. Thus, they might feel less burdened with the possibility of future retaliation when they initiate an AD investigation against a particular exporting market.

6. CONCLUSION

The question of whether FTAs contribute to global trade requires more rigorous and comprehensive analysis. Nevertheless, the result of our analysis can add important insights to that discussion. While AD measures are still widely used to serve as the most popular protectionist instruments in the WTO system, FTAs have inversely affected AD investigations within the boundary of FTA membership. This result appears to be statistically robust for individual countries as well as at an aggregate level. The dynamic effects of FTAs over the pre- and post-FTA periods confirmed the negative relationship between FTAs and AD investigations. However, we found that Argentina and Mexico are exceptions in that they tend to increase AD investigations against FTA parties. The underlying reason for this peculiarity is not clear at this stage.

The empirical finding of our analysis may have interesting economic and legal implications for future FTA negotiations. If this result is globally confirmed, the effect on AD investigations alone can become a crucial element for FTA strategies and policies of WTO members – particularly for Asian countries that have been exceptionally vulnerable to AD measures. Competitive advantages ensued by favourable AD actions may be sometimes a key factor to secure stable access to exporting markets. In addition, the actual effectiveness of FTAs in taming AD investigations may further raise incentives to modify the AD rules in particular and trade remedy rules in general in the context of FTAs in order to create more artificial advantages for FTA parties.

There are numerous other issues to be addressed in relation to the relationship between FTAs and trade remedy actions. For example, whether diversification of trade remedy rules observed in the recent FTAs actually leads to reduction or diversion of trade remedy actions, and if so, how much will be able to shed important light on the future renovation of the trade remedy system. We hope our findings in this study invoke more academic interest regarding the economic and legal effects of FTAs on trade remedy actions.

REFERENCES

Ahn, Dukgeun. 'Restructuring the WTO Safeguard System'. In *The WTO Trade Remedy System: East Asian Perspectives*, edited by M. Matsushita, D. Ahn & T. Chen. London: Cameron May, 2006.

Ahn, Dukgeun. 'Foe or Friend of GATT Article XXIV: Diversity in Trade Remedy Rules'. *Journal of International Economic Law* 11, no. 1 (2008): 107–133.

Allison, Paul D. 'Fixed Effects Regression Models'. *SAGE, Series: Quantitative Applications in the Social Sciences* 160 (2009): 49–69.

Bhagwati, Jagdish & Arvind Panagariya. 'Preferential Trading Areas and Multilateralism – Strangers Friends or Foes?'. In *Chapter 1: The Economics of Preferential Trade Agreement*. The AEI Press and Center for International Economics, University of Maryland, 1996.

Bown, Chad P. 'The WTO and Antidumping in Developing Countries'. *Economics & Politics* 20, no. 2 (2008): 255–288.

Cameron, A.C. & P.K. Trivedi. 'Econometric Models Based on Count Data: Comparison and Applications of Some Estimators and Tests'. *Journal of Applied Econometrics* 1, no. 1 (1986): 29–53.

Cameron, A.C. & P.K. Trivedi. 'Regression-Based Tests for Overdispersion in the Poisson Model'. *Journal of Econometrics* 46, no. 3 (1990): 347–364.

Feinburg, R.M. 'U.S. Anti-dumping Enforcement and Macroeconomic Indicators Revisited: Do Petitioners Learn?'. *Review of World Economics* 141 (2005): 612–622.

Gourieroux, C., A. Monfort, & C. Trognon. 'Pseudo-maximum Likelihood Methods: Applications to Poisson Models'. *Econometrica* 52 (1984): 701–720.

Hallworth, Taro & Matloob Piracha. 'Macroeconomic Fluctuations and Anti-dumping Filings: Evidence from a New Generation of Protectionist Countries'. *Journal of World Trade* 40, no. 3 (2006): 407–417.

Hilbe, J.M. *Negative Binomial Regression*, Ch. 10. UK: Cambridge Univ. Press, 2007.

Knetter, Michael M. & T.J. Prusa. 'Macroeconomic Factors and Antidumping Filings: Evidence from Four Countries'. *Journal of International Economics* 61, no. 1 (2003):1–17.

Mathis, J. *Regional Trade Agreements in the GATT/WTO: Article XXIV and the Internal Trade Requirement*. The Hague: TMC Asser Press, 2002.

Moore, Michael & Maurizio Zanardi. 'Trade Liberalization and Antidumping: Is There a Substitution Effect?'. Working Papers ECARES no. 024. 2008.

Prusa, T.J. 'On the Spread and Impact of Anti-dumping'. *Canadian Journal of Economics* 34, no. 3 (2001): 591–611.

Prusa, T.J. 'Anti-dumping: A Growing Problem in International Trade'. *The World Economy* 28, no. 5 (2005): 683–700.

Sadni-Jallab, Mustapha, R. Sandretto & M. Gbakou. 'Antidumping Procedures and Macroeconomic Factors: A Comparison between the United States and the European Union'. *Global Economy Journal* 6, no. 3 (2006): Art. 5.

Teh, Robert, Michele Budetta & Thomas J. Prusa. 'Mapping Trade Remedy Provisions in Preferential Trading Arrangements'. In *Handbook on Regional Rules in the Global Trading System*. 2007.

Wooldridge, Jeffrey M. 'Quasi-likelihood Methods for Count Data, Ch. 8'. In *Handbook of Applied Econometrics*, edited by M. Hashem Pesaran & P. Schmidt. Massachusetts: Blackwell, 1997.

Zanardi, Maurizio. 'Anti-dumping: What Are the Numbers to Discuss at Doha?'. *The World Economy* 27, no. 3 (2004): 403–433.

APPENDIX 1

TECHNICAL NOTES ON ECONOMETRIC METHODOLOGY

1. Tests for Over-dispersion and Yielding Variance Parameter for Estimation

The Poisson function may be expressed as

$$P(n) = \frac{e^{-\lambda}\lambda^n}{n!}$$

where n is the number of occurrences of the event and λ is the mean and the variance of the distribution. If n is the number of AD investigations initiated by a reporting country i to a partner country j at time t, the parameter λ depends on a set of explanatory variables that affect the probability:

$$\ln \lambda_{ijt} = \beta' X_{ijt}$$

The Poisson model, however, assumes the equality between the mean and the variance of the distribution. For instance, the Poisson model underestimates the variance-covariance matrix in the case of over-dispersion (the variance is bigger than the mean).

The negative binomial model is an extension version of the Poisson model that loosens the restriction of that equality.[30]

Cameron and Trivedi proposed an auxiliary regression for NB QMLE-I and -II.[31] The regression is based on the so-called 'QMLE $\hat{\beta}$ (Pseudo–Maximum Likelihood), which obtains the fitted values of the dependent variable ($\hat{\beta} = \hat{Y}_i$) by estimating the Poisson model. By running this regression, we can diagnose the over-dispersion when the t-statistic of the coefficient is significant, leading us to reject the Poisson restriction.

Since $E[(Y_i - f(X_i, \beta))^z] = \Omega(X_i, \beta, \alpha)$, α could be derived by a regression based on the relation $(Y_i - f(X_i, \beta))^z = \Omega(X_i, \beta, \alpha) + \varepsilon_i$, where ε_i is an independent error with zero mean. For the case $f(X_i, \beta) = \exp(X_i\beta)$, for $\Omega(X_i, \beta, \alpha) = (1+\alpha)\exp(X\beta)$, we could obtain $\hat{\alpha}$ with an auxiliary regression of $e_{oi}^z - Y_i$ on $\hat{Y}_i$ for NB QMLE-I variance parameter, whereas that for NB QMLE-II, it is $\Omega(X_i, \beta, \alpha) = \exp(X\beta)(1 + \alpha\exp(X\beta))$ with an auxiliary regression of $e_{oi}^z - Y_i$ on $\hat{Y}_i^2$.

For the case of our model, the results of the regressions were all significantly positive, meaning all parameters (α) are different from zero.

---

[30] Cameron & Trivedi, (1986).
[31] Ibid.; Cameron & Trivedi, (1990).

2. Calculation for Marginal Effect for Maximum Likelihood Estimation (MLE)

If $E(Y_i) = \lambda_i = \exp(\beta_1 + \beta_2 x_i + \delta D_i)$, then $E(Y_i|D_i = 0) = \exp(\beta_1 + \beta_2 x_i)$, and $E(Y_i|D_i = 1) = \exp(\beta_1 + \beta_2 x_i + \delta)$.

Therefore, the percentage change in the conditional mean is identical to the effect of a dummy variable in a log-linear model; thus, the effect is calculated as

$$100\left[\frac{\exp(\beta_1 + \beta_2 x_i + \delta) - \exp(\beta_1 + \beta_2 x_i)}{\exp(\beta_1 + \beta_2 x_i)}\right]\% = 100[e^\delta - 1]\%$$

APPENDIX 2

FTA EFFECTS ON THE AD INVESTIGATION: THE CASE OF MAJOR AD USERS

Dependent Variable (Number of AD)	Argentina		Brazil		Mexico		Australia		Canada		EC	
	NB I	NB II	NB I	NB II	NB I	NB II	NB I	NB II	NB I	NB II	NB I	NB II
Constant	-11.550***	-11.656***	-10.980***	-11.309**	-4.140***	-4.827***	-18.339***	-17.505***	-15.365***	-14.397***	-17.064***	-15.229***
	(0.978)	(0.579)	(1.395)	(4.407)	(0.656)	(0.591)	(1.755)	(0.823)	(1.530)	(0.787)	(1.164)	(0.651)
Partner_AD	0.062***	0.053***	0.057***	0.043**	0.137***	0.106***	0.046***	0.039***	0.060***	0.051***	0.060***	0.047***
	(0.007)	(0.003)	(0.010)	(0.020)	(0.020)	(0.009)	(0.010)	(0.003)	(0.012)	(0.005)	(0.010)	(0.004)
LnIM ($t-1$) (imports)	0.487***	0.484***	0.306***	0.304*	0.051	0.079*	0.592***	0.548***	0.543***	0.515***	0.435***	0.443***
	(0.071)	(0.043)	(0.051)	(0.175)	(0.051)	(0.046)	(0.101)	(0.050)	(0.124)	(0.072)	(0.118)	(0.079)
LnEX ($t-1$) (exports)	0.033	0.039	0.038	0.068	0.058	0.065	0.065	0.071	-0.043	-0.040	0.258**	0.170**
	(0.069)	(0.044)	(0.059)	(0.204)	(0.046)	(0.040)	(0.099)	(0.050)	(0.112)	(0.065)	(0.124)	(0.081)
GRR_GDP ($t-3-t$)	-0.236***	-0.217***	0.436*	0.403	-2.578***	-2.106***	0.644*	0.650***	0.830***	0.748***	1.568***	1.674***
	(0.063)	(0.036)	(0.261)	(0.817)	(0.839)	(0.631)	(0.330)	(0.165)	(0.310)	(0.144)	(0.344)	(0.210)
FTA	0.718***	0.723***	-0.344	-0.428	0.881**	0.920***	-0.746	-0.747***	-0.401	-0.365*	-0.443**	-0.417**
	(0.260)	(0.134)	(0.423)	(1.314)	(0.374)	(0.282)	(0.508)	(0.268)	(0.457)	(0.234)	(0.243)	(0.163)
Number of observations	2,475	2,805	2,565	2,565	2,535	2,535	2,820	2,820	3,045	3,045	3,198	3,198
Parameters (α)	0.508	0.030	1.480	0.306	2.404	0.633	0.925	0.216	1.539	0.228	1.039	0.088
	(0.028)	(0.003)	(0.035)	(0.008)	(0.057)	(0.013)	(0.034)	(0.012)	(0.025)	(0.004)	(0.046)	(0.007)
Log likelihood	-427.57	-426.25	-627.45	-608.49	-305.82	-301.97	-374.66	-370.84	-341.09	-335.24	-612.15	-630.75

Note: * denotes statistical significance at the 10% level, ** at the 5% level, and *** at the 1% level. Period effect is considered in all models. (Robust) Standard errors are in parenthesis.[32]

[32] However, unlike NB QMLE II, since the NB QMLE I does not assume that the relationship between the mean and variance is linear exponential, it is not possible to do a GLM robust NB QMLE I analysis even when 'α' is fixed ahead of time; Wooldridge (1997).

Dependent Variable (Number of AD)	United States		China		India		Korea		South Africa		Turkey	
	NB I	NB II	NB I	NB II	NB I	NB II	NB I	NB II	NB I	NB II	NB I	NB II
Constant	-18.010***	-18.067***	-105.07	-97.89	-43.787***	-37.124***	-23.987***	-23.812***	-24.181***	-24.074***	-11.922***	-12.152***
	(1.271)	(0.631)	(85.45)	(65.72)	(9.450)	(8.379)	(2.384)	(1.414)	(4.012)	(2.146)	(1.787)	(0.928)
Partner_AD	0.092***	0.043***	0.024	0.018	0.075***	0.039***	0.025*	0.019***	0.074***	0.064***	0.109***	0.061***
	(0.014)	(0.003)	(0.029)	(0.019)	(0.015)	(0.005)	(0.010)	(0.004)	(0.014)	(0.005)	(0.022)	(0.005)
LnIM (t − 1) (imports)	0.418***	0.466***	0.006	0.008	0.239***	0.206***	0.389***	0.394***	0.534***	0.499***	0.540***	0.567***
	(0.096)	(0.054)	(0.046)	(0.036)	(0.041)	(0.031)	(0.118)	(0.073)	(0.104)	(0.054)	(0.113)	(0.054)
LnEX (t − 1) (exports)	0.194**	0.170***	0.620***	0.561***	0.218***	0.219***	0.449***	0.442***	0.080	0.073	-0.088	-0.110***
	(0.096)	(0.054)	(0.079)	(0.058)	(0.055)	(0.041)	(0.145)	(0.088)	(0.106)	(0.056)	(0.091)	(0.037)
GrGDP (t − 1−t − 3)	0.919***	0.876***	9.919	9.270	4.865***	4.005***	0.426**	0.406***	3.946***	4.280***	-0.329	-0.172
	(0.239)	(0.101)	(9.365)	(7.201)	(1.365)	(1.206)	(0.190)	(0.118)	(1.527)	(0.834)	(0.256)	(0.151)
FTA	-0.362	-0.558***	-1.531***	-1.580***	-1.746***	-1.469***	-0.027	-0.010	-0.417	-0.355*	-0.812*	-0.948***
	(0.306)	(0.149)	(0.386)	(0.314)	(0.529)	(0.461)	(0.749)	(0.474)	(0.400)	(0.211)	(0.420)	(0.227)
Number of observations	3,091	3,091	1,295	1,295	2,640	2,640	2,760	2,760	3,015	3,015	2,415	2,415
Parameters (α)	1.317	0.075	0.508	0.030	3.135	0.261	0.564	0.096	1.967	0.563	2.820	0.266
	(0.025)	(0.002)	(0.028)	(0.003)	(0.100)	(0.009)	(0.019)	(0.005)	(0.046)	(0.011)	(0.038)	(0.003)
Log likelihood	-647.19	-639.39	-549.14	-565.31	-1,431.37	-1,566.89	-221.61	-219.04	-346.17	-341.55	-241.76	-250.27

Note: * denotes statistical significance at the 10% level, ** at the 5% level, and *** at the 1% level. Period effect is considered in all models. (Robust) Standard errors are in parenthesis.

APPENDIX 3.1
REGRESSION RESULTS INCLUDING RER AS CONTROL VARIABLE

Table 6 shows the result of NB QMLE regression that includes bilateral 'RER' as a control variable into our model. Basically, the results are identical with the former regression model with export instead of RER; the coefficient signs of FTA dummies and other variables used in the models are all the same with slight differences in their values. In terms of country analysis, the five countries – the United States, Canada, the EU, Argentina, and Mexico – have shown significantly positive signs for the coefficients as expected, in line with previous studies, suggesting that a strong currency creates an environment more attractive to filing AD petitions.

On the other hand, in the case of most other developing countries (Brazil, China, India, South Africa, and Turkey), there is no prevalent pattern related to RER. This result is supported by recent comprehensive studies on determinants of AD use. These papers examined the patterns of AD uses by distinguishing the groups by developed and developing countries. They found that the effects of RERs are inconsistent with earlier studies in the case of developing countries.[33] However, interestingly China and Turkey cases appear to show counter-intuitive results with significantly negative coefficients for RER. This result may be explained by the peculiar trade policies of those countries that are contingent on macroeconomic situations. Given the perception that Chinese Yuan is undervalued, low currency values for Yuan tend to entail more aggressive AD actions against China and in turn provoke more retaliatory AD actions by China. This kind of reactive AD actions by Turkey also seems very plausible particularly considering its aggressive AD uses since the early 2000s.

Table 6. FTA Deterrent Effects on the AD Investigation

Dependent Variable (Number of AD)	QMLE-Negative Binomial Regression			
	(A)	(B)	(C)	(D)
Constant	−9.671***	−9.547***	−10.532***	−10.313***
	(0.287)	(0.281)	(0.997)	(0.971)
Partner_AD	0.108***	0.108***	0.148***	0.151***
	(0.007)	(0.007)	(0.013)	(0.013)
LnIM $(t-1)$ (imports)	0.332***	0.325***	0.351***	0.342***
	(0.013)	(0.012)	(0.040)	(0.038)
LnRER $(t-1)$[34]	−0.046	−0.042	−0.036	−0.036
	(0.031)	(0.031)	(0.046)	(0.047)
GrrGDP $(t-3-t)$	0.157***	0.161***	0.027**	0.027**
	(0.009)	(0.009)	(0.010)	(0.011)

Continued

---

[33] See Moore & Zanardi (2008) and Bown (2008). In Bown's analysis, his Probit model estimation of the industry-level AD use for India, and Mexico does not show statistical significance on the effects of RER.
[34] LnRER: Logarithm of RERs (one year lagged, $t-1$).

342

Table 6. (Cont'd)

Dependent Variable	QMLE-Negative Binomial Regression			
(Number of AD)	(A)	(B)	(C)	(D)
FTA	−0.665***		−0.396***	
	(0.103)		(0.115)	
FTA ($t - 2$)		0.473**		0.596***
		(0.201)		(0.176)
FTA ($t - 1$)		−0.783***		−0.651**
		(0.279)		(0.267)
FTA (t_0) (year in force)		−0.847***		−0.565**
		(0.325)		(0.307)
FTA ($t + 1$)		−0.717***		−0.459*
		(0.264)		(0.275)
FTA ($t + 2$)		−0.423		−0.343
		(0.381)		(0.274)
FTA ($t + 3$)		−0.589**		−0.160
		(0.250)		(0.338)
FTA ($t + 4$)		−0.955***		−0.740***
		(0.282)		(0.271)
FTA ($t + 5$)		−0.992***		−0.797**
		(0.349)		(0.381)
Country fixed effect	No	No	Yes	Yes
Number of observations	28,442	28,422	28,205	28,250
Parameters (α)	4.130	4.090	5.733	5.835
Log likelihood	−7,350.63	−7,349.52	−6,443.96	−7,350.63

Note: * denotes statistical significance at the 10% level, ** at the 5% level, and *** at the 1% level. Robust standard errors are in parenthesis. Period effect is considered in all models. The result is based on NB I, which has a variance that is proportional to the mean, that is, $(1 + \alpha)\lambda$. Refer to the appendix regarding the issues of QML parameter (α), a measure of over-diversion, used for estimations.
Data source of RERs: USDA Economic Research Service.

APPENDIX 3.2

FTA EFFECTS ON THE AD INVESTIGATION: THE CASE OF MAJOR AD USERS

Dependent Variable (Number of AD)	Argentina		Brazil		Mexico		Australia		Canada		EC	
	NB I	NB II	NB I	NB II	NB I	NB II	NB I	NB II	NB I	NB II	NB I	NB II
Constant	−11.106***	−10.981***	−10.655***	−10.749***	−4.395***	−5.055***	−17.810***	−16.913***	−19.102***	−19.295***	−16.898***	−15.009***
	(0.784)	(0.570)	(1.183)	(3.261)	(1.121)	(0.608)	(1.343)	(0.869)	(6.497)	(5.148)	(0.861)	(0.678)
Partner_AD	0.067***	0.054***	0.056***	0.043***	0.128***	0.105***	0.047***	0.040***	0.061***	0.051***	0.054***	0.045***
	(0.009)	(0.003)	(0.009)	(0.015)	(0.021)	(0.009)	(0.008)	(0.004)	(0.008)	(0.005)	(0.009)	(0.004)
LnIM (t − 1) (imports)	0.520***	0.515***	0.340***	0.357***	0.121**	0.150***	0.632***	0.591***	0.499***	0.473***	0.689***	0.605***
	(0.042)	(0.029)	(0.040)	(0.085)	(0.058)	(0.033)	(0.041)	(0.030)	(0.047)	(0.037)	(0.038)	(0.030)
LnRER (t − 1)	0.175**	0.173**	0.017	−0.004	0.494***	0.451***	0.016	−0.168	0.257***	0.273***	0.290***	0.276***
	(0.086)	(0.076)	(0.105)	(0.316)	(0.095)	(0.074)	(0.372)	(0.241)	(0.096)	(0.074)	(0.049)	(0.040)
GRR_GDP (t − 3−t)	−0.207***	−0.171***	0.372	0.341	−2.793***	−2.286***	0.634**	0.637***	1.964	2.237	1.633***	1.727***
	(0.058)	(0.030)	(0.226)	(0.637)	(0.525)	(0.628)	(0.311)	(0.176)	(2.004)	(1.580)	(0.371)	(0.218)
FTA	0.763***	0.789***	−0.361	−0.416	1.085***	1.087***	−0.705	−0.704**	−0.404	−0.379	−0.403*	−0.375**
	(0.228)	(0.135)	(0.322)	(0.995)	(0.387)	(0.273)	(0.513)	(0.282)	(0.356)	(0.249)	(0.230)	(0.175)
Number of observations	2,307	2,307	2,367	2,367	2,367	2,367	2,487	2,487	2,697	2,697	2,412	2,412
Parameters (α)	0.737	0.034	1.470	0.312	2.287	0.630	0.926	0.217	1.645	0.239	1.073	0.11
Log likelihood	−433.62	−439.01	−592.36	−592.36	−294.96	−289.92	−373.51	−369.43	−340.30	−334.20	−575.02	−585.93

Note: * denotes statistical significance at the 10% level, ** at the 5% level, and *** at the 1% level. Period effect is considered in all models. (Robust) Standard errors are in parenthesis.

Dependent Variable (Number of AD)	United States		China		India		Korea		South Africa		Turkey	
	NB I	NB II	NB I	NB II	NB I	NB II	NB I	NB II	NB I	NB II	NB I	NB II
Constant	-17.915***	-18.166***	-10.660***	-9.266**	-2.961	-3.446	-22.850	-28.962***	-14.712***	-13.424***	-13.183***	-13.360***
	(1.262)	(0.682)	(3.944)	(4.466)	(4.244)	(5.528)	(19.867)	(13.026)	(1.966)	(1.151)	(1.357)	(0.989)
Partner_AD	0.092***	0.041***	0.085***	0.069***	0.080***	0.041***	0.037***	0.028***	0.075***	0.064***	0.106***	0.059***
	(0.023)	(0.003)	(0.021)	(0.020)	(0.014)	(0.005)	(0.009)	(0.004)	(0.012)	(0.005)	(0.023)	(0.005)
LnIM ($t - 1$) (imports)	0.601***	0.632***	0.311***	0.300***	0.366***	0.338***	0.707***	0.719***	0.575***	0.537***	0.518***	0.523***
	(0.043)	(0.027)	(0.037)	(0.031)	(0.024)	(0.019)	(0.069)	(0.045)	(0.047)	(0.034)	(0.064)	(0.047)
LnRER ($t - 1$)	0.272***	0.301***	-0.557***	-0.547***	-0.014	-0.063	0.004	0.018	-0.058	-0.074	-0.316	-0.314***
	(0.069)	(0.048)	(0.139)	(0.165)	(0.061)	(0.066)	(0.202)	(0.135)	(0.151)	(0.120)	(0.141)	(0.104)
GrGDP ($t - 1 - t - 3$)	0.939***	0.900***	0.316	0.201	-1.013*	-0.803	0.620	1.358	0.492	0.328	-0.268	-0.111
	(0.259)	(0.105)	(0.414)	(0.469)	(0.593)	(0.791)	(2.374)	(1.601)	(0.584)	(0.306)	(0.226)	(0.148)
FTA	-0.241	-0.463***	-1.539***	-1.482***	-1.551***	-1.303***	-0.143	-0.125	-0.334	-0.287	-1.053***	-1.215***
	(0.213)	(0.153)	(0.437)	(0.337)	(0.514)	(0.464)	(0.584)	(0.467)	(0.324)	(0.218)	(0.349)	(0.225)
Number of observations	2,685	2,685	1,202	1,202	2,412	2,412	2,532	2,532	2,652	2,652	2,322	2,415
Parameters (α)	1.514	0.092	1.513	0.371	3.242	0.269	0.564	0.124	1.989	0.566	2.820	0.266
Log likelihood	-646.19	-631.18	-571.45	-596.06	-1,438.46	-1,572.99	-226.22	-223.72	-340.189	-335.421	-237.11	-246.02

Note: * denotes statistical significance at the 10% level, ** at the 5% level, and *** at the 1% level. Period effect is considered in all models. (Robust) Standard errors are in parenthesis.

Chapter 16

Legal Issues for Korea's "Internal Trade" in the WTO System

Dukgeun Ahn

1. Introduction

Since its inception in 1995, the WTO system has continued to grow to embrace most of the world economy, now encompassing 148 members.[1] The notable exceptions in this broad membership to date include Russia, Saudi Arabia and Vietnam who are currently in the middle of accession negotiations. As of December 2004, 25 countries in total are negotiating for WTO accession.

The WTO, as an international trade organization, demands that an accession applicant be at least a "separate customs territory possessing full autonomy in the conduct of its external commercial relations and of other matters provided for in this Agreement."[2] Accordingly, Hong Kong and Macao secured independent membership status on January 1, 1995 and Chinese Taipei joined the WTO on January 1, 2002 as the "Separate Customs Territory of Taiwan, Penghu, Kinmen and Matsu." It implies that in case North Korea is to be addressed under the WTO system, it would certainly ensure independent membership status. In fact, North Korea already joined the United Nations in 1991, which mandates for membership "peace-loving *states*."[3] It follows that trade involving North Korea would be subject to the same disciplines of the WTO agreements.

This international reality is not, however, coinciding with the domestic constitutional regime in South Korea. For example, Article 5 of the "Special Law on Implementation of the World Trade Organization Agreement," subtitled "Intra-Nation Transaction," provides that "trade between South Korea and North Korea constitutes internal trading within a nation and as such shall not be regarded as that between countries."[4] In other words,

---

[1] Recent accession included less developed countries such as Cambodia and Nepal. Nepal became the 147th member on April 23, 2004, which made Nepal the first less developed country to join the WTO through the full working party process since the WTO was established in 1995. Cambodia joined the WTO on October 13, 2004.

[2] The Marrakesh Agreement Establishing the World Trade Organization, Art.XII.

[3] Charter of the United Nations, Article 4.1.

[4] Public Law No. 4858.

South Korea treats trade with North Korea as internal trade that is not subject to international trade disciplines including WTO agreements. This policy is also reaffirmed by Article 26.2 of the Law on South-North Cooperation that explicitly exempts the application of the Tariff Law to importation from North Korea.[5] Such a discrepancy requires more careful examination and concrete solutions before increasing trade volumes and deepening economic cooperation between South and North Korea raise politically controversial problems.

2. Economic Relations between South and North Korea

Unlike South Korea whose economic structure shows a substantial trade relationship, North Korea has not been visible in terms of international trade.[6] Based on economic statistics for 2004 as shown in Table 17-1, the magnitudes of North Korea's trade volumes are still insignificant compared

Table 17-1. Summary Economic Indicators for South and North Korea

Year	97	98	99	00	01	02	03
Per capital GDP (USD)							
South Korea (SK)	11.176	7,355	9,438	10,841	10,162	11,493	12,646
North Korea (NK)	811	573	714	757	706	762	818
Growth Rate (%)							
SK	4.7	-6.9	9.5	8.5	3.8	7.0	3.1
NK	-6.3	-1.1	6.2	1.3	3.7	1.2	1.8
Total Trade (billion USD)							
SK	280.8	225.6	263.4	332.8	291.5	314.6	372.6
NK	2.2	1.4	1.5	1.9	2.3	2.3	2.4
Exports (billion USD)							
SK	136.2	132.3	143.7	172.3	150.4	162.5	193.8
NK	0.91	0.56	0.51	0.56	0.65	0.74	0.78
Imports (billion USD)							
SK	144.6	93.3	119.7	160.5	141.1	152.1	178.8
NK	1.27	0.88	0.96	1.41	1.62	1.52	1.61

---

[5] Public Law No. 6316. In fact, this principle was maintained from the very first draft of the law, enacted on August 1, 1990. Moreover, this law uses terms such as "carry-in" and "carry-out," instead of "import" and "export," to signify internality of trade between South and North Korea.

[6] The formal titles of South and North Korea are the Republic of Korea and the Democratic People's Republic of Korea, respectively. For simplicity, this paper uses South and North Korea.

[7] Bank of Korea, Comparison of Major Economic Indicators for South and North Korea <http://www.bok.or.kr/template/main/html/index.jsp?tbl=tbl_FM0000000066_CA000000070 1> (visited on December 4, 2004).

Figure 17-1. Trends of Internal Trade between South and North Korea[8]

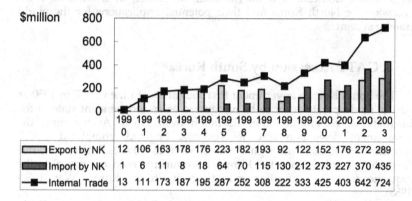

	199 0	199 1	199 2	199 3	199 4	199 5	199 6	199 7	199 8	199 9	200 0	200 1	200 2	200 3
Export by NK	12	106	163	178	176	223	182	193	92	122	152	176	272	289
Import by NK	1	6	11	8	18	64	70	115	130	212	273	227	370	435
Internal Trade	13	111	173	187	195	287	252	308	222	333	425	403	642	724

to those of South Korea.[9] The total trade volume for North Korea is only 13% of itstotal GDP, in contrast to roughly 62% for South Korea in 2003.

This relatively little reliance on trade may partly explain why North Korea has never applied for GATT/WTO membership. Nevertheless, North Korea may need to carefully consider the benefits and costs of WTO membership, particularly after Russia's accession to the WTO in the near future.

On the other hand, as indicated in Figure 17-1, volumes of internal trade between South and North Korea have persistently increased and grown rapidly since 2001. It is also noteworthy that imports by North Korea have considerably increased since the middle 1990s.

The overall benefits and costs of WTO accession for North Korea would require more comprehensive research to assess both imminent and potential long-term economic effects on all economic sectors. But, even a cursory observation of China's recent accession and the current efforts of Russia for WTO accession suggest that the cost of exclusion from the WTO system seems to surpass the price a new member is required to pay. Of course, WTO accession demands huge political as well as economic commitments and subsequent domestic economic restructuring would often entail considerable systemic and legal reform. Therefore, the core part of the question in relation to WTO accession for North Korea would not be whether accession is beneficial to North Korea, but rather when North Korea is properly prepared for such major economic restructuring. That

---

[8] Young-Hoon Lee, "Economic Analysis of Trade Impacts to Economic Growth of North Korea" 13, Financial Economic Research Series No. 201 (Bank of Korea, Nov. 2004; *in Korean*).
[9] Bank of Korea, Comparison of Major Economic Indicators for South and North Korea <http://www.bok.or.kr/template/main/html/index.jsp?tbl=tbl_FM0000000066_CA000000070 1> (visited on December 4, 2004).

question is not addressed in this article. Instead, I will examine what kind of legal issues, domestic and international, are raised in relation to WTO accession for North Korea and their potential implications for the world trading system.

3. GATT Accession by South Korea[10]

The South Korean government first sought to join the GATT in 1950 as part of its desperate effort to be recognized as an independent state in the international community after liberation from Japan. At the time, the government delegation sent to Torquay, England, completed GATT accession negotiation and signed the relevant documents.[11] However, this first attempt failed when the Korean government could not complete the requisite domestic ratification procedures due to the Korean War (1950-1953).[12]

The GATT regime underwent substantial changes to more explicitly encompass development issues during the 1960s. Efforts to demonstrate a more forceful commitment to the interests of developing countries within the GATT system led to the adoption of new provisions, Articles XXXVI – XXXVIII, as Part IV of the GATT.[13] In addition, the GATT as a whole tried to be perceived as a more favorable forum for developing countries. For example, the 1964 GATT publication titled "The Role of GATT in Relation to Trade and Development" emphasized considerable legal freedom for developing countries, such as non-reciprocity, infant industry protection for industrial development, and balance-of-payment protection measures.[14] These factors clearly demonstrated a strong GATT policy to expand its membership with developing countries.

Moreover, in terms of the legal disciplines of the GATT, the late 1960s was probably the lowest point in the GATT's history.[15] During the 1959–1970 period, the GATT dispute settlement activities had dramatically declined, becoming virtually dormant in the late 1960s.[16] Such developments created undoubtedly a more favorable environment for

---

[10] This part was largely drawn from Dukgeun Ahn, "Korea in the GATT/WTO Dispute Settlement System," *Journal of International Economic Law*, Vol. 6, No. 3 (2003).

[11] GATT, BISD II/33-34. At that meeting, Austria, Peru, Philippines and Turkey also finished the accession negotiations. While Austria, Peru and Turkey formally became contracting parties in 1951, the Philippines formally joined the GATT on December 27, 1979.

[12] Tae-Hyuk Hahm, 'Reflections on the GATT Accession Negotiations,' *Diplomatic Negotiation Case* 94-1 (1994, *in Korean*), p.5.

[13] The Protocol Amending the General Agreement on Tariffs and Trade to Introduce a Part IV on Trade and Development, which was adopted on Feb. 8, 1965, entered into force on June 27, 1966. WTO, *Analytical Index: Guide to GATT Law and Practice* (Geneva, 1995) p.1040.

[14] Robert E. Hudec, *Developing Countries in the GATT Legal System* (Trade Policy Research Center, 1987) p. 59-60.

[15] Ibid., at p. 65.

[16] Robert E. Hudec, *The GATT Legal System and World Trade Diplomacy* (2nd edition, Butterworth Legal Publishers, 1990) p. 235-250.

developing countries to consider joining the GATT. In fact, GATT membership increased the most during the 1960s, in which 39 countries acceded.[17]

With such a favorable backdrop to developing countries within the GATT, the South Korean government resumed its effort to accede to the GATT in 1965, when it sought to promote its exports as the primary element of economic development policies. The revision of the GATT to include Part IV to deal with development issues also played an important role in inducing South Korea to reconsider GATT accession at that time. After extensive internal discussions on potential economic benefits and costs, the South Korean government finally submitted its accession application to the GATT Secretariat on May 20, 1966, and conducted tariff negotiations with 12 contracting parties from September to December 2, 1966.[18]

South Korea officially acceded to the GATT in 1967, in accordance with Article XXXIII of the GATT.[19] On December 16, 1966, the Council of Representatives adopted the "Report of the Working Party" for GATT accession.[20] After the South Korean government completed the domestic ratification procedure, the "Protocol for the Accession of Korea" to the GATT entered into force on April 14, 1967.[21] On the other hand, South Korea invoked Article XXXV for non-application of GATT with respect to Cuba,[22] Czechoslovakia,[23] Poland,[24] and Yugoslavia.[25] These Article XXXV invocations were all simultaneously withdrawn in September 1971.[26]

South Korea began its formal participation as a contracting party in multilateral trade negotiations at the Tokyo Round, although it was merely a minor player.[27] Subsequently, South Korea joined the four Tokyo Round Side Codes: Subsidies Code,[28] Standards Code,[29] Customs Valuation

---

[17] The statistics for the accession to the GATT by the period is as follows:

Years	1948-1949	1950s	1960s	1970s	1980s	1990-1994	Total
Number of Acceding Countries	19	17	39	9	11	33	128

The accession to the GATT was also substantially increased in the early 1990s during which the Uruguay Round negotiation had been conducted. See generally WTO, above n. 7, at p. 1136.

[18] The Working Party for Korea's accession included 14 contracting parties. Hahm, above n. 4, p. 23.

[19] GATT, Korea – Accession under Article XXXIII (Decision of 2 March 1967), BISD 15S/60 (1968).

[20] GATT, BISD 15S/106 (1968).

[21] GATT, BISD 15S/44 (1968).

[22] GATT, L/2783 (April 1967).

[23] GATT, L/2783 (April 1967).

[24] GATT, L/2874 (Oct. 1967).

[25] GATT, L/2783 (April 1967).

[26] GATT, L/3580 (1971). See also WTO, above n. 7, p. 1034-1036. On the other hand, it is noted that 50 contracting parties invoked Article XXXV in respect of Japan at its accession in 1955.

[27] Chulsu Kim, 'Korea in the Multilateral Trading System: From Obscurity to Prominence,' in The Kluwer Companion to the WTO Agreement (The Hague: Kluwer Law International, *forthcoming*).

[28] The Agreement on Interpretation and Application of Articles VI, XVI and XXIII. In Korea,

Code[30] and Anti-Dumping Code.[31]

South Korea had never joined the sectoral agreements on bovine meat, dairy products and civil aircraft, nor the "Agreement on Import Licensing Procedures" as a plurilateral agreement. South Korea joined the "Agreement on Government Procurement" during the Uruguay Round and implemented it only from January 1, 1997, while all other signatories except for Hong Kong applied it from January 1, 1996.[32]

4. North-South Trade Issue

(1) MFN Treatment

The imminent legal issues regarding the internal trade of South-North Korea are non-discrimination – specifically, the most-favoured-nation (MFN) – requirement under the WTO Agreements. Indeed, this issue is contingent on how North Korea is considered in the WTO system. In case North Korea is treated as a country or at least an entity that has sufficient legal status to become an independent WTO Member, the WTO Agreements mandate MFN treatment for other members based on "any advantage, favor, privilege or immunity" accorded to the like product originating in or destined for the territories of North Korea.

In terms of strict legal stipulations, there is a subtle difference in the WTO Agreements concerning the MFN obligation. While most other WTO Agreements stipulate MFN obligations on the basis of a "Member" that embraces both states and "separate customs territory possessing full autonomy in the conduct of its external commercial relations,"[33] Article I of the GATT and Article II of the GATS require MFN treatment based on treatment accorded to like products and services of any other "country."[34]

Although there is still domestic controversy about whether South and

---

it was signed on June 10, 1980 and entered into force on July 10, 1980 as Treaty No. 709. See Ministry of Foreign Affairs, Compilation of Multilateral Treaties, Vol.5 (*in Korean*).

[29] The Agreement on Technical Barriers to Trade. In Korea, it was signed on September 3, 1980 and entered into force on October 2, 1980 as Treaty No. 715. Ibid.

[30] The Agreement on Implementation of Article VII. The Customs Valuation Code entered into force on January 1, 1981 while the other three Codes entered into force on Jan. 1, 1980. GATT, BISD 28S/40. In Korea, it was entered into force on January 6, 1981 as Treaty No. 729. Ibid.

[31] The Agreement on Implementation of Article VI. Korea accepted the Anti-Dumping Code on Feb. 24, 1986 and the Code entered into force for Korea on March 26, 1986 as Treaty No. 877. GATT, BISD 33S/207. See also Ministry of Foreign Affairs, Compilation of Multilateral Treaties, Vol.8 (*in Korean*).

[32] WTO, Agreement on Government Procurement, Article XXIV: 3. Hong Kong also had one more year for implementation to apply from January 1, 1997.

[33] Article XII, Marrakesh Agreement Establishing the WTO (hereinafter "WTO Charter").

[34] Article XII of the WTO Charter mentions a State or a separate customs territory. Although there is no clear difference in the legal definition of "state" and "country," the concept of a country is normally understood to have the same meaning of a "state."

North Korea recognize each other as a state within their own constitutional systems, both parties simultaneously joined the United Nations on September 17, 1991 as independent members under the name of "Republic of Korea" and "Democratic People's Republic of Korea." Since the United Nations demands a "state" entity for its membership requirement, the mutual accession to the United Nations seems to imply bilateral as well as international recognition of a "state" status for both parties. Therefore, it is very likely that both parties are treated as independent members in the context of WTO Agreements unless they are substantially reunified. Moreover, considering UN membership, the MFN requirement based on treatment accorded to the other "country" would also be applied.

Despite such international arrangements, South Korea has basically treated products from North Korea as domestic products and has not imposed any tariff or other trade measures on products from North Korea. Article 3 of the Korean Constitution clarifies that the entire territory of the Korean peninsula is the geographical scope of a sovereign Korea. In fact, South Korea enacted a special implementation law for WTO Agreements in 1995,[35] declaring that North Korean products be treated as domestic goods. More specifically, Article 5 of the "Special Law on Implementation of the World Trade Organization Agreement," subtitled "Intra-Nation Transaction," provides that "the trade between South Korea and North Korea constitutes internal trading within a nation and as such shall not be regarded as that between countries."[36] Pursuant to this law, imports from North Korea have never been subject to any trade measures including tariffs and quotas.

Free trade between South and North Korea, however, raises MFN treatment issues for almost 150 WTO Members. In fact, tax-free imports of North Korean products by South Korea already invoked complaints by the United States in March 1991 on the basis of MFN treatment obligation. The United States then suggested that Korea seek a waiver under Article XXV:5 of the GATT to ensure legitimacy under the GATT's legal disciplines.[37] Such a waiver issue is now addressed by Article IX:3 of the WTO Agreement, although waiver arrangements have been rarely made under the WTO system. As of March 2005, most waiver arrangements except for seven waivers relating to regional trade agreements were already expired.[38]

This waiver option, however, does not completely resolve the problem. First, "exceptional circumstances" justifying a waiver decision, and "terms and conditions attached to the waiver" are to be annually reviewed by the Ministerial Conference. On the basis of the annual review, the Ministerial Conference may extend, modify or terminate the waiver. In other words, the

---

[35] See Appendix II.
[36] Public Law No. 4858.
[37] Moon-soo Chung, "Implementation of the Results of the Uruguay Round Agreements: Korea" in *Implementing the Uruguay Round* (eds. by John Jackson & Alan Sykes), p. 375 (1997).
[38] WTO Analytical Index: Guide to WTO Law and Practice, Vol. I, p. 80-88 (2003).

waiver arrangement may be vulnerable to various external factors, economic or political, and thereby be uncertain about whether or how long it can be maintained. Second, other WTO Members can invoke a dispute settlement proceeding when its accrued benefit under GATT 1994 is nullified or impaired regardless of whether a Member to whom a waiver was granted complies with the conditions for waivers or not.[39]

A similar situation concerning a MFN obligation occurred in the context of Germany's accession to the GATT. The Federal Republic of Germany (West Germany) and the German Democratic Republic (East Germany) were simultaneously admitted as members to the United Nations on 18 September 1973.[40] Yet, the two German States had maintained a free trade relationship exempting all customs duties. Accordingly, MFN treatment for other GATT contracting parties was a potentially very controversial issue in international trade, particularly for West Germany.

The legal foundation for intra-German trade was the Berlin Agreement of 20 September 1951, concluded between the two German States, whereby they committed themselves to not impose any customs duties, or charges having equivalent effect on mutually-traded goods originating in one of the two respective countries.[41] Customs duties or charges having equivalent effect had thus never been levied on intra-German trade – trade in goods originating in West Berlin being regarded as trade in goods originating in the Federal Republic of Germany.[42]

Furthermore, at the time of accession to the GATT, West Germany secured agreement of the Contracting Parties that the retention of arrangements for intra-German trade was in conformity with Article I of the General Agreement, and that goods originating in the western sectors of Berlin would be treated as originating in the Federal Republic of Germany.[43]

Upon establishment of the European Economic Community, the parties to the Treaty had stated in the Protocol of 25 March 1957 on German Internal Trade and Connected Problems that the EEC Treaty required no change in the system of intra-German trade. Treaty provisions regulating free trade in goods between EEC member States (Article 9(2) of the Rome Treaty) thus fundamentally also applied to goods traded in intra-German trading and freely circulating in the Federal Republic of Germany.[44]

In the State Treaty of 18 May 1990 between the Federal Republic of Germany and the German Democratic Republic, Article 12(1) provided that

---

[39] Paragraph .2. Understanding in Respect of Waivers of Obligations under the GATT, 1994.

[40] Through the accession of the German Democratic Republic to the Federal Republic of Germany, effective from 3 October 1990, the two German States have united to form one sovereign State, Germany.

[41] GATT, C/M/244, 16 (dated July 31, 1990).

[42] Ibid.

[43] GATT, "Decision of 21 June, 1951 authorizing the Federal Republic of Germany to accede to the General Agreement," Basic Instruments and Selected Documents Vol. II, p. 34 (1952).

[44] This part is mostly drawn from the GATT, C/M/244 (dated July 31, 1990).

intra-German trade in goods originating in either of the two German States would continue to be free of customs duties or charges. Article 13 committed the German Democratic Republic to take account of the principles of free world trade, particularly as expressed in the General Agreement. The German Democratic Republic had also committed itself to adopt the customs laws used in the Federal Republic of Germany and to introduce the Community's Common Customs Tariff. In implementing these commitments, customs authorities of both German States had prepared, and on 1 July 1990 had already enacted, adoption of the Common Customs Tariff, the customs provisions, and the Community's trade policy measures. This had fulfilled one of the conditions for the creation of a de facto customs union between the German Democratic Republic and the Community.

By Council Regulation No. 1794/90 of 28 June 1990, Commission Regulation No. 1795/90 of 29 June 1990, and Commission Decision No. 1796/90/ECSC of 29 June 1990, the Community had acted to remove customs duties and quantitative restrictions for industrial goods vis-à-vis the German Democratic Republic, effective 1 July 1990. In the legal documents just cited, the Community had permitted the German Democratic Republic to honor contracts concluded with countries of the Council for Mutual Economic Assistance (CMEA) under the state-trading system, specifying that customs duties did not need to be applied in these cases. This had been done with the understanding that these imports were intended for use in the German Democratic Republic and that they would remain or be consumed there. Through the enactment of these regulations, the German Democratic Republic had de facto become part of the Community's customs union.

As explained, West Germany secured legitimacy for intra-German trade from the beginning of its GATT accession that was acquiesced and acknowledged in the WTO system. South Korea, however, did not secure legitimacy for intra-Korean trade at the time of GATT accession, nor at the inception of the WTO system. Another plausible opportunity to address this issue in the WTO may be when North Korea begins formal negotiations for WTO accession, since it may be politically premature for South Korea to raise this issue at the WTO without agreement from North Korea. But, the MFN problem indicated above for international trade by South Korea remains until North Korea formally begins WTO accession negotiations and secures agreements from other WTO Members.

(2) Non-market Economy Provision

One of the most serious problems for WTO Members with transition economies or non-market economies are the so-called "non-market economy" provisions applicable for trade remedy actions. In case a WTO Member is designated as a non-market economy, its domestic prices would not be considered appropriate bases for calculating dumping margins or countervailing duties. It would then lead importing Members to use constructed values that typically inflate domestic prices and result in substantially higher antidumping or countervailing duties.

For example, when China acceded to the WTO in December 2001, it made a commitment to be subject to the non-market economy provision for 15 years after the date of accession. In terms of anti-dumping cases, the importing WTO Member shall use Chinese prices or costs for the industry under investigation in determining price comparability only if Chinese producers under investigation can "clearly show that market economy conditions prevail in the industry producing the like product with regard to the manufacture, production and sale of that product."[45] Otherwise, the importing WTO Member may use "a methodology that is not based on a strict comparison with domestic prices or costs in China." [46] Moreover, if there are special difficulties in calculating subsidy amounts, the importing WTO Member may use "methodologies for identifying and measuring the subsidy benefit which takes into account the possibility that prevailing terms and conditions in China may not always be available as appropriate benchmarks."[47] The importing WTO Member should provide notification of those methodologies adopted instead of Chinese prices to the Committee on Anti-Dumping Practices and the Committee on Subsidies and Countervailing Measures. If China establishes, pursuant to the national law of the importing WTO Member, that market economy conditions prevail in a particular industry or sector, the non-market economy provisions shall no longer apply to that industry or sector.

In fact, China is the first Member that acceded to the WTO explicitly agreeing on such a non-market economy provision to be utilized by all WTO Members.[48] The decision on which countries are non-market economies is very arbitrary or at least susceptible to discretionary decisions. For instance, Russia could secure market economy status, at least in the US market since June 6, 2002 when determined as such by the Department of Commerce and in the EU market a little earlier.[49] Practically, the recognition of Russia as a market economy by the United States and the European Communities would facilitate similar treatment by other WTO members. On the other hand, the US Department of Commerce regarded Vietnam as a non-market economy in a recent anti-dumping case concerning catfish products.[50]

---

[45] WTO, WT/ACC/CHN/49, p.79.

[46] *Id.*, p.80.

[47] *Id.*

[48] The Accession Protocol of Cambodia does not include explicitly non-market economy provisions. However, this does not mean that all WTO Members always treat Cambodia as market economy. Pursuant to Members' own domestic regulations, different WTO Members may still treat Cambodian products differently.

[49] See *Peter Slevin*, "U.S. Says Russia Now 'Market Economy," Washington Post, June 7, 2002, p. E01. Also see Russia Weekly, <http://www.cdi.org/russia/211-13.cfm> (visited on August 3, 2003).

[50] US Department of Commerce, "Notice of Final Antidumping Duty Determination of

Considering such diverse practices, it is difficult to anticipate how non-market economy provisions can be applied to North Korea.[51] Yet, it is clear that there is ample possibility for other WTO Members to treat North Korea as a non-market economy and if so, the trade through or by North Korea would be seriously affected thereby.

5. Concluding Remarks

GATT membership for South Korea had played a key role in successfully implementing economic development policies that were closely intertwined with trade promotion policies from the 1970s and throughout the 1980s. The new world trading system centered on the WTO, however, provides not only opportunities but also challenges to many WTO members, particularly new members that have relatively little experience for such a rules-based system. North Korea, currently trying to improve its economic system and structures, may soon find the need to be integrated into the world trading system so as to secure stable and predictable economic environments. Even before that occurs, the strengthened economic relationship and increase of trade between South and North Korea may raise complicated legal problems in terms of WTO obligations. The timely and clear resolution of the current problems would be necessary to prevent perilous confusion at a critical juncture of economic cooperation between South and North Korea.

Sales at Less Than Fair Value and Affirmative Critical Circumstances: Certain Frozen Fish Fillets from the Socialist Republic of Vietnam," A-552-801 (68 FR 37116, June 23, 2003).

[51] Alexander Polouektov, "The Non-market Economy" Issue in International Trade in the Context of WTO Accessions, UNCTAD/DITC/TNCD/MISC.20 (9 October 2002).

APPENDIX I

ACCESSION OF THE FEDERAL REPUBLIC OF GERMANY[52]
Decision of 21 June 1951

The CONTRACTING PARTIES,
Having regard to the results of the negotiations directed toward the accession of the Federal Republic of Germany to the General Agreement on Tariffs and Trade,

Decide, in accordance with Article XXXIII of the General Agreement:

1. (a) The CONTRACTING PARTIES agree to the accession of the Government of the Federal Republic of Germany to the General Agreement on the terms relevant to such accession which are provided for in the Torquay Protocol to the General Agreement.
(b) The CONTRACTING PARTIES further agree that, notwithstanding the provisions of Article I of the General Agreement the accession of the Government of the Federal Republic of Germany will not require any modification in the present arrangements for, or status of, intra-German trade in goods originating within Germany.
(c) In according the benefits of the General Agreement to goods exported from the Federal Republic of Germany, the contracting parties will make no distinction between goods originating in the territory of the Federal Republic and those originating in the western sectors of Berlin.
(d) The provisions of sub-paragraphs 1 (b) and (c) above may be reconsidered at any time at the request of any contracting party, and any decision taken by the CONTRACTING PARTIES in this respect will be taken by a majority of the votes cast.

2. This decision shall be open for signature by contracting parties at Torquay on 21 April 1951, and at the Headquarters of the United Nations from 7 May 1951, until 20 June 1951.

3. This decision shall constitute a decision of the CONTRACTING PARTIES taken on 21 June 1951, provided that it shall then have been signed by two-thirds of the governments which are at that time contracting parties.

4. The Secretary-General of the United Nations shall promptly furnish a notification of each signature to this decision to each Member of the United Nations, to each other government which participated in the United Nations Conference on Trade and Employment, and to any other interested government.

---

[52] GATT, BISD Vol. II, 34-35 (1952).

APPENDIX II

SPECIAL LAW ON IMPLEMENTATION OF THE WORLD TRADE ORGANIZATION AGREEMENT[53]

Article 1   Purpose

The purpose of this law is to ensure the rights and interests of the Republic of Korea (hereinafter called ROK) as a member of the World Trade Organization (hereinafter called a member) in implementing the Marrakesh Agreement Establishing the World Trade Organization (hereinafter called the Agreement), and to secure sound development of the national economy by minimizing the injuries which may be caused by implementation of the Agreement.

Article 2   Protection of Economic Sovereignty

Any article of the Agreement shall not be construed to allow impairment of the legitimate economic rights and interests of ROK as member of the global free trade regime.

Article 3   Security of Rights and Interests under the Agreement

The Government shall exercise and comply with its obligations, in accordance with the basic principles of the Agreement. The government shall enter into renegotiations in accordance with the procedures provided in the Agreement, in the event the results of any trade negotiations are in contravention of the basic principles of the Agreement, or in the event the implementation of any obligations under the Agreement results in material injury to any specific product in the domestic market.

Article 4   Measures against Subsidies

The Government shall take appropriate measures deemed necessary in accordance with the provisions of the Agreement and/or applicable laws of the country, in the event any member exports to ROK any product with subsidies not permissible under the Agreement.

Article 5   Intra-Nation Transaction

Trade between South Korea and North Korea constitutes internal trading within a nation and as such shall not be regarded as that between countries.

Article 6   Special Emergency Tax

The Government may, in accordance with the provisions of the Agreement and the applicable laws of the country, levy a special emergency tariff at a level in excess of the bound tariff schedule for that product, in

---

[53] This English version is not an official translation.

respect of any agricultural/forest/fisheries products, the import of which increases sharply, or the international prices thereof fall substantially.

Article 7   Use of Tariff Proceeds and Import Profits of Agricultural/Forest/ Fisheries Products
The proceeds of tariff and the profits from import of agricultural/forest/fisheries products resulting from implementing the Agreement shall be used for the purpose of increasing the income of the farmers and fishermen people and development of rural/fisheries areas.

Article 8   Protection of Health
In the event there are reasonable grounds to believe that any foodstuff, any container thereof or any other imported product contains bacteria, germs, quarantine laws, foodstuff sanitation laws, plant quarantine laws or domestic animal contagious disease prevention laws, thus causing or threatening to cause national public health problems, the Government may, in accordance with the provisions of the Agreement and/or the applicable laws, prohibit or restrict the importation of the said product, products manufactured or transformed therefrom, or other similar products from the manufacturer or transformer of the said product.

Article 9   Protection of the Environment
In the event there is a danger of environmental pollution causing damage to human, animal or plant life, the Government may, in accordance with the provisions of the Agreement and the applicable laws, prohibit or restrict the importation of the said product and/or the products manufactured or transformed therefrom.

Article 10   Designation of Import Agency
In the event the importation of a certain agricultural/forest/fisheries product is found liable to cause retardation of the relative domestic industry, the Government may, in accordance with the provisions of the Agreement and the applicable laws, designate an agency of the Government, a local autonomous body, a Government-invested corporation or a producers' association to import said product(s).

Article 11   Implementation of Domestic Support Policy
1. Promptly following the effectiveness of the Agreement, the Government shall implement measures facilitating export market exploration including provision of a credit guarantee for export products or provision of information related to export markets to the extent permissible under the Agreement.
2. Promptly following the effectiveness of the Agreement, the Government shall, to the extent permissible under the Agreement, institute the following support measures: direct payment to control production,

support to marginal farmers, support to farmers engaged in organic farming and other environmentally beneficial farming, support against calamities in agriculture/forestry/fisheries, and income support not related to production.

Article 12   Support to Producers' Association for Moderation of Supply and Demand of Agricultural/Forest/Fisheries Products
The Government shall, in accordance with the provisions of the applicable laws, provide support to the producers' associations engaged in moderating the demand and supply of agricultural/forest/fisheries products in respect of their facilities for procurement, storage and processing.

Article 13   Implementation of Structural Adjustment on the Agricultural/Forestry/Fisheries Industries
The Government shall implement structural adjustment of the Agricultural/Forest/Fisheries industries in connection with the implementation of the Agreement, and shall report the status thereof to the National Assembly on an annual basis.

Article 14   Implementing Regulations
Necessary details for implementing this law shall be provided in the Presidential Decree.

Printed in the United States
By Bookmasters